LETTERS TO
Imogene

The Triumph and Tragedy of an American Military Family, 1942-1945

Robert E. Stumpf

outskirts
press

Table of Contents

---◆---

Prologue

The twentieth century was the bloodiest in human history in terms of the sheer level of human suffering at the hands of despots and tyrants. Whether Stalin, Tojo, Mussolini, Hitler himself, or many of the lesser demagogues, such as Saddam Hussein, Idi Amin, or Pol Pot, the brutality had no bounds. This unabated wave of evil reached its zenith in World War II, a six-year holocaust beginning in 1939. It pitted the Axis powers—principally Germany and Japan—against an unlikely coalition led by Great Britain, the Soviet Union, and the United States. The war's name derives from its predecessor, the Great War, 1914–1918, later known as World War I, ostensibly the war to end all wars.

Ironically, the Great War not only did not end all wars, but rather led directly to the rise of Nazism and Fascism, and the next world war only twenty-one years later. Indeed, many strategists, including Dwight Eisenhower and Winston Churchill, actually predicted World War II. They considered it simply an extension of the first war left incomplete by an inadequate peace. The United States, remaining true to its isolationist tendencies at the time, became a principal in World War I only near the end of the struggle that ended in an armistice on

November 11, 1918.

In the midst of these incredible decades of global warfare, the United States came of age as a world power. Even as this era represents the almost unimaginable apex of evil of the twentieth century, it is possible, even likely, that it could have had a different, much worse outcome. If the United States had not intervened in World War I, Germany may well have conquered all of Europe and gotten a head start on eventual world domination. Even so, by 1940, Germany, as the Third Reich, had re-emerged as the world's dominant military power and controlled virtually all of Europe and North Africa. In the Pacific, Germany's ally, Japan, had conquered large parts of Asia and was poised to embark on the bloody expansion of its euphemistically named Southeast Asia Co-Prosperity Sphere. Both powers grew stronger with each additional conquest.

By that time Germany had begun its final solution, the systematic extermination of the Jewish population in Europe. Italy had allied with Germany, invaded Greece and the Balkans, and was expanding its empire in Africa. France had capitulated and formed a quasi-alliance with the Axis. Germany stepped up its aerial assault on Great Britain and threatened imminent invasion across the English Channel. At the same time, Germany was turning its eyes eastward for the conquest of an inadequately prepared Soviet Union.

While these momentous developments seemed lost on much of the general population of the United States, oceans away, President Franklin Roosevelt and other farsighted leaders understood their significance. Politically, it was nearly impossible for Roosevelt to sell immediate intervention on the side of Great Britain to most Americans just beginning to emerge from unprecedented economic depression and steeped in isolationism born out of the tragedy of the Great War. Yet, encouraged by his trusted military and diplomatic advisors, and Britain's Prime Minister Winston Churchill, he persisted with vital materiel and moral support to the British, then fighting virtually alone and for their very survival.

Roosevelt's dilemma was multifaceted. He innately understood the eventual lethal threat to the United States represented by the global designs of the Axis powers. He had to persuade reluctant citizens and political leaders to prepare for war. Meanwhile, even faced with fiscal resources limited by Depression era recovery programs, he knew that significant military support of the British was absolutely essential to their survival and thus the survival of his principal future ally. A similar calculus applied to the Soviet Union, soon to be invaded by Hitler's forces. Meanwhile, he had somehow to form an unprecedented large, effective, well-equipped, and most importantly, well-led fighting force eventually to take the fight to the enemy. Time was not on his side.

After the Great War, in which the United States Army and Navy deployed over a million troops to Europe, the government almost immediately embarked on a protracted contraction of its military forces. Fueled by isolationist antipathy to overseas conflicts, the failure of the United States to ratify the League of Nations treaty, and preoccupation with the boom-then-bust economy, the Army became a mere shadow of its former self. Eventually it shrank to as few as 133,000 soldiers in uniform. As late as June of 1939, the Army consisted of only 190,000 men and five incomplete combat divisions.[1] This compared to 136 divisions of the Wehrmacht that invaded the Low Countries in 1940, and 200 that attacked the Soviet Union in 1941.[2] The future enemy forces were not only large in number, but they were also extremely well equipped with the latest weaponry, well led, fierce, and disciplined. Likewise, they were backed by a sophisticated industrial base, modern air and naval forces, and empires containing vast natural resources.

In contrast, in 1940, the United States Army ranked seventeenth in the world in terms of combat power, just behind the Romanian Army. The Army would grow to more than eight million at war's end, but in 1941 was led by fewer than 14,000 professional officers, including the Air Corps.[3] Many of these were Old Army throwbacks, including a cavalry contingent that was not necessarily convinced that mechanized ground forces were more effective than horses and mule trains.

Still, within this officer cadre was a small group of dedicated military patriots with an uncanny understanding of world events and the nexus of a plan for creating a fighting force capable of defeating the imposing might of the German and Japanese war machines. With vision and fortitude, they tended to gravitate toward positions of leadership in the tradition of great Americans in past national crises. Among this group were several veterans of the Great War and the lean inter-war years who would take their places in the pantheon of heroes alongside Washington, Scott, Jackson, Lee, and Black Jack Pershing. They included Douglas MacArthur, George Marshall, Dwight Eisenhower, George Patton, and Omar Bradley. All West Point graduates (except Marshall, a Virginia Military Institute alumnus), they knew each other to some extent through decades of service in a variety of postings. Each had a circle of colleagues formed in peace and war from Flanders fields to dusty frontier Army posts, from the Philippine Islands to the military bureaucracy in Washington. Many of these professional associates would be carefully selected to serve in key positions of combat leadership in the imminent struggle, especially those who had made it into General Marshall's legendary black book.

One such officer was a forty-eight-year-old Washingtonian, the son of a mid-level manager in the Bureau of Engraving and Printing. Neither a West Pointer nor a veteran of the European battlefields of the Great War, he nevertheless represented the fierce dedication embodied by many of those professional soldiers who, for decades, foresaw war clouds on the horizon and remained true to their calling of service. Together with the two men closest to him, his only son and his only daughter's husband, he would throw his life into the unconditional defeat of the Third Reich. This book is the tragic and triumphant true story of three professional soldiers of World War II. In peace, they were inextricably linked by blood and marriage, and in war, by their common enemy on common battlefields. We will follow them and the specific units in which they served through the war years from November 1942 until August 1945. It is presented for readers three and four generations removed from the war who may not have a background in military history or terminology.

The Axis powers were on the very brink of global domination when the United States finally entered the war after Pearl Harbor at the end of 1941. Without American forces opening second fronts in Europe and the Pacific, only the Soviet Union may have generated the military power to have stymied Germany and Japan. Even so, a world order dominated by Stalin and the Soviets along with Nazi Germany and Imperial Japan may well have signaled the end to democracy throughout the world.

There is no doubt that World War II was the defining event in the history of the United States. While both the American Revolution and the Civil War were paramount in America at the time, neither carried such weight of global consequence. In the twentieth century only the might of American armed forces, backed by its unequaled industrial resources and indomitable spirit, quite literally saved the planet and thereby defined the world order we know today.

1

—•—

Three Soldiers

Donald A. Stroh was born in Harrisburg, Pennsylvania, on November 3, 1892, the son of Harry Lincoln Stroh and Annie Amelia Armpriester. The family moved to Washington, DC in 1896, where Mr. Stroh was employed as a pressman for the Bureau of Engraving and Printing. Donald attended DC public schools. While a member of the Cadet Battalion at Central High School, he developed a lifelong interest in military history and the goal of becoming an army officer. Unable to secure an appointment to West Point, and with his family not in a financial position to fund a private academy prep school, Donald enrolled at Michigan Agricultural College, later Michigan State University, a land grant college that provided financial assistance for members of its Cadet Corps. He was a cadet all four years and majored in horticulture. In September 1914, he was appointed to the rank of cadet major and commanded one of the Corps' battalions. After graduation in 1915 with a bachelor of science degree, he took a job with Sunkist Fruit Company in New York City while maintaining his affiliation with the Army through summer training under the Plattsburgh program.

With the United States' entry into World War I, Stroh applied for and was granted a regular Army Cavalry commission effective June 1917. Prior to receiving his Army commission and frustrated with the Army's slow administrative progress, Stroh accepted a commission in the Marine Corps. He trained as a Marine second lieutenant at Parris Island, South Carolina, and Quantico, Virginia, from June until August, when he was able to effect transfer to the Army. His first Army assignment was the Army Service School at Ft. Leavenworth, Kansas, where, among other things, he learned military horsemanship and cavalry tactics as part of the Third Provisional Battalion. In October, he joined the 17th Cavalry Regiment in Douglas, Arizona, as a troop commander, a position roughly equivalent to an infantry platoon leader.

The mission of the cavalry regiments all along the frontier border was twofold: to maintain security of the border areas against troops of marauding Mexican bandits, and to deter a Mexican alliance with Germany that may have led to a war front in North America. Throughout his service there, the 17th made a series of preparations to ship out to the war in Europe, but much to his disappointment, the regiment maintained border defense for the duration of the war.

Donald Stroh and his future bride, Imogene Finger, whom he called Genie, of Hickory, North Carolina, met in Washington, where she was attending a finishing school. It was the summer of 1914 and she was residing with an acquaintance of Donald's mother. They began a long distance romance which resulted in their marriage in June 1917, days before he reported to Parris Island for duty. Their first child, Imogene, was born in January 1919 in Douglas.

After the war, the 17th Cavalry was transferred to Schofield Barracks, Hawaiian Territory. In 1920, Captain Stroh applied for a transfer to the Infantry and joined the 35th Infantry Regiment as a company commander. While in Hawaii, the Strohs had another child, Harry, in August 1920.

Returning to the United States in September 1922, Capt. Stroh attended the Infantry School at Fort Benning, Georgia, and was subsequently assigned to the National Guard 85th Infantry Division in Detroit, Michigan. The Strohs spent five years there, from June 1923 to May 1928. Capt. Stroh served as the executive officer of the 339th Infantry, and adjutant and assistant chief of staff, G-1(Personnel and Administration) of the 85th Division.

After attending the advanced infantry course at Ft. Benning, where he finished tenth out of a class of 298, Captain Stroh was assigned to the 16th Brigade at Ft. Hunt, Virginia, where he served as the adjutant and S-3 (Operations). During an annual leave, he and Mrs. Stroh retraced the steps of her father's Civil War regiment through Virginia and North Carolina. Capt. Stroh then wrote and published the history of the 42nd North Carolina Infantry. From 1931 to 1933, he attended the Command and General Staff College at Ft. Leavenworth.

The Strohs shipped out for the Philippine Islands in August 1933, where Captain Stroh served as a company commander with the 45th Infantry at Ft. McKinley. He was promoted to major in November 1934 and then served as the executive officer of the 23rd Brigade. While in the Philippines, the Strohs became good friends with Major and Mrs. Lawton Collins. Later, Major General Collins commanded the VII Corps of which General Stroh would be a part while with the 9th Division in Northern Europe.

As the executive officer of the 23rd Brigade, Major Stroh worked directly for Brigadier General J. L. DeWitt, who would later command the U.S. Fourth Army. DeWitt wrote of Stroh on this annual Officer Efficiency Report (OER) dated November 16, 1935:

A superior officer, dependable, thorough, with fine judgement and common sense, conscientious and ambitious, of high professional attainments. One of the most efficient officers I know. This officer should be

given the opportunity to attend the Army War College
so as to make him available to the War Department
General Staff.

This appears to be the beginning of Stroh's grooming for higher
things. DeWitt later brought him to the Fourth Army staff as the G-2,
in the years just prior to the war.

Returning to the United States in January 1936, the Strohs moved
to Plattsburgh Barracks, New York, where Maj. Stroh commanded
a battalion in the 26th Infantry. In June 1936, the Strohs returned
to Washington and Maj. Stroh attended the Army War College, the
Army's senior service school.

Following graduation in June 1937, he was assigned as a tactics instructor at the Infantry School at Ft. Benning. In the summer
of 1938, he became the Chairman of the Attack Committee at the
school, a position he held for two years during the critical pre-war
years of Army tactics development. His OERs of June 1939 and May
1940 were written by then Colonel Courtney Hodges, who later commanded the U.S. First Army in Northern Europe. Of Stroh, Hodges
wrote:

He is an alert, dignified, cooperative and
trustworthy officer. He possesses an analytical mind
and is well grounded in his profession, a rapid and
tireless worker who produces superior results. He
has the highest potentiality for any class of duty or
assignment. He is calm, dignified, serious and open-
minded. He is an original thinker with a keen mind
and thorough knowledge of his profession... He has the
highest present and potential value for any class of
duty.

In June 1939, young Imogene Stroh married Second Lieutenant Robert Stumpf, an infantry officer stationed at Jefferson Barracks, Missouri. In July, Harry Stroh entered the United States Military Academy at West Point.

In June 1940, Lieutenant Colonel Stroh was assigned to the Presidio in San Francisco, where he served as the aide and assistant chief of staff, G-2 (Intelligence) to the commanding general, Fourth Army. In April 1941, he and three other officers were sent to the war-torn United Kingdom to study the British military command structure, operations, and intelligence system. Upon return, he was promoted to full colonel. General DeWitt's endorsement of Col. Stroh's OER dated March 1942: "I concur in this report and recommend Colonel Stroh for appointment as Brigadier General for duties and responsibilities for which he is fully qualified."

In the spring of 1942, Col. Stroh returned to the 85th Division as part of the regular cadre for its wartime activation. He commanded the 339th Infantry Regiment upon its activation until his promotion to brigadier general in July. He was then reassigned as the assistant commanding general of the 9th Infantry Division at Fort Bragg, North Carolina, commanded by Major General Manton S. Eddy.

It may be worthwhile to explore the job description of an assistant division commander. With the benefit of hindsight and a wealth of experience, Gen. Stroh offered his view in a "lessons learned" paper submitted in July 1947.

> The assignment is unfortunate and largely unworkable. The brigadier is neither fish nor fowl, neither a commander or a staff officer. If in combat, he gives his attention to the main effort, or commands a task force, he supplants the regimental commander, and must employ the latter's staff to the detriment of its primary job. If he supervises infantry training out

of combat he becomes a glorified G-3, and is severely handicapped by lack of a staff, or groups of training inspectors of his own.

To my knowledge nothing of an official nature has ever been announced as to the duties of this unfortunate individual. At least nothing has come to my attention. How he is employed is largely up to the division commander.

In the 9th Division...during non-combat phases my responsibility was the training of all combat elements except the artillery. I had no personnel, supply, or disciplinary functions. I wrote the training programs, prepared and conducted demonstrations and schools, and inspected training.... In combat I did everything from commanding a regiment to preparing...the next day's field order.

In the 8th Division, which I later commanded, I used my assistant in much the same way I had been employed in the 9th, except that I kept a much tighter rein on the tactical employment...

Shortly after his arrival, the division began amphibious training, principally near Solomons Island in the Chesapeake Bay, specifically to prepare for Operation Torch, the invasion of North Africa, although only the very most senior leaders had any idea about where they were going. Amphibious operations—the movement of men and equipment from ships to shore—are difficult under the most benign circumstances. Throw in a long sea transit in crowded conditions, adverse weather, heavy seas, large tides, and of course, enemy opposition and it becomes a tall order indeed for even the best trained units. Because, by nature, amphibious operations are joint operations between naval and ground forces, the coordination challenges are significant and must be addressed early in the process.

For the soldiers involved, imagine being terrified, probably sea-sick, loaded down with upwards of sixty pounds of weapons and equipment, cold, wet, possibly hungry, and then having to climb over the side of a moving ship onto a slippery cargo net to slowly lower yourself into an even more unstable craft that will take you and your crowded comrades to a hostile, turbulent shoreline. Then somehow, not drown on the way from the landing craft to the beach, not get shot or blown up, shoot back, find cover, find your unit, and get organized.

In October, while the 9th Division was at Fort Bragg preparing to make the voyage and invasion of North Africa, it was visited by Major General George Patton, the Western Task Force commander under whom much of the division would operate in theater. During the visit, the division assembled to receive one of his fiery speeches made famous in the movie *Patton,* starring George C. Scott. Here is how then 2nd Lieutenant Richard Kent remembered it in a letter to a fellow 9th Division veteran, Donald Lavender, in 1991.

> He gave the officers of the Division his disgusting tirade at Ft. Bragg theater and then went outside where the entire Division and our wives were and repeated the same thing with even more profanity. Then on ships going to Africa we were forced to listen to tapes of the same thing.

One of the speech's memorable lines was given during Patton's direction on how the soldiers were to treat the enemy. "Grab those pusillanimous sons-of-bitches by the nose and kick 'em in the balls." Apparently the division ladies were appalled and offended, as were a group of nurses in the adjacent hospital who had thrown open the windows in order to see and hear Gen. Patton. The sound of windows slamming shut could be heard as his speech progressed.

Gen. Stroh's son-in-law, Robert Henry Stumpf, was born on September 1, 1915 in Barberton, Ohio. His father, Elmer Robert Stumpf, was a physician specializing in heart disease. His mother, Anne Moore, and father were both originally from the St. Louis area.

At Barberton High School, Bob excelled in mathematics and science, and was a football letterman. After high school graduation in 1932, at age sixteen, Bob attended Akron University for one year while competing for an appointment to the United States Military Academy at West Point.

Having received an appointment from Ohio Senator Robert J. Bulkley, Bob reported to West Point in July 1933 with the class of 1937. He was one of the younger members of his class, many of whom had two or more years of college or prep school. He was a large man at six feet four inches tall, who is remembered by his classmates for his robust health and good nature. He played football and boxed at the academy, earning the nickname "Primo" after his striking resemblance to the then world heavyweight champion, Primo Carnera of Italy. One of Cadet Stumpf's infantry tactics instructors was Major Omar Bradley, who would later command the 12th Army Group in Europe, and is said to have made the subject come alive for the cadets. Cadet Stumpf's proclivity in mathematics and science prepared him well for the rigid engineering curriculum at West Point. But his strongest subjects were military tactics, foreign languages, physics, history, law, and economics. Although not among the top cadets, he never faltered academically, finishing 141st out of 298 in his graduating class. He was commissioned a second lieutenant of infantry in June 1937.

Lieutenant Stumpf chose to pursue flight training with the Army Air Corps and reported to Randolph Field, San Antonio, Texas, in August of 1937. After eight months of flight training, normally the point a student would be designated an Army pilot, he opted out of the Air Corps and transferred back to the Infantry. He may have made this decision because he was too tall to be considered for the cramped cockpits of fighter planes.

Subsequently, Lt. Stumpf was assigned as a platoon commander with the 6th Infantry at Jefferson Barracks, Missouri. In the fall of 1938, he met a nineteen-year-old student at Lindenwood College, Imogene "Jerry" Stroh, at a Halloween costume party. The future Mrs. Stumpf, many years later, reminisced that she wore a hula girl costume and that the tall young lieutenant twirled her incessantly as they danced in an attempt to see what she was wearing beneath her grass skirt. They were married the following June at the Ft. Benning chapel on the fiftieth wedding anniversary of the bride's paternal grandparents.

In pursuit of an Army-sponsored master's degree at the Massachusetts Institute of Technology, Lt. Stumpf transferred from the Infantry branch to the Ordnance Department in the summer of 1940. The Ordnance Department was responsible for the development, testing, and supply of munitions, weapons, and armed vehicles. The Stumpfs packed up and moved to Aberdeen Proving Grounds at Havre-de-Grace, Maryland, where Lt. Stumpf attended the Army Ordnance School, learning weapons theory and production.

In August 1941, they moved to Cambridge, Massachusetts, to begin the degree program. But before starting classes, due to looming wartime contingencies, the program was cancelled. Captain Stumpf was then assigned to the Watertown Arsenal in Boston, where he helped supervise the building and testing of new Army weaponry. During these years, the Army was expanding rapidly and opportunities for regular officers abounded. After years of near stagnation, promotions came rapidly for capable soldiers of all ranks.

In early 1942, Capt. Stumpf attended the special staff officer's course at the Command and General Staff College, Ft. Leavenworth, Kansas, was promoted to major, and transferred to the staff of the 76th Infantry Division as the ordnance officer. As plans for the invasion of North Africa began to coalesce, Maj. Stumpf was assigned as the assistant ordnance officer of the Western Task Force under Gen. Patton. Patton was one of the American commanders of Operation Torch, the invasion of French Northwest Africa. They shipped out with the task force from Norfolk, Virginia, on October 24th, 1942 bound for French Morocco. Also in the invasion task force were elements of the 9th Infantry Division whose assistant commanding general was Maj. Stumpf's father-in-law, Gen. Stroh. Mrs. Stumpf and her mother, Mrs. Stroh, moved to Washington, DC for the duration.

Harry Richard Stroh was the son of a career soldier, a cavalry officer, in the Territory of Hawaii, almost two years after the end of The Great War. Shortly thereafter, his father, recognizing the futility of the horse in modern warfare, changed his branch designator to the Infantry. For the next two decades the future soldier traveled the world with his father, mother, and sister as they moved from post to post, the father slowly rising through the ranks in the severely whittled-down Army of the years between the world wars.

He lived at Army posts in Hawaii, Washington, Georgia, Michigan, Kansas, the Philippine Islands, and Virginia. He was an accomplished horseman and avid outdoorsman. He earned the rank of Eagle Scout while in the Philippines. He loved the rhythms of Army life, the call to colors each morning, and the thunder of a howitzer sounding re-treat at the end of each day; the discipline of the soldiers at drill, the somewhat complex social scene centered around the officers' club. He learned to live and breathe the principles of conduct of the soldier written in the West Point motto: duty, honor, country. These were not hollow words to Harry, but a code of life.

His father not surprisingly steered him to follow in his footsteps with a career in the Army. The father forever regretted that he had been un-able to attain an appointment to West Point. Had he done so, he would have graduated in 1915 with his future bosses Dwight Eisenhower and Omar Bradley. Instead, it took him until America's entry in World War I to gain a commission. He was committed to the idea that his son would make it to West Point and accomplish great things, a calling that Harry also embraced. Indeed Dad nicknamed his only son "Chief," as in Chief of Staff, the highest ranking Army position.

So determined were the two of them to gain the coveted appointment that upon graduation from high school, Harry endured a year of study at Millard's Preparatory School in Washington, the curriculum of which was designed expressly for the competitive West Point entry exam. Not a brilliant student, he nevertheless succeeded in securing an appointment from the 7th District of Michigan and entered the Academy in July 1939, achieving his father's elusive dream. Cadet Stroh struggled academically at the Academy, at one point facing expulsion at the Academic Board for insufficient marks in English. He rallied on reexamination, while the rest of Corps of Cadets were home on Christmas leave.

At the completion of his junior year in June of 1942, the country now engaged in global war, Cadet Stroh reported to Army Air Corps flight training. He was skillful in the cockpit, earning his wings in six months, while still a cadet, and gaining a coveted fighter assignment. His West Point class graduated six months early in January 1943, and he was off to advanced fighter training in Texas, Florida, New York, and finally Groton Field, Connecticut. Meanwhile, his father's 9th Division helped throw Rommel out of North Africa and was engaged in the Sicily campaign, which set the stage for the invasion of mainland Italy.

In the fall of 1943, the 9th Infantry Division shipped out of Sicily for England to prepare for the invasion of northern France. In late November, 1st Lt. Stroh arrived in England aboard the troopship *Queen Elizabeth* with his new P-47 Thunderbolt outfit, the 378th Fighter Squadron of the 362nd Fighter Group. At Christmas, he and his father were reunited for a few days, the lieutenant and the general, the young fighter pilot and the old foot soldier, both bursting with pride in the other. Lt. Stroh's brother-in-law, Lt. Col. Bob Stumpf, was able to join them.

2

---◆---

North Africa:
Operation Torch

The Allies' decision to begin the offensive against the Axis powers in North Africa has been debated from the day it was announced by President Roosevelt to his senior military advisors on July 30, 1942. Conversely, in the global strategic context, the inclination of Marshall and the rest of American military leadership was that any attack against Hitler outside the European continent itself was a misuse of time and resources. They would have preferred an overwhelming assault on fortress Europe at the earliest opportunity, followed by a drive straight to Berlin. Of course, the Soviets, too, would have directly benefited by an earlier invasion of the continent, as they were at the time in a desperate struggle against the bulk of the Wehrmacht.

But Churchill's rationale won the debate. He figured, correctly as it turned out, that the Allies simply were not ready militarily for the momentous task of taking on the Wehrmacht on their home turf, especially through an opposed amphibious assault. Churchill's leverage in the debate also may have derived from his credibility as the leader of the only remaining Atlantic country to be actively fighting the Germans. Examining what Churchill considered the disadvantages of an early (1942) invasion of Europe:

* The Germans were masters of the defense as defined by the military philosopher Carl von Clausewitz during the Napoleonic Wars. He reasoned that a defense of maneuver was far superior to a static defense—the movement of forces to points of vulnerability rather than deployed across the entire theater boundary. From the perspective of the continent being one gigantic battlefield, Hitler, using the modern European rail system, could move large military forces efficiently from front to front, the equivalent of the concept of "interior lines" of the traditional battlefield. Forces in the east fighting the Russians could be shifted quickly to the Western front to respond to an amphibious invasion.

* Any invasion of Europe would by definition have to be amphibious. Hitler controlled virtually the entire littoral of Europe. Amphibious invasion against a prepared enemy was and is a very difficult task. The defender has all the advantages, the greatest being the ocean as his moat.

* An essential element in an amphibious assault is the landing craft itself that takes the soldiers and their equipment from the ships to the beach. Thousands would be required. They simply did not exist in those quantities in early 1942.

* Churchill argued that the British people could ill afford another defeat. To try and fail again might prove a fatal blow to their already sorely tested morale.

* The German military was at the height of its power in 1942. It had fought and defeated every foe including the British since the war began in 1939. Its forces were blooded, tactically proficient, well equipped, and supremely confident; a professional army.

* U.S. forces, on the other hand, were green, inexperienced, tactically immature, equipped with inferior weapons, and comprised mostly of conscripts. The will was there, but the means were yet to be developed.

* British forces had been through a lot. They had fought the Germans on the Continent, in the Middle East, and the RAF had stymied the Luftwaffe in the Battle of Britain. These experiences gave the Brits the proficiency to stack up well against the Germans, but also a healthy understanding of the toughness of their foe. But they were too few to go the distance alone.

So venues other than Western Europe were examined as more appropriate to open the second front. The British were already engaged against German and Italian forces in Egypt with some success. Algeria and Morocco in Northwest Africa were controlled by Vichy France, the German surrogate created after French capitulation in 1940. Although the French had agreed to defend this area, Churchill and Roosevelt reasoned that they would be inclined to make such defense perfunctory, especially against Americans with whom they had no particular animosity.

If the Allies could surprise the Germans by landing a significant force in Northwest Africa, they could accomplish much. They would open a second front at the theater level by threatening the Axis rear in Africa, and a global second front from the Soviet perspective. The Axis would be forced to divert forces from the Eastern Front to North Africa to respond to the new threat. This would relieve pressure on both the British in Egypt and the Soviets at home. The ultimate military goal was to trap Rommel and his Africa Corps between the two fronts and destroy all German and Italian forces in Africa. Of course, the accomplishment of this goal would do much for Allied confidence and morale. It would halt Hitler's ambitions of complete global domination by preventing Axis occupation of the Middle East and eventual link-up with the Japanese in India or Burma.

It would be the warm-up for the inevitable invasion of Fortress Europe, allowing the Americans to build their tactical proficiency before entering into the greater struggle. Their first combat would be primarily against less than inspired French forces. The amphibious assault, although certainly challenging, would be less difficult than one on Europe against German defenders. American military commanders and their green troops would gain invaluable combat experience. Inevitable mistakes may not be disastrous, but would allow the formation of combat effectiveness for the fledgling Army.

Many tenets of modern warfare were new to even the professional American soldiers. Although used effectively by the Germans and others, the integration of air forces into the battlefield, especially in direct support of troops, was an untested concept to the Americans. In addition to the air integration problem, the Army had been reorganized at the tactical level to better integrate the more effective modern weapons systems—tanks, artillery, and heavy infantry weapons. And many army units were now more or less mechanized, meaning they maneuvered primarily by truck and tracked vehicles, rather than on foot supported by mules. None of these fundamental changes in modern warfare were in the combat experience of the professional soldiers who would lead the fight.

North Africa provided the proving ground for these men, their weapons, equipment, tactics, and leadership. Going across the beach, they were courageous, but untried. After North Africa, they were blooded, and a much more mature combat force capable of challenging the Germans in their own arena.

Operation Torch was the western half of the grand strategy to defeat and force the withdrawal of Axis forces (German and Italian) in Africa. The British had been fighting the Axis in Egypt and Libya for some time and formed the eastern arm of the giant pincer movement.

The idea was to force the Axis armies to the central Mediterranean coast in Tunisia, with the Torch invasion force attacking from the west and the British from the east. The Allied invasion force consisted of three task forces, the Western Task Force (WTF), Central, and Eastern. They were organized under a convoluted command organization with General Eisenhower as Commander in Chief. Major General George Patton commanded the Western Task Force. Maj. Stumpf served on Patton's staff as the assistant ordnance officer.

As part of the invasion force, the 9th Infantry Division's three regimental combat teams (RCT) were assigned to three separate commands attacking at three different landing zones. The 47th and the 60th Infantry Regiments were in the Western Task Force zone near Casablanca, and the 39th in the Eastern Task Force zone near Algiers, some 850 miles apart. The 39th had shipped out to the UK in late September and would make the voyage to Algeria with an Allied armada. Gen. Stroh and his boss, Gen. Eddy, would remain behind at Fort Bragg with 9th division elements not included in the initial landings, including division artillery, to supervise embarkation of follow-on units and supplies. While Stroh was not physically present to participate in the landings, he was primarily responsible for training the division over the previous several months, so we will briefly describe their participation.

Torch included over 100,000 men, and 800 ships, including hundreds of transports and their warship escorts, one of which was the WTF flagship, cruiser USS *Augusta*, with Patton and part of his staff aboard. The landings on this 800-mile front were designed to be simultaneous, and a surprise to the French defenders. Morocco and Algeria were French colonies, governed by Vichy French officials and defended by Vichy ground, air, and naval forces. D-day was set for dawn on November 8th.

The main body of the Western Task Force departed Hampton Roads on October 24, 1942 and rendezvoused with other ships from different ports. They refueled underway and kept strict radio silence. The Force began to split up into three groups on November 7th as they approached Morocco, one for each of the three landing areas; Port Lyautey to the north, Fedala in the center near Casablanca, and Safi to the south. Gen. Patton and his WTF staff of over 300 men, including Maj. Stumpf, would go ashore at Fedala with the 3rd Infantry Division and other attached units. It is undetermined whether Stumpf was embarked on *Augusta* or a transport ship, probably the latter. He did, however, make it ashore on D-day, November 8th.

The general and part of his staff were prepared to go ashore at 0800 on D-day, but the *Augusta* became involved in a running gun battle with French warships attempting to break out of the port at Casablanca and disrupt the invasion force. During the course of this battle, the landing craft that was to carry them ashore was blown off its davits. Patton eventually made it to shore at 1320.

The port and town of Fedala were fairly quickly secured as the French resistance was overcome. Elements of the French forces began to negotiate a ceasefire with the Americans. Patton set up the WTF headquarters at the Hotel Miramar and supervised the preparations for the taking of Casablanca some eighteen miles to the southwest. From Fedala, Patton's troops moved toward Casablanca, initially clearing light French resistance, but meeting with much stiffer defense on the 10th. The Americans continued forward and were in position to attack the city in strength on the morning of November 11th.

Recognizing their precarious position and with a desire to prevent the destruction of Casablanca, French authorities signaled the Americans that they sought a termination of hostilities. The impending attack on Casablanca was cancelled. By the afternoon, the appropriate commanders had gathered and cobbled together an agreement that set the stage for French/Allied cooperation across French Morocco.

Meanwhile the 47th RCT of the 9th Infantry Division along with units of the 2nd Armored Division landed at the port of Safi, some

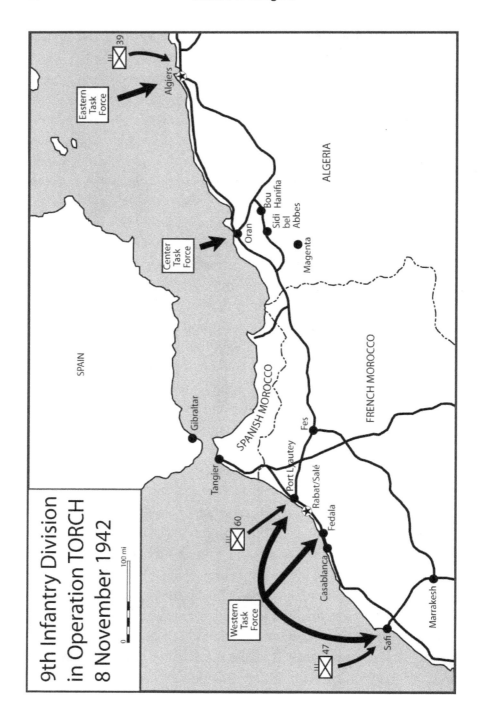

9th Infantry Division in Operation TORCH 8 November 1942

140 miles southwest of Casablanca, in the predawn hours. Safi had been chosen as an objective because its protected harbor provided a safe landing area for the 2nd Armored's medium tanks. The landing force consisted of more than 6,000 men.

Resistance by the French was at first stiff and included heavy artillery as well as rifle and machine gun fire. Naval counter battery gunfire was employed to reduce the enemy artillery. However, it wasn't until some of the American tanks were operational after a few hours that the invaders were able to clear out stubborn sniper fire. By late afternoon, Safi had been secured. The plan was to get the tanks moving north to assist with the battle for Casablanca. The armored column started northeast at 0900 on 10 November.

To the northeast, some seventy-eight miles from Casablanca, the heavily reinforced 60th RCT of the 9th Division formed the backbone of the invasion force at Port Lyautey. During heavy fighting on D-day, the invaders found themselves in a precarious position with some units being driven back to the landing beachheads. The next day, the Americans and reinforced French defenders waged a back-and-forth armor and infantry battle, the Americans supported by the heavy guns of the cruiser *Savannah*. During the night of 9-10 November, offensive operations to capture the airfield produced mixed results, but by dawn, the defenders were beginning to cease operations and surrender.

The airfield was secured by 0800 and by 1030, Army Air Corps P-40 fighters from the escort carrier USS *Chenango* began landing there. As in the famed Dolittle Raid on Tokyo, these Army aircraft were flown off the carrier by specially trained Army pilots. Cleanup operations continued throughout the day supported by naval gunfire. Formal cessation of hostilities at Port Lyautey occurred at 0400, November 11th.

While the 39th RCT (of the 9th Division) was not part of the Western Task Force in Morocco, they played a significant role with the Eastern Task Force in the attack on Algiers. The mission of the 39th, augmented by units of British commandoes, was an amphibious assault east of the city to secure coastal defenses, a strategic airfield, and two small towns while closing on Algiers from the southeast.

At dawn on November 7th about 150 miles northwest of Algiers, the transport *Thomas Stone*, with the 2nd battalion, 39th Infantry embarked, was attacked by German aircraft which disabled the ship's propeller and rudder. The battalion commanding officer, the intrepid Maj. Walter M. Oakes, resourcefully convinced the ship's captain to release twenty-four of his twenty-six landing craft in an attempt to transport the 700-man battalion the remaining 150 miles of open sea to the assault point. The passage was a disaster, the landing craft mechanically not up to the task. Ultimately all boats were abandoned and the entire battalion crammed into the escort corvette, HMS *Spey*. The battalion, and the transport *Thomas Stone*, eventually made it to Algiers, but not in time for the D-day assault.

The 39th's 1st and 3rd battalions successfully completed their missions, landing before dawn on the 8th, capturing their objectives, and closing on Algiers in time for the capitulation of French forces throughout the city.

The first three days of Operation Torch had been a resounding success in that it established a significant Allied foothold in Northwest Africa including the ports of Casablanca and Algiers and several airfields. Additionally, while initially strong, the French resistance had capitulated across the theater of operations. Furthermore, the Allies and French skillfully negotiated cessation terms that set the stage for French cooperation in the ultimate defeat of Germany and liberation of France.

Total Allied casualties were roughly 1,500 killed, wounded, or missing, surprisingly light considering the scope of the operation. And a great deal of combat experience was gained, including tricky amphibious operations. From a strategic perspective, the Allied invasion leading to a solid foothold on the continent put pressure on the Axis forces there, and relieved pressure on the Soviets fiercely engaged with German forces on the eastern front. The presence of substantial American forces in Africa required moving German troops from the eastern front to bolster Field Marshal Erwin Rommel's forces in an attempt to prevent the Allied objective of ejecting all Axis forces from Africa. The Allied leadership recognized that the road ahead would be difficult against experienced German and Italian forces under the leadership of Rommel, the "Desert Fox," on what had become their home turf.

At the end of hostilities in Casablanca on November 11th, a continuing backlog of supplies and equipment were being disembarked from the American transports, many of which were still at anchor. The threat of German submarine attack was a growing concern. On the 11th and 12th, two U-boats torpedoed six American ships off Fedala—four transports, a tanker, and a destroyer. The transports went to the bottom with hundreds of sailors lost or wounded, many with severe burns.

The submarine attacks were witnessed not only by the other ships in the flotilla who were also at high risk, but by many on shore including Gen. Patton and his staff. They were enjoying a celebratory dinner the evening of the 11th; the 24th anniversary of the World War One armistice, the fresh victories in North Africa, and Patton's 57th birthday. When the troop transport USS *Joseph Hewes* was torpedoed by U-173 at about 1930, the huge fiery explosion could be seen from the Hotel Miramar. The transport sank an hour later with the loss of one hundred men, including several wounded evacuees and the captain, Robert M. Smith. The U-173 struck two other ships in the attack, destroyer USS *Hambleton* (DD-455) and oiler USS *Winooski* (AO 38), both of which were damaged, but stayed afloat.

Stumpf's and others' personal belongings had not yet been unloaded from the transports. Except for what he had worn on D-day, he lost everything, including a carefully packed kit of uniforms, equipment, personal items, books, etc. As future letters would bear out, in the months ahead he would request his wife, Jerry (Imogene), to seek out and mail items that were not available in theater. Somehow, he found a way to see the humor in his predicament and dispatched this hastily scrawled, undated note with a Navy man headed back to Norfolk.

> Just caught a naval officer slightly in his cups. Bought him one more to wait for this. He goes back tomorrow and will mail this. I am safe but without personal possessions as a result of our transport being slightly torpedoed and sunk. Everything OK and got some clothes from the Q.M. Will try to cable soon. Tell the old man [Gen. Stroh] am anxious to see him when he gets over on a bit of finagling.
>
> Wrote you a couple of letters on the ship but they blew up. Sorry this has to be short. Don't know when mail goes out.
>
> Not much fighting at present. Miss you. P.S. Tell folks.

3

———•———

Buildup

After the cessation of hostilities with the French, the Americans concentrated on strengthening and expanding their foothold on the continent which included landing vast quantities of war materiel. Undermanned and without sufficient heavy weapons during the invasion, the outcome for the Americans could have been different if the French had put up a more spirited defense and the Germans had more actively supported them.

Now men, tanks, artillery, munitions, vehicles of all sorts, food, fuel, and a thousand other necessities for a modern and growing army were streaming through the ports, including Casablanca. With the reorganization of the Western Task Force during the weeks following the invasion, Maj. Stumpf was reassigned to the staff of the new Area Commander, Brigadier General Hugh J. Gaffey, recently of the 2nd Armored Division, who had been one of the leaders of the successful landings at Safi. Stumpf was the acting S-3 in charge of operations at the Casablanca port, a departure from his duties as an ordnance officer and something he was probably more comfortable with and excited about. He wrote to Jerry on December 5th, "...

prospects are considerably brighter about going either to Infantry or Armored Force." As for liberty in Casablanca, Stumpf was not particularly impressed.

> Not a whole lot of amusement in the town but so
> far haven't had time to mind. On the job seven days a
> week, and the town closes down at 9:30 pm. The Arabs
> here are about the most destitute lot of humans I ever
> hope to see. We have the strange spectacle of camels
> and jackasses getting mixed up in traffic, but not a
> whole lot else that seems strange. Have been trying
> to send something for your Christmas but the famous
> Moroccan leather market is shot because the Germans
> have taken all the leather.

> December 25th, 1942:
> Your dad is here now and I had supper with him.
> He said you got my first letter from me and it was
> quite a relief inasmuch as one of the officers recently
> arrived from the U.S. said I'd been officially listed
> as among the missing. Be sure to tell what's left of
> the old staff the "reports of my death are greatly
> exaggerated."

Remaining behind with the rear echelons of the 9th Division until they could be allocated transport to the theater of operations, Gen. Stroh finally arrived in Casablanca on Christmas Eve, 1942 with the rest of the senior division staff, including Gen. Eddy, after the long ocean transit. He wrote in a letter to daughter Imogene, dated January 3, 1943:

> As I told Mother, nearly the first person I saw
> on the dock when we landed was Bob. He was then

acting as S-3 for the area commander, Gen. Gaffey,
who ordinarily is one of the brigadiers of the 2nd
Armored Division. He was thoroughly disgusted
with this assignment, and with Ordnance in general,
having seen, during the previous few weeks, how the
department really functioned. He gave me a copy of
an official letter he had written, asking to be relieved
of his detail and returned to the Infantry, and also the
endorsement from the Ordnance Officer of the Force,
which referred to him as a superior officer who could
not be spared. I told him that I knew influential officers
at Headquarters and offered to do what I could... Next
morning I called on Gen. Keyes... After leaving his
office, I ran into Bob on the street, and he told me that
Gaffey was going back to his division, and was taking
Bob with him, probably as a battalion commander. This
tickled Bob very much, but I cannot claim any credit...
so I hope by this time that Bob is a doughboy again and
commanding a battalion. [Before the new year, Stumpf
was reassigned to the 2nd Armored Division, whose
headquarters and units were concentrated to the east
of Salé, near the Moroccan capital of Rabat, some sixty
miles northeast of Casablanca.]

Bob looks well. He has a complete new set of
clothing, including a French made blouse [dress
uniform jacket] which isn't at all bad... He is, or was,
living comfortably in a large dorm turned hotel... I
had him to dinner where I was staying, on Christmas
night, when we had a couple of drinks with Gen. Irwin
[9th Division Artillery commander] and Doug Page,
and the meal with them. He gave me a nice Christmas
present in the form of an underarm pistol holster

which he had had made locally. I was sorry that I had nothing to give him, but did give him a few cigars, which are scarce items on this side of the ocean. In his official capacity we had quite a few dealings with him in the next two or three days, and he arranged for our train to bring us here [Port Lyautey]. He was at the station to see us off, and just received the two letters you had written him the weekend I was in Washington last...

We had a thrill here the night Casablanca was bombed, as there was a report that we would get it next, but nothing materialized. There was very little damage done, and very few military personnel wounded.

Gen. Stroh went on to describe his "palatial" living and mess arrangements, that included Gen. Eddy, which indicated that the 9th Division was at last being reunited after having been split up since before the invasion. Before leaving the lines of this remarkable letter, it would be remiss to leave out the following anecdote, a window into Stroh's sometimes facetious sense of humor, one inherited by his daughter.

I had a rare experience New Year's Eve. The officers of a nearby airport invited us over to a dance. There was a terrible mob there, including a flock of local girls, all duly chaperoned with female relatives. You know how I like to dance anyway [he did not], and when I have to do it in about two square feet, with an amateur French orchestra, and with a girl who speaks no English, it is really an ordeal. However, to maintain international relations I was bumping my way around with a particularly homely one when 1943 arrived. With the new year began the kissing. My partner presented her right cheek, and then her left, on which I duly implanted two healthy kisses. This, I thought, would conclude the evening. Not so. She led me over to a row, twelve deep, of beaming relatives, of assorted ages, each of whom I was required to salute in like manner. Hope that 1944 does not find us here.

The disposition of the 9th Division, from after the Torch landing successes to the end of 1942: Division Headquarters, Division Artillery, and various attached units had recently arrived or were on the high seas en route to Casablanca. The 39th Infantry was in Algeria and would remain there for some time. The 60th Infantry was in the Port Lyautey area after their invasion victory there. Lyautey, some seventy-eight miles northeast of Casablanca, would be the location of division headquarters for the next several weeks. The 47th Infantry, after its success at Safi during the invasion, was making the long foot-march northeast from Safi to Port Lyautey, a distance of 238 miles.

In addition to the 9th Division, Port Lyautey was headquarters of the 1st Military District of Morocco, a regional entity also commanded by Gen. Eddy. The significance of this region to the integrity of the Allied positions across North Africa was its proximity to Spanish Morocco and the 130,000 Spanish and native troops stationed there. While Spanish dictator Francisco Franco had declared neutrality, his political bias was clearly with the fascist Axis powers. Were he actively to support the Germans in the coming battles, or intervene militarily on their behalf, it could shift the balance of power to the Axis advantage. Therefore, a healthy portion of the American effort would be dedicated to neutralizing the Spanish potential along the border of French and Spanish Morocco. The 47th and 60th rotated patrolling this frontier for the next several weeks.

The strategic situation for the Axis forces in Africa had become more and more dire. After a long campaign, the British had some successes against the Germans in Egypt and Libya and were keeping the pressure on from the east, while the new American presence in Morocco and Algeria posed a powerful and growing threat from the west. The Germans and Italians were now geographically positioned primarily in Tunisia. It appeared that this would be where the final outcome in Africa would be decided. In response, the Germans and Italians were reinforcing by air and sea at the rate of about 1,500 troops per day, preparing for a massive offensive designed to extricate them from their predicament.

During January of 1943, both the 9th Infantry and 2nd Armored Divisions had similar agendas: regrouping, resupplying, serving as deterrents against the possibility of Spanish intervention, and intensive training for the inevitable combat ahead. Gen. Stroh was heavily engaged with reorganizing the division after it had been so widely dispersed for months. Now it was missing only the 39th Infantry, still on duty with the Eastern Task Force in Algeria, and one battalion of the 47th, holding down the fort in Safi.

Regardless of his professional responsibilities, Stroh maintained a strict letter writing regimen throughout the war, writing his wife, whom he called Genie, and daughter, Imogene (Jerry, to her husband and friends), on alternating weeks. He also wrote his son, Harry, and his mother with regularity. Alas sadly, only the letters to daughter Imogene survive, but they are a complete set, and may contain the broadest description of what he was seeing, thinking, and feeling, albeit within the strict boundaries of what the military censors would allow. His letter of January 17 was wistful about his not being present that week for Harry's early graduation from West Point. He mentions a parade in honor of a recipient of the Distinguished Service Cross for heroism during the Safi landings attended by a large local crowd and many French officers, and more about his son-in-law.

I have heard indirectly from Bob in the past couple of days. On Friday he made me a present of four cakes of soap, "the Soap of Beautiful Women," which is a scarce article in these parts. He sent them up by an officer who came this way. General Keyes was here yesterday on an inspection trip, and spoke of Bob. He said that he was still on the job at the port, but would not be there long. Another officer who arrived today stated that Bob was wearing crossed rifles [infantry insignia], and was hoping for an assignment to a division soon. I believe, as a matter of fact, that he has already been assigned, but is finishing up with the port job pending certain reorganization which is now underway.

This jibes with Stumpf's service record, which shows him on "detached service" 2nd Armored Division, Dec '42–Feb '43. So apparently, he was still in Casablanca at this point.

In his letter to Imogene of January 31st, while discussing the pleasantness of running into so many old friends from throughout his army career and having them as guests in their mess, Gen. Stroh wrote of a significant event for the soldiers of the 9th.

Yesterday we entertained no other than Martha Raye, who has been touring England and Africa for the past couple of months entertaining the boys. I was much surprised by her appearance and actions. She is not larger than you, dresses quietly and acts the part of a lady. She wears a pair of dog tags like any G.I. and seems quite proud of them. During the afternoon she was the main attraction at an open air show for the boys. Here her ladylike demeanor disappeared, and she returned to character, much to the delight

of the audience. Among the stories she told was this.
She attended a dance in Los Angeles for servicemen
at which Lana Turner was also present, attired in a
very revealing gown. During the party a young British
soldier cut in on her and in the course of his dance
asked Lana what the term was that applied to the cut
of her gown. Lana replied that it had a V neck. "Oh,"
said the Limey, "V for victory." "Yes," replied Lana,
"V for victory, but the bundles are not for Britain."
Brought down the house.

Martha Raye of course was the hugely popular comedienne,
movie actress, and singer who spent much of her lifetime entertaining the troops over the course of three wars. Her show for the 9th was
held in the open air at the racetrack at Port Lyautey. In this same letter,
Gen. Stroh went on to discuss Maj. Stumpf's situation:

I am going to try to get down to see Bob sometime
this week. I understand he is back in the infantry,
but is still working with the port. I know this does
not satisfy him. Among our guests today was Jake
Williams, who was at Leavenworth with us, both in
'17 and '31–'33. He is on the staff there [Western Task
Force], and promises to do everything he can to get
Bob to a division. He did not know that he was my son-
in-law, and was very complimentary of his ability.

In his letter to Imogene at a much later date, March 29th, Stroh
went into further detail regarding Stumpf's original request to be reassigned to the Infantry. Referring to his time in Casablanca, he wrote:

I have learned since, from several sources, that
Bob really had been doing a swell job, and it is no

wonder that the Ordnance hated to lose him. But the
staff in which he had gone over [Western Task Force]
was of a size suitable for an Army, such as we had
in Frisco [5th US Army, the Presidio], entirely too
large for the use to which it has been put eventually.
Accordingly most officers have either been doing work
foreign to their specialties, or have been transferred.
Even as early as December, Bob was not performing an
Ordnance mission, and felt that the immediate future
held nothing for him. I quite agree, and am confident
that he will make a name for himself in his present
outfit.

A visitor of the 9th Division even more prominent than Martha
Raye arrived at Port Lyautey with his entourage on January 22nd,
the Commander in Chief, President Franklin Roosevelt. This was co-
incident with his famous conference with Prime Minister Winston
Churchill in Casablanca to plan the next stages of the war. The division marched in review for the president, who took in the parade
from his jeep. He later received a briefing from the commanding officer of the 60th Infantry describing the battle for Port Lyautey during
the November invasion.

In the meantime, Maj. Stumpf had departed Casablanca for
the 2nd Armored Division headquartered at Salé, just north of the
Moroccan capital of Rabat, where he was assigned Executive Officer
of the 66th Armored Regiment. This location is only about twenty
miles southwest of Port Lyautey. In Gen. Stroh's next letter to Imogene
of February 14th, he described the set-up:

Finally caught up with Bob yesterday, a week
ago, and it was a good thing... After anticipating an
additional week at our last place, we were suddenly

ordered out on Tuesday [to reinforce the Allies at
the Kasserine Pass], and goodness knows when he
and I will be able to get together again. First called
on his division headquarters, and was told he was
in the 3rd battalion of a certain regiment [66th
Armored]. After dashing about in the woods looking
for this outfit, we learned that he was in regimental
headquarters instead, regimental executive in fact...
Arrived eventually at the CP [command post] and
found that it must have been bath day. The regimental
commander...named Collier, whom I have never known
before, received me graciously in his birthday suit,
and told me that Bob was similarly attired behind a
nearby tent. I modestly refrained from disturbing him
at the moment, but waited until he appeared in his
undershirt and trousers. He had bathed luxuriously
under a #10 can, punched full of holes in the bottom,
and suspended from a tree... He was very proud of the
layout. He is also luxuriously housed in a pyramidal
tent with three or four other young officers who I
suppose are fellow members of the staff. They appear
to be congenial tent mates. Bob and I swapped a can of
tobacco for a box of cigars, which he claimed was not
quite just, inasmuch as he had received the tobacco as
a present which he didn't like anyhow. Needless to say,
he is tickled pink about his present job, and it is almost
ideal, as he is the first to admit that he knows little
or nothing of the details of his particular unit, and a
staff position will give him every opportunity to learn
before he gets an outfit to command. Incidentally, it
also carries with it a lieutenant colonelcy...

This position outside of Salé was the headquarters of the 2nd Armored Division for much of the rest of the African Campaign. While not seeing action, the division provided a valuable deterrent to any idea the Axis might have of opening a second front from Spanish Morocco. It also provided Stumpf valuable time to re-hone his infantry and armor leadership skills, having served with the Ordnance Department for over two years, and get to know his men. The 2nd Armored would play a major role in the invasion of Sicily, four months hence.

On April 4th, Stumpf wrote his father-in-law, who at the time was in the thick of the El Guettar battle in Tunisia, about developments at 2nd Armored.

> I know you'll be glad to hear that I've never regretted going back to the line since I left the old job. As a matter of fact I've been so darn pleased at just being back again and so busy learning about my new outfit that I've hardly had time to join the rest at "the wailing wall" over our being left out of the action so long. I'll admit that my feet are beginning to itch again, but feel on the other hand that I can make good use of all the time that remains.
>
> Not sure whether it's because I did a good job at exec O, or whether I was so bad they had to move me, but was given a battalion of mediums [tanks] effective today. [2nd battalion/66th Armored] Whatever the reason, I'm naturally tickled pink. Only rub is that I have to practically start over again on the midnight oil just as I felt I was getting to know my job well. My only worry now is enough time to get the "feel" before we start carrying the ball into pay dirt. The outfit is a darn good one as might argue from the officer I took over from—Charlie Rau. He was with you in the

Philippines and at Benning, told me he wanted to be remembered when I wrote.

We've only been getting driblets of news from the front... but I gather you've had the pleasure of several good cracks at the Germans to date. Won't be sorry when we can join you.

Between what the folks at home are doing without and what you're doing up at the front, I almost feel like a slacker sitting here in my small wall [tent] equipped with desk, light, and cot, but don't worry about our being ready when the time comes.

So the former infantryman and recent ordnance officer became an armor commander. At full strength, an armored battalion consisted of fifty-three Sherman medium tanks, seventeen light tanks, six assault guns or 105-mm Shermans, three self-propelled 81-mm mortars, and numerous other service and support vehicles. Total manpower was roughly thirty-nine officers and 710 enlisted men. It is no wonder that Maj. Stumpf would find this assignment quite challenging and welcomed this time in the rear to learn armor tactics and his role as a battalion commander. As we shall see, his experience with armored units in Africa and Sicily will give him a leg up later on as an infantry commander when employing tanks assigned to infantry units. Likewise, he was learning how to exploit the weaknesses of armor when opposing it on the battlefield.

Two influential and colorful officers of the 2nd Armored Division during this period were then Colonel Maurice Rose and Colonel Harry A. "Paddy" Flint. Rose selected Stumpf as his executive officer in the division's Combat Command A, which spearheaded the armored thrust across Sicily to Palermo. Flint went on to command the 39th Infantry in Sicily, England, and Normandy, where Stumpf served as one of his battalion commanders.

4

---•---

The Kasserine Pass
and El Guettar

A s previously mentioned, the 39th Infantry had been assigned to
the Eastern Task Force in Algeria since the invasion in November,
and had been further divided by battalions and supporting units
which were assigned to various Allied groups. The participation of
some of these units at the famous battle at the Kasserine Pass is worth
mentioning, as the survivors rejoined the 9th Division in due time.
Further, keeping abreast of their exploits is warranted because the
39th is where Maj. Stumpf eventually found his home and his most
significant combat time. The 9th Division Artillery played a pivotal
role at Kasserine Pass. As a reference, we will rely to a large extent on
The Making of a Professional, a biography of Gen. Eddy by Lieutenant
Colonel Henry Gerard "Red" Phillips, a 9th Division veteran of North
Africa.

By the end of January, the strategic situation in North Africa was
becoming more solidified, as the British continued relentless pressure on the Germans and Italians from the east, while the Americans

built up forces and supplies to the west, essentially defining Tunisia
as the focus of the coming major battles. Meanwhile the Axis forces
continued to reinforce and reorganize for an all-out spirited defense.

In early February, the 9th Division began its movement eastward
from Morocco toward Tunisia, eventually to rendezvous with the
long-detached 39th Infantry. First the 60th Infantry made their way to
the Oran area, riding across the Atlas Mountains in "forty and eights,"
railcars used throughout the French sphere since World War I, aptly
named because they were designed to accommodate forty men or
eight horses. Outside of Oran, they were assigned to guard airfields
and supply depots. The 47th Infantry followed and received orders
to proceed to Tunisia by its own means of transportation, on foot, in
trucks and various other vehicles. Division artillery followed.

On the morning of February 17th, the division received urgent orders to dispatch all available artillery to Tebessa, a supply base on the
Algeria/Tunisia border. Later that day, the column of all division artillery plus the 60th's cannon company moved out under the command
of Brigadier General Leroy Irwin, the 9th Division Artillery commander. Three days later the column was joined by the 84th Field Artillery
Battalion of the 47th RCT.

Meanwhile the battle at Kasserine Pass had been raging in earnest. Rommel had first struck in force on February 15th in the vicinity
of Sidi bou Zid east of the Kasserine Pass against the 34th Division's
168th RCT, supported by the 39th Infantry's Cannon Company. Both
units were overrun and lost.

Also engaged was the 1st Armored Division Combat Command
B supported by the 39th Infantry's 3rd Battalion and Anti-tank
Company. The 39th set up on the flanks of the pass and awaited the
main German armored thrust. On February 19th, they watched as
two veteran Panzer Divisions engaged Combat Command B in an
epic armored mismatch. The American armor was routed and the
39th Infantry units were overrun inside the pass on the road to Thala,

some twelve miles to the north.

In spite of these crushing blows to the Americans a.
allies, reinforcements were on the way, 9th Division Arti.
the charge. It is remarkable that Rommel did not follow up h.
tage by continuing to advance toward Tebessa immediately. The
forces in front of him were the remnants of a British regiment, the .
Leister, and some scattered British artillery. According to Red Phillips.

The 9th Division Artillery's column arrived at
Thala after dark on the night of February 21 and went
into firing positions already selected by the British.
They had completed the 777-mile journey in less than
100 hours, but there was no rest for the bone-tired
artillerymen. They dug in and dumped ammunition in
order to send the trucks back to Tebessa for more.
At 7 A.M., the Germans resumed their advance
against the remainder of the 2nd Battalion, 5th Leister
Regiment, weakened in the previous day's fighting.
Stuka dive-bombers began hitting the American arrivals.
Inexplicably, although the 10th Panzer had several
infantry battalions in its column, Rommel let his tanks
carry the ball that day, and they began to duel with
British and American artillery. At one point the 84th
Field Artillery Battalion displaced a battery of its 105-
mm howitzers forward in order to bore-sight the enemy's
tanks; the battery lost two guns but its opponents were
stopped. Finally the Panzers had enough.
After the enemy's rapid but orderly withdrawal
from Kasserine Pass...the 9th Division took up
defensive positions extending south from Kasserine.
Fragments of the 39th Infantry's units that had
battled Rommel's forces welcomed the rest of their

ɹiment when it arrived clean and fresh from the ɡar, to complete the 9th's reunification. The 47th's 3rd Battalion was sent eastward thirty miles to S'beitla to outpost the division's defenses.[1]

The next several weeks were spent defending the gains made following the battles around Kasserine Pass and consolidating division units, including reforming the lost units of the 39th Infantry. Gen. Patton had taken command of the US II Corps and was, some might say, ruthlessly forcing his "fighting spirit" into the soldiers under his command. His principle forces included the 1st and 9th Infantry Divisions and the 1st Armored Division. He believed that the best use of his troops after the blood-letting at Kasserine was to get them back into battle, while simultaneously enforcing disciplinary standards that he believed were somewhat lacking. These included maintaining proper uniforms, consistently saluting where appropriate, and proper maintenance of quarters and equipment.

Patton also promulgated a new tactical doctrine whereby infantry units would open a path through which armor units could race. This idea was to be the basis for the next big battle for the 9th Division near the village of El Guettar beginning in late March.

At some point during these weeks, Gen. Stroh was diagnosed with Bell's palsy, and was evacuated to an Army hospital, probably the 21st General at Bou Hanifia, a spa town at an oasis about a forty-mile drive southeast of Oran. Bell's palsy is a form of paralysis of the facial muscles, including those of the eye, normally afflicting just one side of the face. Most patients improve after a period of two weeks or more. He wrote home on March 14th describing his and the staff's conditions at the hospital and, although appearing to be in relatively good spirits, expressed anxiousness about getting back to work, especially since things appeared to be heating up. He wrote to Imogene on March 29th.

I am here for a day en route back to the job, having left the hospital yesterday. The road here was a rocky one, due to several days of terrific rains... Expect to see some old friends here and to transact some official business before taking off tomorrow for the last two laps.

That would place him back at the front perhaps late on the 31st. Meanwhile, the 60th RCT had been fully motorized and was detached from the 9th Division and assigned to the 1st Armored Division to the north to aid in its drive from Gafsa to Maknassy. They first encountered the enemy the night of March 18th at Djebel Gousa, which was well fortified by its German defenders. The 60th was able to outflank the enemy and attack from its rear, taking the *djebel* (hill mass) and routing the Germans. The armored column followed and units of the 60th continued to support them in taking the towns of Gafsa and Maknassy, although they were stopped short of taking the strategic Maknassy Pass.

Meanwhile the 1st Infantry Division, supported by the attached 1st Ranger Battalion, had succeeded in capturing the village of El Guettar and had advanced to high ground to the southeast in the vicinity of Djebel Berda. On the morning of the 23rd, the 10th Panzer Division responded by charging up the Gafsa-Gabes road under the cover of Stuka dive-bombers. Around noon they received a brutal American artillery barrage that slowed their advance, then executed a cautious withdrawal. Later they attacked again but were again stopped by the American artillery and infantry.

Part of the master plan to defeat the Axis forces in Africa was for Patton's II Corps to strike them from the west. The table was set southeast of El Guettar, where the 1st Infantry Division had turned back the 10th Panzer on March 23rd. Patton's plan was to advance eastward to the El Guettar Pass, about twelve miles from the village, along the Gafsa-to-Gabes highway with two infantry divisions, the 1st to the north of the road and the 9th to the south. After securing the pass, the tanks of Task Force Benson, 1st Armored Division would strike through the pass, its flanks secured by the infantry, and attack the Axis rear.

The attack was to begin on March 27th or 28th depending on the readiness of the units involved. The 9th Infantry Division was minus its 60th RCT, which was still engaged fifty miles to the north at the battle for Maknassy. It was also minus one of the battalions of the 39th Infantry, which had been engaged at Kasserine Pass and was in need of complete reorganization. That gave Gen. Eddy a total of only five of his nine infantry battalions at the beginning of the battle, three of which would be seeing combat under 9th Division control for the first time. Further, the division was still many miles away to the north and was delayed getting to and organizing at the starting point. Gen. Eddy's chief tactician and battle planner, Gen. Stroh, was in the hospital and unavailable at the beginning of the battle. Another problem was poor reconnaissance of the battlefield and poor assessment of enemy troop strength; the division's recon troop was assigned elsewhere. Furthermore, coordination with other units was inadequate; during the 9th's delay, the 1st Infantry Division and its attached ranger battalion had withdrawn from their positions around Djebel Berda, south of the highway. This development had not been transmitted to the 9th. The area maps provided to the unit commanders were extremely poor to the extent of being, in some cases, unusable. There was no indication as to the severity of the rugged terrain that was to be the 9th's route of advance.

Gen. Eddy planned a night approach to his objectives on Hill 369, which was at the far eastern end of the Djebel Berda massif. (As in this case, the hill names often reflect their elevation in meters as indicated on topographic maps.) En route to that objective was Hill 772 to the south of the approach, an area he assumed was still occupied

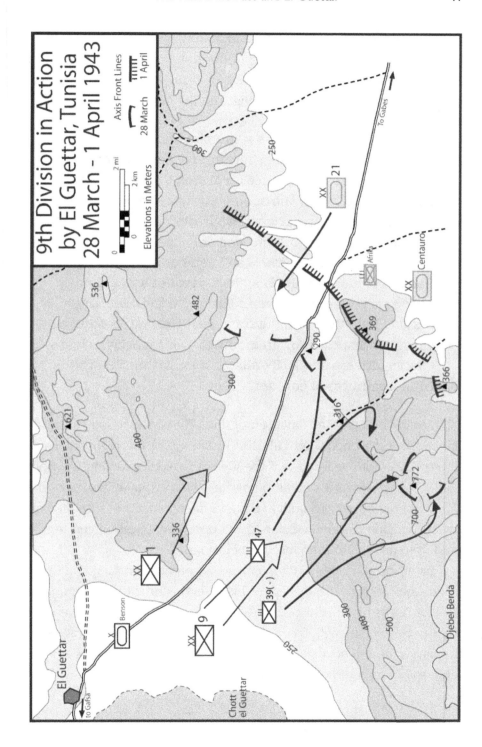

9th Division in Action by El Guettar, Tunisia 28 March - 1 April 1943

Axis Front Lines
28 March
1 April

Elevations in Meters

0   2 km
0   2 mi

by the Rangers. The 47th was to lead, followed by the 39th. At dawn on March 29th, they were to be in position for bayonet attacks on the enemy occupying Hill 369. Red Phillips, who incidentally was wounded in the battle while serving with the 47th Infantry, wrote:

> The 47th's attack was a complete failure due to poor coordination with other units in the area and inept prior reconnaissance on March 28 which not only failed to locate the enemy but warned him. To gain surprise, no artillery preparation was fired. On the assumption that he was only up against demoralized Italians who had been running since Gafsa, Colonel Randle thought a bayonet assault would terrorize them even further. To the contrary, his 2nd Battalion found a fully alert German battalion carefully disposed for an ambush. The Americans lost twelve officers and 218 enlisted men within the first fifteen minutes of contact...[2]

Meanwhile the 3rd Battalion of the 47th was meeting stiff resistance from the enemy on Hill 290 just south of the highway. From there, Gen. Eddy learned that the Germans were directing fire from Hill 772. He ordered a battalion of the 39th to go take it out, but the hill was not neutralized until two nights later, in part because the battalion became disoriented due to the poorly mapped rugged terrain and from taking fire from the higher ground.

Later, on the 29th, Eddy received an order from Gen. Patton to send one motorized battalion of his reserve straight down the road to just north of Hill 369, dismount, and attack the objective with bayonets at first light. The commander of the 2nd Battalion, 39th Infantry determined that Hill 290 was still occupied by the enemy and was an impediment to his proceeding directly to Hill 369 without neutralizing it. The battalion stopped to dismount for an assault on 290. According to Red Phillips, as they approached the enemy positions, "on a flare signal the enemy cut loose with their machine guns and dropped a mortar barrage among the trucks. The battalion was instantly demoralized. Some men ran forward. Others ran to the rear. Most got out their entrenching tools and began to dig. The battalion commander and members of his staff were taken prisoner." It is likely that much of the enemy fire was from Hill 369. For much of the battle there was confusion about which hill was which.

There was much discussion after the demise of the 2nd Battalion as to the propriety of this rather ill-conceived attack, fraught as it was with basic weaknesses, such as the lack of good reconnaissance, and bad information about the positions of both friendly and enemy elements. Beforehand, Gen. Eddy, to his credit, attempted to point these issues out to Gen. Patton, but the latter would have none of it and insisted that the attack proceed. The 9th Division G-3 liaison at Patton's headquarters, then Captain Richard Kent, in a 1991 letter to 39th Infantry veteran Col. Donald Lavender remembers it this way:

> This view is from the Western Task Force and the II Corps in southern Tunisia experience. Tragically, the Patton movie shows him winning a very picturesque battle against the Africa Corps Germans. No such battle ever occurred. I know, I was the Div. G-3 liaison with II Corps and knew everything that was going on. In fact the Germans kicked the hell out of us from the coast through the Kasserine Pass and everywhere else we tried anything in southern Tunisia. No history records that he threw away 800 or 900 good Americans of the 2nd Bn 39th Reg't commanded by Lt Col Oakes in an angry fit one afternoon and night. He ordered them to get on trucks and drive into the

El Guettar pass until contact, then go through the
Germans. His favorite, Benson's Task Force of armor,
had failed for a week or so and never cleared their
cover. The Germans were looking down our throats
from 772 meters above. We found about 150 men of
E Co. dead in a wadi. A few got out to tell the tale. The
rest of the battalion went straight to a prison camp
in Germany. There is no history of this in any history
I've ever seen including Patton's book, Bradley's
two books, the official Dept. of the Army history or
elsewhere.... Boy, were we glad when Bradley took
over. It was like a breath of fresh air.

Kent later went on to become the executive officer of the 3rd
Battalion 39th Infantry in France, Belgium, and Germany, and com-
manded that battalion for the last three months of the war in Germany.
He retired in 1970 as a full colonel after a distinguished career.

The battle continued for another week as the 47th and the 39th
continued to slug it out with the entrenched enemy, making steady,
but very slow progress toward capturing Hill 369. Gen. Stroh arrived
back at the front probably on the 1st of April and things began to sort
themselves out for the division. On April 3rd, a heavy concentration
by all available artillery was laid down on Hill 369 to prepare for an
assault by the 47th Infantry. But the infantry was slow to follow on the
artillery preparation, and the attack was repulsed.

The battle finally ended on April 7th after the enemy had withdrawn to the east and the infantry of the 9th occupied Hill 369. All
three regiments were exhausted, including the 60th, which had continued to battle the enemy at Maknassy Pass, where the previous night
the 10th Panzers and the Italian Centauro Division had withdrawn
from the field and retreated east.

The armor of Task Force Benson had proceeded down the highway toward El Guettar Pass on more than one occasion during the battle, but because the high-ground objectives of the infantry had not been secured, Benson was unable to break through the pass and attack the enemy rear. By the time the pass was secured, the enemy was gone.

Gen. Stroh supervised writing a rather extensive after-action report of the Battle of El Guettar, some of which we will examine for the valuable, and costly, lessons learned by the 9th Division in this, its first major battle under division control.

Intelligence reports indicated that the eastern extremities of Djebel Berda...were but lightly held by the Germans and could be captured with relative ease... [However] this area had been heavily fortified over a long period and developed into a virtual fortress. The natural strength of the position had been augmented by numerous emplacements many of which had been dug into solid rock.

An examination of this area will at once indicate the dominating characteristics of hill 772, which was undoubtedly the key... Had the initial attack been planned to capture hill 772 and then to work generally east along the connecting ridges toward hill 369 it is possible that the position might have been captured despite the handicaps under which the division was laboring. As the battle progressed this fact was realized and attempts were made to develop the tactical plan accordingly. But resistance by the Germans on the dominating terrain and lack of numbers...of the attacking infantry made all efforts fruitless.

The battle of El Guettar was at an end. The division had sustained losses of 151 killed, 962 wounded, and

360 missing, a total of nearly 1,500. It had captured a large number of prisoners [forty-eight, according to Phillips] and had learned many valuable lessons...

1. Early seizure of the dominating observation is an essential prerequisite for a successful advance. As long as such observation remains in the hands of the enemy, further progress is impossible.

2. Early reconnaissance and an opportunity for commanders, of all grades, to perfect their plans and to issue their orders are essential.

3. A determined enemy cannot be blasted out of a prepared position with artillery fire, however effective it might be... The artillery concentration must be followed so closely by the advance of the infantry that the defenders, forced into their holes by the artillery fire, will be unable to man their weapons after the artillery fire lifts in time to effectively withstand the infantry assault.

Gen. Stroh's letter to Imogene dated April 10 sheds some light on his state of mind and morale following El Guettar, and indicates his whereabouts, Oran and Algiers, before returning to the front while en route from his absence in the hospital.

This has been a perfectly scrumptious two weeks as far as mail from home is concerned. I have had at least two letters from everybody, and a regular stack from you, no less than seven since I last wrote. [March 29] These were those of February 1, 15, and 22, and March 1, 7, 15, and 22, so you see the sequence for that eight-week period is complete. And believe me I appreciate them...

Yes, we have had some practical experience during the past week or two, and not all of it pleasant. But so far, so good. The situation looks quite encouraging at the moment... There's no use walking around with a long face because some of us are a bit out on a limb. We'll lick this thing eventually, but it will be no pushover...

My musings have been interrupted by the arrival of Torres [Gen. Stroh's orderly] with the bath water, so now I am sweet and clean again after ablutions in three pints of water in the cute little canvas basin. After a week without a bath, and sleeping in your clothes, things begin to stick together.

You're not far wrong about our activities since March 17 and later. This censorship has me licked. You'll just have to piece together stray bits of information and read between the lines. The silly part about it is that we can't write about what you read about in the paper and illustrated in Life, complete with all the details.

Torres adopted a dog during our stay in Oran... Torres has proven himself a jewel, and I would not know what to do without him. After an interlude of a month, during which he did not receive a single letter, he received six yesterday and his morale is now superfine.

I'm sending in a separate envelope a couple of trinkets that I picked up in Algiers recently.

Shortly after posting this letter, Stroh was on the ground in northern Tunisia in advance of the division, coordinating with the British 46th Division, whose positions were to be assumed by the 9th Division, and the British First Army for the coming campaigns to capture the port cities of Bizerte and Tunis.

Letters from Imogene during these first months in Africa were generally newsy with regard to household arrangements, the weather, and the social scene with most of the men away. She described her attempts to find meaningful work to contribute to household expenses and the war effort. She also expressed some frustration with the mail situation, not being able to predict when letters would arrive and their lack of specificity due to security requirements, as well as delays in receiving and sending news. Still, she and her father kept to their strict weekly regimen of correspondence. These are excerpts from the home front:

> 3349 Runnymede Pl.
> Washington, D.C.
> January 24, 1943
> We haven't heard a word from you since your Dec. 30th letter to Mother. I was so anxious to get your letter about your association with Bob, but we believe those intermediate letters must be lost.
>
> I hear Bob is back in the Infantry, awaiting orders to the Armored Force. Of course we don't know who he is with, where he is, what he's doing or any of the particulars. I guess one of his letters has been lost. I haven't told any of his Ordnance friends the news because I know I'll be blamed for his cancellation... but I knew nothing about it.
>
> I want a job, but for the life of me I can't decide what to do or what to study to get a job. I'd like to learn a trade during this absence from my regular occupation.

February 7

Last week I got fingerprinted and gave my history countless times to the Civilian Voluntary Defense and FBI. I'm starting tomorrow a class to teach me how to plane spot for the Anti-Aircraft voluntary something or other. It is very vague and so secret...something I've never heard before and sounds pretty interesting.

Then I read that nurses' aides are wanted at Army hospitals so tomorrow I'm investigating a way to do aiding at Walter Reed. That is what I've wanted to do all along, so I'll get there, never fear. The only thing I just couldn't stand to do is bathe a corpse. I'll empty bed pans for a month if they don't make me do that.

February 14

This afternoon I start plane spotting and it is a gorgeous day so there will be lots of activity. I was hoping my first day would be overcast so that I would have plenty of time to think. This week we had classes to learn how to operate and they rush us through so fast that we don't have a chance to get a lot of confidence.

We have a map of Africa hanging over the desk in the den. It looks so appropriate. If Harry should go to the Far East we'll have a well-rounded education in geography trying to keep up with all the fronts. Of course everything revolves around North Africa in our minds.

"Life" is beginning to show some pretty horrible pictures of the front and everyone is publishing at last the facts of maybe yes and maybe no we'll win this thing. The longer it lasts the more frightening it becomes what you'll have to accomplish.

February 21

Yesterday I put in at the Weather Bureau for an appointment to work as an assistant meteorologist. It is a steady job earning $1400 a year to begin with and learn my trade at the same time. Walter Reed had nothing for me and this is closer than any other positions I found for which I'm qualified.

February 28

We were a little worried last week about the turn of events at the front over there, but are relieved now. [Kasserine Pass]

We received our no. 2 ration book Friday and start the point system tomorrow on all canned goods, catsup, vegetables and fruits, and dried beans.

March 15

The other day our cord of wood arrived and was dumped in the backyard. We couldn't find anyone to put it away...but between the two of us we got it neatly stacked away. Mother said she saw neighbors peeking behind curtains while the general's wife and daughter did manual labor.

To tell the truth we are living so luxuriously. We've gotten almost used to the cold. The fireplace has been used all the time while we're sitting. The den is still uninhabitable. Our coal is exhausted and there is no more, so we have wood which makes a good hot fire. But this house is so grand. Col. Kelly has lowered the rent to $145.00 voluntarily as suggested by the Rental Board and he also gave us permission to have a fire.

I was pretty happy to get your news of Bob. His letters are so much happier since his new assignment and he seems so satisfied.

March 21

Bob is catching up on his new job so I heard in a Feb. 26th letter. He is "spoiling" for a try at his knowledge. We feel that you are in the push we are reading about and wonder if you are in the part that captured Gafsa.

March 28

We'll have 24 gal. of gas until July 22nd. How do you like that? 1 1/2 gal. a week.

We are very concerned about you since we've read about the big push. I guess you are satisfied to finally see actual fighting; though you'll never want the experience again you'd never have been satisfied not to have witnessed the excitement.

We had a big surprise when Harry called from the Levys that he was passing through on the way from Selma to Mitchell Field for a couple of weeks. We were so excited to see him and his new secondhand grey four-door Ford sedan. He will be flying P-47s now.

April 4

Tomorrow I start at the Weather Bureau at 24th and M. The hours are from 8:30 A.M. to 5:00 P.M. and I'm dreading working and giving up my free time. I've always wanted to work and here is my chance.

April 11

I started working Monday morning and ended Saturday evening, and how the week did fly. The work isn't hard physically, but mentally it is terrific! I read weather maps covered with isobars, make graphs form the maps, do all kinds of computing. We're in a department called the Extrapolation Forecast Research working for some Navy Commander. The work is pretty wonderful when you figure that though we are aiming at the present for better ways to forecast the weather for war, also we are giving data that will be used always. We work on charts sent from all over the world.

Tomorrow I start back on an evening four-hour shift as an anti-aircraft volunteer to see if I can work all day and do this voluntary work, too, every third night.

Received a free V mail from Bob yesterday written March 21st. He doesn't give an inkling where he is or what he is doing.

April 18

We hope that you are out of the hospital and back with the division. We are reading that you are right in there. Hope all goes well.

Received a letter from Bob written April 4th—V mail free—unphotographed. He says he is a bat. commander of the 66th and taking Charlie Rau's place who has moved ahead. Bob seemed very tickled.

Friday, I received my first paycheck for $18.66 after 11 days of work with a $25 war bond deducted. Now isn't that wonderful?

May 2

We're so anxious to hear your first account of a battle. Guess the only difference between maneuvers and the real stuff is that when the soldiers fall over and play dead, they never get up.

Bob sent a letter April 18 that came V mail and is first one that has been photographed. It is as big, just slightly larger than a postage stamp... I'm so glad Mother has a magnifying glass. I knew V mail develops to a small stage, but never dreamed it was so minute.

5

———◆———

Sedjenane to Bizerte

Even before the 9th Division had committed to the battle at El Guettar, it had orders to move to northern Tunisia for the Allied campaign to capture the port cities of Bizerte and Tunis. After the El Guettar action, Gen. Stroh was dispatched with an advance party to coordinate with the British First Army, and specifically the British 46th Division, whose current positions the 9th would occupy for the start of the battle. From this vantage point, Stroh evaluated the German defensive positions holding the ground through which the division were to advance. The 9th, with attached units, would hold the extreme northern flank of the allied armies, moving west to east along the Mediterranean coast toward Bizerte. The following conversation between Gen. Eddy and Gen. Stroh is from Red Phillips's book *Sedjenane: The Pay-off Battle:*

> Don Stroh was pushing for a holding attack by one
> of the 9th's three regiments against the main German
> defenses on the two hills west of the village of Jefna,
> then using the division's other two regiments to flank

those positions to the north. The hill positions blocked the principal and most direct approach to Bizerte.

Stroh reported how the British had previously attacked Green and Bald Hills, as they had named them, directly without success. The Germans had well-prepared positions and plenty of firepower. Another head-on attack of these hills would be a re-run of what the 9th had just been through at El Guettar, slowly grinding away against determined defenders possessing adequate means and superior observation.

"We gotta hold 'em by the nose with one regiment and kick 'em in the tail with the others," Stroh suggested with a grin at this reminder of General Patton. [From his famous speech to the division some months earlier at Fort Bragg.] "One of our envelopments should be shallow and add to the threat of Jefna," he explained. "The other would go in further north and strike deeper, cutting the Germans' means of supporting the Jefna defenses."

"What about the Krauts' reserves?" Eddy asked.

Stroh replied that the Germans were going to be stretched thin when the entire Allied force struck together across their front:

"The British will kick off a day ahead of us and the enemy won't have anything left with which to counterattack. With our attachments we'll have them outnumbered four-and-a-half to one and our advantage in guns is even greater," Stroh asserted. "We'll smother them."[1]

Eddy was concerned that either "attacking or defending, the Germans almost always held back a reserve, and they could be depended upon to counterattack." With the 9th holding nothing substantial in reserve to repulse a counterattack, the results could be devastating. But in the end, Stroh's daring plan was approved.

In addition to its three infantry regiments (the 39th, 47th, and 60th), the 9th Division included the following units: 26th, 60th, 84th, and 34th Field Artillery Battalions; 15th Engineer Battalion; 9th Quartermaster Company; 9th Medical Battalion; 9th Cavalry Reconnaissance Troop; 9th Signal Company; 709th Ordnance Company. Additionally attached to the division for this operation: 62nd Armored Field Artillery Battalion; 434th Coast Artillery (AA); Battery H 67th Coast Artillery (AA) Regiment; 894th Tank Destroyer Battalion; Corps Franc d'Afrique; Air Support Party.

This is how Gen. Stroh's plan was described in the division after-action report:

> The division commander early decided that a frontal assault on the Green Hill-Bald Hill position would be so costly as to be unwarranted. He therefore decided on a bold scheme of maneuver, whereby the bulk of the division would be employed in a wide flanking movement through the extremely difficult terrain to the north of the main road, with the object of outflanking the hostile position and cutting the enemy's line of communication to the north and northeast. It was realized from the start that such a maneuver would be hampered by the almost total lack of communications through the area to be traversed. Further, secrecy was an essential since it was anticipated that the Germans would not suspect that a maneuver of this difficulty would be attempted if troops could be moved into position without their presence being disclosed.

In preparation for the attack a meticulous study of the terrain was made and dominating observation was selected for each of its several intermediate objectives to be captured by each regiment each day.

By daylight 22 April all units [would be] in their attack positions and all plans...perfected... On the extreme left (north) flank the Corps Franc d'Afrique was to move forward between the 60th Infantry on their right and the coast of the Mediterranean, through an area where it was thought resistance would be the least. One of their main objectives was the seizure of the dominating observation afforded by Kef En Nsour.

The 60th Infantry, moving forward by stages under the cover of darkness on the night of 19-20 April, was to initiate its attack from an area generally west of the 30 grid line and north of the Sedjenane Valley... It was assigned four intermediate objectives and one final objective to be captured within a period of five days. Its final objective completely dominated the main road.

The 39th Infantry, moving forward a short distance to the area generally west of the 28 grid line and south of the Sedjenane Valley, was to attack for the capture of three intermediate and one final objective during a period of five days. Its final objective likewise dominated the main road.

The 47th Infantry, to the area just west of the 32 grid line and astride the main road, was to conduct a holding attack against the main enemy position on Green and Bald Hills. It was to employ one battalion on its right (south) flank for a limited objective attack on D-Day, but no serious attempt was to be made for the reduction of the German main position until the advance of the 39th and 60th Infantry had outflanked these positions to the northeast.

The 1st American [Infantry] Division was on the right (south) flank of the 9th Division but a gap of some 6 1/2 miles separated the two units. To cover this gap the 91st Reconnaissance Squadron was to be employed with instructions to maintain contact with the 47th Infantry on the north and the 1st Infantry Division on the south, and to reconnoiter vigorously to the east in an effort to convince the Germans that the main attack of the division was to be made against their south flank.

The extreme width of the front, approximately 24 miles, posed a difficult problem for the artillery commander, who was forced to scatter his units widely. The light battalions were employed in their normal roles in direct support of the three infantry regiments. The medium and heavy artillery were divided into two groups, one to be employed on the south and the other to the north. Many of the artillery positions were inadequately protected by infantry. This was particularly true in the Sedjenane Valley. In an effort to relieve this situation the 9th Reconnaissance Troop and the 894th and 601st Tank Destroyer Battalions were attached to the division artillery and largely employed on protective missions in the Sedjenane Valley.

Gen. Stroh had learned much about the local idiosyncrasies facing the division during his time reconnoitering with the British. The Corps Franc d'Afrique (CFA), which was attached to the division and holding down its left flank during the advance, was an irregular force, rather ill equipped compared to regular French units with which the 9th had been in contact up until this time. They were somewhat shunned by the regular French army for a variety of reasons including race, citizenship, and prison records, and had not been allowed to join the regular forces of the French XIX Corps. But their commander, Colonel Pierre J. Magnan, had welcomed the Allied invasion from the beginning and finally persuaded Eisenhower's staff to let them join the Allied cause. They had been stationed along the coast in the months prior to this offensive, keeping the Germans off-guard and helping to protect the British northern flank. Col. Magnan's troops were organized into five infantry battalions, augmented by several sections of Goumiers, native Berber tribesmen who functioned as scouts. The "Goums," as they were called by the doughboys, were tough and fierce-looking and very capable of operating in rough terrain and forest environments. They operated in groups of about twelve, led by a French noncommissioned officer, often a Legionnaire. Allegedly they were paid by the number of enemy ears they harvested.

Another unique aspect of the Sedjenane experience was the American use of mules to augment the difficult nature of supplying the forward troops in rugged terrain with only one useable road. Gen. Stroh assumed that among his troops were many men raised in rural environments who had experience with the pack animals. He likely harkened back to his cavalry days when he once served as the regimental supply officer of the 17th Cavalry along Arizona's border with Mexico where mule pack trains were part of his daily responsibilities. But in fact, the 300-some mules utilized during the campaign proved to be quite a challenge, not easily overcome. Red Phillips quoted PFC Trevor Jones of the 9th Quartermaster Company.

I became part of the mule-skinning brigade hauling
rations and ammo forward to the troops. Those mules
were probably nasty and stubborn under normal

conditions. With our inexperience and ineptness, along with the occasional shelling that came our way, they were almost impossible to handle.

My only experience with this sort of thing was at the local park's pony ride back in Scranton, but gradually I learned how to tie granny knots and load the pack saddles. Then we would set out, sometimes on trails, often through the brush and thorns, over the hills and down the wadis. Eventually we'd arrive at some point occupied by the 60th guys or their Goum friends. We'd rest and then head back, sometimes packing litters with the wounded.[2]

Despite the initial awkwardness of the mule teams and their green-horn handlers, they played a key role during the battle, overcoming terrain obstacles to keep the forward troops supplied with food and ammunition. The mules would supplement the primary supply effort of having the division engineers build jeep trails on either side of the Sedjenane River as the flanking regiments advanced. At times, they were not able to keep pace, in which case the forward units held their positions temporarily.

Gen. Stroh's advance work with the British enabled the turnover of positions between the Brits and Americans to go relatively smooth-ly. The relief took place in darkness and the various commanders of all echelons were given thorough briefings of what they were facing in terms of terrain, observation, and enemy strength. Likewise, Stroh was confident in the quality of intelligence he received, much of it supplied by local herdsmen who moved their flocks throughout the area, including adjacent to enemy positions. 1st Lieutenant Chester Braune, Jr., Gen. Stroh's aide-de-camp, recalled the final planning phase for the impending action:

After talking to the British and looking things over, General Stroh asked me what I would do with the 9th. I said: "General, I'd put one regiment on the line and flank with the other, keeping one in reserve." I had learned that in ROTC.

The general said: "That's fine, but we need one regiment on the line and it must make big enough waves so that we can flank with two regiments." He then had me color the contours on his map so that he could pick out the highest ground at a glance and plan the routes of advance for the attacking regiments.

Outside the town of Sedjenane the command post was in a two-story villa and we went to some lengths to maintain its innocence. MPs stationed out on the road were dressed as Arabs. No one was allowed to use the front door. We went around to the back and climbed a ladder to a second-story window. Despite this we were strafed by a Messerschmidt 109 one day. It blew a large hole in the roof and scattered tiles around.[3]

Facing the Americans was the Manteuffel Division, named for its commander, Generalmajor Hasso E. von Manteuffel, a seasoned combat veteran of Poland, France, and Russia before his assignment in Africa. He organized a hodgepodge group of German and Italian units during the reinforcement period, late in 1942 after the American invasion, into the division he now commanded. It had been fighting the British in northern Tunisia for some time including from the Germans' current fortified positions guarding the approaches to Jefna. The Manteuffel consisted of only about 5,000 men including 1,000 Italian troops, organized into nine battalions, the total only about a quarter the size of the reinforced 9th Division. But the terrain greatly favored the defense, and the veteran Axis troops were well dug in, much like they were at El Guettar. They had proven a tough nut to crack, turning back at least three British assaults on their positions around Green and Bald Hills during the previous weeks.

Gen. Eddy assigned the holding action along the enemy front to the 47th Infantry commanded by Colonel Edwin H. Randle, who had led the regiment through the successful invasion and action at Safi, as well as the battle at El Guettar. Eddy considered the 47th, which had performed well at El Guettar despite its many handicaps, his best regiment at the time, and Randle his best commander. Likewise he considered the mission of holding the enemy front the most crucial of the battle plan, possibly because the 47th would be exposed to enemy fire for the entire time it would take the battle to unfold. Eddy had not yet seen firsthand the fighting qualities of the 60th Infantry, commanded by Colonel Frederick J. de Rohan, which had been deployed with the British at Maknassy while the rest of the division was at El Guettar.

The 39th Infantry had not performed especially well at El Guettar and had taken a beating, both there and previously at Kasserine Pass. Gens. Eddy and Stroh were concerned about the morale of the regiment and the competence of its commander, Colonel J. Trimble Brown. Red Phillips's words regarding Col. Brown: "Among his pre-war assignments were two turns as aide-de-camp to...a mentor of George C. Marshall and, subsequently, Dwight D. Eisenhower. Whatever else this service may have done for Brown's professional development, it seems to have expanded his self-esteem to the extent that nearly everyone in the 39th Infantry found him to be insufferable."

Returning to the division after-action report as the battle kicked off:

The attack started at 0530, 23 April. By 1100 it was reported that all regiments had reached their D-Day objectives with little opposition. Orders were

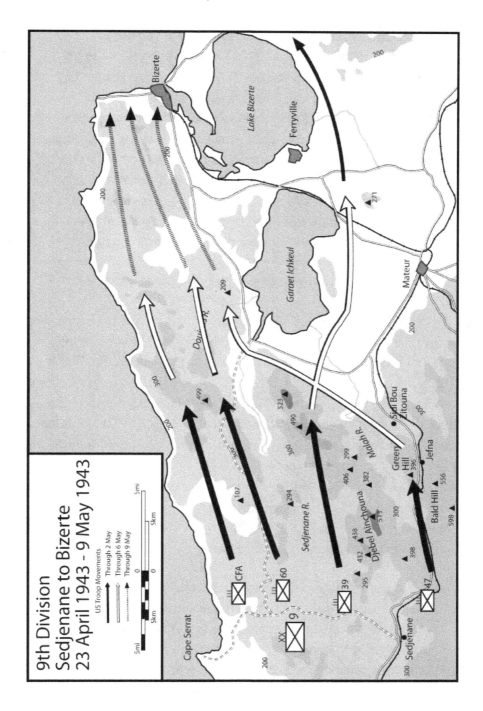

9th Division
Sedjenane to Bizerte
23 April 1943 - 9 May 1943

US Troop Movements
Through 2 May
Through 6 May
Through 9 May

5mi
5km
0
5km
0
5mi

Bizerte
Lake Bizerte
Ferryville
Garaet Ichkeul
Mateur
Sidi Bou Zitouna
200
Douar R.
209
523
490
300
406
299
382
Malah R.
300
Green Hill
396
Jefna
Bald Hill
556
598
598
200
300
300
Sedjenane
398
295
432
438
575
Djebel Ainchouna
294
Sedjenane R.
107
499
200
300
200
Cape Serrat
CFA
60
9
39
47

accordingly issued to press on to the D plus one
objective. This satisfactory development was true on
the north and south flanks. [60th and 47th Infantry]
It was not true in the center where the 39th Infantry
had encountered heavy resistance on the dominating
hill Djebel Ainchouna. By nightfall its leading elements
were in a state of confusion and had reached only the
lower slopes of the djebel. During the afternoon the
60th Infantry on the left, meeting increased terrain
difficulties but little opposition, reached a point
about mid-way between their D-Day and D plus one
objectives. The Corps Franc by evening of the first day
were held up by resistance on Hill 107-3493.

During the 39th's action at Djebel Ainchouna, Col. Brown and
several senior members of his staff were captured by a German patrol, but soon after, repatriated by American troops. At the time there
was some speculation that the 9th's battle plan had been lost and
recovered by the Germans. With the 39th halted before Ainchouna
and its commander and senior staff shaken up, Gen. Eddy made the
decision to relieve Col. Brown of his command. Just before midnight,
Gen. Stroh arrived at the regimental command post, formally relieved
Col. Brown in private, and, there being no ready replacement, took
command of the regiment himself. After conferring with the staff and
reviewing the next day's operational orders, which he left intact, he
returned to the division CP. Lt. Braune:

In connection with Colonel Brown's capture I heard
many rumors about missing orders and a situation
map, but Generals Eddy and Stroh did not attach much
importance to that, or the fact that he'd been captured.
Most of their concern centered on what they perceived

as poor morale in the 39th. This was the primary
reason for his being relieved. As for Stroh's command of
the 39th for those few days before a replacement could
be brought in, we went up there each day and he ran
the show. Then, when things were buttoned up, he'd
turn things over to [Lt. Col. Van H.] Bond, the executive
officer, and we'd return to the 9th CP.

One incident that occurred when moving back
and forth gives some insight into the character of
the general. We were driving across a field following
the tracks of previous traffic when we came upon a
weapons carrier which had just hit a mine. There was
nothing to be done. Stroh told the driver to pull around
the wreck and continue. I admit my knuckles were
white as we did so.[4]

For the next several days, Gen. Stroh did double duty at the height
of the yet most consequential battle for the division and of his career;
days at the front leading the 39th Infantry, nights at the division command post, reviewing the events of the day and going through the
next day's orders. After a lifetime of preparing for this moment, Stroh
was commanding troops in battle for the first time. Now age fifty, and
thirty-two years from when he began military training as a college
cadet, he was relying on command experiences at all levels, from a
cavalry troop to infantry units; company, battalion, and regiment. But
he had never commanded under fire, with the responsibility for the
lives of over 3,000 men directly under his control.

Returning to the after-action report:

On 24 April the Corps Franc, with the support of
an additional battalion of light artillery, captured hill
107. The 60th Infantry occupied Djebel Dardys-3489.

Progress was slow due to the steepness of the hills and the thickness of the vegetation which was so bad at times that the men had to crawl on hands and knees to penetrate it. The 39th Infantry resumed its attack on Ainchouna and reached the summit. Here its leading battalion was seriously opposed by heavy enemy fire from the north and east. Several senior officers became casualties and it was only by the superior leadership of a junior captain [Capt. Conrad V. Anderson, CO of C Company] that the battalion was able to retain its precarious hold on the mountain. The 47th Infantry, in accordance with the plan, made no advance during that day. Activities on the front of the 91st Reconnaissance Squadron were again limited to patrol action.

On 25 April ... the 60th Infantry and Corps Franc held their positions. The 39th Infantry, employing a fresh battalion with excellent field artillery support, completed the occupation of the summit of Djebel Ainchouna, driving out strong German defense forces. The 47th Infantry advanced two companies about a mile to the east without serious difficulty and seized hills 502 and 598. The fall of Ainchouna deprived the Germans of much of their observation over the Sedjenane Valley. It was possible thereafter to push reconnaissance with mechanized elements well to the east in this valley...

On the morning of 26 April the Germans counterattacked the 2nd Battalion 60th Infantry in considerable force but were repulsed with the loss of 116 [German] dead. This counterattack, true to the German practice, was evidently to cover a withdrawal from their Sedjenane positions, which had been outflanked by the double envelopment... The 39th Infantry advanced two battalions to Djebel El Aleat, the D plus one objective for this regiment, thus resuming the step by step advance as planned...

Little progress was made on 27 April except in the zone of the 39th Infantry where a battalion was successfully advanced to the Hill 382... German reaction to the advance of the 39th Infantry now became more marked and the 2nd Battalion, which continued to hold this position for the next week, was constantly subjected to artillery and mortar fire.

On 27 April a replacement commanding officer for the 39th Infantry arrived, Colonel William L. Ritter, and Gen. Stroh was able to return full time to his divisional duties. Major Robert B. Cobb, commanding officer of the 2/39th, who would become one of the most decorated battalion and regimental commanders of the entire war, recalled Gen. Stroh's brief command of the regiment.

Regarding General Stroh's command of the regiment I would rate him as one of the most caring and knowledgeable infantry leaders the 9th Division had. After he took over he came up every day to help me carry out orders and listen to my concerns.[5]

Maj. Cobb had been one of the officers captured and repatriated on April 23 with Col. Brown. He went on to lead the 2/39th through the Sicily campaign, and later commanded a regiment in the 87th Infantry Division in Europe. Another 9th Division veteran, Colonel Dean Vanderhoef, USA (ret), later remembered Gen. Stroh in a similar light.

General Stroh was a complete gentleman in the finest sense of the word. Add to this, strength of

character and professional competence of the first
degree. He was in my mind "Mr. Fort Benning," the
desired product of the Infantry School. In our personal
contacts he was pleasant and open to whatever I had
to say.[6]

Despite his packed schedule during his time commanding the
39th Infantry, Gen. Stroh refused even to temporarily abandon his
schedule of writing home. So as the battle raged on, he dashed off
a short letter to Imogene dated April 25th. (It was not postmarked
until May 2nd.) Clearly he believed that regular mail helped ease the
worry of those who maintained the home front. From this short letter
in a somewhat slap-dash cursive, a deviation from his usual meticulous hand:

We are not exactly celebrating Easter this year
with eggs and rabbits, at least not using the same
sort of eggs we used to have. So in view of the current
excitement will have to limit this note to a line or two.
   ...had a nice letter from Bob last week... I'll enclose
it and you will receive a bit of news from him...
Managed to get off a brief reply to him just before the
present unpleasantness started...
   Things are poppin', so must away.

Back to the division after-action account:

By 28 April supply difficulties in the zone of
the 60th Infantry [according to the plan the 60th's
objectives required covering the most ground] had
become so serious that it was hoped to continue
the advance in the northeast... along a reasonably
passable road. Such an advance, however, neglected

the capture of the dominating terrain to the east...

For the moment, logistics triumphed over tactical operations and the 60th Infantry was directed to move to the northeast, astride the [Sedjenane] river valley, with the Corps Franc advancing on their left. The 60th was successful in occupying Kef Sahan on this date. During the afternoon the 1st Battalion 39th Infantry was moved from its position on Djebel Ainchouna by a circuitous route to the northeast and successfully occupied a position on hill 377, preparatory to an advance the following day to hill 406...

On 29 April it became clear that the Germans were occupying in considerable force the dominating observation east of the zone of advance of the 60th Infantry and unless these observers were driven off, the advance of the regiment would be impossible. Accordingly, plans were made to turn one battalion to the east against Kef En Nsour, which it was hoped could be reached by darkness. So great were the supply difficulties, however, and so difficult the terrain, that it sometimes required two days to progress a mile and to bring up supplies for further progress. Enemy resistance was not great, but nature provided the greatest impediment. The 3rd Battalion 60th Infantry was unable to occupy Kef En Nsour for three days. Meanwhile, the 39th Infantry on this date was preparing plans for a coordinated attack on hill 406, which was to prove one of the turning points of the entire campaign. The 47th Infantry in its zone continued patrol activity against Bald and Green hills and succeeded in holding down the German fire from those hills with their own supporting weapons.

The 39th Infantry's looming attack on Hill 406 proved to be a gem of tactical planning and execution. German prisoners had confirmed that the enemy considered this dominant terrain feature critical to its defense and had declared it to be defended to the last man. Col. Ritter and his staff incorporated a plan in microcosm of the overall division operational plan. Lt. Col. Bond's 3rd Battalion, with supporting artillery, would assault the hill directly from the west, up a gently rising slope against good fields of fire for the enemy. Meanwhile, Capt. Anderson's 1st Battalion would flank around to the north and assault up the steep northeast face of the hill, betting that the Germans' attention would be focused to the west and not to the difficult northeast terrain. Timing was critical so that the two assaults would occur near simultaneously and immediately be preceded by the artillery barrage; speed was of the essence for the 1st Battalion. The regiment executed near perfectly. The 1st Battalion was able to scale the steep northeast face and attack the enemy's rear while his attention was focused on the frontal attack by the 3rd Battalion. Back to the after-action report:

> The attack of the 39th Infantry on Hill 406 on
> 30 April was completely successful. [The 39th also
> captured Spur 29 and Hill 382.] This area completely
> dominates the complicated terrain just to the south
> as well as the road leading northwest toward the
> head of the Sedjenane Valley. It was evidently in this
> area that the Germans had concentrated many of
> their supply dumps and other installations for the
> support of their Bald-Green hill positions. With the
> necessary observation in our possession, effective
> shelling of these installations was possible. In a
> single day the 26th Field Artillery Battalion fired
> over 4,000 rounds with devastating effect. The main
> German defenses had now been out-flanked and two

days later he began withdrawing to the northeast.
Meanwhile, events in the 60th Infantry zone were
moving along satisfactorily. The 1st Battalion occupied
Djebel Guermach and prepared to advance on to the
east to assist the attack of the 3rd Battalion. The 2nd
Battalion, moving to the northeast, was abreast of the
French, on their left, in a position to assist our allies
in seizing the high ground at the eastern exit of the
Sedjenane Valley....

The 47th Infantry had perfected plans and had
made the necessary reconnaissance to move one
battalion into the valley north of Green hill and to
attack that hill from the north on 2 May in connection
with the advance by the 39th Infantry.

On 1 May, orders were received from II Corps to
suspend all further offensive action pending certain
regrouping on the remainder of the Corps front.
Accordingly, plans for the attack on Green hill were
suspended and all units prepared to hold positions
then occupied...

This interlude did not last long. On 2 May there
were definite indications that the Germans were
pulling out in the direction of Mateur. The Corps
commander [Major General Omar Bradley] directed
the 9th Division to pursue vigorously to the northeast,
leaving one infantry regiment to guard approaches
on the south. A rapid advance was begun all along the
line.

[On 4 May] Having now advanced approximately
12 miles in 13 days and captured a total of 815
prisoners, together with much materiel and
equipment, the division had reached the last of the

hills overlooking Bizerte. It had captured both of its assigned objectives, the Bald-Green Hill area and the road junction at 5094. It was again confronted with the difficult task of fighting its way out of these hills with very inadequate lines of communications. It will be noted that there is but a single road which leads to the east from the Sedjenane Valley. Movements south of this road were impossible due to the Caret El Ichkeul [a large lake]. The hills north of the road as far as the seacoast were strongly held by the Germans. Progress on the road, even if it could be made under fire, was impossible for wheeled vehicles due to the fact that the bridge over the Luted Douimiss...had been blown. In other words, the division was confronted with the necessity of advancing across an isthmus less than eight miles wide with but a single road on the extreme south flank. Of the German positions confronting us, that on Cheniti appeared the most formidable. The Germans here adopted their usual tactics of holding strongly the exits of all bottlenecks.

Confronted with these facts, it was apparent that efforts must be made to fight for elbow room, to drive the Germans from Cheniti and the hills to the north, and to construct a new road to the northeast, along which artillery could be displaced and supplies moved as the attack progressed.

It was recognized that a frontal assault on Cheniti would probably be unnecessarily costly, whereas an advance north of that hill might result in outflanking it and making its subsequent capture relatively easy. Accordingly the 47th Infantry was directed to attack on 5 May for the capture of...Hill 131, Hill 158, Hill

125. This attack occurred early on 5 May, but by dark on that date had made insufficient progress to warrant a direct attack on Cheniti. The 1st Battalion of the 60th Infantry had relieved elements of the Corps Franc west of Cheniti on the night of 5-6 May and had thoroughly reconnoitered approaches from the hill and position areas for supporting weapons. Shortly after noon 6 May this battalion assaulted the northwest slopes of Cheniti with the bayonet, the men following artillery concentrations at 100 yards or less. The attack was completely successful and by evening Hill 168 and the [adjacent] saddle...were in our possession...

Early on 7 May the 47th Infantry continued its advance to the east against weak opposition and was soon in possession of its objective. 1st Battalion 60th Infantry completed the capture of Cheniti... The 3rd Battalion 60th Infantry moved along the southern slopes of Cheniti and took position on Hill 114...

The capture of Cheniti permitted the repair of the crossing over the Oued Douimiss. Prior to noon Company A, 751 Tank Battalion (M) and the 894th Tank Destroyer Battalion passed the crossing, moved east and thence north under orders to reconnoiter the hills to the north and overcome any opposition therein.

The 9th Reconnaissance Squadron moved east along the road to Bizerte, removing a minefield...and continued its reconnaissance to the east.

By mid-afternoon all indications pointed to the fact that the Germans not only had withdrawn on the division front but also had evacuated Bizerte.

Accordingly the mechanized force...was ordered into the town which it entered at 1615. They discovered street sniping in progress and were subject to artillery fire from enemy positions across the channel to the southeast. They accordingly withdrew early on the night of 7 May to the vicinity of the airport.

Just before dark the 47th Infantry was directed to assemble and to move at once to the high ground northwest of Bizerte... At the same hour, one battalion Corps Franc, motorized, was ordered into position on the left (east) flank of the 47th Infantry. By daylight 8 May the French forces were along the northern exits of Bizerte.

The 60th Infantry was also moved to the east and occupied the high ground generally along the 61 grid line.

The entire 39th combat team was attached to the 1st Armored Division and thereafter did not operate under [9th] division control [for the rest of this campaign].

For the next several days, the 9th reconnaissance troop and patrols from the infantry thoroughly scoured the country northwest of Bizerte and brought in a few scattered prisoners...

The Sedjenane-Bizerte campaign was at an end. The division had successfully taken advantage of the lessons learned at El Guettar. It had substituted sweat for blood. With a minimum of loss it had maneuvered the Germans out of one position after another. The wide envelopment to the north undoubtedly was a complete surprise to the enemy. It had seized the dominating observation fast, making the German position untenable. With one exception, when coordinated attacks became necessary, as at Ainchouna on 25 April and Cheniti on 6 May, commanders were given ample opportunity to make detailed plans and reconnaissance. And finally the infantry had learned the important lesson of following artillery concentration closely as was exemplified in the capture of Cheniti, the last remaining German defensive position west of Bizerte.

The "minimal losses" of the 9th Division mentioned in the report were not insignificant: eighty-two killed, 548 wounded, and twenty missing, out of a force of nearly 20,000 men. These casualties compare with 1st Division numbers: 103, 1,245, and 682; and 34th Division: eighty-five, 470, and seventy-nine. Both the 1st and 34th advanced along the front to the south of the 9th. Total II Corps losses in equipment were nine light tanks, forty medium tanks, nineteen half-tracks, one 155-mm gun (which took a direct hit from a 500-pound bomb), thirteen mortars, sixty-nine automatic weapons, and about 400 other small arms.

On the German side, the casualty figures are less precise. They include 34,934 German and 5,861 Italian prisoners of war, and approximately 3,000 killed. Large amounts of enemy equipment and supplies were destroyed in battle or by the retreating enemy. Equipment and supplies seized by American troops include 750 motor vehicles, forty-five half-tracks, 250 artillery pieces, seventy-five mortars, 750 machine guns, fifty tanks, 30,000 small arms, 1,000 tons of ammunition, 1,600 tons of rations, 1,000 tons of clothing and equipment, and seventy-five tons of medical supplies.[7]

The 9th Division had coalesced into a cohesive fighting machine for the first time, accomplished under difficult circumstances in terms of terrain, supply, and lines of communication. It had also

successfully employed a variety of attached units including six battalions of the Corps Franc d'Afrique, an irregular force with a different
language and culture. It was the coming of age for the 9th Infantry
Division. Red Phillips's aptly named "pay-off battle" opened the door
to the next two years of hard-fought campaigns which would eventually take them across the Rhine and into the heart of Germany.

The following poem, "Sedjenane," was written by John D. Day, a
9th Division veteran of the battle.

> Death's swift flight, through the April rain,
> Paused at a place called Sedjenane.
> With a cold hand he marked his prey
> And picked the ones who were to stay, forever
> At a place called Sedjenane.
> In a brief moment, they gave their all,
> Life, and all it meant, beyond recall.
> Never to be bothered by the rain, they sleep
> At a place called Sedjenane.
> Wooden crosses mark each hallowed grave
> And above the sleeping ranks, red poppies wave.
> The fight is over, there in peace, they'll ever remain
> The ones we left behind us at a place called Sedjenane.

Gen. Stroh was instrumentally involved with the entire course of
this major battle, from initial coordination with the British, to personal reconnaissance of the terrain and German positions, to con-
ceptualizing and delineating the battle plan. During the battle itself,
he materially assisted the division commander with the proper uti-
lization of forces even to the extent of taking command of and reorganizing one of the frontline regiments at the height of the fighting.
He surely must have felt relieved after the division's rough going at
El Guettar and the mauling that some of the units had experienced
at Kasserine Pass. After Sedjenane, he was clearly now quite proud

of the division, and he related as much in a letter to Imogene dated May 10th:

Well, it looks as if we have gotten to the end of the trail as far as the African campaign is concerned. Our division has captured all of its objectives, including a seaport which I cannot name but which you have doubtless read about in the paper. Things began to crack definitely on Friday [May 8], and we pushed some mobile outfits out fast, entering the city just ten minutes before the British entered the other seaport. [Tunis] I followed that night with some reinforcements through a night of inky blackness and rain squalls, and on a road on which numerous bridges had been blown and mines planted. By Saturday morning we were in possession of all the hills overlooking the city and it was all over but the shouting. The bulk of German prisoners were trapped between us and the Allied troops to the north and east. Yesterday afternoon the roads were said to be jammed with prisoners going to the rear, many of them driving or otherwise being transported in their own vehicles. A report had just been received that the Corps "cage" already contains 18,000 prisoners, with more coming in.

We had quite a jollification here last evening, slightly marred by the arrival of a German plane which dropped an egg not too far away as a gentle reminder that the war was not yet over.

I was appointed Military Governor of the city yesterday, and that afternoon General Eddy and I went in to pose briefly for Fox News. That will be one strip which will certainly be deleted before being shown. The place, which in normal times must have been quite beautiful, is a complete wreck, having been pounded for months by American and British planes. My job as governor will be very brief, as I'll probably be relieved today by the British. This will suit me just fine, since what I don't know about military governing will fill a large book.

Don't know how long we will stay here, or where we'll go next. But it now appears that the men will have a short time to get rested, reclothed, and bathed for the first time in many weeks. The division has done a magnificent job. I hope it receives due credit.

The last line of Stroh's letter begins a narrative that persisted throughout the early combat history of the 9th Infantry Division in World War II; that, despite its performance, many perceived it did not receive the level of recognition as other divisions in similar circumstances. In Gen. Bradley's report on operations of his II Corps in the Bizerte campaign, he wrote:

French units under the command of their efficient commander, Colonel Magnan, fought with courage and determination...in mountainous terrain and suffered many casualties. Even though exhausted at the end, they still had but one purpose in mind—to drive the enemy from their shores. Their determination, their courage, and their devotion to their cause were an inspiration to our troops.

Some of the II Corps, namely the 1st Infantry Division and elements of the 1st Armored and 34th Infantry Divisions, have been fighting in North Africa almost continuously since they landed at Oran on 8

November. Other units have been in action in Tunisia
for varying periods from 18 January onward.[9]

Bradley went on to praise the Corps at large for their splendid
success in the campaign. So of his five major units, all of which made
significant contributions to the Bizerte Campaign, he mentions four
by name, omitting what arguably may have been the most efficient
unit in the campaign; the one that had to be ordered to slow down to
wait for others to catch up despite having the most remote and rugged
route of advance; the one that was in direct control of and coordination with the French Corps Franc d'Afrique; the one that first entered
and secured the ultimate objective, the city of Bizerte. It was the 9th
Infantry Division, the division that landed all of its combat teams on
the beaches of North Africa on November 8, albeit attached to various other higher headquarters at the time. It must have stung, for the
rewards of a combat soldier in relation to the sacrifices he makes
are slim indeed, and recognition is one of the few. There would be
much discussion and speculation on this peculiar phenomenon in the
months ahead. Some attribute it to the personality of the commanding general, the somewhat taciturn Manton Eddy, who was a very
careful and meticulous commander, unlike some of the other, more
flashy and flamboyant division commanders. Perhaps the omission of
the 9th was an unintentional snub by the Corps commander, for after
the action was over, he sent this message to the division, probably
well before the report of operations was written.

During the recent operations which began on
April 23rd and ended on May 9th, the work of the
9th Infantry Division has been most commendable.
The Division was faced with a wide sector, which was
extremely rugged and largely covered with an almost
impenetrable growth of vegetation. In spite of the

tremendous handicaps confronting the Division, it pushed ahead, overcoming every obstacle. Its efforts were rewarded by the capture of Bizerte. The Division is to be congratulated on its brilliant performance.

6

---◆---

African Interlude

After May 9th with the surrender of all German forces in the II Corps sector, the 9th Division assumed new and different duties, one of which was the supervision and guarding of nearly 25,000 German and Italian prisoners of war. Patrols in the areas around Bizerte continued to bring in stragglers to add to the totals. In addition, repairs to the port and battered city infrastructure, as well as debris removal, were undertaken by the division's 15th Engineer Combat Battalion. During the campaign, this resourceful outfit had built seventy miles of roads and repaired another 126 miles. They repaired many bridges and constructed mountain trails for supply and evacuation of the wounded.

Following a brief stay in the Bizerte area during which the men were able to clean up and get some rest, the 9th Division packed up and moved to Magenta, Algeria, a small town about eighty miles south of Oran on the edge of the Sahara Desert. This would be the beginning of an intense seven-week training period in primitive conditions and intense daytime heat so disabling that midday siestas were ordered for everyone. The closest town was Sidi bel Abbes, some fifty miles north, headquarters of the French Foreign Legion. Passes were issued on a rotating basis and the men got to enjoy some R and R on the town.

Training included basic infantry drills, but also more complex regimental-size tactical drills with live artillery to further hone the combat skills developed at El Guettar and Sedjenane. They worked on an especially important skill, "leaning in" to artillery barrages. This meant, following very closely behind softening up barrages before the enemy has time to come out of their holes into effective fighting positions.

The letter from Gen. Stroh to Imogene while en route to Magenta, dated May 23, gives an interesting perspective on some of the locals:

I am slowly beginning to cook as the sun rises higher on the parched desert valley where we bivouacked last night. Our convoy has gone ahead and left us, but I remained behind with my little trouble-shooting circus to write letters and enjoy the calm and peace of a perfect Sunday morning. After lunch we will pack up and set out in pursuit of the column which doesn't have very far to go today. We expect to rejoin the remainder of the division on Tuesday afternoon at a location not far from where we were in February. You may be able to draw your own conclusions.

These Arabs are really becoming a pest. They not only congest all the roads with themselves, their sheep, goats, cows, donkeys and camels, but they sit around every bivouac area like vultures, ready to steal anything on which a soldier is not sitting, and dig up our kitchen sumps in search of tin cans and scrap food the minute we move away. They are becoming bolder every day and I sometimes wish for a big bull

whip. I suppose that American soldiers have given
away literally tons of cigarettes, matches, and candy
to the kids along the roads, and they show no more
appreciation than mummies.

One of the officers of the 39th Infantry, 1st. Lt. Charles Scheffel, a veteran of El Guettar and Sedjenane, was in charge of a platoon of twenty men delivering 200 POWs to Oran on a forty-and-eight boxcar train. The prisoners were some of the thousands taken in the Bizerte campaign and included a German colonel. Scheffel said Gen. Stroh had arranged the train and equipped it with machine guns on top of the passenger cars. Before Sedjenane, Scheffel had attended the British 18th Army Group Battle School to learn their "battle drill." He paints a riveting picture of desert life for the 9th Division at Magenta in this narrative from his book, *Crack and Thump*.

I delivered my prisoners at Oran and found out
the 9th Division was encamped south of Sid-bel Abbes
near Magenta, a small isolated oasis. The division
was trying to stay hidden from German spies and
sympathizers while it restocked with troops and
supplies for the next invasion.

We headed for the bivouac area, catching rides on
supply trucks, grinding along through the increasing
heat, the dusty landscape becoming more desolate
and barren as we made our way south. The sun
burned down from an empty blue sky, waves of heat
shimmering in from the distant hills.

At noon on the second day, we reached a gigantic
tent city at the edge of the Sahara Desert, a forlorn place
to bed down the division. The temperature was over a
hundred, with none of the sea breezes that cooled Oran.

Shortly after I arrived, an epidemic of diarrhea broke out, caused by drinking contaminated water. Some men had to be evacuated back to the hospital at Oran. As one of the most senior lieutenants, I became S-3, plans and operations officer, of the 1st Battalion, normally a major's slot.

I was determined to make the most of my opportunity, and during the last days of May 1943, I trained the battalion on what I'd learned from the Brits. I doubt if Brigadier General Stroh, the 9th Division assistant commander, knew who Lieutenant Scheffel was, but one morning he watched me demonstrate the British battle drill for squads. That afternoon I was ordered to report to his office.

"I've heard about the stuff you're doing with the companies in 1st Battalion," he said. "I want you to teach this to your whole regiment."

That became my full-time job for the next week. I went over why two-man foxholes work best, how to maneuver an infantry squad under fire, what a batman is—all the important little things the Brits had taught me, stuff that helped keep me alive.[1]

After a couple of weeks in camp at Magenta, Gen. Stroh's mood had darkened considerably, which is manifested in his June 6 letter to Imogene. Though he couches his funk in terms of not getting promoted, it was more likely a combination of circumstances across a broader scope of concerns, including perhaps Gen. Bradley's glaring omission of the 9th Division in the report of operations. His promotion concerns, with the benefit of hindsight, appear to be misplaced. After all, he had been a brigadier for less than a year, and the division had improved dramatically due in no small part to his efforts. He had a good working relationship with his boss, and finally, it was clearly to be a long war. The army was still rapidly expanding. He would get his chance. As evidenced by the words of his lessons learned report of 1947, he simply did not like his job as assistant division commander. Like most good soldiers, including his son-in-law, he wanted his own command. In a backhanded compliment sort of way, it might be argued that Gen. Eddy considered Stroh too valuable to let go. By the end of this missive to Imogene, he has recovered some of his normal upbeat tone.

A year ago today was a big date. It was the day we presented the colors to the 339th Infantry. I was a big shot then [regimental commander] with a real job and a bright future. How things can slip in a mere twelve months.

Red Irwin [9th Division artillery commander, recently promoted to major general] has promised to take this letter home with him when he leaves tomorrow, and while it will have to go through censors as usual you should receive it somewhat sooner than usual... I'd give a thousand dollars to be in his shoes. What with disappointment, homesickness, and wounded pride, this promotion muddle has left me in a very low state, and I find it difficult to think of anything else.

Doug Page also received a cruel blow when he was refused the logical promotion to Irwin's vacancy. We are getting an outsider [Brig. Gen. Reece M. Howell] who will probably be good enough, but Doug has been with the outfit for nearly three years, knows it and everybody in it thoroughly, has done a fine job for the past three months, and well deserves the place...

Certainly appreciate you writing so often, so regularly, and at such length, when you are so busy otherwise. Your letters always bring a ray of sunshine into a dark and gloomy world.

...Stars on campaign ribbons during the last war were awarded for participation in battles... In that case Bob will undoubtedly be entitled to one for the initial landing. [at Fedala, Morocco]

No, sorry, you'll probably have to wait for another war before having a "Major Dear" [family slang for major general] in the family. I have been given the brush off, and it makes me mad as hades. I know what you are saying, that it's all for the best...but unfortunately I can't think of it in that way, despite the fact that I'll concede that you're usually right.

Lowell Thomas wasn't too far wrong in his announcement except that the 894th Tank Destroyer Battalion was our first unit to enter Bizerte, instead of the 826th...

Two weeks ago today we passed Bob's outfit [Combat Command A, 2nd Armored Division] on the road going the opposite direction. Looked hard for Bob, but couldn't find him. Compared with our battle-scarred and weather-beaten equipment, theirs looked neat and shiny. I know where Bob is now, but unfortunately cannot tell you by this means. Perhaps a little bird will visit you soon with the news.

I am spending most of the weekend at our Eve-less Eden [Ain el Turk] on the shore of the Deleted Sea [Mediterranean]. Came up yesterday afternoon and will go back tonight. It is a place to loaf, read, sleep, sun bathe and cool off and all hands enjoy it hugely. We had

a wonderful dinner last night in honor of Irwin and
Randle, who is also going back to become a bigger dear.
Tonight we will be the guests of the division artillery at
a blowout honoring Irwin. It is almost as exciting as in
the old days when the transports used to leave.

Had the pleasure of seeing "Yankee Doodle Dandy"
for the second time on Friday night, when we attended
the movies in a nearby city [Oran] as the guests of the
local French big shot. Not the least of our enjoyment
came from sitting in big upholstered leather chairs
in the front row of the balcony. This was a relief after
sitting on jagged rocks on the side of a hill where we
see our camp movies. The camp movie machines leave
much to be desired too. The sound is off a large share
of the time... The other night we saw a complete short
of an orchestra in action without a peep of sound.

In June, the division received word that the 39th Infantry and
Division Artillery were both to be detached from the 9th for the Sicily
Operation; the 39th attached to the 1st Infantry Division, and Division
Artillery in support of the 2nd Armored Division. This was, of course,
probably considered another slap in the face to Gens. Eddy and
Stroh. On June 29, the 39th Infantry (minus the 26th Field Artillery
Battalion) moved out for the 910-mile trip back to Bizerte, followed
by Division Artillery the next day. The rest of the division continued
training and conditioning until July 8th when it packed up and began
the foot march some eighty miles to Ain el Turk. The journey was a
slog in debilitating summer desert heat. After a 123-degree scorcher,
they marched only at night. The new staging area at Bou Sfer near
the beach was a huge improvement over the conditions at Magenta,
but the training continued and plans for the 9th Division's role in
Operation Husky, the invasion of Sicily, began to take shape.

With the Axis forces expelled from the continent, the 2nd Armored Division, where Maj. Stumpf commanded a medium tank battalion in the 66th Armored Regiment, had completed its role as the guardian of the Spanish/French Moroccan border. The months on the Moroccan frontier had provided opportunities for extended periods of training which were of great benefit to Stumpf, who was learning his job on the fly. He got some good news on May 17th and shared it in a V-mail to his folks:

> Busy tonight but just wanted to take a minute to let you know that I've been promoted [to lieutenant colonel]... It's the first time since I hit old Jefferson Barracks in '38 that my rank has caught up with my job and I certainly appreciate it. Doubt if I'll get another one in the war and I'm just as well satisfied for I certainly have my hands full on this job. Only draw-back is that now I'll have to pay income tax.

After passing his father-in-law who was going in the opposite direction on the road to Magenta, he again wrote to his parents in a letter dated May 27th.

> ...We're in quite a comfortable location now but have no definite idea as to how long it will last. Something is "cooking" but no details have been released and everyone is a bit curious. We are seeing a good bit of the British now and personally I much prefer working with them than with the French. That's...as far as I'd better go, at least until we have a fair combat comparison... Got a good chuckle at Dad's letter saying the African campaign would be over by winter. Got the letter several days after the last surrender. A town near us is catching nearly nightly

visits from the Germans but so far they've slighted us
without hurting our feelings a bit.

Something was indeed "cooking" at the 2nd Armored Division.
Colonel Maurice Rose, Chief of Staff, had been on special assignment in Tunisia during the II Corps campaign on Bizerte as an aide
to Gen. Earnest Harmon, especially to observe the operations of the
1st Armored Division. He was a dashing former cavalry officer, well
respected by his peers and superiors. For his actions during the drive
to take Mateur, he was later awarded the Silver Star. Days later, he
was designated as the American representative to negotiate surrender
terms with the German command in the II Corps sector. Under Gen.
Bradley's instructions, he delivered terms for unconditional surrender
to the Germans, which they reluctantly accepted.[2]

When Rose returned to the division on May 27th, he was selected
for promotion to brigadier general and given command of Combat
Command A, one of three in the division. CCA was to be attached
to Gen. Lucien Truscott's 3rd Infantry Division for the initial phase of
Operation Husky. The outfit left for Bizerte on June 3 to prepare for
the amphibious assault. Gen. Rose selected Lt. Col. Stumpf to be his
executive officer. Stumpf had mixed feelings about the assignment,
although it was clearly a feather in his professional cap. In a letter to
his folks dated June 20th, he wrote:

> ... Sorry to say I lost the battalion just as I feared
> I would. The regimental commander came back to
> take it over and we got our old regimental commander
> back. Didn't go back to my job as regimental executive
> but have taken over the same job for Combat
> Command 'A' of the Division. When we're operating
> alone we have a good sized staff and it's more work
> than when I was with the regiment. Would have been

quite pleased with the assignment if it would not
have meant giving up a command. Hope to have one,
though, when the opening rolls around again. Expect
to be quite busy for the next few weeks so don't worry
if I have to skip a letter now and then.

In later correspondence, it would become more clear that Stumpf's disappointment in losing the battalion back to his predecessor, Lt. Col. Charlie Rau, was more of a blow than indicated in the letter above. Rau, who had been in the Philippines with Gen. Stroh, had taken command of the regiment, thus creating the opening for Stumpf. When the old regimental commander returned, Rau was simply reassigned to his old unit. Apparently, there was some bad blood shed over the whole rigamarole. For the rest of his time in the 2nd Armored Division, Stumpf would lament his staff job, although, in retrospect, it provided him valuable experience, and earned him high praise from his new boss. It is possible that his unhappiness with the job may have been in part attributable to Gen. Rose's leadership style. A future staff officer for Rose, Major William A. Castille, during a transition period in England, would later write: "Our entire staff spent three very difficult weeks trying to please a very demanding Brigadier General." He went on to describe Rose as "tough, impatient, terse, and hard to satisfy."

The week prior, during a planned tour of some of the American forces in the Bizerte area, Gen. Stroh was in the vicinity of the 2nd Armored Division and took a detour to locate his son-in-law. Thinking that Stumpf was still a major commanding a battalion in the 66th Armored, he had no luck at all finding him until he went directly to the regimental headquarters, which informed him of the changes. In a letter to Imogene, dated June 20th, he gave his take on the turn of events.

Bob was so busy that I only spent a few minutes
with him. He looks well and has a very responsible

job, although sorry to lose his battalion. His present
boss is the former chief of staff of his division, on the
verge of promotion to brigadier. He [Rose] did not
know of our relationship and seemed interested when
I told him. He told me that he had selected Bob as his
executive from among all of the field grade officers of
this command, so your judgment of the lad's ability is
vindicated. He is about to dispense with his footlocker,
and will hereafter live out of a barrack bag and a
musette bag, but there are worse misfortunes.

Stumpf's duties as Rose's executive technically included being
second-in-command, ready to take over in the commander's absence
or disability. For everyday operations, though, he functioned as a
chief of staff for the combat command, ensuring that all staff duties
were being carried out properly: personnel, intelligence, operations,
and supply. In addition, he was the commander's senior aide, advisor,
and personal confidant. He had to be on top of the tactical situation
and assist the commander with communications with his forward
units. On occasion, he was the personal liaison to those units when
the commander felt it necessary to have a senior presence at the front.
If the commander needed to be two places at once, the exec filled in
for one of them. When Gen. Rose felt it necessary to be at the front
himself, Stumpf ran the headquarters. It is worth noting that the 66th
Armored Regiment was part of CCA, and that Stumpf had been serving in that regiment since January, first as regimental exec and most
recently as a tank battalion commander. So he knew many of the
soldiers and was familiar with the organization of his new unit.

On June 25, CCA participated in Operation Bookmark near
Bizerte, a full-scale rehearsal for the invasion. Their landing beach
was to be near the city of Licata on the south central coast of Sicily,
planned for July 10, 1943.

7

---•---

Sicily: Operation Husky

Combat Command A, 2nd Armored Division landed on the beaches at Licata on July 10th as part of the American provisional corps under Maj. Gen. Lucian Truscott. In addition to CCA, this group included the reinforced 3rd Infantry Division, elements of the 82nd Airborne Division, and the 3rd Ranger Battalion. The American forces advanced up the center and western parts of the island, while the British attacked up the eastern coast. The Allies immediate threat was a total force of about 200,000 Italians, organized into four infantry divisions and various other units, and 32,000 Germans. The latter were organized primarily into two crack divisions, the Herman Göring and the 15th Panzer Grenadier. The landings went fairly smoothly despite opposition by coastal artillery and enemy aircraft. Heavy weather delayed and dispersed some of the landings, although it also hindered enemy attempts to reinforce coastal defenses as the landings progressed. D-Day objectives were the capture of the port at Licata, and the airfield, some three miles west.

During the amphibious operation, the American landing ship LST *313*, on which Lt. Col. Stumpf was embarked, came under German

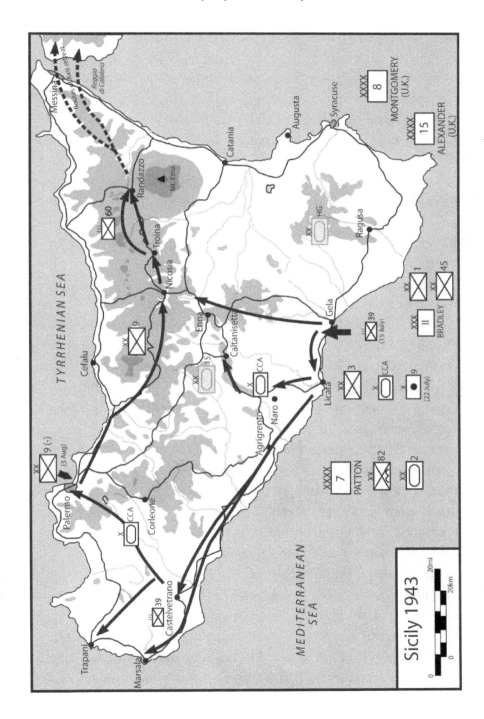

Sicily 1943

aerial attack, was bombed, set afire, and sunk. Stumpf took command of the stricken vessel briefly after its captain became a casualty. He eventually climbed down the stern anchor chain while his command car and equipment were burning, up forward. He made it to shore without injury, but again lost all his personal kit. Other ships sunk by German and Italian aircraft were the minesweeper USS *Sentinel* and destroyer USS *Maddox*.

By nightfall the D-Day objectives had been taken, although aerial reconnaissance had detected the 15th Panzer moving from the northwest toward the coast. At midnight, Gen. Truscott ordered CCA commander, Gen. Rose, to attack at daybreak and capture the town of Naro, about fifteen miles northwest of Licata.

The attack jumped off at 0600 July 11th. The armored column met light resistance along very rugged terrain, including a strafing attack by two Focke-Wulf 190s. The column used tanks as infantry carriers for the first time in combat. Naro was secured before noon and the troops took up positions in the surrounding woods. As they were launching a strong reconnaissance force toward the town of Canicatti, about eight miles north, Naro was attacked by a squadron of American B-26 bombers, which partially destroyed the town. Fortunately, the dispersed Americans escaped serious damage. Facing German anti-tank fire, and more friendly fire from American aircraft, the push toward Canicatti got the column to about four miles short of the town by dark on July 11th. The next day, the attack on Canicatti continued and met some strong German resistance from artillery and anti-tank weapons. By 1500, the town was in American hands.

CCA was placed in reserve for the 3rd Infantry Division the next morning, July 13th. The next several days included armed reconnaissance patrols, routine equipment maintenance, and rest, food, and hot showers for the troops.

On July 17th, CCA resumed its advance to the northeast, capturing the town of Serradifalco. The next day it continued its advance capturing the towns of San Cataldo and Caltanissetta. At that point, CCA was detached from the 3rd Infantry Division and rejoined the 2nd Armored Division as 7th Army reserve.

For the first week of the campaign, CCA casualties were twenty-five killed, 154 wounded, and thirty captured. The CCA captured more than 3,900 enemy troops. More than 35 percent of the American casualties were from friendly air attacks.

On July 19th, 2nd Armored learned that Palermo, Sicily's largest city, had been declared the highest priority objective in the campaign and that the outfit would be a part of the northward thrust across the western part of the island to the seaport on the northwestern coast. The assembly area for the advance was in the vicinity of Agrigento, some twenty-five miles west of Licata. The 100-mile advance to Palermo kicked off to the west at 0600 on July 22nd, meeting light resistance along the coast to Castelvetrano, then turned north across the island, arriving at the approaches to Palermo at around 1800. As it turned out, the city was ready to surrender. A patrol from CCA entered the city and returned with Major General Giuseppe Molinero, who surrendered all military forces in the area to Major General Geoffrey Keyes, Provisional Corps commander, and Gen. Gaffey, commander of the 2nd Armored Division. Gen. Patton and Gen. Rose entered the city about an hour later to crowds cheering them as conquering heroes. Then there was a formal surrender at the Royal Palace.[1]

Within the next few days, the entire western half of Sicily had been secured by the American forces. CCA set up headquarters in a comfortable villa near Mondello Beach, several miles north of Palermo. They then embarked on a period of occupation duty, vehicle repair, and preparation for transport to England. On July 27th Gen. Rose submitted a Legion of Merit recommendation for Lt. Col. Stumpf to the Commanding General, 7th Army (Patton) that reads in part:

...for exceptionally meritorious conduct in
performance of outstanding service. Since June
20, 1943, in the capacity of Executive Officer of the
Combat Command, Colonel Stumpf has functioned
tirelessly to facilitate the proper functioning
of the Combat Command. Through his efforts a
comparatively green staff was whipped into shape
and functioned in a superior manner through the
planning stages of the invasion operations and
combat operations subsequent to the invasion. During
the operations against the enemy, Colonel Stumpf
performed... in such a manner as to ease the burden
of responsibility of the ... Commander and kept the
operations moving forward in an expeditious manner.

During the period stated in the above citation,
Colonel Stumpf was subjected to all types of weather
and several times was subjected to enemy fire by
being bombed, strafed and machine gunned in the
performance of his duties.

Lt. Col. Stumpf's account of events is stated somewhat less elabo-
rately in a V-mail letter to Jerry dated the same day.

We hit the south coast of Sicily July 10. You
probably know how the whole operation is progressing
better than we do as publications are not reaching
us—not even mail to date. Usually too busy to listen
for news flashes on the radio. Lost all my equipment
again, dammit, but was not hurt although have been
well dusted off a couple of times. Have already sent
you a list of stuff to send, principally v-mail, as we
can't get the stuff—blank I mean. Writing this in the

midst of considerable hubbub, but will try to make some sense between interruptions. The outfit has done mighty well and should be due for a rest soon—all but the staff as usual. Don't like my present job worth a damn as it keeps me back from the fighting most of the time. Your poppy might be over by now but am not sure. They put his outfit in piecemeal. I saw some of the artillery on several occasions. Hope to get back for some tall tales one of these days. We spent a short time after a long drive billeted in some Duke's palace. Still miss you much....

Meanwhile, the 39th Infantry in Bizerte had been preparing for its amphibious landing in Sicily. They departed on July 14th and arrived at the Gela beachhead some fifteen miles east of Licata. After the landing, they were attached to the 82nd Airborne Division and began a drive westward along the coast all the way to Marsala on the westernmost tip of Sicily. Action was swift as they passed through town after town, destroying defenses and capturing prisoners. By July 21st, they had captured the town of Castelvetrano, enabling the 2nd Armored division to hook north on their final drive to Palermo.

The first battalion continued westward where, later on the 21st, they occupied Campobello. They proceeded onward and, approaching sunset, captured Mazara and took 3,456 Italian prisoners. The 39th Infantry took Marsala on July 24th after a heavy American artillery barrage. Meanwhile, the 39th's 34th Field Artillery Battalion had been attached to the 82nd Airborne division at Agrigento for its drive on the important Axis port of Trapani, some ten miles north of Marsala. They blasted the enemy defenses there, enabling the 82nd paratroopers to capture the city.

The 9th Division Artillery departed Bizerte on July 21st and debarked at the port of Licata the following day. Within a few days they were in support of the 1st Infantry Division near Enna, some forty miles northeast of Licata in the mountainous central region. At the same time, the 34th Field Artillery in Trapani reverted to 9th Division Artillery control.

The provisional corps, consisting of the 3rd Infantry, 2nd Armored, and 82nd Airborne Divisions, took up occupation duty, and the 39th Infantry was transferred to Gen. Bradley's II Corps, where he put them in the line with the 1st Division near Nicosia, about ten miles north of Enna, near the 9th Division Artillery. As the Italian defense of Sicily began to collapse, the Germans made preparations to evacuate the island. This included fighting a spirited withdrawal eastward toward Messina. There they would embark for crossing the Strait of Messina into mainland Italy. They utilized two lines of withdrawal and fortified them heavily to prevent the Americans from easily chasing them down. The southerly route through the center was in very mountainous terrain where the 39th Infantry and 9th Division Artillery found themselves deployed. The German fortifications on the high ground surrounding this route to Messina were similar to those at Sedjenane, heavily dug into solid ground.

During this time, the 39th gained a new commander, the legendary Colonel Harry "Paddy" Flint, a flamboyant ex-cavalryman and old friend of Gen. Patton. Flint replaced Col. William L. Ritter, who had broken his leg jumping from a jeep. The morale of the 39th had been a concern of Gens. Eddy and Stroh for some time. Caught as they would be in the bitter struggle at Troina, they needed strong leadership to see them through.

By July 30th, the 39th Infantry was moving out of Nicosia northeastward alongside the 1st Infantry Division; objective, the town of Cerami, about ten miles away. After a two-day battle the regiment had cleared the enemy out of the town and the surrounding hills. The next objective was the German strongpoint of Troina, another eight miles of winding road away.

Troina was especially well fortified, defended by hardened troops of the 29th Panzer Grenadier Division with lots of firepower and excellent points of observation all around, some as high as 3,000 feet above the surrounding terrain. At each objective, the 39th, fighting as part of the 1st Infantry Division, faced considerable challenges and was subject to heavy casualties. Time after time they attacked uphill into the teeth of the enemy weapons. When the Germans withdrew from a position, they counterattacked each time. The roads and fields of advance were mined. All the bridges had been blown. Waves of Allied bombers and heavy concentrations of artillery were unable to crack the defenses.

As the battle raged on, help was on the way. Finally en route to Sicily, the remaining units of the 9th Infantry Division, which had been II Corps reserve, were making their way to Sicily. Soon after Palermo was captured, the 9th, minus the 39th RCT and Division Artillery, already in the fight, began boarding twelve ships near Oran for the voyage to Palermo, where it would debark and enter the fray. Gen. Eddy and some of his staff flew ahead to plan with Gen. Bradley and II Corps regarding the 9th's role. Gen. Stroh remained with the main body to oversee the transport operations. He described the voyage in a letter to Imogene.

At Sea July 31, 1943

On another one of those conducted tours at government expense which, under normal conditions, would have cost us hundreds of dollars. I hope that the censor will not take too violent exception to the heading of this letter, but since I honestly don't know where we're going, and will not be able to tell you where or when we started, there should not be too serious a crime committed.

The trip so far has had many of the pleasant attributes of the usual transport journey, of which we have had so many enjoyable ones together [including to the Philippines and return in the mid-thirties]— good food, plenty of relaxation, enjoyable bridge games in the evening, and pleasant companionship, less of course the fair sex. We are even reveling in New York drinking water, which is a real treat after seven months of drinking from African mud holes, streams and wells. Also we have had fresh oranges and apples, a real menu affording a selection of food and a set of chimes to summon us to the meals. It's a great life until more exciting adventures overtake us.

I am writing this letter in the Captain's cabin, by his kind indulgence...

We were sorry to give up our comfortable villa at the last stop [Ain El Turk, Algeria], but at the same time glad to get underway again after a more or less lazy interlude of over two months. All was not so hunky dory during the last few days there, at that. The sewage system began to go haywire, and something happened to the antiquated and inefficient plumbing so that we could get scarcely any water at all. Matt [Gen. Eddy], while trying to take a bath one day, found that the tub was full of what he described as small fish. Actually, they were mosquito larvae, which apparently had been accumulating in the open tank on the roof. How many of these things we had been drinking, I shudder to think.

"More exciting adventures" did indeed overtake them, that very night. The ships arrived after dark and dropped anchor in Palermo harbor awaiting daylight to disembark. Enemy aircraft raided the convoy at dawn the next morning for nearly two hours. In the melee, no ships were lost and several aircraft were downed by anti-aircraft fire.

The troops disembarked after the air raid, made their way to bivouac east of the city, then began a motorized march to positions just west of Cerami, near the approaches to the Troina battlefield. With the 1st Infantry Division still stalled before Troina, Gens. Eddy and Bradley had planned another bold flanking maneuver by sending the 60th RCT around the enemy's right, through terrain not considered passable by an armed force. Meanwhile the 47th demonstrated before the enemy in support of the 1st Infantry Division, which at the time still included Eddy's third RCT, the 39th.

The 60th began its advance early on the morning of August 5th and successfully maneuvered to the enemy's rear, northeast of the town, where it threatened his crucial artillery observation positions. Without requiring a direct assault, the Germans determined their position untenable and withdrew eastward from Troina that night. The contributions of the 39th Infantry to the victory at Troina did not go unnoticed. Major General Terry Allen, commanding the 1st Infantry Division, wrote this in a letter to Gen. Patton dated August 6th.

The 39th Infantry entered the lines and executed a brilliant attack against Cerami, just west of Nicosia, on July 29th. It continued in the lines as an integral part of the 1st Infantry Division in the advance... against Troina, which culminated in the capture of that locality and the destruction of the German troops therein. Throughout the latter phase of this operation, the 39th Infantry was given a punishing role to continue the pressure against Troina from the west....

The 39th Infantry executed its assigned mission with the utmost efficiency and gallantry. The

personal leadership of Colonel H. A. Flint in the close
supervision and direction of front line battalions...
greatly influenced the combat operations of his
Regiment. His personal example was an inspiration to
the officers and men of his command.[2]

After the fall of Troina, the 39th reverted to 9th Division control
and was placed in reserve for a well-deserved rest. The 47th Infantry
passed through the positions held by 1st Division units and prepared
to advance to the east. Gens. Eddy and Stroh had designed another
variation of their plan at Sedjenane using a flanking maneuver to
keep the enemy off balance. Instead of having the entire bulk of the
division advance along the main road, they sent the 60th RCT to the
left on a parallel route to take the high ground from the Germans. The
60th began a hundred-hour march along the ridge lines to the north
of the route to Messina, putting continuous pressure on the German
defense of the main highway eastward. As the 47th began to advance
along the main artery to Messina, they ran into stiff German resistance featuring the familiar 88s and the new-to-them *Nebelwerfer,*
also known as the "Screamin' Mimi." This weapon was a multi-tubed
rocket launcher whose large explosive rounds were augmented with
noise-enhancing devices giving them a characteristic scream designed to strike fear in their targets. They were very mobile and hard
to pin down. In addition, the roadway was heavily mined and all the
bridges had been destroyed by the retreating Germans. Still the 47th
made steady progress the first day, August 7th.

On the morning of that day, the 60th's lead 1st Battalion, on its
approach to Monte Camolato, received a devastating mortar and artillery attack that caused heavy casualties and stopped them in their
tracks. After getting good counter battery fire from supporting artillery, the regiment was able to clear the enemy from Monte Camolato
by the end of August 8th.

The 47th occupied Cesaro on the morning of the 8th after the enemy had withdrawn the night before. It pushed on eastward toward the next major division objective, Randazzo, another twelve miles down the road. The regiment spent two days gaining objectives south of their line of advance, Hill 1003 and Casto di Bolo. By August 10th, the 39th Infantry had moved up and was in position to pass through the 47th in pursuit of the Germans' retreat toward Randazzo. Division artillery units were somehow able to move forward with practically no roads available and be in position to support the attacking battalions of the 39th.

The 39th began its final advance on August 12th supported by the 60th Infantry on the north and British forces to the south. Col. Flint's plan was a double envelopment using the 1st and 3rd Battalions, while the 2nd was holding down the front. Going was tough the first day, with a maze of mines along the roadways which forced the infantry off road. At the end of the day, the 39th was taking heavy fire from the defenders at Randazzo and pulled up still a few miles short of the objective. Next morning, the town fell to the 1st Battalion, who entered the town with no resistance. The Germans had pulled out during the night. That day the British 78th Division passed through Randazzo replacing the 39th there. At the same time, the 60th Infantry was in contact with the 3rd Infantry Division, which had been advancing along the coastal road to the north. Just like that, the 9th Division had been "pinched out" of the race to Messina. Although they did not know it at the time, combat in the Sicily campaign was over for them. After mopping up operations, Gen. Eisenhower declared victory in Sicily on August 20th.

There were significant factors that assisted the division's success on that final drive to Randazzo. First, two of the division's three RCTs were fresh, having just entered combat from reserve status. That allowed Gen. Eddy to place the 39th Infantry in division reserve to give them a little rest after their brutal ordeal at Troina. Second, the brilliant left flanking maneuver to take the Germans' positions on the high ground allowed the 60th RCT to put pressure on the enemy's flank all along the route of advance. Third, because the 60th was off the main road, maintaining lines of supply and communication was extremely difficult. Once again, they put their experience from North Africa to good use. The combat engineers were building roads behind the infantry nearly as fast as they were advancing. Where roads were not an option, they built jeep trails. When even that was not possible, the soldiers used mule pack trains to haul essential ammunition and supplies and to evacuate the wounded, much as they had done in northern Tunisia.

After two weeks of constant movement and combat and not knowing what was next in store for the division—rumor was that the 9th was to be part of the imminent invasion of mainland Italy—Gen. Stroh took some time to reflect on his surroundings and recent experiences. While encamped outside of Randazzo, he penned a letter to Imogene dated August 14th, the first day off the line and on reserve.

We are getting plenty of scenery out of this war, if nothing else. Our last two locations have really been something to write home about, and that is exactly what I'm going to do. The night before last we felt as if we were living in a picture postcard. Our tents were pitched in a Sicilian farm yard, constructed on a series of terraces, each just large enough to hold one tent. We dined off a table erected on a stone structure resembling those on which the old Romans used to eat, on the top of which a German poet, who'd evacuated the place only a short time before, had scribbled some verses in his native language. A grapevine over the place added a picturesque touch. The view over the valleys and mountains in the distance was magnificent, with a backdrop of a perfectly shaped active volcano, many hundreds of feet higher than the surrounding mountains, and from the summit of which curled a perpetual column of yellowish smoke [Monte Etna]. Nestled in the intervening valleys were two or three little towns, some still in German possession, and over which the smoke of battle still hung. Today we are encamped in a large grove of big pine trees and a species of cedar resembling Lombardy poplars in shape. Close beside us is a stone building which looks like a medieval castle, very austere and forbidding from the outside, but said to be very luxurious within. Nobody has had sufficient curiosity to investigate, however, since the Germans have just vacated it, and it is supposed to be well booby-trapped. You have no doubt read about these pleasant little devices, the construction of which the Heinies are very adept. You sit down on a chair, open a door, pull out a drawer, or pick up a book, and they blow up in your face. Somebody ought to pass a law.

We have been hacking our way through the mountains for some time, building roads as we go, and the result is no boulevard. I am rapidly developing callouses in a place where they are usually expected least, as the result of daily jeep rides, during which we bounce from rut to stump to boulder and back again. It is somewhat difficult to maintain a desirable appearance of dignity, and to salute with the snappy one-two motion required by regulations while attired in a large pair of rubber rimmed goggles, a dust respirator, and while clinging to various portions of the vehicle with both hands to avoid being dumped out on your ear. I may recover, but I'll never be the same.

The jeep was never designed for comfort anyway, and when the bottom is filled with a layer of sandbags (to decrease the effect of being thrown skyward when the jeep hits a mine) the joy of riding therein is by no means enhanced. Dust is everywhere, and in quantities more than somewhat. I am beginning to like the flavor, and am thinking of going into business here after retirement, putting the stuff up in fancy bottles, giving it an intriguing name, and selling it as face powder. Something like Sicilian Delight or L'Amore de Mussolini.

Rene, Torres' dog, is no longer a virgin, and the headquarters group is now agog concerning what the outcome will be. Not satisfied with African suitors, she had to wait until her arrival in Sicily before falling from grace, the accepted male being reported as a small wooly specimen. Since Rene is of ancient African descent, this presents an international puzzle of no mean proportions.

Braune, in addition to his other duties, has recently been appointed as mess officer in charge of the generals' mess. One of his first acts was to trade a pair of his shoes with a farmer for six dozen eggs and four young turkeys. The latter, looking very downhearted, are now tethered near the mess tent, being fattened on miscellaneous tidbits pending that happy day when they will be big enough to roast.

Enough of this drivel. Some time I may be able to give you some real news.

The commanders were clearly pleased with the division's work. They had used their lessons from Tunisia to complete a short but decisive advance against a stubborn veteran enemy. The commanding general sent this letter to "All Troops, 9th Infantry Division" on August 18th.

> With the campaign in Sicily drawing to a close, I can tell you that once AGAIN you have brilliantly justified my confidence and pride in you as a courageous, efficient fighting organization.
>
> The mountainous terrain over which you so successfully attacked must have been a challenge to your spirit and stamina—a challenge, I want to say, you met in the highest traditions of the United States Army. The problems you were forced to solve in supply alone would have stopped a less determined division. You have accomplished almost impossible feats of engineering, communication, and evacuation. The lessons you learned in Tunisia have served you well in Sicily.
>
> In every branch you have well earned in the minds of your commanders, your country, AND YOUR ENEMIES, the title of "the VETERAN Ninth Division."
>
> You have witnessed the wretchedness, the suffering, and the want that war brings to the people of the land in which the war is fought. God forbid that our loved ones at home will have to experience what the peoples of Sicily, Italy, and Germany are now experiencing. It is up to everyone to see that this war is brought to a quick and successful conclusion. This can be brought about only by determination for vigorous action in that direction by every individual of this command.
>
> Major General Manton S. Eddy[3]

After several days, the 9th Division marched westward to the beach area near Cefalu on the northern coast, about halfway from Randazzo to Palermo, arriving and setting up camp about August 26th. There they would rest, regroup, repair, and enjoy some recreation as they prepared for their next exciting adventure.

8

——— ✦ ———

Sicilian Interlude

A s it turned out, the 9th Division remained in Sicily for another couple of months after the fighting ended in August. The Mussolini
government had capitulated and the Allied invasion of mainland Italy
had begun. The 9th was one of the divisions being held in Sicily in
strategic reserve pending the situation in Italy. Meanwhile, they went
back to work repairing, replacing, and restoring equipment, receiving
replacement troops, and beginning another training program. In addition, somewhat sadly, all of the units in Sicily were required to supply
replacements for the divisions fighting on the mainland.

One of the highlights of a soldier's life during this time was the
appearance of the "donut girls" of the American Red Cross. Over
170,000 donuts were distributed to the hungry doughboys of the 9th
Division alone. Post Exchange (PX) supplies improved as did the rations, including fresh meat. There were USO shows including stars Al
Jolson, Jack Benny, Adolphe Menjou, as well as movies and shows
by the division's own soldiers.[1] Passes were given to sons of Sicilian
descent to search for relatives. The 7th Army commander, Lieutenant
General George Patton, addressed the division on August 26th, part

of his apology tour ordered by Gen. Eisenhower, punishment for slapping two soldiers in an army field hospital. Gen. Patton considered them cowards and malingerers. They had been hospitalized for "combat fatigue," now known as PTSD.

During the first weeks following the ceasefire, Gen. Stroh and Lt. Col. Stumpf, in relatively nearby encampments, met several times and began an interesting dialogue about the latter's career path. Stumpf was adamant about his dissatisfaction with his current billet, and made it clear that he was yearning to return to a command of his own. His father-in-law was empathetic as he, too, was anxious for his own command. In his August 29th letter to Imogene, Stroh wrote:

> I saw your O.A.O. [one and only] yesterday and had the devil's own time finding him as usual, spending most of the day speeding over the roads looking for his CP. Saw some new country while doing it, so the trip was not without its compensations. When I walked into his office, what do you think he was doing? You guessed it, sleeping. It was a warm Saturday afternoon, when most of the Army doesn't ordinarily work very hard anyway, and the boss was away, so he shouldn't be blamed too much. There he was, with his head on his desk, peacefully sleeping the war away. I hadn't forgotten his twenty-eighth birthday, so took him a box of cigars, which, believe me represented a far more valuable gift than a bucket of diamonds. There isn't a cigar in Sicily, and my precious stock is rapidly reaching the vanishing point, with no fresh increments yet arriving from home. But because it was Bob, I was happy to do it. Small enough, under the circumstances.
>
> He has no doubt written you that for the second

time he lost nearly all of his possessions when his ship was sunk. I doubt if he has given you all the details, and would probably not want me to, but I feel that you would want to know now that it is all over. He evidently had a very close call with his life, as he was still on the ship at the time, and it caught fire, forcing him to go down the stern anchor chain while his command car and equipment burned merrily on the other end of the ship. He seems no worse for the wear, however, and is his own cheerful, smiling self. His command has been reduced to about the vanishing point, at least temporarily, and while he did not intimate it in any way I am afraid he does not have much to do, and is accordingly not too happy.

Gen. Stroh was keeping his eye out for a battalion commander job that Stumpf could fill, almost certainly throughout the entire Corps, but also within the 9th Division itself. Stumpf had under his belt the recent experiences of battalion command, combat, and executive duties at the regimental and combat command levels. The 39th Infantry had taken a beating in North Africa and in Sicily despite having performed well. Their new commander, Paddy Flint, had led them in an inspirational manner through the tough battle of Troina and the final drive toward Messina. He was in a position to make some changes and was familiar with Stumpf's various roles in the 2nd Armored Division, where Flint had previously served. When a position opened up in the 39th, Gens. Stroh and Eddy, and Col. Flint undoubtedly powwowed about bringing Stumpf on. There could have been potential issues regarding nepotism and favoritism, on which both Stroh and Stumpf commented in various correspondence. In the end, Stumpf got the nod, which leads one to believe that they really wanted him in spite of any appearance of conflict of interest. In a V-mail letter to his parents on September 15th, Stumpf wrote:

> Just got my orders today to report to the 39th Inf. 9th Division. Jerry's dad arranged the deal and I think I'll get a battalion. Will let you know as soon as I get specific information as to my assignment so I can give you a more complete address. I was getting so darn fed up with the desk job when the "old man" offered me a battalion, I jumped at the chance. I hope I can stay put now for a while and get started picking up my old doughboy tactics again. Would have been glad to stay with the 66th, but things didn't work out that way. By the way, understand my new regimental commander was formerly C.O. of the 66th, so we'll have something to talk about. Naturally I'm tickled to get a command (if I do) again and only hope I can do a good job. Will try to cable you from the new outfit when I get there tomorrow. Sent one to Jerry from here today and I know she'll pass the word along. I have some studying to do, then pack a little, say goodbye to the staff, and get some sleep.

September 18, 1943

> Just wanted to let you know that I've been assigned as the C.O. 3d Bn. Have hardly had a minute since I arrived and expect to be just as busy for a while. Have already been on one 24 hour problem with the battalion and its former C.O. and go out again Monday in charge myself. In for reconnaissance and have some classes tomorrow. Will have to teach some stuff I haven't had for several years... Am well pleased

to get a shot at this job and know I'll be happier with
the work even if it will be hard at first.

September 26

Still in Sicily but have plenty to do now with my
battalion and only hope I can keep it long enough to
see a little action in command instead of on someone
else's staff. Our regimental commander was awarded
the D.S.C. last week for action in the Sicilian campaign,
and a good many of the officers including my 23
year old exec have been decorated so I feel rather
inconspicuous.

Jerry sent me two photos of Harry taken when the
wings were new, so thought I'd send one along.

Have put the battalion through one problem and a
corps inspection, both of which came off all right so I
feel a little more at home now.

Don't know where or when we'll go from here but
the sooner we get at it, the sooner we can be on our
way home and I hope it won't be long.

Gen. Stroh chimed in on his new battalion commander in a letter
to Imogene dated September 27th.

Bob joined the division since I last wrote you and
seems well satisfied with his new job. I believe he
escaped from his former one just in time. He joined
at a very hectic time, when it appeared we might be
going places. [Italy campaign] This has simmered
out, but he did have to get his battalion ready for the
corps commander's inspection last week, from which
he emerged with flying colors, as his battalion was

especially commended in the critique. He has his old
M Co. [his company at West Point] under his command
again which pleases him, I will have to be very
careful as to an official relationship in order to avoid
any criticism on the part of officers on the charge
of favoritism. This is always liable to crop up when
personal relationships are involved. His regimental
commander and I have a working agreement on the
matter, so that my official relations with Bob will be
exactly those of any other battalion commander. I am
certain that Bob would not want it any other way. It is
a fine opportunity for him, and I'm sure he'll do a fine
job.

Stroh probably debated with himself over making the suggestion to offer his son-in-law an essential job in the division. If it were
not to work out, it would reflect poorly on him. It would have been
easier to lobby for a similar position in another division where there
would have been no potential conflict of interest. On the other hand,
Stroh clearly had great confidence in Stumpf based on his familiarity
with the work he had done in other capacities in North Africa and
Sicily, that and Col. Flint's firsthand knowledge of his work in the
66th Armored. While it appears the command's initial impression of
Stumpf's performance was highly favorable, the true test would come
only when the bullets began to fly again.

Here is Imogene/Jerry's reflection on her husband joining her father's division, written September 29th, the word "extra" indicating
that she was writing in addition to her normal one-week interval,
having written only three days prior.

This is just a frothy dessert extra to thank you
for fixing Bob up so wonderfully. Frankly, I never

dreamed you'd ever get together on that or that Bob
would consent to being in the same outfit. He hopes he
can be worth your opinion of him, but I know he'll do
you credit just as your own son. He certainly is tickled
and both Mother and I can't get over it. A.P.O. 9 to
both. Gee whiz we'll get ranks all tied up now.

We still think Harry made a wise choice taking Air
Corps because he's his own boss and he does love his
work. You'll understand when and if you get to see
him. Wish he could go your way. We're expecting him
home this weekend.

Thanks for making Bob happy, and in turn making
me very proud.

After receiving Imogene's letter, above, Gen. Stroh replied on October
24th.

I must confess that I was happier to get this one
than any of the others. I was not at all certain how you
would take Bob's transfer to the division, and this nice
little note completely cleared up the situation, and
made me happy to know that you are happy and proud
about it. When I saw him last week, we found we were
in complete agreement as to our official relationship,
which removes any remaining faint trace of doubt as
to the desirability of his coming here. I was somewhat
fearful, as I have mentioned to you before, that he
would not understand my rather formal contacts with
him officially, but I should have known that his good
common sense would not have tolerated any other
treatment.

Bob, Bob Robb, and Hank Royall gathered with me

for dinner last week during Matt's absence. It was a congenial crowd, a grand meal, and a happy evening. What we did to a bottle of Scotch was pitiful, not to mention two kinds of wine at the table and brandy afterwards. But the thing that really brought tears to our eyes were the charcoal broiled tenderloin steaks, five inches in diameter and nearly two inches thick, neatly surrounded by French fried potatoes. All the boys could do during the first few minutes was to feast their eyes and inhale the aroma. The ice cream with chocolate sauce was not bad either. While talking over old times at McKinley [the Philippines], Hank stated that you were then the most beautiful girl he had ever known. Bob and I replied simultaneously, "She still is." You get your good looks from your mother.

We are getting our first issue of winter longs, only one per man so far, but as they are O.D. [olive drab] in color, Bob's colonel would say, "Hit don't make no difference." With that color they won't need to be washed all winter.

Gen. Stroh reflected further on Stumpf's assignment to the division and the fine line he was walking. He also related another harrowing experience that his son-in-law had recently gone through in a letter to Imogene dated October 10th.

We had an instructive field exercise last week. Bob's battalion was one of three in division reserve, so came directly under my command. He handled the situation with his usual efficiency. I hope he doesn't get the idea that I am neglecting him personally and socially, but I am so afraid that both he and I will be hurt by criticism of favoritism that I am bending over backward to deal with him exactly as I would any other battalion commander. In doing so, I may be overdoing it, but I think this attitude is better than if an opportunity were given to others to accuse him of being a fair haired boy.

If you don't tell Bob everything I tell you, I'll let you in on little secrets from time to time, about which I doubt that he'd write... While out on reconnaissance last week in a light cub plane they landed on a road, which is not unusual. On attempting to take off again, the ship left the high crown, hit a pile of crushed rock, and nosed over, completely wrecking it. Neither Bob nor the pilot were scratched. These planes land and take off so slowly that it's hard to get hurt. Thought you'd like to know, but I know he'd not tell you.

All was not work and drudgery for the 9th Division soldiers as they awaited their next exciting adventure. The generals and their staff were quartered in a rather nice villa with a view of the Tyrrhenian Sea. They often entertained other officers and their guests, sometimes local officials. Here is Gen. Stroh's description of one such event, written to Imogene on October 10th.

Quite a party last night... A couple of nearby evac. hospitals, or at least a bunch of nurses attached thereto, are breaking the boys' hearts no end, not to say three attached Red Cross doughnut girls, who, deprived of flour to make doughnuts, have to spend their time in other pursuits. Most of these women are definitely past their prime, but...after ten months or more away from home anything in skirts begins to look like Hedy Lamar. Anyway, two of our handsome young staff officers have built up a pretty solid acquaintance with a nurse who may be identified as Olivia, and a Red Cross doughnut dispenser who rejoices in the name of Becky. The headquarters mess was planning a special feed last evening, and these two couples were planning to attend... We had a rather uproarious evening. Olivia is known for her ability to say anything that comes into her head and proceeded to do so. The chief WOW [worn out wolf, Gen. Eddy] she called Butch. After the second highball she began to display some of her parlor tricks, including an attempt to pull off the table cloth without first removing the objects d'art thereon. This was highly unsuccessful and we face the prospect of eating out of our mess kits for some time to come. From a BBC program blaring from the radio in one room, and a scratchy phonograph going full tilt in another, you couldn't hear yourself think. Naturally I was outranked by my host, and out-glamoured by the aforementioned staff officers, not to mention two aides, so I took myself to a quiet smoke on the terrace. If this kind of thing keeps up, I'm going to revert to tent life in the bivouac area.

Lt. Col. Stumpf made good use of the time to get to know his soldiers and brush up on infantry tactics. He drilled with the battalion and "burned the midnight oil" studying. In a V-mail letter to his parents dated October 24th, he wrote:

Doesn't look as though will make it home this Christmas but everyone is betting on the next one. No definite information as to our next operation has come down this far yet but everyone thinks he can call the shot. Don't think I'd better do any guessing on paper... Have been busy as usual and don't have much of a spare time problem. The days just aren't long enough. Had dinner with Jerry's dad the other night and stuffed myself on steak. Don't get to see much of him but it's just as well as long as I'm in the outfit... Have restocked on all essential clothing and equipment and my trunk locker finally caught up from Africa—a bit battered but all in one piece, so don't worry about my getting along all right on that score.

After the inevitable rumors of impending deployments and operations, all of which petered out, by mid-October it was becoming clear that a move was imminent for the 9th Division. Vehicles and heavy weapons were turned in, and replacement soldiers ceased reporting in. Two significant events occurred at the end of the month. On October 25th, thirty-four 9th Division soldiers were sworn in as naturalized American citizens, earned by fighting for their new country in battle. The next day, the division passed in review before Gen. Patton, the first time the 9th had marched in review together as a whole unit. It was followed by the presentation of medals by the Seventh Army commander.[2]

Just before breaking camp for their next destination, on November 1st, Lt. Col. Stumpf mailed a 9th Division Christmas card to Jerry. It featured the division shoulder insignia, an eight-sided red, white, and blue patch called the Octofoil, with the inscription, "Greetings from overseas. The officers and men of the Ninth Infantry Division wish you a very Merry Christmas and a victorious New Year." On the back, he wrote, "Will miss you more than ever this Christmas, and am giving you strict orders to have a good time for both of us. Hope will be just one more apart." Apparently he was getting used to giving orders.

Separately, he sent her a 39th Infantry V-mail Christmas Card that read, "Just six little words/ But backed with good cheer/ And sent to you now/ As a greeting sincere/ Merry Christmas and Happy New Year."

In the beginning of November, the division marched from Cefalu about forty miles to the muddy town of Mondello on the outskirts of Palermo. In terrible weather, they prepared for embarkation on troop ships, destination England. The word was out that the 9th would be part of Gen. Eisenhower's massive invasion force for northern Europe. From Mondello, Lt. Col. Stumpf commented on the staging situation in a V-mail to his parents dated November 7th.

> Apparently we're in the midst of a rainy season now and it's running true to form. In spite of recent improvements, they still haven't developed a war without rain and mud. Expect we'll see a good deal more of it before I can curl up and look out of a window again. Not working too hard—just training and waiting. But the latter gets harder as it goes along and I'm certain everyone will feel better when we can get busy terminating this end of the rat race once more.

Cold, wet, and muddy, the troops finally made their way aboard the transports and got underway on November 11th. The flotilla consisted of twenty troop ships escorted by eight destroyers. Meanwhile, Gen. Stroh led a small advanced party to England by air. He described the circuitous journey, along with other observations, in a letter to Imogene dated November 6th.

> Somewhere in England
> Learned last Sunday night [October 31] that two other officers and I would make the trip by air, so we took off early Wednesday morning and arrived here

this morning making three plane hops and one by train last night. Never thought I'd see Africa again but spent Wednesday night in a town in southern French Morocco. [Casablanca?] The longest hop came on Thursday night, eleven hours mostly over water in a big four-motored C-54A, which resulted in the most uncomfortable night I believe I've ever experienced. We had nothing but "bucket" seats, lengthwise of the fuselage, with no arm or backrests. It was bitterly cold and no opportunity to sleep. While off Lisbon we encountered a sixty-mile headwind which caused the civilian crew plenty of worry as to whether there would be enough gas to complete the trip, with the possibility of having to land in Portugal and being interned. However the headwind switched and we got in all right. I had another uncomfortable moment when I noticed considerable activity in the rear of the fuselage and in my semi-awake consciousness came to the conclusion that they were inflating the rubber life rafts piled there, preparatory to abandoning ship. Shortly afterwards, still half awake I saw a lot of sparks from a motor flying past the window, and could think nothing but that the Germans were attacking us with tracer ammunition. All very humorous afterward but a little disturbing at the time. We finished the trip last night on the Royal Scot, a crack train, my first experience with a British sleeper car. Not bad.

Found out today that Harry has not arrived yet, but will be here shortly. I'll keep in touch with his outfit, and will plan to go see him if I have to bust a gut. Have not seen the kid for nearly fourteen months.

I don't know if it was wise for Mother to tell you what I wrote to her concerning Bob... a man is just a grown up kid after all, and when he doesn't have his women folk around to sympathize with him it makes his troubles almost unbearable. But he's alright now and has made a hit with the division and his regimental commander, as I knew he would.

To we battle-scarred field soldiers these specimens around here make us entirely nauseated. They still have the Pentagon pallor, and the seats of their pants are all shiny from rubbing around on swivel chairs... They all wear cute caps covered with rubber covers to protect them from the rain, well pressed blouses and pink pants. I'd like to get them in a slit trench for about fifteen minutes. Majors, lieutenant colonels and colonels are about as thick as raindrops in a thunderstorm. Honestly, some of them are so young they haven't shaved yet, and most of them don't even know how to salute.

Imogene's reply:

December 5, 1943

Were we ever glad to receive your letter of Nov. 6th from somewhere in England. It was the first actual news we have had from you that you were there.

And we do hope Harry's destination is what you think. We have just been keeping our fingers crossed and know how thrilled you'd be to see him.

Mother surely makes a knockout figure when we step out. She had on her lovely bright red suit, with new cocky red hat and flattering black veil. When we met her [for dinner] I saw a "major-dear" eyeing her. Small wonder.

It is interesting to note that Gen. Stroh seemed to have a good handle on his son's whereabouts, schedule, and destination weeks before Lt. Stroh had a clue about even to which theater his outfit was going.

For the rest of the 9th Division, the passage to England covered 2,800 miles and took about two weeks. This would indicate an average speed of only a little over eight miles per hour, much slower than normal convoy speed. To account for this time, it is likely that the flotilla performed significant evasive maneuvering, re-routing, or both, to evade enemy submarine and air attack. Conditions on the ship were generally bearable, although the enlisted men were crowded into berthing spaces well below deck. Two meals a day were served, with only snacks for lunch. Reading, movies, and gambling were the primary pastimes, although there was some official training on social relations with their British hosts who were suffering the deprivations of nearly four years of war. One group of ships arrived at Liverpool on Thanksgiving Day, November 25th. Others groups disembarked at Swansea, Wales, and Gourock, Scotland. By the end of the next day, most of the division had arrived by rail at their new homes in the vicinity of the cathedral city of Winchester, about forty-five miles southwest of London. Lt. Col. Stumpf described the situation in a V-mail to his folks dated November 24th, probably written while still at sea.

> Sorry I haven't been able to send any letters for the past couple of weeks or receive any for that matter, but we should start catching up on back mail soon. The outfit has been on the move again and I'll let you know where we are as soon as it's authorized. One more day until Thanksgiving and it looks like a toss-up as to whether we'll have a good meal or "C" ration. Hope there won't be any doubt about the next one.

9

———◆———

The Army Air Corps

The next two chapters will chronicle the journey of Cadet Harry Stroh as he prepared for his role in the war beginning with his first class (senior) year at West Point, which started at the end of May 1942, through his deployment to the European theater in late 1943. We are fortunate to have all of Harry's letters to his mother, father, and sister during this period. They tell a nearly complete account of the adventure, so they will be quoted extensively and without much elaboration.

Because of war exigencies, the West Point class of '43 graduated about five months early, in January 1943. For Cadet Stroh, most of the time from the end of his junior year until graduation was devoted to flight training. It was somewhat surprising that he chose Air Corps over Infantry, given his father's career-long devotion to the latter. As we shall see, Gen. Stroh initially was not happy about Harry's decision, although he tried to soften, or even withhold his disapproval. Perhaps there was an element of youthful rebelliousness in the choice. After all, Harry had essentially acquiesced to his father's career suggestions all along, and this gave him the opportunity to step out on his own and differentiate himself from his father. In any event, his decision would have profound implications for father and son.

The first indication of Cadet Stroh's interest in the Air Corps presented itself in a letter to his parents from West Point, dated January 18, 1942, while his father was stationed in San Francisco.

> We've been getting a lot of poop on the Air Corps lately. As a matter of fact it's definite that we will have extensive flying training every other day starting real soon. Friday all the cows [juniors] got a poop sheet to fill out as to whether they wanted to get in the Air Corps or not. It is a final and irrevocable choice as of June 1942. The choice has got me stumped because I don't know if I want the Air Corps or not. My first choice is Infantry but if any of our class is going to be ranked [drafted] into the Q.M. [Quartermaster Corps; supply] I want Air Corps because my class standing isn't very high and I would probably be ranked into the Q.M. I don't know what to do. I want to get in the Air Corps long enough to fly a short time but I wouldn't want to stay in—my mind has always been set on the Doughboys. Wish I knew whether we would be ranked into the Q.M. I'll have to decide soon cause the poop sheet goes in on Thursday.

Two weeks later, it appeared Harry had made a decision. In a letter home he wrote, "Starting Tuesday we start a two-hour tactics course to replace drawing. It's about Infantry tactics so I might as well start boning up on that stuff since I'm going to get in the Doughboys. New sections [class standings] are going to come up pretty soon and I'm anxious to see where I go." On February 8, he elaborated on his decision to join the Infantry.

I thought I told you that I rejected the application for the Air Corps—turned it down flat—didn't even want to see if I could pass the physical. However, during the past week there have been a few rumors going around that all the present 1st Class are going to be required to take the physical and those who pass will be ranked into the A.C. whether they want it or not. I don't know how true that is, but being ranked into the A.C. is still better than the Q.M. However, if I do as well in the next few months as I did this past month, I won't have any fears of being ranked into the Q.M. I think I am higher this month than I have ever been since I started academics. I went up 4 sections in Elect. and up 2 sections in Thermodynamics.

February 23, 1942

There is going to be an early graduation—May 29th. That's about three weeks early... The men in my class who are taking Air Corps leave here on the 30th of May and go to certain basic schools all over the U.S. and take the basic and primary courses until Oct. 7th. I don't know what they are going to do with the men taking branch schools but there are rumors that we will go to our branch schools for a three-month course. That means Benning [Infantry] for me I hope.

Had quite a surprise last Sunday night. Les [roommate Lester Taylor] and I were listening to the radio and writing letters when all of a sudden there was a pound on the door and Les and I popped to attention and we saw a uniform walk in and thought it was the O.C. [Officer in Charge, a roving watch officer] Then we glanced over toward the door and there was

Bob [Stumpf]. Les and I almost keeled over we were
so relieved—thought we would be walking the area for
playing our radio during C.Q. [confined to quarters]
Had a long talk with him until 9:30 and then it was
time for bed so we didn't get a bit of studying done. Bob
seems to be glad of this chance to get away and I don't
blame him. He gave me 8 pair of 2d Louie bars and 1
brand new pair of 1st Louie bars—said I would be using
them pretty soon.

March 1, 1942

This Air Corps poop sure is making me envious.
Getting out of a whole month of academics next fall is
enough but now there is more than that. While they
are away this summer they will have their pay sent
to them in cash and will have unlimited weekends.
Now they are trying to get pay and a half for the ones
taking the Air Corps. In the days they don't attend
class they will go to Stewart Field and fly. And what do
we poor land boys get—nothing.

March 8, 1942

Well, get set for the news! My name came up to
take the Air Corps physical and for some reason or
other I passed without any catches. So now I'm going
to take the Air Corps... I don't know whether you will
like this news or not... All the cows have been kidding
me about changing from the doughboys to the Air
Corps but that will die down pretty soon.

March 29, 1942

Dear Dad:

What do you think of my changing over to the Air
Corps? Well, as I said before I don't think I'll be staying
in it very long. Eventually they will catch up in my
eyes and I will be a doughboy again. I'm not overly
enthusiastic about flying as some of the boys are—I
don't care one way or the other but I always did want
to know how to fly and get the thrill of it and then
get out... The poop came out yesterday that we would
receive $75 a month instead of the usual $65 and also
be given free insurance. That shows that we are going
to be taken care of for the four months we are away.

April 13, 1942

Well, we drew for Air Corps schools last Tuesday
and by the time they got down to my name there
wasn't much left. The two schools I wanted near Miss.
[Where his parents were going] were filled up, so I
took the next best thing—Avon Park, Fla.

There are no surviving letters from Col. Stroh to Cadet Stroh that
might have shed light on Harry's father's feeling about his service
selection. Based on correspondence a year later, it may be surmised
that the colonel was none too happy about it. It is interesting to
note Harry's nonchalant references to possibly washing out of flying school for one reason or another, and switching to Infantry. The
washout-plus-fatality rate for military flight training was exceedingly
high—approximately 40 percent.

Air Corps flight school was designed around three phases:
Primary, Basic, and Advanced. Each phase was nine weeks in duration and together totaled about 200 flight hours. Cadets and officer

trainees flew increasingly faster and more complex aircraft as they proceeded through the course. Except for Primary, they were taught by Army pilots. As the war approached, with the huge expansion of the program, some changes were inevitable. Primary students were taught by civilian instructors at civilian flight academies. The duration of flight training was reduced by nearly 50 percent, to six months, although the amount of flying and the overall curriculum was not.

The plan to include West Point cadets in flight training began with Cadet Stroh's class of 1943. They were to complete the Primary and Basic phases during the summer, return to West Point in early October, graduate and be commissioned in January, then complete the Advanced Phase and be designated Army Pilots. Of course, it being wartime, plans changed.

Stroh finished up his junior year as manager of the varsity lacrosse team, allowing him to miss out on all the graduation-week parades, about which he was most happy. He struggled through final exams, received his longed-for class ring, became a "firstie," and shipped out on a troop train for primary flight training at Avon Park. His comment to his folks in a letter dated May 31st, "Oh, it's a wonderful feeling! First-classmen and rings—there isn't much more a person could ask for."

After a hot, crowded journey on the troop train to Florida, and sitting around for two days of bad weather, Harry finally got his a crack at flying an airplane, the venerable Stearman PT-13 "Kaydet" biplane. From Lodwick Aviation Military Academy, he wrote his folks in a letter dated June 7, 1942.

> There are about 150 men in my class—42-K—so we only fly about 30 minutes a day and then sit around on the flight line the rest of the morning while the rest fly... They didn't waste any time once we started flying. The instructor took the plane off and then turned the

controls over to me. It was quite a thrill flying it and know that everything you did the plane would react. Saturday we also flew and I have about 58 minutes flying time. Another 9 hours and I should solo! The more I fly the better I like it—I didn't realize it could be so much fun. Tomorrow we are supposed to take off without the aid of an instructor and then learn how to do a spin. They really move along and when you drop behind you don't catch up and then out you go.

June 14

I have only about 2 1/2 hours of flight time so far which isn't so good. In two weeks we should have had our 5 hour check flight with an Army pilot. I'm not sorry I'm a little behind though because I don't seem to be getting this flying business any too well. Some days I feel as though I were a "hot" pilot and other days I can't keep the plane steady to save my soul.

June 21

If I fly like I did last Friday... I think the instructor will let me solo [with] under 8 hours because I was really hot. I felt so relaxed and at home in the plane that day—first time I have ever felt like that. Nobody has washed out yet, but one flying cadet has a check ride Saturday, so I suppose he will be leaving us soon. Flying hasn't been so hard yet but you really have to stay on your toes every minute.

July 8

Well, there is a hot pilot in the family now. I soloed last week much to my surprise. I took the check ride last Monday and didn't do any too well. It is a great feeling to fly around the field all by yourself and not have anyone in the front cockpit.

July 13

Last week I almost doubled up my flying hours. After you solo, the time really adds up... To tell the truth the more I fly the less I like it. It was fun the first few weeks, but my heart just isn't in it I guess. Maybe I'm an old doughboy after all.

I haven't heard from Les [in Oklahoma, at a different flying school] for over a month now—I'm beginning to think he washed out or something. So far there have been only 3 Pointers washed out down here and that's not bad—3 out of 46 and primary almost over.

July 26

...so I haven't had my 40 hour check yet and I have 53 hours—ready for my 60 hour check—the final one. Maybe I'll be able to get my 40 and 60 together.

...Joe and I went to the Sebring Air Base and looked over the B-17E's—the best of the Flying Fortresses. While we were looking at one, the crew came out and were going to take a flight and they said we could come along... it turned out to be 5 hours of formation flying. It was quite an experience to ride in one of those big babies. The pilot let us take the controls for a few minutes and I was rather surprised how easily they handled. It got rather monotonous though after 5 hours. I don't think I would enjoy flying the big boys for a career.

Cadet Stroh completed primary training and was transferred to Shaw Field near Sumter, South Carolina, for the basic phase where he flew the low wing BT-9 or BT-13 Valiant. Meanwhile, his father had been promoted to brigadier general, left command of the 339th Infantry in Hattiesburg, Mississippi, and transferred to Fort Bragg, North Carolina, as the Assistant Commanding General of the 9th Infantry Division. Cadet Stroh was able to visit his folks at Fort Bragg during his transfer to Shaw.

Initially pleased with the military seriousness of the Army air base compared with the civilian laxity of Avon Park, Stroh and the other West Pointers became bitter over their treatment by the newly commissioned officers on the base who ridiculed them in subtle ways and put them on report regularly. In a letter home dated August 16th, he wrote, "…it won't take much more before one of us takes a swing at one of these 2nd Lts. that think they are so high and mighty." In the same letter he went on to tell them about the new airplane.

> This Basic ship is quite a job—fast and plenty heavy. It is just like learning to fly all over again— nothing is handled the same as was operated in the primary ship. I only got in two hours last week and in that time I still hadn't the feel of the plane. It will be many a day before I solo in this plane. I have been so busy in the air—turning this and pulling that—that I haven't even had a chance to look over the country and orient myself. But with a little time I guess I'll get used to flying it.

As the exigencies of war drove the realities of wartime training, the expectations of Cadet Stroh and his West Point classmates with regard to their return to West Point were being dashed by plans to send Air Corps cadets directly to advanced training. They were originally to return to West Point after Basic in early October. The beginning of his letter home of September 6th underscored his frustrations.

Right now there are 36 very bitter cadets here at Shaw. We will get back to the Point in Dec. and will graduate on Jan. 26.... There is only one cadet here who doesn't care if we go back or not, but everybody else are counting the days until we go back. After looking forward to the 1st Class year for 3 years and then have it taken away makes us pretty sore. This is war I guess so we have to take the bitter with the sweet.

Had my first formation ride in the plane the other day. It was only a three plane Vee formation but you have to stay on the ball or you run down the lead plane. We fly only 3 feet from the lead plane's wings and that isn't far, especially in rough air. It's a lot of fun though—the best type of flying I have had as yet. This week we start night flying and cross country...

September 20

They have already made the selection of single or twin-engine school and the whole selection was based on nothing but height and weight—everybody 5' 9" and 160# [and below] is going in single engine. So I go to single engine and fly the hot stuff.

I was kinda doubtful whether I would get down in one piece last night because there was a strong wind blowing and it rained nearly all the time. And to top that off we were landing with no lights. The old plane bounced around like a balloon all the time. I made it all right though and all the better for the experience.

Guess Imogene has gone home now. It sure was
swell having the whole family together again even
though it was only just for a few days. She sure doesn't
look like a major's wife.

Took quite a long cross country trip last week. The
greatest surprise was that I didn't even get off course.
Two men in the squadron did get lost and ended up
about 100 miles away from the field. That didn't
go over so big with the C.O. We have another cross
country tomorrow...it's about 400 miles long... All you
have to do though is follow the map.

During the last week of Basic with only seven flight hours left to
complete the course, Harry came down with pneumonia and was
admitted to the hospital. The day he was to be released, the rest of
his class left Shaw Field for advanced training. The doctors and his
C.O. tried to get him a two-week sick leave, which would probably
have meant he would be too far behind to catch up with his class
and would be going back to West Point. "...I'm afraid they will send
me back to the Point and then go to Advanced after I graduate. That
won't be too bad, but I would like to get my wings with the rest." But
the sick leave was not approved and he was ordered to proceed directly to advanced training at Spence Field, Moultrie, Georgia, where
he would fly the AT-6 Texan. The operational tempo for Harry's class
continued to pick up, surely a reflection of the accelerating pace of
wartime operations. His first impressions of the new plane and flying
curriculum are conveyed in a letter home dated October 18th.

Yesterday, after having been grounded all week,
I flew for the first time. They didn't waste any time
once I got started. The first trip up and the instructor
expects you to operate and land the plane all by

yourself... The second the plane leaves the ground you have to do about three things at once including retracting your wheels and then your ship is really moving... This is the sweetest ship I have flown yet... I flew about 4 hours yesterday and the last hour, the instructor let me take it up alone so now I ought to be able to catch up with the boys in quick order.

October 25

Here it is, 1:30 A.M. and we are down at the flight line doing a little night flying. We were lucky tonight and got the graveyard shift. At least we have all tomorrow morning to sleep.

I have been here over two weeks now and haven't been off the post yet. In fact the only part of the post I have seen is the road from the barracks to the flight line. We are positively on the go from the minute we get up until we hit the hay. Basic was a dead boat compared to this and I thought Basic was bad... 14 days in a row of flying is beginning to tell too. They had better give us a little rest or some of the boys flying will certainly fall off.

So Bob has gone for good, eh! He must have had quick orders.

November 1

...The time seems to go by more quickly all the time—especially when we are busy every minute of the day as we are... This weekend we had it pretty easy though. We had all Sat. and Sun. off. I don't know what got into the brass hats by giving us all that time off but it was mighty good.

Friday we got a poop sheet stating what part of the Air Corps we wanted. Most of the boys, including myself, put in for fighters and then photo recon. The instructor said that both of these had a pretty good chance of going across [to war] pretty quick and that is what I want.

Every day now I am beginning to like flying better. Friday we went up North about 30 miles and then did low altitude formation flying. I swear our ships weren't over 4 ft. from the tops of the trees. When I landed I got out to see if there were any pine needles in my landing gear. It was more fun than I have had so far.

November 8

Well, Dad, I am beginning to feel that you are right about the Air Corps... Wednesday and Thursday we went out on maneuvers... I have never seen anything so disorganized in my life...

Now I have something to tell you which I don't know whether you will like or not. Friday eight men from each of the five squadrons were picked to fly the P-39 [Airacobra] for the next two weeks. These eight are supposed to be the best in each squadron, but I don't see why I was picked because I know there are more than 8 men who can fly better than I in my squadron. Anyway, I was picked so now I'm going to fly one of the Army's best pursuits.

November 15

I'm flying P-39's this morning and this afternoon I am flying an AT6 to Atlanta and come back tonight. This Atlanta trip is the longest cross country we take and the best.

Boy, these 39's are some ships. The more I fly them the better I like them. I have 5 hours' time in them now and need only 5 more until I can go to any field and take one up. You see, before you can take a ship up you have to be "checked" out in that ship which consists of a 10 hour transition period.

We had a few accidents in the 39's the other day— Friday 13. One of them was a fatal accident and one of my classmates at the Point. Then about 5 minutes after the first accident another boy spun in but he managed to bail out and wasn't hurt. That was the second West Pointer that was killed in 2 days so we Pointers down here don't feel too good. Those were the first accidents we have had and we were figuring on having a perfect record.

If Bob is in Casablanca it looks as though he is having a pretty good time. Kinda envy him myself but I guess it won't be long now until I can get across myself. Flying these 39's I think my chances of getting into a fighter outfit are pretty good.

November 22

We are still flying the 39's. We have been flying them for two weeks and still haven't got 10 hours... Either the weather is bad or else there aren't any ships to fly. I don't see how they fly these 39's in combat. They go up for one hop and then they go into the shop for a few days for repair.

You got the wrong impression on how McMullin was killed. He was flying an AT doing some night work... He lost the horizon and spun in. We have had a

few accidents in the 39's though—four to be exact. Two
bailed out and two were killed. If anything goes wrong
with one while I'm in it the first thing I will do is bail
out.

Wednesday all the 42K goes to Eglin Field, Fla. for
about 9 days for a little actual gunnery—aerial and
ground.

Eglin Field, Fl.
November 29, 1942
Dear Mother and Jerry,

We left Spence Wednesday and got down here that
night. Thursday went out and fired our first hundred
rounds and out of that number of bullets I got 9 hits
in the target. It was rather rough and hard to hold
the sight on the target—but 9 out of 100—that's pretty
bad. Friday was just as bad if not worse, I hit 8 out of
100. Sat., after listening to the Army lose a game to
Navy again, I went up and did much better—27 hits out
of 100. That's not bad either because the instructors
are hitting about 30 and 35. Today I shot 27 out of
100 again so now I'm in a rut. Tomorrow is the last
day of ground gunnery so I am going to try to break
30. Tuesday we change fields again and shoot a little
aerial gunnery. We go back to Spence on next Sunday I
think.

Just got back from a meeting where the officers
told us that we were the worst shots they had ever
seen—and here we were breaking the Eglin Field
record. These officers really have some funny ideas.

November 29, 1942

Dear Dad:

Got a letter from Imogene today and she said that you were going to Dix [Fort Dix, New Jersey]. If it isn't a military secret can you tell me how long you'll be at Dix?... I would like to see you before you go because there is no telling how long it will be before I see you again.

Been down here at Eglin for 4 days now and I really think this is the best part of our training—especially for men going into combat soon. This gunnery is a lot harder than it sounds on the surface—as I found out in the first two days. You just can't fly the plane and pull the trigger and expect to hit anything. I have fired about 400 rounds on ground targets so far and I have only about 20% hits. However that's right up among the top... Tuesday we change fields and fire a little aerial gunnery. They say this is a little harder than ground but I don't see why it should be.

Eglin field is the Air Corps' proving ground and they have every make of plane in the Army down here. We were allowed to look the planes over this morning and some of them looked pretty good. That P-51 looks like a swell plane to me—the best the Army has.

December 6

Dear Mother and Jerry,

For the past week we have had nothing but overcast. I don't think I have flown over 2 hours during the whole past week. I did finish up my ground gunnery finally—final average for 500 rounds was 29% hits. That was about 4th or 5th highest in the squadron. We went to aerial gunnery then, but I fired only 148 rounds and hit the target 11 times which isn't good. We were supposed to get 900 rounds of aerial but the boys flying the 39's had to come back to Spence and finish flying in order to be through by graduation. All in all though it was a nice rest—all we did most of the day was play cards or sleep. I even tried growing a beard but it wasn't very satisfactory.

After a bruising nine-hour ride in the backs of Army trucks, the student pilots arrived back at Spence Field on December 5th. The West Pointers were scrambling to finish the rest of their flying requirements in time for flight school graduation on the 13th. But the date was moved up to the 11th, so they were flying literally day and night to get it done. Knowing of his father's impending departure overseas, Harry was trying to coordinate a visit on his trip back to West Point. Gen. Stroh had just executed orders to Fort Dix, staging point for his ocean voyage to Casablanca with the remaining elements of the 9th Division. Harry's plan was to get off the train at Trenton and meet his father there, then make his own way to West Point. By the afternoon of December 11th, Cadet Stroh was sporting silver pilots wings on his chest. He and his West Point classmates left on the train for the Point that evening. His plan to see his father was not to be, as the general would be at sea before Harry could get there. So he executed Plan B. His mother and sister had recently moved in to a rented house in NW Washington, D.C. In a letter to her father dated December 13th, Imogene wrote:

We had a surprise last night about 3:00 A.M. The doorbell rang and there stood Harry in a beautiful Luxembourg cap, lovely O.D. blouse and trousers. He looked just like an officer except for the fried egg on the cap and W.P. insignia on his shoulders. The first thing he did was throw open his coat to show us the silver wings on his chest.

He presented Mother with the set of wings presented to him because there is a superstition that it is bad luck for him to wear them. Guess he thought I looked hurt because he gave me a pair too.

We put him on a plane this afternoon after picking Grandma up to see him off.

Cadet Stroh's version of his surprise visit is included in a letter to his father from West Point dated December 20th while Gen. Stroh was still at sea en route to Casablanca.

Sorry I couldn't get to see you in New York or somewhere. Got your telegram and also one from Mother before I left Spence Field. Now I don't know when we'll see each other again—hope soon though. I'm really sorry that you won't be here for graduation next month. I've been hoping all year that your orders would be put off long enough for that occasion. It won't seem right without you here.

It was quite a thrill to get my wings on the 11th but not as much of a thrill as getting the diploma next month. Now I'm a rated pilot—all I have to do is find a plane to fly.

Started back for the Point on the 11th and got to Washington on the morning of the 13th—early in the morning (about 3 A.M.) Had to ring the doorbell about 10 minutes to get anybody up in the house. They were really surprised to see me. Stayed in Washington until the 13th and saw Grandma and then on to New York and on to the Point the next morning.

The academic course we are getting now is really a hot one—one year's work in one month. However, it is really interesting stuff and all of it can be used when we get out.

Cadet Stroh enjoyed a brief but joyous Christmas leave in Washington. To his father he wrote, "Somehow or other it didn't seem like Christmas though without you there. We all missed you." He returned to West Point on December 30th. Early in January he and his pilot classmates got their initial assignments following graduation. After a twenty-two-day leave, he reported to Craig Field near Selma, Alabama, for a four-plus-week course flying P-40s, a frontline fighter aircraft then in combat in Africa and the Pacific. Next stop was to be a course in air-ground coordination in Orlando. And finally, to a new combat squadron, training on what he hoped would be the Air Corps' latest fighter, the P-51 Mustang. After completion of training and qualifications, the squadron was to ship overseas and into the war. He had grandiose ideas of being in the war by the end of summer as a captain or major commanding his own squadron.

Stroh's class completed academics on January 14th. He was elated to at last be free of the academic burdens that had plagued him for over three years. He graduated ranked 382 out of 409. One of his classmates failed to make the academic cutoff on the last day, but was retained for a June graduation. The class of "January 1943," as it came to be known, graduated on January 19th.

10

———— ✦ ————

Fighter Pilot

Second Lieutenant Stroh enjoyed most of his well-deserved twenty-two-day graduation leave in Washington, staying with his mother and sister, sleeping every morning until eleven, eating like a horse, and generally decompressing. He left Washington on February 7th, made a stop in Hattiesburg to visit friends of the family, and reported in at Craig Field near Selma, Alabama, on the 10th. He began his fighter career with 200 hours and five minutes of pilot time. He wrote to his father on February 14th.

> We were on the line the first three days all day long, just going over technical orders and looking the P-40s over. We flew a few hours in an AT-6 just to get us back in the feel of flying after our two-month layoff. But here it is the fourth day on the line and I still haven't been up. I am flying the P-40E's and there are only 5 on the field... These ships don't look any different from the P-39—as far as flying goes—so I don't think I will have much trouble. We stay here for

4 weeks, then to another field somewhere for another
4 weeks and then down to Florida.

We have swell quarters on the post and a swell
club—not bad being a commissioned officer...

February 17, 1943
Dear Mother and Jerry,

These P-40s are much better than the P-39. At
least that's my opinion. They are much bigger and
much more stable. The flight characteristics are much
better than the P-39.

February 21
Dear Dad:

We have been here over 10 days so far and haven't
had over 8 hours flying time. There are 23 of us down
here and 11 of the 23 have had an accident of one kind
or another. We are even ashamed to hold our heads
up around here now... I haven't had any accidents yet
(knock on wood), but if I ever do I know it won't be a
gross mistake like some have had. Personally I don't
see why they don't ship some of these boys out—just
because of their attitude if for no other reason. If I ever
become a squadron commander and run across a man
with that attitude I won't lose any time transferring
him out of my outfit. Pretty soon some of these boys
will be German aces! In the meantime we sit around
on the ground because there are only 2 or 3 planes in
flying condition. It sure is a sad affair.

Well if the situation continues around Tunis I guess
they will be sending the 9th up to the thick of it. I know
you are getting eager to get into it. I know I would.

If you ever get back for a while I will make it a
point to take leave or something and see you. I am still
disappointed that I didn't get to see you in Dec...

For the next several weeks, Lt. Stroh and his P-40 classmates endured a dearth of serviceable aircraft, which meant a lot of sitting
around and not much flying. To make matters worse, they were rack-
ing up a good many minor accidents, which tarnished their reputation and exacerbated the airplane problem. Eventually they were told
that not all of them would continue on track to a combat squadron,
but would become instructors for a while. Stroh was so frustrated that
he wrote his father that he would quit the Air Corps if that happened
to him. For the month of February, he logged eleven hours in the P-40
and another five in the AT-6.

At one point he took a four-day pass to Baton Rouge to visit his
old flame, Jeanne Kendall, whose folks he had visited in Hattiesburg.
He wrote that they had a wonderful time despite the fact that she was
engaged to a Navy pilot in Corpus Christi. "It certainly was nice seeing her again—don't know when I'll ever see her again though... I'm
still mighty fond of her even after what she has done to me."

The flight schedule eventually picked up with the arrival of more
P-40s on the airfield. The latest word was that after completing their
time in the P-40s, they would proceed to Mitchel Field, New York, for
transition to their combat aircraft. During the increased operational
tempo, Lt. Stroh had his first accident, a ground loop, which is where
a wingtip drops on landing, scrapes on the ground, and spins the
aircraft around. Apparently there was minimal damage, but it was a
blow to his pride and a blemish on his permanent flight record. His
flight time totals for March were twenty hours in the P-40 and four in
the AT-6.

After finally completing the P-40 course, the lieutenants got orders on March 24th to Mitchel Field on Long Island. Lt. Stroh thought

that Mitchel was just a processing stop and that he would soon ship out to another field in the area, perhaps Westover, Massachusetts. He had bought a car from a nurse at Craig Field for $700 and would be making the trip to Long Island in it, hoping to swing by to see his mother and sister on the way. He wrote to his father March 24th, the night before hitting the road.

> Went over to Montgomery yesterday to watch a big air review for [Army Chief of Staff] Gen. Marshall and [British Foreign Secretary] Anthony Eden. There were 108 ships in the formation and was very impressive. The ships were flown by old timers and they were pretty good at formation flying.
>
> About 6 of our group were washed out of flying pursuit type aircraft and are going to Texas to be instructors. All of us were given check rides by several of the big wigs on the field. I sure do feel sorry for the men who got washed out. The thing that gets most of us is that two of the worst flyers weren't washed out. They will be in Texas until they prove good enough and then sent to combat. If I had been washed out I believe I would transfer to the doughboys. Couldn't stand being an instructor.
>
> Well, keep pushing them back over there. Am thinking about you a lot.

Driving day and night, including a brief stop in Washington, Lt. Stroh made it to Mitchel Field by the deadline on March 27th. After a few days, he and five of his group were sent to Westover Field, near Springfield, Massachusetts, for a flying course on the P-47, after which he expected to be shipped to a combat outfit. While at Westover, he ran into his West Point roommate Les Taylor, who had been flying the P-47 for a couple of weeks. A few days later, he was ordered to Orlando for a four-week tactics course. He and another close friend from West Point were on the train that afternoon and in Orlando two days later. He reported to his father about the course in a letter dated April 6th.

It looks as though the Air Corps is bucking up, Dad—at least, if this school is any indication. I am in the first class of this "School of Applied Tactics," and things seem to be pretty well organized. The first four days are devoted to tactics and techniques of all branches... I admit it covers quite a broad stroke... but is more than most Air Corps personnel have had before. Then a week and a half of tactical training in day fighting. Then for two weeks we move out into the field and practice what we learned—real combat conditions—guns loaded and all. So far it has been mighty interesting. If this school clicks it looks as though the doughboys will be getting a little of the support they have been yelling for.

April 16

...I sure would like a crack at those Japs—I'm afraid I wouldn't be too humane—not after what they have been doing to our boys. But then, I'd like to go to Africa also...

...I was talking to a Capt. in our barracks and I learned that he was out at the Presidio at the same time as you were. He remembered you very well—in fact he spoke very highly of you—said you were about the finest man he had run across in both the 4th Army and 9th Corps Area Headquarters. He made me feel pretty proud I tell you.

Hope you are feeling fit now and stay out of the hospital.

On May 5th, Lt. Stroh took his first three flights in the Republic P-47 Thunderbolt. For the next six months, he flew the P-47 at a furious rate up until preparations began for his squadron's deployment to England. He was pleased with the increased pace of flying, especially on days when the weather was good. For the first six weeks, the syllabus included continued instrument training flights in the AT-6 and BT-8 aircraft at regular intervals between P-47 flights.

In a newsy letter to his father dated May 6th, Harry described the increased tempo, and reported that he finally received letters from his dad and brother-in-law. He lamented not having been promoted to first lieutenant yet, as he had been led to believe he would, and that he had lost one of his front teeth in "a little accident last week." It is unclear what kind of accident, but he was happy with his dentist's treatment and repair. In a letter to his mother and sister dated May 10th, he noted that he also broke his nose, but "they took a piece of cartilage out of it so you wouldn't even know it had been broken."

> ...And next week at this time I expect to have a
> full complement of teeth. They have swell dentists
> here... They seem to be much better than the usual
> run of dentists. All of them have girl assistants so I
> don't mind going up there at all—they are pretty good
> looking too—have to get a date one of these fine days
> when I get my tooth.

His tone turned much darker only a week or so later in a letter to his father dated May 19th about the state of the Air Corps and a flying incident brought about by his own irresponsibility.

Well, now that all the excitement is over in Africa I guess you will be looking for newer fields to conquer. Can't say that I blame you, either—keep 'em on the run I always say.

I'm in a very depressed state of mind about now—sometimes I wonder why I didn't listen to you last summer and go back to the Doughboys. The more I see of the Air Corps the more I understand why there weren't any planes in the air at Pearl Harbor and in the Philippines. What chance has a mere 2nd Lt. got of voicing any opinion on how to do things—especially to these Reserves who naturally scorn a West Pointer anyway. I'm beginning to think the only thing we got out of the Point was the ring... If something doesn't hurry up and happen pretty soon I might even transfer now—even if it does mean another wait before I can get across.

Maybe all this bitterness was brought about by my little accident the other day. Jim Rippin and I were flying around in an AT-6—flying instruments. Well, we got tired of that so we went down and flew along the treetops for a while. I was flying the ship and keeping a pretty close eye on things, but not close enough I guess because I hit a telephone wire and the wire kinda cut up the tail surfaces. The plane flew OK and the damage was very slight. But as punishment the CO charged me a $20 fine, be OD for an indefinite period, grounded, and then write a memorandum, from Wing, on low flying, 50 times. That's the thing that got me—just as though we were in the eighth grade or something.

Enough of my troubles now—you are the one with the only troubles that count anyway...

May 23

Dear Mother and Jerry,

...Guess what! I now have bars to match my wings —silver. Ain't that something! Apparently the whole class got promoted because all the boys in my class got their promotions on the same day. I immediately broke out the pair Bob gave me way back in '42. Some of the boys in the Sqd. didn't like our promotion much but that is tough. It took us 4 years and they have been in only about 4 months...

Hope you didn't read anything in the paper about the wreck we had at the field yesterday and start worrying... It was a pretty nasty collision—two planes locked wings and fell right in the middle of the town— killed a cit [civilian], too.

Despite his being grounded for part of the month, in May, 1st Lt. Stroh logged 37.6 hours in the P-47 and another four in the trainers according to his flight log. If he and his West Point class had not been accelerated, he would still have been a cadet and would not yet have begun flight training. Imogene related a visit from her brother to Washington in a letter to her father dated May 20th.

Harry arrived one night while I was working and the minute I opened the front door I knew he was home from the tobacco smoke, so I woke everyone and even aroused the cat... Harry looks much older and wiser. It was so good to have him. We took a couple pictures of him to send to you all dressed in his snappy tropical worsted... He doesn't seem to like the P-47's too much because he says who will be at an altitude of 33,000 feet to fight with? Mother says at least he'll be above them. By the way I probably plotted Harry coming down in his Commercial [airliner]. He had a lot of criticism as to the way the plane landed. It was so funny to hear him.

No news from Bob this week. He's sending the 76th [Infantry Division] patch that he wore on the landing [at Fedala, Morocco in November] so that I can sew it on his "memory black felt."

For goodness sake where do you get the idea we are suffering from rationing? We are regimented a little but we have all we want to eat and wear. You and Bob have us so well off financially that we can have this beautiful home and just buy anything we want. We have so much we can't spend it all. When we had the leg of lamb and ice cream with chocolate sauce for Harry we said you all surely would love to sink your teeth in it. It will be wonderful when we all sit around the table again together.

The promotion, his eventual release from being in hack, a new tooth, and the visit to Washington seemed to have restored Lt. Stroh's good spirits. He received two letters from his father and quipped in a letter to his mother and sister dated June 6th, "By the sound of his letters Dad seems to be doing all the work in the division." He also "met a pretty nice gal downtown the other day—the best one I have met in a long time." He mentioned flying over West Point during June Week and planned to again to "watch the Plebes work (if they work anymore since the Corps has gone to hell!)" He also mentioned flying at very high altitude in the P-47.

Had a lot of fun yesterday—went up to 30,000 feet and flew around and did some acrobatics. Things sure

look small from that height. A clear day too—I could
see all the way to Boston. I still wouldn't like to fly at
that altitude in combat though.

Lt. Stroh continued to build up time in the P-47 and began to
appreciate the capabilities of the airplane more. But he still dreamed
of going to a P-51 squadron. His opinion of the P-47 was that it was
good only for high altitude operations whereas the P-51 was a better
low altitude fighter. He became an assistant flight leader with designs
on being a flight leader within a month or so. With that qualification,
he figured he would then move to a combat squadron and prepare for
deployment overseas. Although he now figured it would not be until
"the end of the year at best."

Both of his close friends, West Point roommate Les Taylor, and Jim
Rippin, got married on the same day and each asked him to be his
best man. Harry opted for Les in New York rather than making the trip
to Detroit for Rip. He was intrigued that his friends got married while
on the verge of being shipped out to war.

He saw the first mention of the 9th Division in *Time* magazine
but carped to his father in a letter dated June 5th, "They seem to favor the 1st Div. though, which I didn't like very much." In that same
letter he fretted about what he saw as the delay in his deployment
overseas:

Had a letter from Les Taylor the other day. He is
at another field now and his outfit is about ready to
go across. Wish I were in his shoes. Nothing to do but
just wait I guess. The more time I get here though the
better I will be when I get to combat.

Not all was gloom and doom, though. In letters to his mother and
sister dated June 14th and 21st, he wrote:

You know that girl I told you about last week—well, things are really progressing. She is a swell girl and I really like her a lot. I think both of you would like her too. She is really set on becoming a graduate nurse which will take another year and a half.

Guess I'll have to put the old bus on blocks pretty soon. I have about 3 gals. of gas left to last me until the 21st of July. I'll have to do that unless I can find the black market someplace.

Well, another bunch [of new pilots] has gone out now and here I sit. The way I figure I will be ready to go out [to a combat squadron] about Aug. By that time I will have about 150 hours [in the P-47] and that will give me enough experience to be a flight leader. By that time maybe they will get rid of these 47's and get a good plane in this field—P-51's maybe. There is a good rumor going around that we are going to get P-51's in here.

Perhaps he was rationalizing that his continuing delay going to a combat squadron would pay off by him getting into a P-51 squadron. He further expressed this sentiment in a letter to his father dated June 22nd.

At least I am progressing a little—I'm an asst. flight leader now. In another month maybe I'll be a flight leader and then it won't be long until I get moved out. There have been some rumors...that they aren't going to form many more 47's groups, and then they are going to start in on 51's. Now that is the plane I have always wanted to fly. It looks like the P-40 but it is a better ship than the 40. These 47's might be OK at high altitudes, but we would be shot down before we ever got to that altitude. The 47's have seen combat for about a month now and I haven't heard very good reports of them.

Had a letter from Les the other day. His group has moved down to New York. I don't know whether that is a staging area or not. I don't believe it is, but they are about ready to go across. This group asked for about 8 replacement pilots the other day... I just about put my name in for it but then I don't like the idea of going over as a wing man and have a poor chance of getting through. Been looking in the paper every day looking forward to the new activity on the Continent. Mother said you were back in Oran now. Must be pretty good to get back to that part of the country again.

In a letter to her father dated June 27th, Imogene mentioned Harry's current flame.

Did Harry tell you about some nice girl he's met there in Springfield who is hoping to finish nursing [school] next year? She's the first girl he's mentioned twice in succession since Jean. Wish he'd find a nice girl to marry so he'll feel he's got something to come home to. I hate to hear him say "fighter pilots are expendable."

In June Lt. Stroh flew twenty-nine sorties for 37.7 hours in the P-47, and another four sorties for 3.3 hours in the trainers. That gave him a total of 74.3 P-47 hours. It appears he may have been exaggerating his flight hours to his folks, or maybe he was just rounding up. The regular flying continued into July, and Harry seemed to be more at ease with his situation as his experience in the plane grew, knowing that skill and experience translate into success in combat. He discussed this and a range of other topics in a couple of informative letters to Gen. Stroh dated July 18th and 25th.

Things look like they are really popping over there. See in the paper that Patton has the original 7th Army plus more Inf. and armored units attached. Does that mean that you are in it or did the 9th get moved out?

Been doing a lot of flying lately. Most of the pilots have left for a newly activated Group [362nd Fighter] so now since there are not many around here we get a lot of time in. I have over 100 hours now [96, according to his flight log] in the 47 so I feel as though I know quite a bit about it. I figure that we will be pulling out of here in Aug. or Sept.—if we are lucky. Feel more like a permanent fixture around here every day. Maybe I ought to do what Jim Rippin and Les Taylor did—get married and settle down for the duration. Can't find anybody to marry though—that's the only trouble.

Mother must be getting tired of waiting for me to come down to see her so she and Imogene are coming up here this week for a few days. Maybe I can take Mother up for a short hop... Don't know if I can take Imogene up or not, but I will try.

Now that summer is here I've been looking for a convertible. I saw a nice '41 Chevy downtown...for a pretty good price. So sometime this week I am going down and get it. I figure I can put it in storage when I go across and then have it when I get back since no new cars will be made for two years after the war.

Been having a lot of fun around here with the

Navy. We were fighting with some down at Long Island
Sound and one of the Navy boys spun in and forgot
to bail out. So now the Navy is out looking for blood
and attacks every Army plane they see. Wouldn't be
surprised to see a few more accidents happen because
of that little incident.

Anxious to see the pistol you sent me. Mother
said she would bring it up with her when she comes.
Probably shoot somebody before I figure out how it
works.

The latest rumor is that the whole group is going to
be moved to Savannah Ga. next month so we can get
a little flying done. [due to persistent bad weather in
New England] That won't be bad at all.

Mother and Jerry came up last Tuesday and
stayed until Thursday. It was really nice seeing them
again. They both look well and seem to be getting along
pretty well at home.

Had a little trouble up here last week. One of our
boys got in a simulated dog fight with a Navy plane
and the Navy plane cracked up killing the pilot. It was
entirely the Navy pilot's fault but apparently some
Admiral brought pressure so now they are going to
court martial our boy. He is sure being railroaded. The
court has already come to a verdict even before the
trial begins. Then two generals were flying up here the
other day and a couple of ships from the field attacked
the generals' ship, which the generals did not seem to
like in the least. So now we have to watch our "p's and
q's" around here for the next few weeks.

Mother brought the Luger you sent me. Thank you
very, very much. It is sure a swell gun. It feels much

better than the .45 does—seems to fit your grip better. It took me two days to figure out how to disassemble it... Took it down to the armament section and cleaned it up. Now I'm waiting for when our squadron goes out to the pistol range and try the gun out. By the looks of the holster the German Lt. must have been through the whole African campaign. If and when I go overseas I think I will take it with me rather than get a .45.

Looks like the boys are really going to town in Sicily. Would really like to know if the 9th is in it.

The first of my close friends got killed the other day—one that lived right down the hall from me at the Point. He has been married only three weeks, too—I sure feel sorry for his wife. They were on their honeymoon when I went to Les's wedding and were pretty happy—and now he has gone. Guess it happens to the best of them.

Imogene wrote her father all about their trip up to see Harry in a letter dated July 25th.

Well, Harry surely does enjoy his work. He told us more this trip than ever before. He certainly knows all about his little ship which by the way isn't so little. It is a very heavy thing and quite thick through the fuselage. I was surprised to notice four blades on the propeller which he says has to be 'cause the motor is so powerful.

Did he tell you he was a flight leader now leading four ships and the last we saw him he had 101 hours to his credit. Be prepared for him to call you a "paddle foot." All land forces are paddle feet. Tried to get a picture of him in the sloppy A.C. hat and hope it turns out. You'll just faint away.

The nicest family out in the nicest suburb of Springfield has just taken Harry all in. They entertain him all the time. They even had us over for a picnic dinner on the lawn. It was lots of fun and since they are Southerners we had good food.

What tickled me most was entering Westover Field for the first time. The sentry popped the prettiest salute you ever saw and sir'd Harry with every other word. Honestly I just had to laugh right then and there, but I did turn my face. It was so funny and did Harry ever soak it all in. He just puffed up. He still looks pretty young to be a 1st Lt., but he has settled down a lot and talked about what he'll do when the war is over. He is really planning for a future, so we feel much better.

In July 1943, Lt. Stroh accumulated 34.1 more P-47 hours in twenty-nine sorties and another 1.1 hours in one trainer flight. He now had 108.4 total P-47 hours and 349.8 total flight hours. He was a qualified flight leader and was ready to move on to a combat squadron. On August 13th, he was transferred to the 378th Fighter Squadron of the 362nd Fighter Group, an already formed outfit that was in the final stages of combat training for deployment to the European theater, and rumored to be shipping out in mid-October. He defined this milestone and other intriguing developments in a series of letters to his family, the first dated August 8th to his mother and sister:

Well, the old zoot buggy [his new car] seems to be pretty unlucky. The other day I was out with a little gal and she said she would like to learn to drive. Well,

I was a sucker and let her. She did OK for a while and then a tree got in the way when she took a corner too fast. Instead of putting on the brakes, she jammed down on the gas and let go the wheel. So now the old buggy is in the shop... I was pretty mad at first, but, goodnight, she wasn't to blame—the first time to drive and all that.

You ought to see this little gal—name's Jerry too! Boy, she is pretty as a picture and has everything to go with it. I had met her about a month ago, and didn't pay much attention to her. Then I saw her downtown one day and she really did look good. Too bad I wasn't with her when you were up here so you could give your approval—which I'm sure you would. She is blond which is something new for me. She is a trim little thing —5 feet and weighs about 100 pounds—kinda small, eh!

Been getting a lot of time lately now that most of the pilots have left.

378th Fighter Squadron,
Groton Field, Conn.
August 17, 1943
Dear Mother and Jerry,

Well, the best has finally happened. I have finally left Westover, and none too soon either. There were four of us that left the 320th for this group—the lucky four, too. You see this Group has been in training for the last two months and are quite a good way through their program. So you see I am glad that I didn't have to go to a group that is just forming...

Got down here today and got all settled and even

got some flying in—didn't waste any time at all... The field isn't much—three runways and some tar paper buildings—but at least it's a combat outfit.

But it's a funny thing—when I wanted to leave Westover I couldn't, and when I didn't want to leave they ship me out. You know if I had stayed there another week you would probably have a daughter-in-law on your hands, Mother. You should have met that little gal—bet you really would have gone for her. We are supposed to go back to Westover next month so maybe I will get hooked, but I doubt it—not when I'm leaving in Oct. Sure have gone off the deep end though—what a woman!

Guess I'll hit the hay since we have to get up at 5 tomorrow—in a hot outfit now so I'll have to get eager for the big time.

378th Fighter Squadron
Groton Field, Conn.
August 24, 1943
Dear Dad:

You see I am now in a hot combat outfit—and I mean hot outfit... I came down here about a week ago and have been flying almost continually since. As a matter of fact I have been out of my flying clothes only once since I came here. They are trying to rush us through and cut off two weeks of our training. And in the meantime the brass hats have increased the number of hours we need for training from 150 hours to 225 hours. I am not a flight leader down here, but I am not kicking—at least it's a combat outfit.

Saw in Time this week that you were in Sicily after

all. By the sounds of the article you must have relieved the great(?) 1st Div. The 9th ought to be due for a rest itself—that makes two campaigns under the belt—old timers now, eh!

Told you about my new car didn't I—my convertible... I figured I ought to get it now and put it in storage when I go across and then I can get it out when I get back.

You know if I had stayed in Westover very long you might have had a daughter-in-law by this time. Yep things were really getting that way—cutest little trick you have ever seen... Now that I will be going across pretty soon I don't see getting married so if things are the same when I get back, maybe I will lose that $5 bet I have with you—won't mind losing though.

August 24
Dear Mother and Jerry,

In the past week I have flown as much as I got in the whole month up at Westover... Working from 6 in the morning until midnight you are bound to get a little time in. We are scheduled to get in 12 hours of night flying and as far as I am concerned that is 12 hours too many. So far I have 6 hours.

The weather did close in the other night so we got off at six o'clock. So I decided to go up to Springfield and see that little gal I was telling you about. When I see you next time I'll really have to tell you about her.

Lt. Stroh completed his first wartime mission at the end of August which he described rather nonchalantly to his mother and sister in a letter dated September 1st.

Went up to Stewart Field [New York] last Wed.
when the President and Churchill stopped by Hyde
Park on the way back from Canada. I thought it would
just be a few days, but apparently Frankie wanted
to take a rest. He stayed until Sunday afternoon and
we came back Monday. It was rather boring waiting
around for something to do. We were just an alert
flight, ready to take off at a minute's notice in case
anybody started fooling around Hyde Park. We were
never sent up...

Don't worry about buying new dresses for my
wedding because there won't be any—not because I
don't want it but there are other complications. No, as
far as I'm concerned I would have taken the final steps
by this time.

It was truly a banner month for Lt. Stroh's flying in August; 54.3
hours including 49.8 in the P-47 for a total of 158.2 P-47 hours. For
the first time, about half of Stroh's forty-one P-47 flights were in the
P-47D model, the latest version of the Thunderbolt. Before moving
to the 378th, he had flown only the B and C models. His previously
frequent musings about the P-51 Mustang, his dream machine, disappeared from his letters. It is likely that being immersed in the culture
of a war-bound frontline squadron, with a group of like-minded hot-
shot young fighter pilots, and operating at such a hectic pace instilled
in him a sense of pride in his outfit and his airplane. It was apparent
that he was going to war in the P-47 and there was no use wishing
otherwise.

The P-47 initially was designed as a high altitude escort for large
bomber formations, for which it was well suited. It was the largest
fighter aircraft in World War II, weighing in at 10,600 pounds empty,
and was produced in the greatest numbers, over 15,000 in all. The

Thunderbolt was heavy, powerful, and armed with eight fifty-caliber machine guns, two more than other fighters, including the P-51. It could carry up to 2,500 pounds of externally mounted bombs and rockets; up to 425 rounds of fifty-caliber per gun.

Initially, it was the primary escort for B-17 formations flying out of England to targets in northern Europe. But its eighteen-cylinder, 2000-plus horsepower radial engine was quite thirsty, burning about 100 gallons of high octane aviation gasoline per hour at cruise speeds, much more than that in combat scenarios. As such, its range of about 475 miles was limited compared to the bombers it escorted. Additional range was gained by adding external fuel tanks, but they had to be jettisoned to maintain maneuverability when dueling with enemy fighters. The Germans learned quickly to attack the bomber formations early in the mission thereby forcing the escorts to release their tanks and give up some of their extended range. About the time Lt. Stroh's outfit was making its way to England, P-51 Mustang groups had entered the fray. Their greater range capability determined that they would become the escort of choice. Hence, the primary mission of the P-47 changed from high altitude escort to ground interdiction, a role in which, ironically, it excelled.

The frenetic pace of flying for the 362nd Fighter Group continued into September even though the first week had them grounded due to bad weather. This put the group under even greater pressure to reach their flight hour goals in time for their scheduled deployment. During the slack time, Lt. Stroh slipped up to Springfield to see his two best friends, Les Taylor and Jim Rippin, and their new brides who all went out and had a big time on the town. "That will probably be the last time we will see each other. Les expects to leave pretty soon…" He made no mention of seeing his blonde girlfriend, Jerry. He took a tour of a new submarine at the base across the river in New London and remarked, "Those sure are big boats. That's not the life for me though—I'll fly any day than spend 3 months at a crack in one of those things." To his father he wrote on September 16th about his plans to see the family in Washington.

> As soon as we finish our program we are supposed to get a little leave... We will have about 15 days in which we won't be doing a thing... I'm going to drive my car down to Wash. and have nice visit with the family and then leave the car in storage there. It will be a swell car to have when I get back.
> Guess I told you that I fired the pistol you sent me. It sure is a nice weapon—much better than the .45 I think... lighter and as good a defensive weapon...
> There sure are a swell bunch of boys in the squadron I'm in. Couldn't have wanted better... I am mighty thankful to just to be in a combat outfit and close to getting across. Had a mighty nice birthday last month.... Mother sent a swell cake up which arrived right on the day and went over big. Still don't feel that I'm getting old—not 23 anyway.
> Wish we could have the whole family together when I go home in the next few weeks—would be swell to have a big reunion. We'll be thinking of you.

Imogene was still volunteering with the Coast Artillery Anti-Aircraft Volunteers (AAV). She wrote to her father about a bit of excitement for her and her mother in a letter dated September 19th:

> I've changed my volunteer job to the 3 to 7 shift, the one I began with. It is a grand routine. When I reached home Mother had a nice supper ready and gave me three guesses of whom I plotted that afternoon. I ended with Harry, not dreaming it could

have been, but it was... we had a flight of two circling
the field about the time he landed. He flew out over the
house and she said he nosed up into the blue gaining
altitude as soon as he passed over. So she has seen him
fly. Isn't that exciting!

378th Fighter Squadron
September 23, 1943
Dear Mother and Jerry,
    Sorry I couldn't get out to see you the other day but
I had to get right back—before it got dark. Would have
dived on the house again, but our planes were very
distinctive from Bolling and I was afraid we would be
turned in for buzzing.

Harry finished September while on five days' leave. It was another
productive month of flying. He flew all but one of his forty-one sorties
in the P-47, thirty-two of those in the D model, for 50.6 more P-47
hours. His total was now 208.8 hours, close to the 225 goal prior to
deployment. He wrote his father an upbeat letter on October 6th.

    Had a pretty nice time during the past week. Had
my final leave for five days. All spent at home. It
was really swell being at home again... Mother and
Imogene are looking swell. Mother looks as though she
is gaining a little weight.
    Guess by the time you get this letter I should be
over there myself. We are all through with our training
and are just marking time right now. I don't know
when we'll go across but I hope it will be soon.
    Went over to Mrs. Irwin and got all the Luger
shells. Also got a picture of the owner. He looks like a

kid to me—about 15 or 16.

Glad to hear that there is another possibility of getting your second star. I know darn well you deserve it. I'm kinda thinking that Eddy is afraid that you'll relieve him of the 9th so he won't put your promotion through. Hope you get that D.S.M. too.

Hear that Bob is now in the old 9th. Well, if you keep it up you will have the whole family in the 9th. Well, they could have done worse.

Well, never can tell, Dad, I might be seeing you soon—can't tell about things like that.

Runnymede Pl.

Washington, D.C.

October 3, 1943

Harry has been with us since Wednesday and golly it is good to have a man around. He smokes cigars now, Daddy, if you can picture it and the house has smelled wonderful for the first time since you left.

Mother paid all our points for a couple weeks for a wonderful steak that practically melted in our mouths. Harry eats a lot and enjoys being home so much. He pitches right in helping us with the meals and serving at the table.

I can't get over what you wrote Mother about Bob's immediate past. It makes me awfully sad and I know why Bob hated his job now. I hate missing all of Bob's disappointments and joys, but can't tell how glad that he is nearer to you so that you can get to know each other better and share a few things. I've never known so completely what a home has meant until this last year. It is a little word with a bottomless meaning, and

I hope I can make a better one when this is all over.

Received your letter of Sept. 12 about your dinner with Bob. Hope Harry will be joining you for a dinner soon.

378th Fighter Squadron
Groton Field, Conn.
October 10, 1943

Well, back again and nothing has changed. The only thing that is changed is not having a car to step out in... Almost everyone here has gotten rid of their cars also.

I want to thank both of you for the swell time I had while at home. Don't know when I appreciated it so much. Felt just like old times!

Had two letters from Dad this week—first I've had for quite a while. He said something about his having another chance of getting his second star... He told me all about Bob... Seems as though the 7th Army is just staying in Sicily and doing more training—as if they need it. Guess you just can't get too much training though. Would be nice if they sent us to Africa or Sicily—they seem to be using 47's in that area.

Got a card from Les giving his APO number so I guess he is on his way. I'll probably run into him again though somewhere over there. I'll have to look up his wife when I get to New York.

October 15
Dear Dad,

It was nice being home... never have appreciated it so much as I did during my last visit.

Those black airplanes you spoke about were probably night fighters. Don't think I would like that type of flying much—don't like flying at night one bit. These 47's seem to be making a pretty good name for themselves on these raids to Germany. The more I fly them the better I like them—don't think I would even trade them for a P-51 now.

Take good care of yourself. I'll be looking for some good reports of action by the 9th now that there are two great men in it.

The comment about Lt. Stroh's growing appreciation for the P-47 is certainly a turn-around from his previous assessment, especially the quip about not trading it for a P-51. The tactics being developed for the airplane in combat over Europe took advantage of its unique capabilities; exceptional speed in a dive, good high altitude maneuverability, heavy firepower, and the ability to absorb punishment. In air-to-air combat they endeavored to fly high and attack their adversaries from above using slashing maneuvers rather than getting into a "fur ball." These successful tactics were very likely filtering back to the combat groups training stateside.

The 362nd Fighter Group continued to fly through most of October; Lt. Stroh's last P-47 flight for the month was October 22nd after which they began to divest their airplanes, received new personal combat gear, and shifted to different sorts of training activities. They finally moved to their staging base, Mitchel Field on Long Island. Harry wrote to his father on October 26th, "The last stop at last. After 9 months of waiting I am getting set to get on that old boat. This is pretty good staging at Mitchel—we can have a pretty good time in New York before going across." He made one more short trip to Washington to surprise his mother on her birthday, October 27th.

Even with the short flying month and some stretches of bad

weather, Lt. Stroh managed to fly twenty-eight P-47 sorties, all but four in the D model, for 35.3 flight hours. He also had one flight in a BT-13 trainer and one in a UC-78 Bobcat, a light twin engine aircraft used extensively for training bomber pilots. His total P-47 time was 244.1 hours, well over the goal of 225 for combat deployment. He picked up two more flights on November 2nd adding another four hours. With this much time in the airplane, he and his squadron mates must have been very comfortable with the P-47 in all flight regimes and conditions.

Lt. Stroh discussed his new activities in squadron life with his father in letters dated October 26th and November 5th.

Guess you know that the Air Corps isn't as bad as it used to be. We have been issued all kinds of field equipment and on Wed. we are to go out in the field for a few days—strictly Inf... I get a big kick out of watching these pilots trying to figure out how to adjust and fit their equipment. Guess you were right when you said that they know only how to fly an airplane. They're pretty good boys though—like them a lot.

Oh, my poor back. Don't you ever say anything about the Air Corps doing nothing but sit on their bottoms all the time. Today makes the second hike we have gone on in the past three days. The first one was only 5 miles with nothing but strip packs, but today we had full field packs and walked at least 12 miles— complete with 2 blankets and a complete pup tent. You should have heard the boys voicing their opinion about the whole deal. They don't seem to see any sense in the march but I have a good idea it was for a reason. Not having hiked for a long time I was a little tired when it was over, but it did feel good to get out on the old feet again—makes one feel like a real soldier again—even made me a little homesick for the doughboys.

No, we aren't on the way yet but the time is drawing nigh. We have been issued jungle kits to attach to our parachutes which makes it look like we might go to the South Pacific area. As a matter of fact our P of E [port of embarkation] has been changed. So there is no telling where we may end up.

378th Fitr. Sqd., APO 9020
% Postmaster, New York
November 15, 1943
Dear Mother and Jerry,

Well, here it is the middle of Nov. and we are still in the States—eastern coast. At least we are getting someplace because we now have an A.P.O. number and that is something. No telling I might be having Christmas dinner with Dad and Bob yet.

Received all the Christmas packages the other day. Thank you so much for the bars and cigars. Don't you think you are a little optimistic sending so many [captain's] bars? The C.O. of the outfit doesn't believe in promoting anybody until they have proved themselves in combat. At least he doesn't promote any pilots—all the ground officers have gotten all their promotions. Those cigars look like pretty good ones... when I see Dad I will give him some of them.

All we have been doing for the past two weeks is marching and taking hikes. Nobody likes these hikes, but I don't mind them at all. As a matter of fact, it makes me a little homesick for the old Inf. Jim Rippin and I are seriously considering getting in the Inf. after the war...

On the morning of November 12th, a truck convoy transported the group from Mitchel Filed across the George Washington Bridge, then to Camp Shanks in preparation for going to their Port of Embarkation. Restrictions on all personnel were ramped up. No one was allowed off post. The mail was censored. The last days were spent in endless inspections, physicals, abandon ship drills, more hikes, and watching training films. After all requirements were complete, passes off post were allocated for about four days. Then everyone was locked down again. On the evening of November 21st, everyone marched the length of the post with full packs and boarded the train for Hoboken. On arrival, they schlepped their complete baggage the length of the station and pier, then boarded ferries taking them to their ship, the Cunard liner *Queen Elizabeth*.[1]

The ship got underway the following afternoon. The voyage to Britain was a quick one, at a speedy thirty-two knots. This was too fast for a convoy-type crossing and too fast for the German U-boat wolfpacks. Initially there was some evasive maneuvering, but for the most part it was an uneventful crossing. The ship was very crowded and especially uncomfortable for the enlisted men berthed low in the ship with poor air circulation. They arrived in the Firth of Clyde off Greenock, Scotland, on November 29th, spent the day disembarking, getting supper, and then finally boarding a train around midnight for the two-day trip to their new home in Wormingford, near Colchester, England, about thirty-five miles northeast of London.[2]

In a letter to his mother and sister written while still at sea, but not postmarked until December 5th, Lt. Stroh discussed the voyage.

> Don't know how well this letter will be written as I am writing on board and the sea is a little rough about now. You won't believe it, but I have gone this far without getting the least bit seasick, and the trip is just about over. Maybe the boat has something to do with that...

When this little war is over and I have a lot of money and a long vacation, I'm going to take another ride on this very boat and travel in style... This is real class with a capital "C"—just like the movies. Of course it is a little crowded on this crossing...

The food is especially good. There are only two meals a day but they are mighty big. Can you imagine having fish every morning for breakfast? When I get back I'm going to have a big breakfast just as a matter of habit.

Haven't had any excitement so far—very quiet crossing...

Hope to see Dad sometime—he might possibly be just where we are going.

Had some pretty warm weather for a few days on the trip [in the Gulf Stream] and we were beginning to wonder just where we were headed. However, today and last night it turned cold and a strong wind started blowing so there is not much question in anyone's minds just where we are going.

There are quite a few "U.S.O." and "Camp Show" personnel on board so they got together and gave a big show for the men. It was quite good, but no big name personages were around.

11

———◆———

England

General Stroh had been in England for several weeks, moving back and forth between his quarters in Winchester and London, where he was involved in military planning with Allied leadership. He knew his way around the city, having been there on a liaison trip with the British military for several weeks in 1941. He was intrigued by the air defense blackout conditions throughout the country and wrote about them to Imogene from his London hotel in a letter dated November 21, 1943.

> Take equal parts of the dark of the moon, the blackout, and a heavy fog and you really have something that it's hard to get about in. That's what we had here last night, the darkest that I can remember. I had gone downtown while it was still fairly light for dinner, but by the time I got back all traffic had been stopped and it took me about twenty minutes to make the four or five short blocks from the nearest subway station to the hotel, even with the help of a powerful flashlight.

I suppose these people after more than four years of
it, think nothing of it, but to a tenderfoot it is quite an
adventure.

Haven't seen Bob, of course, for about three weeks,
but expect to be around before many days have
passed. His outfit will be quartered in about the best
accommodation available, but that isn't saying much.

In between trips here I've been living in the town
of Deleted [Winchester], one of the most historic in
the country. There's been no opportunity to explore
the place yet, but I'll have to do that before long.
Preliminary contacts with the townspeople have been
very cordial. There seems to be a sincere desire to
become chummy and to make us feel at home.

After disembarking at Swansea on Thanksgiving day, the
39th Infantry arrived by rail at the little village of Barton Stacey
on November 26th. There, they moved into awaiting Nissen huts
and barracks. They were about eight miles north of 9th Division
headquarters in historic Winchester. The other division units were
quartered in Winchester and other surrounding communities. The
first order of business was a week-long course on manners; how
to behave when interacting with the locals, British customs, traditions, and local history. After passing written exams, soldiers were
given passes, and later, leaves and furloughs up to ten days, including trips to London. Other benefits included Red Cross clubs, USO
shows, dances, movies, boxing matches, newspapers in English,
and English radio stations. Tons of back mail were catching up with
all the troops, and the delivery time was reduced considerably from
what it had been in Africa and Sicily.[1]

In his first V-mail to his parents since arriving at Barton Stacey,
dated December 1st with the header "England," Lt. Col. Stumpf

discussed receiving a backlog of mail and Christmas packages, and how he and his boys were enjoying the luxuries of camp life.

> Received two packages from the Prentices and was slightly mystified by the baby powder. One package had split open and gave a fine delicate flavor to the nuts, cigars and socks... We're quite comfortable now and enjoying a barracks for a change. Won't get to see much as we're practically restricted because of transportation and crowding but we expect to be fattened up for a while. Just enjoying camp experiences. Looks like the jinx is broken too. Left one ship in sailing condition. Hope it lasts.

> December 4, 1943
> Dearest Jerry,
> Wanted to write you again tonight to thank you for all the good things you've been sending me... Feel guilty opening Christmas presents this early but don't I deserve it after waiting until March for last Christmas?
> Looks like I'll be busy most of tomorrow working out a training schedule. What a directive! Just finished looking over some back issues of "Time." They come in micro-film editions now and a lot faster.
> Still restricted so haven't seen much of the country except on a short drive on business and a short march. Now that we're...comfortable once more, I seem to miss you even more.

Gen. Stroh's Winchester quarters were in a private home on an estate called "Pitt Manor" whose owner, Lady Ley (pronounced "lee"), made a room available for the American Army's use. On December 5th, he wrote a long, informative letter to Imogene updating, among other things, his and Bob's accommodations, and plans for seeing Harry.

> Have seen Bob for only a couple of minutes during a conference at division headquarters, since he arrived about a week ago. I think his outfit is well settled in as good accommodations as are available for any of us, and he should personally be reasonably comfortable while we are here. To achieve a trip without loss of his personal equipment is a step in the right direction at any rate.
>
> Sent Braune off last week to try to locate Harry. He came back with a pretty good lead on which I plan to follow up tomorrow, in hopes of actually finding the kid. Haven't seen him, as you know, for nearly fifteen months, and I doubt if he knows I'm in England. The meeting, if it occurs tomorrow, should be a real surprise. Maybe I can get him here to spend Christmas.
>
> This has been a record week for the receipt of mail, and it is still coming in. A total of about thirty letters, fourteen packages, magazines, Christmas cards, etc. So good to be alive when things like this happen.
>
> I guess Bob can't tell you the name of his regimental commander because it is prohibited to disclose the name of any commander from colonel up... I am sure that you would not know him, but he is a rare egg. Don't know how many people know of our relationship, but I'm sure that nobody can accuse Bob of having received any favoritism because of it. In fact,

I may be bending over backwards too far in the other
direction. I know Bob's good sense will understand the
reason.

This is really a swell dump I'm in now, and the
people seem to want to do everything in their power to
make me comfortable. I don't want to intrude on their
hospitality, and yet I don't want to appear high hat.
It is hard to determine just where to draw the line.
The two ladies of the house have been away visiting
friends most of the week, leaving the old retired major
to hold down the roost alone. I was his guest at dinner
last Monday evening. He is a veteran of the Boer War
[1899-1902, South Africa] and retired in 1920, so
I should judge he is close to 70. Quite an interesting
old duck... Lady Ley and her daughter are apparently
very horsey. There are hunting pictures all over the
place...

Although this is a modern house in every sense of
the word, the English certainly have funny ideas about
heat. The throne room is a little cubical just large
enough for the purpose, without a particle of heat in
it. As a result, you might as well be outdoors. Whether
by accident or design there is a small framed motto
on the wall of this enclosure all about "If you have a
job to do, do it now!" Believe me, in that atmosphere,
you don't need to be urged. The room containing
the bathtub is likewise without heat. I can never
determine which is worse, a warm room and cold
water, or a cold room with hot water.

Gen. Stroh followed through on his plan to find his son the
very next day. Lt. Stroh penned a letter to his mother and sister on

December 7th describing what surely must have been an emotional reunion for both men.

> Bet you can't guess what happened yesterday. The squadron went on a little trip for the day and got back to the base about five o'clock last night. I walked into the officers mess and who should be standing by the fire than Dad. I almost dropped in my tracks—and I thought he was in Ireland. He sure was a sight for sore eyes to say the least. Haven't seen him for over a year. He hasn't changed much considering what he has been through. Of course there are a few more lines on his face and a few more gray hairs... The face distortion that I noticed on one of his pictures after his hospitalization has disappeared completely. He drove up in a big Buick just like yours except the steering wheel is on the right side. Torres was also along and a driver that Dad had acquired. Torres sends you both his best regards... I talked with Torres and the driver coming back to the field and they spoke of nothing but praise for Dad—and they said they were speaking for the whole Div. It was certainly nice to see a real soldier again—a little snap and neatness.
>
> Dad and I went to the local hotel and had a fine dinner considering what you can get in England. We had a long talk together which was very interesting— all about the action in Africa and Sicily...
>
> Went to the big city [London] the other day. We made the big mistake of reaching the city at night so consequently we didn't have any idea where we were or how to get anywhere—it's so black you can't see your hand in front of your face...

Nothing doing as far as flying goes yet.

3349 Runnymede Pl.

Washington, D.C.

January 2, 1944

You don't know how tickled we were to hear from Harry through Grandma [Gen. Stroh's mother] that you two had met and are near each other. Hope he buzzes you out of bed some day with that powerful motor of his.

We're so glad to hear from Harry at last and to know you've smoked cigars and had meals together. We've talked about it so much and it makes us so happy.

The city of Winchester continued to show its congeniality toward the 15,000-plus men of the 9th Division. The city's mayor, retired Royal Marines Lieutenant General Francis Griffiths, befriended Gen. Eddy. He arranged for a Christmas ball for the officers of the 9th at the Winchester Guildhall, which was a roaring success and the beginning of many such friendships. The mayor proclaimed Sunday, January 20th, an Allied day of prayer, and services were held in Winchester Cathedral for representative personnel from all 9th Division units.[2]

All was not wine and roses, however. Shortly after settling in, the division got down to the serious business of training for the impending "main event." The weather was frightful: cold, wet, and often foggy. Field exercises included cross training between the infantry and more specialized units such as the combat engineers. The doughboys learned about mine laying and detection, and the employment of various weapons against fixed emplacements. They also worked closely with armor and anti-tank units, how to employ them and how to attack enemy armor with infantry weapons like bazookas. The special units practiced small unit infantry tactics. Everyone practiced calling for artillery and adjusting mortar and artillery fire.

The division began to develop a more comprehensive and effective means of coordinating tactical air support, a specialty that was rife with problems in their previous campaigns. Air liaison officers cross pollinated between the division and Air Corps units to develop procedures for rapid and accurate close air support; to get rounds squarely on the enemy while scrupulously avoiding friendly troops,

At the heart of all this military activity was the realization by everyone, from Gen. Eddy to the newest replacement soldier, that the next combat operation would be more challenging than anything they had faced before. They had no idea when or where it would take place, but that it would surely happen before too long, and that they would be facing the best of a very competent and determined enemy.

In late December, Lieutenant General Omar Bradley, now commander of the First U.S. Army, paid a visit to the 9th Division for the purpose of presenting the Distinguished Unit Citation to the 2nd Battalion 60th Infantry for action at Djebel Dardyss in Tunisia. The ceremony was held in the quadrangle at Winchester Barracks, where Gen. Bradley attached the award streamer to the battalion guidon. He no doubt sat down with the division leadership to discuss preparations for the invasion.[3]

On the home front, Imogene and her mother were facing another house move as their landlord, Colonel Kelly, a friend of the family, had the house painted with the intention of selling it. This had Gen. Stroh very concerned, on top of all the other things he had to worry about. If life in Winchester was more comfortable than what he had experienced for the past year, he was still away from home and it would appear would remain in that situation for a long time yet. He discussed this and other events in a letter to Imogene dated December 19th.

Keep Mother cheered up as much as you can. She's a brave woman and never complains, but I know her heart is heavy many times. The absence of her men folk is only part of the game and won't last forever. I tried to put into effect the very plan you suggest to get a few days at home early in November by volunteering as a sort of high powered messenger or something, but of course there was no chance. Only the big shots and the Air Corps get that opportunity. Good plan to have the Stumpfs over for Christmas. If all goes well, will have our family concentrated in two places anyway, even if they are a good many thousand miles apart.

Did I tell you or Mother that Torres had received his box from you? He'll no doubt acknowledge it after he opens it Christmas. He seemed thrilled and duly impressed.

I see by the morning paper that you have 90,000 cases [of the flu] in Washington. Hope it avoids Runnymede Place and Donner Avenue [his mother's residence].

Good news about the house. As I told Mother, even if he sells now he can't put you out until the latter part of March, and you don't let him give you that six weeks song and dance. The law says three months.

No more word from Harry since last Monday, so I hope that nothing will prevent his arriving here next Friday. If he doesn't come I'll be one disappointed papa.

I think I'll give Bob my Rolls razor for Christmas. Hate to give him something six or eight years old, but I guess you know that he lost his once, or maybe twice [when the ships he was on were sunk] and they are practically unattainable. He has a brand new blade, which he gave me for my birthday, so I'll give that back to him so he'll have a complete outfit. I've been using another type of razor for eight or nine months, and find it more convenient for field service.

My landlady is doing her best to promote Anglo-American relations even to putting crossed American and British flags over the fireplace. She went all the way to London last week to get an American flag, but was unable to find one, so she made one by hand, on the needlepoint basis. She proudly exhibited it this evening when I had tea with them and asked if it was all right, as she had no pattern but a tiny one on a Christmas card. I found that she had left off the bottom red stripe and six stars, so she is now pulling it all apart so as to add the missing parts. Quite an experience living here.

December 21, 1943 near Colchester
Dear Mother and Jerry,

I'm really looking forward to this weekend with Dad and Bob. I have two days off but am going to take a third, though. We ought to have a big celebration. It will seem rather funny—three on one side and three on the other. Well, maybe next year we will all be together again. Saw Les the other day. He flew down here on his day off and stayed one afternoon. He has been on several missions, but hasn't knocked any planes down yet.

We've been having pretty good food over here—even better than what we got at Groton. Of course there isn't much variety but still it is mighty choice—only things I miss are milk and eggs.

Write you all about the big Christmas doings Sunday. Wish there were some way to call you as per custom.

3349 Runnymede Pl.

Washington, D.C.

December 26, 1943

What a wonderful Christmas we've had. Knowing that you were getting your gifts and were probably together made it especially happy. The Stumpfs arrived about 5:30 P.M. Christmas Eve and Union Station was so crowded I had trouble finding a place to sit. That evening after a delicious fish dinner here at home, about 14 people gathered to trim the tree. We had sort of an eggnog party, sang carols and then went to the Cathedral for the midnight service. We had to stand, but the music was so beautiful and really heavenly that we didn't mind standing.

V-mail

December 27, 1943

Dear Mother and Dad,

Had dinner Christmas with Jerry's dad and Harry. We thought of you folks together at home and it made the day seem a lot better. Know you enjoyed being together as much as we did. Thanks so much for the food. As far as immediate Christmas was concerned, I opened your Christmas cake (the big one) at midnight and had some more Christmas morning. It certainly is good. Have allowed a few choice morsels as gifts, but not much of that cake! That's mine. Jerry's dad gave me a Rolls razor which will be a welcome replacement. Fritz finished off the one you gave me, Dad, but he'll pay hell getting this one.

December 28, 1943
Dear Mother and Jerry,

The big reunion is a thing of the past now—just a fond memory. I left my field Friday morning—the 24th and reached Dad's Hq. that afternoon about three o'clock. Dad wasn't at the office, but Braune was there and put me in Dad's big Buick and drove me out to Dad's palatial home. He has only one room in the house but he has a standing invitation to use the rest of the house. He has the most comfortable bed I think I have ever been in—you sink down about 3 feet when you get in it. We went to the staff mess and met all of the brains of the outfit. I felt kind of out of place—a mere Lt. among so much rank, especially sitting at a private table with Dad. We then went to a show downtown. I was surprised at the theater—it was almost as classy as the Radio City Music Hall in NYC.

Christmas morning I had a great treat—a fresh fried egg—out of the shell too! A friend of Dad's gave him three fresh eggs for a present. Then Dad took me for a trip around the countryside visiting his various units. We missed Bob at the time; however that afternoon we met at Gen. Eddy's house for dinner. Also two of my classmates were there so we had a big time talking over old times. Bob had on his African blouse— the one with the shoe string for arm braid. It's really not a bad blouse though. Then later that night Lady Ley had another dinner for Dad, Bob, and I—English style—everybody dressed as though they are going to a ball. Sunday we did some sightseeing again.

It was really great seeing Bob and Dad again—wasn't quite complete though without you. Next year we hope it will be different.

Big day today—we finally got some airplanes. So now I hope things will start popping.

Runnymede Place
Washington, D.C.
January 9, 1944
Dear Daddy,

It certainly was very nice of you to part with your Rolls razor to give Bob. He was certainly pleased. You're very nice to him. And now that we've heard that you and Bob and Harry had Christmas together we really are happy. Harry just raved about everything and Bob must have gained a few pounds from what he writes. You must have had a merry Christmas.

Received your letter of Dec. 19th last week and enjoyed the talk about the American flag. It is so nice the people you live with have taken you in so much. It makes it seem almost like a home then.

We went to a cocktail party at the Collins' last evening and it is funny to have Gen. Collins back. We got so used to you men being absent that when one comes back it gives us the strangest feeling. Almost like seeing a ghost. What will it be like when you or Bob gets back? Golly, it is a long time.

The Collins' and the Strohs had been good friends since being stationed together in the Philippines in the mid-thirties. Gen. Collins had recently commanded the 25th Infantry Division in the Pacific against the Japanese, including campaigns in Guadalcanal and New Georgia. His superior performance resulted in selection by Eisenhower as a corps commander for the impending Northern Europe campaign.

In a letter to Imogene dated January 2, 1944, Gen. Stroh described in most humorous terms his newfound place in English society.

It's not me of course, but the novelty of the uniform. An American general in England, outside the immediate vicinity of the golden throne, is a rare bird, and until the newness wears off I guess I can expect plenty of social attention. It's all right with me, as we've been starved for female companionship for the past year that this frivolity is the next best thing to being home. I find that English women are just as catty, and that they love their little morsels of scandal, just as much as the Ladies' Aid Society at home. I circulate around in a rather closed circle in which all the women have been friends for years, and my every movement is duly reported through the grapevine. Everything is hotsy-totsy, but it is amusing, and a new experience for me to watch these folks trying to outdo each other in entertainment.

It was amusing to meet two war widows of the British Regular Army whom Matt entertained on New Year's Eve. They are exactly like army women at home, with a fine disdain for everything civilian, and a line of shop talk which is reminiscent of a cocktail party at Benning.

Friday evening [New Year's Eve] was a big time... The boys at the mess threw a dance that evening which I attended briefly just before midnight, and then went to Matt's in time to toast the new year with champagne.

Had a delightful luncheon with a couple in the country this afternoon. The husband is a big banker and so rich that he donated the yacht which raced for the America's Cup a few years ago. The other guests included a retired British general who was in command in India just before the war. Forget his name, but strangely enough it was not the same as his wife, who, more strange yet, was Lady Cantaloupe... All the lady cats call her Lady Melon, of course. In fact, the same lady cats call my landlady Gypsy Lee, because she was born in part of the country where a lot of gypsies live. They cannot understand why I smile at this name, not knowing of the famous striptease.

A feature of this meal was real, stiff, whipped cream on the chocolate pudding and the most delicious port, vintage 1900, that I have ever tasted. The lady of the house calls herself a farmer, and indeed has a herd of thirty or forty guernsey cows, which explains the whipped cream.

I told Mother of my very fine Christmas with Harry and Bob, so there is little to add now, except to thank you for these wonderful pictures of you and Harry. Nothing could have been more of a surprise or more welcome... The canteen soap will be very useful when I start bathing again under an oil drum or tin can. I have the picture folder on my desk in the office, and show it to all visitors. Yours and Bob's card... was one of the nicest I received.

Torres started off the year right by getting busted in the kisser at about 7:00 A.M. January 1. Although he is only a corporal, and a questionable one at that, he is the senior of the small group of men who work in my mess. The morning after a big party is not a very happy occasion anyway, and I guess Torres tried to push the boys around a bit and one of them took a swing at him. I've had to make different arrangements. He's a fine looking sight right now.

The boys of the 378th Fighter Squadron were relearning that flying is a perishable skill, especially fast-paced, high-powered fighter plane flying; proficiency begins to erode in a matter of days after laying off. For Harry and his squadron mates it had been two months since they gave up their planes stateside. The new P-47s the squadron was now receiving had been shipped over and required considerable reassembly and inspection by maintenance personnel before being released for pilot acceptance checks. So, combined with the rustiness of the pilots, the initial flights were somewhat benign and bereft of tactical maneuvering. Still, getting back in the air had a profound effect on the morale of the squadron. Lt. Stroh's first flight since November 2nd, was scheduled for January 5th. He wrote his father that night.

Well, it looks as though things are finally happening around here. We received 14 planes in the other day—not much but enough to give the boys a little something to do. They have been giving them an acceptance check for the past few days, but today we took them up for the first time. Almost everybody got a flight except me. I had my engine all running and ready to taxi out for the takeoff when I ran off the taxi strip and found myself stuck in the mud. So I had to get out and didn't get in the air all day.

APO 638, England

January 6, 1944

Dear Mother and Jerry,

Another thing, we finally got some airplanes—not many but enough to give the boys a ride once a day. Went up today for an hour. It really felt mighty funny flying again—first time for two months. Soon I guess it will feel just as usual though.

January 9, 1944

Only word I had from you this week was a V-mail from you, Sis. Glad to have that much—at least I learned that everyone has gotten over the flu. That must have been a pretty bad epidemic in Washington.

This week passed considerably faster than any of the previous ones. We are slowly getting more planes now—almost enough for each pilot to get a flight every day. The days are so short here that we don't have too many hours to fly in. Ordinarily we start flying about nine o'clock and quit about 5. Also the planes are new so we don't do many fancy maneuvers—nothing but straight and level. At least we're getting a pretty good view of England. I've never seen so many airfields in my life.

Receiving planes and getting in the air again has really improved the old morale of the whole outfit. I've never seen so much change in such a short time.

Back at the 9th Division, the training and preparations continued. Gen. Eddy reorganized his staff along the German model to perform with greater efficiency in combat. He directed Gen. Stroh, as a routine, to be present at the main command post, while he made his way to the more forward positions for direct interactions with regimental and battalion commanders. Gen. Stroh would run the operational headquarters and make decisions in the commander's absence, as well as supervise the G-2 (intelligence) and G-3 (operations) activities. The rear CP would be the charge of the chief of staff, Col. Barth, who would supervise the administrative group, G-1 (personnel) and G-4 (supply).[4]

Another of Gen. Eddy's initiatives was to meet privately over dinner at his mess with all nine of his infantry battalion commanders, among them Lt. Col. Stumpf, in order to get to know them better and determine what they needed for the greater effectiveness of their units. He was aware that many of them might be casualties in the coming months, and also anticipated losses from this group as replacements for regimental commanders.[5]

The division was notified to make ready for a visit on January 19th by Gen. Eisenhower's invasion ground force commander, General Sir Bernard Law Montgomery. Most of the men at this point did not know precisely who he was or where he fit in the grand military hierarchy, but he would in many ways hold their fate in his hands, and vice versa. Red Phillips:

> Montgomery ordered each of the various combat battalions to be in formation at their various training areas at an appointed time. He wished to speak with the men. No voice-amplifying equipment was required.
>
> The general arrived precisely on time in a jeep accompanied by General Eddy's aide. They pulled up before the formation and "Monty," in British battle dress with his trademark beret, hopped up on the jeep's hood and said, "Good morning, men, please break ranks and gather round me here."
>
> That done, he asked the men to remove their

helmets because he wanted to see their faces. No one
had ever told them to do that before. Montgomery
then said a few words recalling the 9th's help to him
in Africa and how they were all in it together again
to beat the "Hun," as they had in Tunisia. He spoke
rapidly. His voice was high pitched like General
Patton's, but there the comparison ended. "Monty" did
not curse or weep.

After about five minutes of such pep talk,
Montgomery bid the troops "cheerio" and was off to
his next appointment. From beginning to end it was
an altogether different introduction than anything the
9th's soldiers had ever heard before, and they enjoyed
it immensely.

...the visit had no great effect upon the 9th's
combat effectiveness. The men simply saw him as a
winner and were flattered that this famous person felt
it worthwhile to come to see them.[6]

According to his flight log, Lt. Stroh had flown five sorties in
England by January 9th. He and the other pilots of the 378th were
about through with the re-familiarization stage and beginning to re-
hone their tactical proficiency. One new skill to learn was the art of
dive-bombing, which Stroh sensed was to play a large role in future
operations. He discussed this, the group's first combat casualty, and
other less critical topics in a series of letters to his father, mother, and
sister, the first one dated January 14, 1944.

Dear Dad,
I know now how you must have felt in the past
year when you didn't receive any mail for weeks at a
time. I haven't received a letter from home for over

two weeks now... I'm beginning to think the greatest morale booster is "mail."

See in the paper that your old friend [Lieutenant General Walter Bedell "Beetle"] Smith is the C. of S. to the big boss. [Eisenhower] Wasn't he a Capt. back in '39 when he was at Benning—maybe a major. Sure does seem funny to read about all the big shots and then look back a few years when they were just another one of the boys.

Been flying pretty regularly now—at least once a day, weather permitting. Ships are slowly coming to the Group. Guess by next month we ought to have a full quota and then really start operating. As yet I haven't been assigned a private plane, but in some ways I am glad I don't have one. When I get mine I want to break it in myself and not let everybody and their brother fly it all day.

I'm beginning to see what you mean about saving money over here—can't seem to get rid of it. Guess I'll have to spend some on Imogene's birthday gift.

January 16, 1944
Dear Mother and Jerry:

Having a big time listening to the radio right now—have Jack Benny doing his stuff. There is a Forces Network over here which transcribes all the best programs from the States—Hit Parade, etc. Usually, however, somebody (you guess) jams the frequency and drowns out the station.

Been having all kinds of surprises this week as far as food is concerned. Starting about 4 days ago we have been having mighty good meat every day—steak, pork chops, turkey, lamb—all kind of stuff. If this keeps up we will be spoiled by the time we go back to the good old "C" ration (Spam and corned beef). Also, now that we are flying, there is an additional ration of 3 eggs (fresh) per pilot per week. How about that! The mess officer is everybody's friend now.

I thought San Fran. always had bad fog, but this stuff over here takes the cake. For the past two days we have had one solid fog bank around us—can't see ten feet in front of you. Practically have to file an instrument flight plan to go from the barracks to the mess hall.

Just about a year ago you arrived at the Point, didn't you [for his graduation]. Good night, that seems ages ago—only one year. Wonder what the next will bring forth.

Dad writes that he is up for his second star again— fourth attempt. Hope he gets it soon.

January 24, 1944
Dear Mother and Jerry:

Dad came to the Field to pick me up on Friday and we left for his place in the afternoon. We had a quiet evening at home that night. Slept late the next morning... Dad arranged a "shoot" for me—hunting to you, using beaters instead of dogs... I managed to get 3 pheasants which isn't bad for a beginner.

Sat. night we got asked out to dinner. Talk about putting on the dog—that dinner was it. I've never seen so much silverware in my life. The main event I believe was the lobster—a real honest lobster—and did it taste good.

Sunday we went out and had dinner with Bob. He certainly does seem to like his job and seems to be doing a wonderful job.

I gave Dad my Parker "51" [fountain pen, not available for civilian purchase during the war] since I have that other Parker I got in Benning. So you needn't look any further, Mother.

Getting more and more planes every day. First thing you know we will be going across the drink.

January 30, 1944
Dear Dad,

Getting in a few more planes —almost enough to make a mission [typically 36 on a Group mission, 12 from each squadron]. Tomorrow I am taking a few boys to pick up some more planes and then we will be fat.

This Group had its first casualty the other day. Lately we have been sending the ranking flyers of the Group to other Groups to get a little experience by going on missions. He went out on his first mission and failed to return. That would be pretty hard to take I think—first mission and all that.

Been doing quite a bit of [practice] dive-bombing lately. You would be surprised at the results. I don't know of anyone who has made a direct hit, but most of them are only 50 or 75 yards away and that would make a lot of damage with a big bomb. Maybe there is something to this fighter bomber.

January 30, 1944
Dear Mother and Jerry,

We are doing a bit of dive-bombing now —quite a bit as a matter of fact. Apparently that is about the only thing that we might be doing. I'm trying to get all that

I can out of it because we are supposed to be used in support of the landing forces. So I'm going to show Dad that the Air Corps can give the ground forces a little support.

The Group had its first casualty the other day. That was his first trip across too—poor guy. Well, it probably won't be the last. By the way, I am in the 9th Air Force. So if you ever read about the 9th you might know that I was with it.

According to his flight log for the month of January, Lt. Stroh flew twelve sorties for 15.5 flight hours. He also flew three Link trainer simulator sessions for instrument work. The Squadron was approaching its wartime quota of airplanes, and the anticipation of impending combat was growing among the pilots. His first letter of February was to his mother and sister dated the 8th.

Spent the majority of last week going to southern England to pick up a few planes. We had to stay at the other field for a few days because of bad weather. The English had a wild idea when they built that field on top of a hill which is almost in the clouds. Had a nice vacation out of it, but that is about all. We flew quite a number of ships back and I was lucky enough to get hold of one. So now I have something I have been working for for over a year. I don't know what it is, but I feel kind of important now—something to take care of and something of responsibility. Been working hard to get the old bus ready to go on missions. Speaking of missions the Group went on their first mission across the channel today— saw no opposition and lost none. As soon as my plane is ready I'll be going along with the boys.

So, along with the notion of impending combat, Lt. Stroh was assigned his own airplane, designated P-47D-11. This would be his primary ride until it was destroyed or otherwise taken out of commission, or as newer model replacements made their way to the squadron. His first taste of combat came on February 10th, an escort mission across Holland to just inside Germany. This eventful flight was led by the then double ace, Lieutenant Colonel Francis Gabreski, who would go on to become the leading American ace in the ETO with twenty-eight aerial victories. Gabreski, who at the time was CO of the 56th Fighter Group, was on loan to lead the 362nd's first five group missions because of his considerable combat experience. On this, the group's second mission, Gabreski was flying with the 378th Squadron. Lt. Stroh described the action in a letter to his father dated February 10th, followed by the 378th's Mission Report and another letter home.

Well, I feel like an old-timer now. I've seen the best the Germans have in the air and came back to tell about it. Went up on my first mission today, and a mighty exciting one it turned out to be. It was a rather hot affair for quite a time—until we got relieved by another group. We lost one man in the group which everybody regrets. At first there were eleven missing, but finally all but one showed up. At least we are even on the score—one for one. The C.O. of one of the squadrons knocked one down. At least I now know there is a war going on. It's just a little dangerous, isn't it, but it's a new life—something different.

February 10
    Mission No. 2—Lieutenant Colonel Gabreski leading this squadron on escort. Squadron made

R/V [rendezvous] as briefed at 1030 at 27,000 feet. Crossed Zuider Zee thirty miles east of that point. Blue flight was jumped near Balkberg (5040N-0630E) as it was making left turn to leave escort by 2 or 3 ME-109's from above and in the sun at four o'clock. No. 3 had just turned back due to oil on the canopy. Nos. 2 and 4 were seen to spin down. No hits visible, time—1055. Lead of the flight came home alone and made L/F [landfall] out at Noowijout at 1120 after circling and looking for the others. All others were early returns or radio relays. Lieutenant Hall NYR [not yet returned].

February 13, 1944
Dear Mother and Jerry,

This week our group went operational and has 4 missions under its belt now. Three of the missions were uneventful and rather short. However one was right into Hitler's back door and was rather exciting at times... I never realized how big the sky was until I got over there and got separated from the flight. You sit there with all the power you have in the airplane going at full blast trying to get with the flight again and all the time waiting for a couple of Jerries to come down at you. After a few missions though I guess it will come second nature as what to do at various times.

After being on a few missions I have a lot more confidence in my airplane and spend most of my time fixing things and getting it ready for the next day. I have been using sandpaper on it recently and smoothing down the rough paint so the air resistance will be less. When I get through with that I want to put some wax on it. Since there isn't any wax to be had in England I was wondering if you would... get me a few cans of Simonize. Putting this wax on adds about 3 or 4 mph to the plane and sometimes that's what counts.

Dad wanted to see me in London this week but I can't get away nowadays.

That first mission clearly got Lt. Stroh's attention. The downed pilot was in his flight that day, so he must have been in the thick of the dog-fight. It appears the formation got badly separated, a grave situation with enemy fighters in the vicinity. The debrief was probably quite colorful. Col. Gabreski would not have pulled any punches as he pressed home the necessity for formation discipline and mutual support. Fortunately the next several missions were less eventful, with lessons learned on all of them, including fuel management of the thirsty P-47s.

Being a history buff, in early January Gen. Stroh took leave to tour some of the famous and historical sites in England, including Kensington Castle, Stratford-on-Avon, and Windsor Castle, among others. The weather was frightful: cold, damp, and dreary. He had been warned as much by his British acquaintances, but clearly his timetable would not have permitted a later sightseeing schedule. In letters to Imogene, he complained about the lack of heat in the hotel rooms and terrible hotel food. But overall, he declared it a successful trip. He did, however, suggest feeling a little guilty when thinking about the troops.

Jan. 16

We are trying to see England in eight days, which, you must admit, is a pretty big order. While poor Bob, and hundreds like him labor from dawn until dark, and later, to get his outfit proficient on the range, here am I, gallivanting around in a nice big Buick with a private chauffeur and an aide to find hotel rooms, pay the bills, and read the map, while I sit back and enjoy myself. Sure great to be a general.

Jan. 30

Last Sunday morning, I called Bob to tell him that Harry and I would be out to see him... by the time we arrived he was ready for us, and we spent a pleasant hour with him before going to his mess for dinner at twelve thirty. He has a very comfortable room as camp rooms go, well heated with a rusty iron coal stove, two clothing closets, three reasonably easy chairs, a cot which is too short for him as usual, table, etc. He had your beautiful colored photograph prominently displayed on a shelf. It is really a beauty. Bob eats in a mess with about seventy-five other officers, those of his own battalion and several other companies. We had a very good meal including steak. I think Harry enjoyed eating there, and was impressed by the number of young officers who were wearing the Purple Heart, Silver Star and other ribbons.

I guess the handicap under which Bob was writing in November was that he was just getting settled in a new place, and was probably balancing the paper on his knee. He finally succeeded in making a voyage without getting torpedoed, and I don't know what else could have been the matter with him.

Did I tell you I met Bob's old boss, Reinhart, during a trip a couple of weeks ago? He was surprised to learn that Bob was still alive, having heard that he had been drowned during the African landings, and was very complimentary of his ability.

1849 Runnymede Pl.

Washington, D.C.

February 21, 1944

Why sure Bob's got plenty of ability. I always knew that and I really don't have to have generals tell me about it, but I certainly love to hear it and it makes me very proud. I wish he could come home soon, but that is only wishful thinking.

As February rolled around, training continued to intensify for the ground forces throughout Britain even as the number of U.S. Army units grew. At Allied headquarters, planning for the invasion went on amidst extremely tight security. The big questions for the troops were twofold: when would the invasion occur, and where would the landings take place? Understandably, rumors were rampant; landing sites from Norway to Germany to France, all the way to Spain, and invasion dates from a few weeks hence, to summer. For the 9th Division an exclamation point on D-Day anticipation occurred February 23rd when Gen. Stroh's old friend, Major General J. Lawton Collins, visited Barton Stacey to address the troops. After returning from the Pacific and a stop-over in Washington, Gen. Collins was now the VII Corps Commanding General, and the 9th Division was part of his command. In his speech, Collins stressed the historical importance of what they would soon embark upon, and complimented the troops on what they had already accomplished in Africa and Sicily. He impressed the men as credible and energetic, a dynamic leader, and he fed their confidence.

Gen. Stroh admired and respected his younger friend, now his boss. He also considered him a little on the brash side, but understood that, for him, it only enhanced his leadership ability. He reflected this in a letter to Imogene dated February 26th.

Have written Mother in full about Joe's visit here early in the week. He spoke of driving you and Mother somewhere on a slippery, snowy night while he was home. You write that you were glad he was driving. It wouldn't have made any difference. He would have taken complete charge from the back seat. He is certainly a dominant duck, but a great guy.

12

———•———

England Phase Two

While the ground troops ramped up preparations for D-Day, still months away, the fighter-bomber boys of the 378th continued to gain combat experience in the skies over Europe as they escorted large formations of American bombers. Lt. Stroh described the routine in letters to his mother and sister, the first one dated February 21st.

> Starting last Monday, we had rain and snow every day until yesterday. So the Germans in Berlin must have had a pretty good rest from the bombs since none of the daylight raids were pulled. Yesterday the day was still bad but we took off anyway for a little trip across. The C.O. took us a little too far in to suit me since nearly everybody got back to the field with only about 10 gals. of gas and that is calling it a little too close. That trip took three hours and then we grabbed something to eat and met the bombers coming out— another three-hour job. Six hours of flying is no easy job—sounds easy but you sure tire easily at those high

altitudes. I still haven't taken a shot at a Hun yet—seen plenty, but not close enough to take a shot. Plenty of time for that I guess.

Dad dropped by for a few hours the other day. I tried to meet him in London but it is kinda hard to get days off now. I'm trying now to get a couple of days next month to visit him.

Had a pretty exciting air raid the other night—the first in a long time now. A bunch of flares were dropped and we just waited for the bombs to start falling, but apparently they didn't want to waste them on us.

Got a letter from Les the other day—he's a Capt. now. Also heard that one of my "classmates" (June '43) is also a Capt. Boy I'm really disgusted.

February 27, 1944

I have ten sorties in now and am in for the Air Medal. That doesn't mean much because that is just automatic—every five missions or ten sorties you get an Air Medal and at 50 sorties you get the D.F.C. Every mission you carry a belly tank you get two sorties and a mission without a belly tank you get one sortie. So you see how fast you can build up your sorties.

Had a mighty big mission the other day. Our C.O. believes in going the limit of gas capacity. So the other day we went almost to the Swiss border which is over 300 miles. That makes over 600 miles round trip and some of the boys just barely made it. We were lucky enough not to get jumped over there or there wouldn't be many to come back. I think the C.O. learned his lesson though and was mighty glad to see everybody get back—don't think he will try that again.

Lost another boy the other day—that makes two in
the squadron and one was wounded in combat, the 1st
purple heart in the Sqd. That makes the Hun two up
on us so I guess we will have to get busy.

The Purple Heart recipient was Stroh's pal, Lt. Bob Kennedy, who
had taken hits from an ME-109 in the cockpit, one of which grazed
his skull. The 600-mile mission Stroh described was led by the Group
CO, Lieutenant Colonel Morton D. Magoffin, a West Point '37 classmate of Stroh's brother-in-law. That flight was on February 25th and
was Stroh's last mission of the month. In his first month as a combat
pilot, he logged 20.1 P-47D flight hours, 13.2 of which were "operational," on six combat missions.

During the month, the Group's P-47s were equipped with wing
fuel tank stations to extend their range. At first some pilots were not
happy about the very small loss of speed and maneuverability due
to the increased drag, but eventually were won over because of improvement in range capability.

For Lt. Stroh, the month of March started out very intensely, flying
seven operational sorties in the first week. He then took a few days off
to visit his father and brother-in-law. When he returned, there were
big changes in his routine. His letter home of March 6th describes the
scene that first week:

Another very tiring day and they are coming more
and more often. Almost every time we have very good
weather we go out at least twice a day—give support
to the bombers as they go to the target and then pick
them up when they come back. That gives us just
enough time to come back to the field, gas up, and get
something to eat and then back in the air. In the past

four days I have gotten more missions than I did the whole first month of operations. I don't know why I should get so tired flying only 6 hours a day but at the end of that time I can hardly crawl out of the cockpit. Maybe being at high altitude tires you faster than when working on the ground. Had a pretty good look at Paris the other day. It's a pretty good looking town—just like the pictures. Maybe it won't be long until we will be over there.

Was supposed to visit Dad over the weekend, but we were a little short of pilots because of sickness and transfers, so I couldn't go down. However I hope to go down sometime this week.

Went up to see Les the other day. He's a Capt. now or have I told you that. We are trying to get our 7 day leave together, but I don't think it will be possible... I think we have to get 3 months of operational time before getting a 7 day leave.

March 12, 1944
Dear Dad,

I want to thank you for a very enjoyable two days—it was the best so far. The riding and tennis sure did feel strange—especially playing them under the existing conditions—didn't seem as though there were a war.

Hope you told Braune what happened to his cap. I sent it back today along with 4 oranges which I hope aren't spoiled when they reach you. That is the first batch of Sunkist we have received so don't think we get them all the time. Sorry I can't send enough for the whole staff.

When I got back I found there had been many
changes made in the Group. The first person I saw
said, "Hello, Group snoop!" Much to my surprise
and dismay I found out that I have been transferred
to Asst. Group S-3. That is a good job as far as
advancement goes, but I don't want any part of it. I
might just as well be a ground officer rather than have
wings—only go on one out of every five missions. Of
course it is just temporary, but if I do the job well the
Col. will probably make it permanent. I don't want
the job yet I hate to be lax on the job so I'm between
two crossfires—just let time decide I guess. Also Jim
Rippin went up to Sqd. operations officer and Beeson
(my classmate) became a Sqd. C.O. (1st Lt. to Sqd. C.O.
in one short hop—not bad!). Beeson was immediately
promoted to Capt. of course. This is a pretty good
break for the three of us of course and we are all
trying to make good just to show the Col. that we can
do it. Another thing—as S-3 I don't get any days off so
I won't be seeing you for some time. Maybe after we
move to our advanced base I will get a day off and run
over to pay you a little visit.

March 12, 1944
Dear Mother and Jerry,
    Had a nice visit with Dad the other day—one of
the best so far. Tuesday I left the field early and got to
Dad in time for supper. That night the 9th was boxing
the 1st Div, and it was a bloody affair—the 9th coming
out on top. Dad was very pleased and proud of the
division—said that also reflects on the differences
of the way each division stood up in battle. The next

day we went out horseback riding for the first time
in two years. I was a little out of practice so didn't sit
exactly right on the horse. However, it was a very
enjoyable ride. That afternoon Dad invited the two
ladies of the house out for a little tennis. I didn't prove
too bad after my layoff and had a mighty fine time.
Dad's not so old yet—he can still get around the court
in great style. Then on Thursday, Dad and I visited
one of the regiments in the field and tried to find Bob.
However Bob was at some other spot so we just had
some C ration and went on our way. Next stop was
Sandhurst—the West Point of England. I was certainly
disappointed in it—maybe in wartime it has changed
somewhat—now it is an OCS [officer candidate school]
for the tanks. Went into the chapel and just below the
altar was a stone presented by West Point after the
last war. That was something new to me—that would
make good poop to ask plebes at the Point.

March 20, 1944

They still have me pushing a desk around here
at Group Hq. It's really not a bad job and it has a lot
of responsibilities... but I don't get to fly on many
missions.

The Group has been doing some dive-bombing
lately and haven't lost a single person in the process.
It's a mighty fine feeling to pull up from a dive and
look back to see a big explosion and know that even
though it wasn't a direct hit you at least scared the
Jerries a little.

Really sorry to hear that you had to move. Only
hope the new place is half as good as the last. Even if it

isn't I know the combined talents of you two will have it in top shape before long.

March 27, 1944

Right now the boys are coming back from a little mission and are having quite a time getting into the field. The visibility is about a quarter mile and the ceiling about 500 feet so the planes are just milling around the field. We will be lucky if nobody is killed when we have to fly at a time like this. But when the big dogs say get in the air there isn't much we can say.

I had a big time myself during this mission. While the boys were away another boy and myself took up a twin engine job [British AS.10 Oxford] and checked me out in it. He showed me how to fly it and told me take it around myself. Personally much prefer single engine. All the extra gadgets get in the way.

Guess you have read in the papers lately about the Thunderbombers bombing airdromes in France—well, that's your little boy Harry doing some of that. We had our first dive-bombing mission the other day. It sure is a lot of fun—the best we have had so far.

March 29, 1944
Dear Dad:

Here we are still at the old base... Guess the person who started that rumor didn't know what they were talking about... After looking at the new base, though, I would just as soon stay here.

Glad to hear you received the oranges OK... That bunch of oranges was the best we have ever had—since we had been getting some from South Africa which aren't up to the Sunkist variety.

Still holding down the desk job as yet. Things are beginning to pop around here now and there will be a few changes in the Group pretty soon. So I should know if this job will be permanent or not in a very few days. I'm getting pretty used to it now and get to fly on every other mission so I don't have much to complain about.

We have been going out pretty regular now—dive-bombing and strafing besides an occasional escort mission. It's old stuff now—feel like a veteran. By the way the Air Corps has picked up. There will be no more D.F.C.'s given out except for exceptional heroism. So I guess the air medal will be all I will be wearing.

Lt. Stroh's last P-47 flight of the month occurred on March 26th, a dive-bombing mission of an airfield near Gorenflos in northern France. The mission report states that the formation flew past the target, then set up for a southeast to northwest run-in, began the dive at 12,000 feet with a sixty-degree dive angle, and pulled out at 4,500 feet "with good results."

For the month of March, Lt. Stroh flew 35.8 P-47D hours, and twelve combat sorties including his first combat dive-bombing mission. And he checked out and flew three hops in the Oxford, which was very similar to the C-78 he had flown previously in the States. Each fighter group was issued a transport aircraft, typically a small twin engine model, to expedite movement of parts and personnel and other various cargo requirements.

On the home front during March, Imogene and her mother took on the task of finding and moving in to another house when their landlord sold the house on Runnymede out from under them. Imogene discussed the move and other items of interest in a series of letters to her father.

3349 Runnymede Pl.
Washington, D.C.
March 6, 1944

It is almost impossible to find an apartment. We'll probably end up going to Arlington... We'd like to rent another house but Washington is only for sale and rentals are scarcer than men. But don't worry 'cause we always get what we're after and by golly nothing can stop us this time either. You just wait and see.

That was a pretty nice letter you wrote about Gen. Collins, but I hope you don't really mean or think that your family loses any respect for you just because you don't get another star right off the bat. You're the kind of man that wins the wars and you don't have to be covered with a bunch of hardware for us to be proved. We believe that you deserve twice as much as you've gotten and you're so much more capable than some of these friends of yours that we just don't understand.

3614 Ingomar Pl.
Washington, D.C.
March 12, 1944

What a big mess we're in! If you could only see us females making this move without you males, you wouldn't believe it. Honestly, I'm getting to feel so independent—earning a salary and making moves. Even packed books and rolled rugs...

You should see this horrible house... the wallpaper is gaudy and loud, and the oil tank is empty. I'm going to the ration board to beg them to give us a 100 gal. until our request for coupons goes through. Mother has a bad cold now and I'm just getting over one so we have to have heat. But the house has a good roof, it is pre-war, it has a beautiful big double garage, one bathtub in each of the two bathrooms. It will be alright and today, after seeing it a second time, it isn't as bad as the first time I saw it. I'll build a fire in the fireplace tomorrow to see if it draws.

Received a letter from Bob that took seven days to journey. I've never heard him so enthusiastic as he was about that sightseeing trip you gave him. What does it mean sending him out on bivouac? It sound as if things are getting to important matters. Kind of toughening them up.

I certainly wish you were home. I really think that Mother misses you more than you miss her.

I can't imagine Harry even so much as acting as your aide [on a business trip to London], but I hope he pulled your chair out at least once and has popped you a good salute by now.

March 20, 1944

We've been working... this last week getting settled. We've scrubbed floors, walls, rolled and unrolled rugs, moved heavy furniture around... the house isn't bad with all our nice things in it.

What do you know! Henry Ford predicts the war will be over in two months. We certainly won't have finished what should be if it is.

For the 9th Division, March 24th was a red letter day when they were paid a visit by Prime Minister Sir Winston Churchill, Supreme Allied Commander General Dwight Eisenhower, and First Army Commanding General Omar Bradley. Red Phillips:

Coming by train, he [Churchill] was accompanied by Generals Eisenhower and Bradley. They were met by Generals Collins and Eddy about five miles from the division area and transferred to cars for touring the twenty-seven miles of roads between camps of the division's components. The first stop was the Barton Stacey camp of the 39th Infantry and Division Artillery. A full battalion of impeccably uniformed and polished infantry did the welcoming honors for Mr. Churchill, who refused to merely drive past. He dismounted and slowly walked down each rank, stopping and gazing into the face of each soldier as he passed. As one of them said later, "It was as if he was saluting us instead of the other way."

The artillery was displayed with the howitzers arranged hub-to-hub in a horseshoe shape with muzzles uplifted. Churchill again refused to ride by but got out of the car and examined the men and equipment carefully. He asked questions about the American artillery specialty of bringing coordinated mass fire on a target and instantly grasped its implications as explained by an articulate young battalion commander, Lieutenant Colonel William C. Westmoreland.

On the way to Winchester, the entourage passed the other two infantry regiments spread along each side of the road... Each soldier individually executed Present Arms and Eyes Right or Left, and followed the approach of the lead vehicle. "I've never seen anything like it," Churchill exclaimed.

At Winchester Barracks, Churchill watched a parade of the 9th Division Special Troops and spoke briefly but eloquently, reminding the soldiers of their past exploits in the Mediterranean and his own ties with the United States. He was amazed to learn that "Special Troops" consisted of what he termed "the odds and sods of the division." The Prime Minister beamed: "Our divisions have them, of course, but yours march properly, like Guardsmen."[1]

The party visited one other division location that afternoon. In the evening, the prime minister held a dinner party on his train, which had remained at Winchester. Gens. Eisenhower and Eddy were in attendance and there were an additional seven guests. They ate, drank, and talked for three and a half hours. It is unclear whether Gen. Stroh was there. His letter to Imogene dated the next day mentioned nothing of the visit whatsoever.

April 1944 began true to character; rain, rain, and more rain; that and the beginning of British "double summertime," where the clocks were set back two hours, giving the fighter-bombers plenty of daylight in which to operate. At the 362nd Fighter Group, Assistant S-3 Lt. Stroh spent his time in the office planning missions, few of which were flown because of the foul weather. His only flight of the first week of April was in the Oxford. His one exciting mission of that time was on April 8th when the squadron was scrambled at short notice to strafe a number of enemy locomotives traveling west toward Rouen. It was the second mission of the day for many of the pilots who had not had a meal since breakfast. Sleep came easy for them that night.

The Group was preparing to move to a new field, some forty miles south in Kent and that much closer to the enemy. It involved more rustic conditions; accommodation in tents rather than huts, a pierced steel plank rather than concrete runway, and other changes. For Lt. Stroh, a benefit of the move was that it would put him considerably closer to his father. He was careful to get his new APO address to his mother and Imogene to avoid any delays in mail delivery. In a letter to them dated April 3, 1944, he wrote:

> Had a mighty nice surprise yesterday. I went to the mess hall at dinner and just got through washing my hands when who should walk in but Dad. I was never so surprised in my life. The only trouble with him coming here is that he never stays very long—a few hours and then right back. We have a big time exchanging letters that we have received from the two of you.
>
> Now I have another change in my address. Instead of sending it to the 378th F.S., just put down 362nd F.G. The APO is still 595. You can see by this that I am a permanent member of the Group staff. A group is comparable to a battalion. I have gotten pretty used to this job by now. Also I am in for Captain so I'm not kicking.

APO 595, England

April 9, 1944

> I want to thank you for the wax. It looks like pretty good stuff. However, now that I have the wax, I have nothing to put it on. Since I am now a permanent member of the Group Hq. I don't need a plane to call my own. So they took my plane and gave it to some replacement pilot who just joined the squadron which made me very mad.
>
> Had all the intentions in the world of going to church today, but we had a mission and I was rather busy plotting the course. This must be the first time I have missed Easter church for many a year.

APO 141, England (near Headcorn)

April 16, 1944

Seems as though I change APO's almost monthly, doesn't it? Well, maybe this will be the last change for some time.

We're real soldiers now—living in tents under full field conditions. I left our other field a few days before the main body moved and really had a big time setting up a new field. Of course the runway matting was already laid, but we had to find sites for the living tents and also space to park the planes.

It sure does feel good to get out in the field again. Guess a thing like that gets in your blood. The fresh air will do everybody a world of good though. I know my appetite has picked up 100% since I have been out here—the food itself is much better than we had at the other base.

Now that I am only about 40 miles from Dad I might be able to drop over and see him every once in a while.

APO 141, England

April 16, 1944

Dear Dad,

The big move has taken place and now we are real field soldiers. I came down about 3 days before the main party to get things organized for operations... and it's a good thing I did. I've never seen anything so poorly organized as this move has been. The one man who knew anything about who got what in the way of equipment was away so you can imagine the condition of things around here. Besides, a lowly 1st Lt. didn't have a chance

against several Majors. So I was just forced to go out
and steal things I needed rather than ask for them. I lost
several friends that way but I did my job.

The move was rather bad for the main body for it
started raining the minute they arrived and has been
raining ever since. But that will make real soldiers out
of some of these people.

Imogene's weekly letters to her father continued to keep him abreast
of life on the home front, and encouraged him when he was down.
She correctly deduced that he was intensely homesick and clearly frustrated with his position as assistant division commander when he felt
that he deserved promotion to major general and a division of his own.
One could reasonably speculate that his boss, Gen. Eddy, relied on
him to such great extent that he really did not want to let him go, and
maybe did not push hard enough for promotion, although Gen. Eddy
did put him in for promotion again and again, and recommended him
for the Distinguished Service Medal. In fact, Gen. Eisenhower, in a cable to Army Chief of Staff Gen. Marshall dated March 27, 1944, when
discussing possible replacement division commanders for the looming
invasion, wrote, "The only brigadier I now have here who I consider
fully capable of a division command who is not actually in command
of a division is Brigadier General Stroh."

Relevant passages of letters from Imogene to her father during the
month of April represent her grasp of the situation, alternately chiding
and encouraging him as he prepared for the invasion to come.

3614 Ingomar Place
Washington, D.C.
April 2, 1944
We just read in the paper today that John Eckert
was killed in Germany piloting a B-26. He had a six

weeks old son.

...we got some ice cream and went by to see Grandma. She showed us the picture of you with the three other brains of the division [Eddy, Howell, Barth]. You look like the fatted calf and we'll never be able to feed you so well when you come back. I never saw such a contented smirk on anyone's face as you had. Guess war isn't so bad as Sherman says in some ways.

We got a big kick out of you lying awake the night when you heard we had moved. Gee whiz, it was all over but the shouting when you all heard. It was pretty bad at that, but when something has to be done it always gets done and there is no use worrying about it.

And if you don't stop worrying about that star I'll do something really drastic. Everyone that knows you knows what a fine officer you are and probably can't understand why you don't have it. And you know you don't care what your enemies think. Or do you? Your lucky star just hasn't shown yet, Daddy, just as Gen. Collins wrote you... Please don't worry so, because we worry back here 'cause you're worried.

A luxury tax of 20% has gone into effect on jewelry, leathers, cosmetics, and liquors. Uncle Sam is getting down to brass tacks.

April 10, 1944

We just received Harry's letter of April 3rd telling us of your surprise visit of the 2nd. He always seems to hate to see you go.

In Harry's letter it sounded almost as if the bigger dear will move up a notch. I shall have to keep an account of how long that will keep you satisfied before you want even greater heights. It is a good thing to be that way because you don't get stale or in a rut, but it makes you so unhappy at times.

April 16, 1944

The announcement of you receiving the Legion of Merit came out in the Wash. Post the other morning. It was a nice write-up and made you sound like a real soldier. None of the chair-polishing soldiering either. Your hardware is starting to accumulate.

I haven't heard from Bob since March 29th which arrived in 5 days. You give his activities in a concise way so that I can pass it on to the Stumpfs. Bob never has been so terribly regular about letter writing and with time going by so fast I guess he doesn't realize how many days go by between letters. Can't complain though, he's been better than I ever expected when he left.

Start thinking about coming home. This is beginning to seem so long.

April 22, 1944

Did I tell you I finished 500 hours at Anti-Aircraft [Volunteers]? To celebrate I bought a new pair of Wave's slacks to wear on duty. They are cut so nicely and the girls on my shift call me "fancy pants."

We received a letter from Harry written the 16th giving his new APO... It's grand to know he is only 40 miles from you. Wish you could say in what direction from you and we can really pin him down.

Much of the 9th Division was in the field for Easter weekend working a battle problem. Even the higher-ups were not immune to some of the unpleasantries of wartime training. Gen. Stroh described one such drill at 9th Division headquarters in a letter to Imogene written on Saturday, April 8th, but only in a way that educes a chuckle rather than a tear.

Having just withstood one of Colonel Barth's depressing little idiosyncrasies, a surprise gas and smoke "attack" in the command post, during which everyone had to run about with his gas mask on, I can now settle down to some serious letter writing.

You should have seen the reaction of our camp follower dogs when the gas arrived. I don't know whether dogs can cry or not, but I imagine they are just as uncomfortable as humans are under the circumstances, and have no way of protecting themselves. But the most distressing feature to them was no doubt seeing their late human friends running about disguised in snouts like some visitors from Mars. Between the gas and the strange apparitions suddenly inhabiting their world, the poor beasts didn't know which way to turn, and ran about whimpering and yelping, with their tails between their legs. In addition to Rene, who... has long since become a permanent member of the headquarters, with three campaigns and two sea voyages behind her, we have acquired a new member of the official family, or at least Matt has; a roan cocker spaniel, now about four months old, named Kippy. Rene and Kippy don't get along too well together yet, but as this trip is their first experience together, their relations may improve.

The emasculated division marched into the field yesterday and parts of it will remain until

Wednesday... One regiment doesn't participate at all,
and another doesn't arrive until Monday night. It
seems that Bob's outfit never misses a formation, and
they are in bivouac close by as I write, ready to start
maneuvers in the wee small hours tomorrow. They will
then have a busy time until Tuesday noon, with little
rest at night, and will return to their usual location
on Wednesday. A fine way to spend Easter and the
Easter holidays. Another division, located near here,
is going to stage an Easter sunrise service tomorrow.
I wouldn't be surprised to see our "battle" pass right
through the layout.

My favorite English cat, Timmy, is about to have
kittens. Lady Ley expects to drown them all, but I'd
like very much to keep one... Guess that's out of the
question.

We had a large ceremony last Tuesday when
a regular convoy of Red Cross trucks arrived for
attachment to the division. They consisted of four
independent groups, each of three or four vehicles of
assorted sizes, and each manned by three or four Red
Cross women, whose principal job in life from now on
will be to smile, bake doughnuts, and hand out the same
to the hungry soldiers. The doughnut baking truck is a
wonder of efficiency. It makes its own power, bakes 150
doughnuts per hour automatically, and plays records
over a loudspeaker. The girls do all the work of cleaning
up, dispensing the products, and greeting the boys with
a cheery smile and warm handclasp of greeting... Wish I
had a doughnut right now.

A couple of Thunderbolts just flew over. Wonder if
Harry was in one of them.

Harry was not in one of the Thunderbolts that day. His monthly flying was severely curtailed by several factors: bad weather, his duties at the Group, the big move to the new field, and an unexpected week-long assignment away from the field. He was given orders to attend "Camouflage School" located at a picturesque river town that he was not at liberty to divulge. He was none too keen on the school "except that I did learn a great respect for land mines and booby traps." But the town he fell in love with and thoroughly enjoyed himself. On the way back from the school, he spent the weekend with his father and brother-in-law, including a side trip to Portsmouth to visit Admiral Horatio Nelson's flagship, HMS *Victory*, about which he remarked, "Those were really the days of iron men and wooden ships." Up until April 26th Lt. Stroh had flown only one P-47 mission, but had flown the Oxford ten times, probably in support of the station move. Gen. Stroh wrote about Harry's visit in a letter to Imogene dated April 24th.

Harry paid me a surprise visit for nearly 48 hours beginning Friday night... we did have the usual grand time together, and for the first time succeeded in including Bob in most of our activities which added greatly to the enjoyment of both of us. On Saturday afternoon we had an All-American male quartet on the tennis court for the first time. Picked up Bob at his camp about three o'clock, and George Smythe [47th Infantry CO], the fourth member of the group, joined us a little later. We all changed into our "tennis" clothes in my room, and were a sight to behold by the time we were all equipped. Bob's feet are entirely too big for any available tennis shoes, so he played in leather soled GI's, and a one piece fatigue suit of herringbone twill. Smythe wore an old West Point sweat shirt with drawer-like trousers to match, and rubber soled sandals. Harry was becomingly attired in OD trousers and shirt, and I did manage to find some tennis shoes that would fit him. I was practically a fashion plate, with khaki trousers, cotton OD shirt, and light tan sweater. We played five sets with every possible combination of partners and had a fine time. Smythe was in charge of gymnastics at the Academy in Bob's time and was an outstanding athlete there, being All-American quarterback about '24, so it was a pleasure for the youngsters to beat him in three of the five sets played.

After a short round of drinks Smythe departed, but Bob and Harry… had dinner with me at the mess, together with two visiting major generals. Fortunately, the menu happened to be an excellent one, and the boys enjoyed a fine meal. The three of us then returned to Pitt manor, and sat for a while on a bench in front of the house, enjoying the sunset, and the beautiful peaceful valley in front. None of us could imagine that we were in the front yard of a war. After it became chilly, we went up to my room, lighted a cheerful fire, had a round of port and chewed the fat until about nine, then Bob went home in the Buick.

Bob had dinner again with us yesterday at one o'clock, and went along to take Harry back to his field, where we had supper and where Bob met Harry's group commander [Magoffin], a classmate of his. En route, we paid a visit to the "Victory" at Portsmouth.

Had a nice Easter card from my second daughter, Jean Thompson. She is a sweet kid. Wish I could get Harry interested.

Bob proudly showed me the most recent picture which you sent him, taken either in front of the Capitol, or with an artificial background, we can't determine which... The picture is a bit rumpled by virtue of much carrying about in Bob's shirt pocket during the recent maneuvers and at other times, but he thinks the world of it.

General [Courtney] Hodges was with us for two or three days last week. He inspected Bob's battalion and renewed old acquaintances made when he attended your wedding. The old man seemed much pleased to see Bob again, and to note how his professional prospects have changed since the old lieutenant days.

Four of your nice letters arrived since I last wrote, ranging from March 21 to April 10. You are the best young cheerer-upper that I know, and I want you to know how much I appreciate your sympathy. Everything you say about my military prospects is true, and I'll not burden either you or Mother again with the subject. It was a close call, but I'll grin and bear it from now on, strengthened by the knowledge that you folks at home at least have not lost faith in me.

Lt. Stroh got back in the saddle on April 26th when he flew a dive-bombing mission to a storage facility at Nantes, France. The thirteen squadron aircraft were carrying two 500-pound bombs each and made their runs from east to west from 8,000 feet, pulling out at 1,500 feet amidst some light flak. They saw one enemy aircraft high over the target area, but were not engaged.

On the 29th, Stroh flew in a sixteen-plane formation on a bombing and strafing mission to an airfield near Gardelegen, Germany, only about fifty miles west of Berlin. The squadron claimed two ME-410s destroyed and one damaged, and three Stukas as probables. The weather was 2,000 feet overcast, so the attack was conducted at low altitude. For the abbreviated flying month, Lt. Stroh flew three combat missions for 8.8 hours, and a total of 22.5 hours including his non-combat flight time. He now had over 600 flight hours total.

On April 15th, the 362nd Fighter Group was reassigned from the 70th Fighter Wing to the 100th Fighter Wing of the XIX Tactical Air Command. The Group strength on April 30th was 153 officers and 824 enlisted men. After its move from AAF Station 159, Wormingford, Essex, its official location was now AAF 412, Headcorn, Kent. During the month, Lt. Stroh was awarded his first Air Medal.[2] He commented about his most recent mission in these letters home:

APO 141, England
April 30, 1944
Dear Mother and Jerry,

Almost made it to Berlin the other day—didn't quite have enough gas for that though. Wouldn't want to try that trip too often—we really have to ration the gas to the engine on the way home. Also, we were up for 4 1/2 hours and that is quite a time sitting on a rubber boat—deflated but still hard.

I can't get over the swell weather we've been having lately. Wish we would have a little rain now though—it would get rid of a little of this dust. Every time the Group takes off it feels and looks like the desert in a dust storm.

I still haven't been able to get another ship. Glad I hadn't though, because nice new jobs are coming in as replacements. They haven't any paint on them and are really beauties to look at.

The boys are just getting back from a mission so I will have to sweat them out and see if any are missing. I'm getting grey hair worrying about them coming home.

May 1, 1944
Dear Dad,

Sure is hard getting back in the saddle after my week of so-called vacation. Reminds me of going back to the Point after Christmas furlough.

There have been a few changes around since I left though. My old C.O. of the 378th was promoted and shipped out to another group. Then a few days after you brought me back the Col. [Magoffin] got his chickens [full colonel]. The old man immediately went out and bought himself a swagger stick.

The other day we almost went to Berlin—within 50 miles of it—the first 47 group to go that far. I was really sweating my gas out though—England never looked so good as it did that day. This dive-bombing is the most fun—especially when you drop a ton from each plane.

The month of May started out with a bang for the Group. On the morning of the 1st, they flew a re-strike mission to Haine St. Pierre, a target they had previously hit. On the return leg, they noted that the marshaling yards at Valenciennes were full of rail cars. Lt. Stroh returned with the Group that evening back to the yards, one squadron escorting B-26s and the other two, including the 378th, each aircraft dropping two 1,000-pound bombs. Results were good; the yards were very heavily damaged.

On the 2nd and 3rd, Lt. Stroh flew acceptance tests on two new replacement aircraft, silver ones with no paint, and bigger propellers for better climb performance; designated P-47D-22 and P-47D-23. Number 22 would become his new ride. He wrote about this in letters to his family, the first to his mother and sister, dated May 7th.

Haven't heard from Dad since I saw him several weeks ago. Guess he is getting ready for the big day. I flew over his Hq. the other day and gave him a good buzz job.

The Group has been sitting on the ground as of late. Both our runways are torn up and getting repaired. By the time we leave this field, the runways will be in perfect condition.

May 8, 1944
Dear Dad,

If you were in the office last Tuesday about five o'clock—I was about fifty feet from you. I was up testing a brand new silver job so I thought I would pay you a little visit. I flew over the Hq. building then over the house—not knowing where you would be. Then I went out and buzzed Bob a couple of times—I know he doesn't like that, but I couldn't pass up the chance.

By the way—congratulations on receiving the Legion of Merit. You deserve more than that, I know—maybe the DSM is coming also. I have run across several Lts. in your division who swear by you and how you are the best damn general officer they have run across. So if you have the support of the subordinates, you must have some respect among the higher boys.

Stroh's next combat mission was on May 10th, dive-bombing the airfield at Rheims with 500-pounders. The squadron used a variety of bomb types including fragmentation, incendiaries, and smoke bombs. On return to the field, one P-47 was destroyed when his hung-up frag bombs fell off and blew up on the runway. Earlier in the day, one of the squadron's P-47s was hit by flak and went down in the Channel. The pilot, Capt. Desens, survived and was picked up by an air-sea rescue unit. Also on that day, Stroh's log book indicates that he went up in a light observation L-4B Grasshopper, the military version of a Piper Cub. With operational flying somewhat curtailed, he managed to slip away to London for a few days with his buddy, Jim Rippin. They stayed at an apartment that Rippin's squadron kept for just such sojourns. Upon returning from a band concert in Hyde Park, "...who should be there but Dad. He shows up at some of the funniest places. He didn't stay too long—an hour or so and then he had to go."

On May 20th, by order of the Ninth Air Force, the Group was re-christened the 362nd Fighter-Bomber Group, a clear indication of the growing emphasis on P-47 air-to-ground operations, and a portent of the role they would play in direct support of ground forces after the impending invasion. The arbitrary name change didn't seem to stick, however. Decades later, the veterans of the Group were members of the 362nd Fighter Group Association.

The weather during May was fickle. During the first week or so it was so cold that the boys lamented the possibility of losing the local apple crop. There were ten days during the month when no missions at all were flown, including nine scheduled missions that were scrubbed for weather. In preparation for the invasion, the emphasis on those that were flown was on the destruction of transportation infrastructure such as railroads, marshaling yards, trucks, bridges, and airfields.

Earlier in the month, Lt. Stroh had been approached by a pilot in one of the other squadrons about getting a job at the group. Stroh jumped at the prospect of returning to the squadron, and the two of them presented their proposal to Col. Magoffin, who said he would mull it over. By the end of the month, Stroh was back at the 378th and back on the regular flying rotation. On May 26th he flew in a fourteen-ship escort of medium bombers to and from an airfield at Beaumont-sur-Oise, about twenty miles due north of Paris. Excellent hits were observed in the dispersal area. One flight went low only to discover that the planes were dummies and found real JU-88s in the woods. The pilots also observed a westbound locomotive with fifteen boxcars taking refuge in a tunnel and noted that the west end of the tunnel would be a good skip bomb target.

On May 28th, it was a twelve-plane return escort of heavies from Magdeburg, about eighty miles west of Berlin. One bomber crashed and exploded about twenty miles southeast of Liege; eight parachutes were observed. Lt. Stroh's last flight of the month was an escort of heavies to the yards in Jamelle, France. His squadron-mate, Lt. Gough, went down in the channel and was picked up, but had not survived.

It was another abbreviated flying month for Lt. Stroh. He was despondent over not having been promoted to captain, as had all of his West Point classmates in the Group. His plan to use superior performance in his Group job as a springboard for promotion had obviously failed. But now he was happily back with the squadron and ready for the biggest adventure of his life. In May he flew five combat missions for 12.4 hours, another two P-47 test flights, and three C-78 flights for a total of 18.7 hours. The months ahead would be much busier in the air.

Back home, Genie and Jerry soldiered on, fixing up the new house and creating vegetable and rock gardens. Jerry continued with the Anti-aircraft Volunteers and working part time at the Weather Bureau, but was making plans for a big trip to Texas, St. Louis, and Barberton to visit friends and relatives. She also had the urge to go back to school. She explained some of her plans in letters to her father, the first one dated May 2nd.

All of a sudden, as usual with me, I have a tremendous urge to get my degree. I hear that if I take intensive studies this summer and winter I can finish my last two years at George Washington University. I'll go on with Home Ec. for a minor and since I like Botany so much I'll take that for a major.

Of course, I'll drop my job and only do a little substituting at anti-aircraft. Mother thinks it is a fine idea and this couldn't be a better chance to get it for me. Even if Bob comes back before I'm through, at least I'll have that many more credits and hours which I might be able to complete gradually. I hope you don't think I'm absolutely crazy...

It was wonderful that Harry got to fly you, and if you're not careful you're going to let it slip how much you think of the A.C. and how proud you are that Harry is in it.

May 7, 1944

Today, we anti-aircraft volunteers had a treat by riding in Army trucks inspecting the Military Defense of Washington. Since our section chief couldn't go on the tour and I'm asst. chief of section I was allowed to ride in one of the command cars with our commanding officer, a graduate of Annapolis, class of '24. Also, I had the honor of eating with the MDWCO Gen. Lewis at one of the gun batteries. All the soldiers had cleaned their barracks, rest rooms, etc. so they shone and were at attention for our inspection. They were alerted at each of the various positions we went to and after a demonstration we were free to handle all the weapons and practice aiming the big guns and even watch the

various radars operate. I even had the great pleasure
of enjoying a peep ride. By golly, with all the big shots
and brass hats in my immediate family, I had to ask
a lowly lieutenant to take me. It was as much fun as
riding the rolly coaster at Glen Echo.

Texas
May 14, 1944

There is a soldier sitting in my Pullman section and
wants to talk my head off, so I've moved to the parlor
car.

This has been a busy week. I handed in my
resignation to the Weather Bureau without regrets.
Also, I've made my plans for the summer session
at G.W. The Dean won't let me take more than two
subjects, so at 7:10 A.M. I take the required history
course and at 9:00 I take one of the two required years
of Spanish. But, isn't that a wonderful schedule?

All my plans to see everyone have been working
out just as I had hoped... We're waiting for the Fort
Worth train here in Waco. All you see far and wide are
men in khaki and men, too old, in cits.

Many people have complimented me on your
receiving the Legion of Merit and I guess Mother
wrote you about her receiving a letter from Gen.
Quesada saying how pleased he was to present Harry
with the Air Medal. That is a nice thing to do, Pappy,
when you are the big chief.

You'll never, never know how happy we are you
didn't send in that letter when you were right on the
ledge. You would have been miserable for the rest of
your life full of regrets for doing it. You're much too

valuable a soldier and leader to waste your time here at home at times like these.

En route to Cleveland, Ohio
May 28, 1944

[In San Antonio] met lots of girls whose husbands were overseas. Homer [Euglow, a former beau] and Traeger are in Prison Camp 2 in Davao, Mindanao. I think that is pretty good news since the most fit of the prisoners from Luzon were sent there to work the fields. The wives keep in touch with each other and every so often one of the men mentions another on his form card. The girls can only write 25 word typewritten messages. Rilla Colvert hasn't heard a word from P.K. but some mentioned that he was O.K. All the girls continue to receive their allotment.

[June's husband] Bob took me on a tour of the Ger. Prison Camp and that was really interesting. They were Tunisia prisoners. They are a fine looking bunch of men and are getting excellent care with the most up-to-date equipment.

Barberton, Ohio
May 29, 1944
Dearest Mother,

It is so cute when I read that Harry had buzzed Bob, because Bob griped in one of his letters that a Thunderbolt was buzzing his area much to his disgust. Bob says it's alright for me to go to school but that he bets I won't learn anything to help him get what he wants most. Wonder what he's talking about.

For the 9th Division, the month of May was spent in final preparation for the invasion, much of it on field exercises and in direct
coordination with other units. The weather in the field was typically
cold and wet, and the soldiers had to deal with the mud, much like
the conditions they could expect across the channel. They worked
tirelessly to ensure their weapons, vehicles, and equipment were in
absolutely pristine condition. New personal equipment was issued.
They noticed a sizable increase in the masses of military aircraft passing overhead. Leaves and furloughs were cancelled and the excitement level increased commensurately. A big morale boost occurred
when the veterans of North Africa and Sicily were issued the highly
coveted Combat Infantryman Badge. This gesture included most of
the men in the division who had been in the fight since late 1942,
and who had been with the division for months before that. After
the campaigns in Tunisia and Sicily, they considered themselves seasoned warfighters and were brimming with confidence.[3]

Though only the most senior commanders and intelligence personnel were privy to any of the plans, the role of the 9th was to deploy
as VII Corps reserve afloat, as a ready strike force off one of the assault
beaches. Their planned landing date was D plus four, although the
actual date of the invasion was determined only a few days out. The
lead divisions began embarking as early as May 30th.

13

—————•—————

Normandy:
Operation Overlord

During the planning, build-up, and transport phases of the Allied invasion of Northern Europe, the operation was code-named Neptune. Once the actual amphibious operation began, it was referred to as Overlord.

Gen. Eddy departed Winchester on June 3rd and turned the 9th Division over to Gen. Stroh. Chief of Staff Colonel George B. Barth was to lead a small advance party with the 4th Division landing on D plus one to set up the 9th Division assembly areas. Gen. Eddy would accompany the 90th Division and go ashore on D plus two.[1] Also on June 3rd, Gen. Stroh moved out of his quarters at Pitt Manor for good and returned once more to London. Given the events unfolding around him, and that he was embarking on the climax of a twenty-seven-year military career, it is somewhat remarkable that he sat down that night to write a somewhat newsy letter to Imogene. After commenting on her recent trip and other mundane subjects, he wrote:

I'm writing you a day early this time, not knowing what tomorrow may bring forth, and in the same room which I first occupied in Deleted [London] when we arrived here in November. Moved out of my comfortable billet this morning as to be closer to the center of things, and it almost made me homesick, I've been there so long, and they were so kind to me.

[at a recent social function in Winchester] ... I did meet one interesting couple, a recently retired British colonel and his wife, as clearly Regular Army as are those at home. It is remarkable what common interests we all have. The lady had spent her life in the service, being an Army brat. I struck one very sad note, however. She was wearing a small silver replica of the R.A.F. wings, and I asked her the significance. Tears came to her eyes when she said they had lost their 19-year-old son in flight combat. I was terribly sorry that I had brought up the subject.

Bob looked well when I saw him last Tuesday. Busy as usual, and more excitement ahead.

One of our greatest invasion problems is what to do with Rene. She is very evidently about to become a mother. I cannot think of a less fortunate time. As close as we can figure the father is a large wooly-haired beast, and as Rene is neither large nor wooly-haired the result will be interesting. When I begin to [share a] mess with Matt again, I am afraid something will have to be done with the dog situation, as he has recently become high hat with dogs, not deigning to associate with any which are not blue-blooded.

Keep rooting for us. We'll probably need it. But if the shortest way home lies to the east, we might as

well get started and get it over with. It should be an
interesting show—if you enjoy that sort of thing.

The 9th Division moved into six-hour alert status on May 27th,
which meant that they had to be ready to deploy within six hours. They
got the order on June 3rd and began moving out by truck and rail to
staging areas at Southampton, Dorchester, and Weymouth. The men
began loading onto their ships on the morning of D-Day, June 6th.
The 39th Infantry embarked at Southampton. In all, the 9th Division
soldiers were dispersed among forty-seven Liberty ships, eight LSTs,
and twelve LCTs, none of which were known to be comfortable rides.
They got underway for Normandy on June 7th, arrived twenty-four
hours ahead of their scheduled land time at Utah Beach, and waited
offshore for their turn to disembark, scheduled for June 10th. During
their time at anchor, the ships occasionally came under attack from
German shore batteries and aircraft. In one instance twelve ME-109s
strafed a ship with elements of the 39th Infantry on board, wounding
several who required evacuation.[2]

General Eddy went ashore on June 8th and toured the battlefront
with VII Corps commander, Gen. Collins. He finished the supervision
of Col. Barth's advance party preparations for the arrival of the main
body of the division.

At the 362nd Fighter-Bomber Group, the action picked up in the
days leading up to the invasion. Lt. Stroh was flying on practically
every mission, his 378th Squadron schedulers apparently taking care
of him after his limited flying time while at the group. On June 1st,
he flew another acceptance flight on his new airplane. On the 2nd,
the squadron launched fourteen P-47s, each with two 500-pounders,
for a dive-bombing attack on the railroad from Amiens to Criel. They
cut the track in three places, destroyed one bridge, and dropped eight
bombs in a railroad marshaling yard. On the 3rd, they launched thirteen on a fighter sweep of the Rouen area with no ensuing action. On

June 4th, they escorted B-26s to the Seine River bridge at Courelles, which was destroyed. The escort mission on the 5th was aborted due to weather.[3] Lt. Stroh took time out to write letters to his family on the 4th, the first one to his mother and sister.

> Well! Things are really picking up around here now. I am back with the squadron....and perfectly happy—I have a flight [as leader] and am back with the boys. At least we all talk the same language and don't run across all the bootlicking that goes on in Group Hq.
>
> Took off... last Monday Tuesday and visited Dad— for the last time maybe. We had a big feast Monday night —fried chicken, fresh asparagus, and ice cream. Tuesday we went out to see Bob and then we played a little tennis. All in all it was a mighty nice time.
>
> Came mighty close to getting my first victory the other day. A couple of Jerries came diving down on the bombers we were escorting and I started after them. However I apparently didn't have enough head start because I couldn't quite catch the guys. But while I was down on deck I saw a train and put a couple of squirts in the engine and saw the steam pouring out the holes. Feel kinda sorry for the Frenchmen who run those engines, but those trains have to be stopped.

Dear Dad,

> Don't know what's up but I have a feeling this might be the eve of something big. Don't see why it should as a matter of fact, but I just have that feeling.
>
> Finally got myself a beautiful airplane—all silver job with a big paddle-blade propeller which is about

twice as wide as the ordinary props which gets much better climb characteristics. As yet I haven't taken it on a mission because we are still pulling an acceptance check. But it won't be long 'til I go with my nice new shiny pride and joy.

Been going out regularly lately—at least once a day. We are supposed to go on one a day until the big day so we won't be tired and also to get our planes in the best of condition. The C.O. has been pretty nice so far by letting me go on every mission. The boys are going to catch on soon and I'll be sitting on the ground for a while.

All the crew chiefs in my flight got hold of about 20 good size steaks and invited all the pilots of the flight over for a big feast. They sure did taste good regardless of where they came from.

Flew my new aircraft on its first mission this morning [June 5th]. Only trouble was the bombers didn't show up—said they couldn't get through the overcast. Those bomber boys don't seem to be very good at instrument flying.

On the big day, June 6, 1944, the 362nd was in a ready reserve status, to be called for whatever mission might be required. They waited, disappointed, all day before getting the call to escort a group of troop-carrying C-47 tugs and gliders to the battle area inland from Utah Beach. They expected swarms of enemy fighters to go after the easy transport targets, but no air opposition materialized and the mission was uneventful.

The 7th was a much busier day. The Group flew three missions and Lt. Stroh was on two of them, almost certainly the first two. The first one was a 4:10 A.M. launch, again escorting tug and glider groups to the Carentan area, about six miles southeast of Utah Beach. Sixteen aircraft were dispatched, but one crashed on takeoff. The pilot suffered injuries but miraculously escaped death. The C-47s dropped provisions and gliders in the designated area. Three C-47s were seen to hit the ground and explode. On the way out several C-47s were seen in the water, each with various small numbers of dinghies and rescue operations in progress. The second launch of the day was a dive-bombing mission on the railroad and a bridge at Le Guillone and marshaling yards at Argentan. Bombing was done from 3,000 feet with little angle of dive. Hits were good. The action that followed was narrated by Lt. Stroh in an official MIA witness report.

> Green flight was attacked by three ME-109s at 3,000 feet. E.A. came in from six o'clock and below. Evidently they had been higher in the clouds. They dove below and came up shooting. Lt. Gilbert's plane was hit and dove to the ground, where it exploded... As Green Flight approached the bombing area, and with the bombs still attached, tracers were seen coming up, apparently from the ground. On looking back, three enemy craft were seen. "Break" was given immediately and executed. While I was jettisoning my bombs, I noticed a big explosion, which apparently was Lt. Gilbert crashing into the ground. Two other ships of the flight were damaged.

Two other group airplanes and pilots were lost. A fourth pilot was rescued from the Channel. All of the P-47s were configured with bombs. There was no fighter cover. After this, group policy was changed to include additional aircraft with no bombs as cover on all bombing missions.

The third mission was an evening sixteen-plane launch, twelve bombers and four as escort, on the Seine bridge at Oissel, one of the few bridges remaining between Paris and the sea. The bombs were armed with delay fuses which allowed for very low releases—down to fifty feet—with great accuracy. The bridge was put out of action. Of course, the downside of this type of delivery is the higher susceptibility to flak. The next day, the squadron launched a sixteen-plane afternoon fighter sweep of Northern France with no enemy aircraft encountered. There followed two days of rest, due in large part to foul weather.

On D-Day, the 4th Infantry Division succeeded in pushing ashore at Utah Beach and fighting inland to link up with the 82nd Airborne Division, elements of which had parachuted in behind enemy lines the night before in the vicinity of St. Mere Eglise. This successful establishment of an extended beachhead allowed for the organization of assembly areas for follow-on units including the 9th Division. Col. Barth and his advance party had come ashore with the 4th Division on D plus one, thereby giving them several days to get things set up. When Gen. Eddy arrived on June 8th, he found that the situation on the beach was a mess. It was as if no one was in charge of the ship-to-shore operations: unloading men, weapons, ammunition, vehicles, and equipment from the ships to landing craft, and then to the beach. In many cases, individual unit commanders took the initiative to commandeer landing craft and crews to get their men and equipment to the beach. The good news was that the 9th Division assembly area was organized and ready for the main body to arrive on the 10th.

Ships transporting the bulk of the 9th Division arrived twenty-four hours ahead of their scheduled debarkation hour, as planned, to be ready to surge ashore early if required. As the men made their way ashore on the morning of June 10th, they were greeted by an otherworldly scene of controlled chaos. Ships of every size and description were all over the approaches to the beach: some foundered, some at anchor, some with extensive battle damage. The debris of battle was everywhere—smashed vehicles and equipment, discarded personal items, medics moving wounded seaward for evacuation, enemy beach obstacles. The engineers were still at work clearing mines and other impediments to progress. Small craft loaded with troops and equipment streamed inexorably to the beachfront to disembark their loads, then backed off for another trip. Small unit leaders beckoned their charges and tried to keep track of everybody as individual soldiers searched for their units. Not all, maybe most, landing craft crews were unsuccessful in depositing their loads at precisely the correct spot, adding to the turmoil. All this was punctuated by the sounds of battle not far off, and the occasional shellfire from enemy batteries as they slogged ashore.

It took several days to get the entire division ashore and organized, but by the end of June 11th, the Falcons of the 39th Infantry, except for some vehicles and supporting weapons, were completely ashore and ready for combat. Shortly after he landed, the C.O., Col. "Paddy" Flint, was called to Division CP for a conference with Gen. Eddy and Gen. Barton, commander of the 4th Division. Because the 4th was having difficulty moving north up the coastline before the strong enemy fortifications in and around Quineville, Gen. Collins beefed up the 4th Division by attaching the 39th Infantry to it. And so the first combat for the 9th Division on continental Europe since the First World War was accomplished by the 39th Infantry, ironically and similarly to the invasion of North Africa, under the command of a different division.[4] General Eddy noted wryly in his diary, "Looks like the usual disintegration of my division has started."[5]

On June 12th, Col. Flint unleashed his three battalions northward against the Germans in a line abreast attack with 1st Battalion along the beach, 2nd and 3rd Battalions arrayed further inland, all three supported by two batteries of division artillery. Lt. Col. Stumpf's 3rd Battalion was ordered to push the Germans out of the village of Fontenay-sur-Mer slightly ahead and to the west of the other units. His soldiers ran into heavy sniper fire coming from the town, but by the end of the day had eliminated the snipers. The battalion took up positions in the town. Earlier in the day, Stumpf's friend, commander of 1st Battalion, Philip Tinley, had been severely wounded, accentuating the gravity of the situation. Not only had a fellow battalion commander been hit, but Stumpf would be giving up his able executive officer, Maj. Frank Gunn, upon whom he had so much relied, to assume command of 2nd Battalion.

After the first day's battle, as darkness enveloped their blacked-out positions, Stumpf made a final check of each of his four companies' dispositions in and about the town, then reported to Col. Flint's command post for further orders. The plan for 3rd Battalion on the 13th was to attack east of Fontenay-sur-Mer to the marsh, then wheel north, clearing the German resistance south of the Quineville-Montebourg highway in conjunction with the 22nd Infantry of the 4th Division. Returning to his own CP, he met with his staff and company commanders to perfect the assault plan, afterwards falling exhausted to the ground for a few hours of fitful sleep.

The next day neither the 39th Infantry nor the 22nd Infantry were able to make significant progress. The 3rd Battalion of the 39th advanced to the northeast about 1,000 yards before being stopped by a combination of German and friendly artillery fire falling on its forward elements.[6]

On the morning of the 14th, the 3rd Battalion was to continue the attack toward Quineville with the 3rd Battalion 22nd Infantry and be pinched out at the bend of the road south of the town. Stumpf directed the attack to the north with I and M Companies in the lead, then wheeled to the east using heretofore reserve K Company to lead the assault in the new direction. At 1400 a group formation of thirty-six 9th Air Force A-20 bombers laid down a barrage of 500-pound bombs against the German positions in and to the east of the town. Col. Flint realized the opportunity to capitalize on this bombardment by following it as soon as possible with an infantry assault. Meanwhile, the

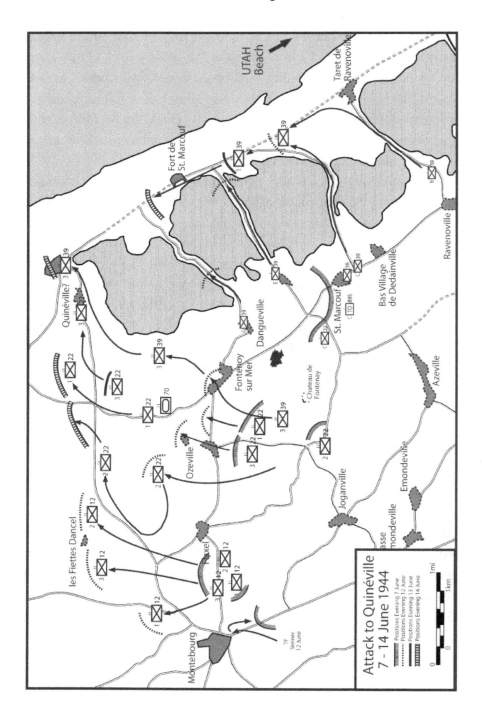

Attack to Quinéville
7 - 14 June 1944

Positions Evening 7 June
Positions Evening 12 June
Positions Evening 13 June
Positions Evening 14 June

22nd Infantry had been ordered to hold their positions until 1700. Third Battalion was in position and ready. Col. Flint did not hesitate to request and receive approval from 4th Division to send it independently against Quineville.

It was a tall order. The German defenders were dug in deeply amongst the masonry buildings, basements, and fortifications in and to the east of the town. They were well equipped with heavy weapons and ammunition, had clear fields of fire and, unbeknownst to the Americans at the time, their commanding general had been ordered to hold the Quineville ridge at all costs. This position was anchored by the town of Quineville adjacent to the beach and extended about 4,000 yards westward along high ground.

The battalion jumped off at 1600 hours with K Company leading the assault. Initial movement to the town was rapid, and the battalion captured sixty-eight German soldiers. On the heights just southwest of Quineville, the leading elements of K Company attacked from the rear a German 88-mm gun in a concrete emplacement. The gun crew set off demolitions, destroying the weapon, then surrendered. About the same time, tanks of the 70th Tank Battalion, operating in support of 3rd Battalion, opened fire at long range at what appeared to be enemy vehicles on the right flank. They received anti-tank fire in return. This was another "blue-on-blue" engagement as the vehicles were in fact tank destroyers of the 1st Battalion, fighting its way up the beach in the vicinity of Fort San Marcouf. Fire ceased when identification was confirmed by flare signals and radio.

As K Company entered the town it received mortar fire, but continued on to the first intersection. Here, 3rd Platoon, which had been leading the attack, turned to the east and advanced toward the beach. A tank ditch cut through their line of advance. As the platoon approached it, they came under heavy mortar, anti-tank gun, and machine gun fire, forcing the lead elements back and driving the rest to cover in ditches and buildings. The platoon leader directed a firing line to be built up, but this was not effective, as the enemy was firing from prepared concrete emplacements with clear fields of fire.

Meanwhile, the 1st Platoon pushed into the northeast part of the town with the intent of clearing out resistance and proceeding on to the beach. K Company's weapons platoon emplaced 60-mm mortars to the south of town. Col. Stumpf rushed up eight machine guns and one section of heavy machine guns from M Company (heavy weapons) through heavy fire to join the 1st Platoon. Together they secured the built-up area in the northeast of town, but were forced to take cover after receiving heavy casualties when they attempted to advance across relatively exposed positions toward the beach fortifications. Simultaneously, 2nd Platoon succeeded in clearing out the western part of the town with little opposition other than mortar fire. The enemy's strength was concentrated on protecting the beach fortifications.

During this action Stumpf halted his other two rifle companies, I and L, under the last cover before the town, about 400 yards southwest. He alerted them to take up the attack on either flank of K Company on order, although there was little room for their deployment except in the open and across wire entanglements that were strung across the flanks of their line of advance. Stumpf had placed M Company heavy mortars to cover the original mission of the battalion before the independent assault on Quineville, positions that were now out of accurate range of the town itself. Those elements were in the process of moving forward over difficult terrain and mined roads. During this movement, communications with the mortar elements went out. About this time Stumpf learned that the leaders of K Company's 1st and 3rd Platoons were casualties.

To cover the reorganization of K Company and the approach of supporting tanks, as well as to soften up the enemy fortifications, Stumpf requested artillery on the enemy positions to be followed by a covering smoke barrage. The plan was for K Company to assault the fortifications under the cover of smoke, supported by the 70th Tank Battalion. Radio communications were difficult but the requested fire was relayed through the 39th Infantry Cannon Company radio and delivered by Ninth Division Artillery. The fire was generally ineffective against the concrete emplacements, but did result in a temporary cessation of mortar fire. Smoke was not available. What happened next is described in the 39th Infantry After Action report.

Lt Col Stumpf was calling for artillery, tanks, anything he could get. Artillery fired once along the beach, but higher hqs denied using it any further. The Col then called for the tanks. Lt. Schneider came down with two tanks, turned the corner at the main cross road, got mortar fire, backed out and returned down the trail. (Col Stumpf was thoroughly disgusted with the way the tanks acted. In fact all the officers I talked to laughed when tanks were mentioned, all of them insisting that the tanks were of no use whatsoever, that they turned and ran at the first sign of opposition.) It had been hoped to use the tanks in the town to shoot up some of the houses where the MGs were emplaced. Someone *insisted* (at the point of a gun, some of the officers say) that Schneider return to aid K Co in clearing out the town. Schneider then returned, but with no more success than the 1st time, according to K Co officers.

Stumpf again urgently requested smoke from any available 4th or 9th Division artillery or mortar units. Shortly afterward one round of 81-mm mortar white phosphorous, used for artillery ranging, struck his battalion command post, and the mortars suspended fire.

Things were not looking good. Apparently, smoke would not be available before dark. The tanks were not able to give any meaningful support. K Company, after a difficult assault and hours of street fighting, was hunkered down in the town after sustaining heavy casualties. More artillery on the town might do as much harm as good. Stumpf was still collecting his wits after surviving the various mortar barrages on his CP. He was down to his last option to take the town and free K Company from their precarious positions: launch an infantry assault with his other two rifle companies.

He ordered L and I Companies to attack on either flank of K Company into the fortifications, supported by a platoon of heavy machine guns from M Company. L Company led the assault on the left, with K Company moving abreast of L Company as the lead elements came up. As L Company approached the town drawing heavy mortar fire, a heavy concentration of smoke from 4th Division artillery fell squarely on the enemy fortifications. Stumpf ordered K Company to attack immediately to take advantage of the smoke. As the 1st and 3rd Platoons reached the fortifications, led by a rifle squad under SSGT Bruce Perry, Jr., all enemy positions within the Quineville area surrendered. It was 2130, just prior to sunset.

The battalion captured over 100 additional German soldiers. But K Company alone suffered five killed and twenty-eight wounded. With the guns of Quineville and its surrounding fortifications silenced, movement of American supply tonnage across Utah Beach nearly tripled in efficiency, from 1,500 tons to 4,000 tons per day, combined with increased efficiency moving troops and vehicles across. These actions were rapidly reinforcing the Allied salient, setting the stage for the breakout to the west and capture of Cherbourg.[7]

The 362nd fighter group got back to it on the 11th on a group dive-bombing mission on targets of opportunity on the Cherbourg peninsula; each squadron providing twelve bombers with two 500-pounders, and four cover airplanes. Good results were scored against road and railroad targets. The weather was marginal and nine airplanes initially were reported as missing, although most eventually made it back.

On the 12th, the group flew two more dive-bombing missions, the second of which was in close proximity to American troops, a first for the group. All squadron configurations were similar to the previous missions. Lt. Stroh reflected on the events of the past week in a letter to his mother and sister dated June 11, 1944.

Well, this has been a very memorable week. Guess it will long live in the memory of everybody for many years. Kinda had a feeling the big event would take place this week—maybe just watching Dad's actions. I am a little disappointed... that we didn't get off the ground until late in the evening of D-Day.

We have been on about six missions over the beachhead so far and it is a wonderful sight. I can see now what the higher headquarters have been doing for the past year or so. Things are really organized. Dad is over there now I guess. He can't complain about air cover—never seen so many planes over such a small area in my life—just a continuous umbrella.

You might see my name in the paper one of these days. One of the boys in my flight was a little short of gas today so we went into one of the emergency landing strips on the beach. We were the first Americans to land on that side of the front. A war correspondent took our names and addresses....Even if I don't get any further I can say I've been in France.

I have been keeping up with Dad's movements since we get wireless reports back about every hour. So now I won't need a letter from him to keep up with him.

APO 141, England
June 12, 1944
Dear Dad,

So after the long awaited day, we finally did it... So what do you think of the air support. Is it better than the other two campaigns?

Had a nice experience the other day. We had been flying up and down the roads strafing anything we saw when my wingman said he was low on gas. So I started to look for one of those emergency landing strips over there. I was just about to sit down right about where you were, but the strip there isn't very long and I was afraid one of us would overshoot and wreck a good plane. I went down to a British strip and gassed up. I found out I was the first American plane to land in that field and the crews wrote all over my plane.

Guess you are mighty busy now. I keep up with the outfit every day when the ALO [air liaison officer] gets in his reports—at least I'll know where to give extra support if you ever call for it.

The pilots clearly had been briefed on the availability of these emergency strips in the event they could not make it back across the Channel. It appears that in this case, the young wingman got a little carried away with the exciting armed reconnaissance and lost track of his fuel situation. As the flight leader, Lt. Stroh made the decision to get him on the ground quickly, and then land himself so that his wingman would not have to make it back to England solo, a dangerous prospect if he got jumped all alone.

The United Press war correspondent who Stroh mentioned in his letters to his family, Richard D. McMillan, did write a somewhat embellished story that appeared in newspapers back home on June 15th. The article mentions Stroh and his wingman by name and how they had spotted RAF Spitfires on the strip. Their British brethren fueled them up quickly and sent them on their way.

14

———— ◆ ————

The Cherbourg Campaign

T he port city of Cherbourg lies at the northern end of the Cotentin Peninsula, almost due south across the English Channel from the port of Southampton and roughly twenty-five miles northwest of Utah Beach. As such, it was of significant strategic importance to the invasion because of the need to open a large, deep-water, protected port to funnel essential men, equipment, and supplies to the growing salient. It was close to England and close to the expanding front. Cherbourg became *objective one* after the beach-head became relatively secure, and the Germans knew it. The following paragraphs describe the movements and battles of the 9th Division as a whole as well as its subordinate units, with emphasis on the 39th Infantry.[1]

On June 14th, the 9th Division, less the 39th Infantry, which was busy at Quineville, began cutting the Cotentin Peninsula from the vicinity of Utah Beach in the east to the towns of Barneville-sur-Mer and Port Bail in the west, a distance of about twenty-three miles. The 47th and 60th Infantry attacked westward beginning at 1000 between the 82nd Airborne Division to the south and the 90th Division to the north. This drive was against the slowly retreating German 91st Division, which was fighting a delaying action to buy time for possible major reinforcements and a counterattack. The initial objective was the Douvre River, about halfway across the Peninsula. Resistance in the north of the front was somewhat stronger than in the south, so the moving front became echeloned to the right as the southerly units covered more ground.

The next day, the 9th Division welcomed back the 39th Infantry, minus 3rd Battalion, which remained with the 4th Division for the rest of the day. Gen. Collins decided to throw the entire VII Corps forward to the Douvre as rapidly as possible to prevent the enemy from establishing an organized defense along the river. Both the 47th and the 60th made intermediate objectives on June 15th with the 39th in reserve. On the 16th, enemy resistance stiffened as the Americans closed on the river. The 39th swung around to the right to support elements of the 90th Division and cover the right flank. The 2nd/60th supported by the 746th tank battalion raced ahead and began crossing the river over a series of three small bridges. The third bridge was out, so the tanks had to turn back. Direct enemy artillery fire began to rain in on the three rifle companies now dug in at bridgeheads. It was not until after dark that reinforcements caught up to relieve the battered companies. By the end of the day, the 9th Division had broken all of the enemy resistance in its sector of the front all the way to the Douvre and set up what looked to be the enemy's rapid withdrawal westward to the sea. The retreating German 91st Division by this time had effectively ceased to exist as an organized fighting unit.

Throughout June 17th, with the 90th Division to the north and the 82nd Airborne Division to the south, all three 9th Division regiments continued the rapid advance southwest to the sea in a race to keep the German 77th Division bottled up on the peninsula. That evening Gen. Stroh took a moment to write this letter to Imogene.

Will take advantage of a few quiet moments this evening to get off a few brief lines to you. Was up all last night, and today has been busy, so that the old hole in the ground will be very welcome tonight...

We made the third change in command post location in four days, so you can judge that we have been moving. We are now in one of the many apple orchards with which this country abounds, surrounded by the thick, thorny hedges, and carpeted with high, green timothy grass, daisies and clover. Several fat cows are peacefully grazing in the next field, giving scant indication that this area was fought over yesterday. In fact, there are many evidences of German occupation—cleverly constructed foxholes with covers of sticks, earth and grass, and much abandoned equipment of all sorts. It will take months to clean up all the junk. Some of the German individual equipment, carried by each soldier, is very clever and unique. For instance, each man carries an orange plastic box, about the size and shape of a shoe polish box, in which he carries his daily 30 gram ration of fresh butter.

Bob's regiment has made the headlines, and he personally has been responsible for most of the glory. One troublesome little village [Quineville] was holding out, despite the best efforts of a regiment from another division to capture it. Bob's battalion was sent in after a heavy bombardment from the air which I witnessed from a grandstand seat. He captured the place, was driven out by intense mortar fire, but came back within an hour to take it the second time, and hold it. It was one of the most noteworthy acts of the campaign to date, and he will no doubt get adequate recognition. We have a flock of high power newspapermen living with us at the moment, who, I hope, at long last, will go to town on stories of this kind...

It is almost too dark to see, and with Jerry over every night, lights are distinctly unpopular. So I will have to stop. Maybe the war will be over by the time I write again. Hope so.

On the morning of June 18th, the 47th Infantry fought their way to the Atlantic Coast towns of Port Bail and Neuville-Beaumont, followed shortly thereafter by the 60th Infantry capturing the port of Barneville-sur-Mer about three miles to the north. This completed the cutting of the Cotentin Peninsula, effectively ending the opportunity of any remaining German forces to retreat from Cherbourg. The American Army was now established in strength along the line from Quineville on the English Channel southwest across the peninsula to the Atlantic Ocean. The next major objective was Cherbourg itself, twenty or so miles to the north.

This spectacular drive by the 9th Division was materially aided by the fighter-bomber boys, practicing close air support techniques that were still relatively new. In one instance during intense ground combat in the vicinity of St. Jacques-de-Nehou, the commanding general of the German 77th Division was killed by an attacking P-47. The 362nd Fighter Group was instrumentally involved. On June 13th, the group flew two armed reconnaissance missions along the highway south of Argentan with good results, especially by strafing. The 378th lost two pilots that day, Lt. Skeen, who bellied in deep in enemy territory, and Lt. Bentley, who was blown up by his own bomb. Of late, the squadron had been using very low altitude delivery tactics with delay fuses which allowed the delivery aircraft to escape from its bomb blast. This day, however, they were using instantaneous fuses.

On the 14th, the group flew four more interdiction missions to targets in northwestern France, some on the Cotentin Peninsula, as the VII Corps prepared to kick off its drive to the sea. On the 16th, there were two C-47 escort missions to and from the expanding beachhead area. On the 17th, during the thick of the fighting on the peninsula, all three squadrons were gone all day, flying a series of support missions out of a remote field in France, from early in the morning until nearly midnight. Four pilots of the Group were lost that day, although two survived, evaded, and made it back. Lt. Frank Glover of the 378th took flak in his right wing, which detonated his fragmentary bomb. He bailed out and his plane exploded in the air. The day's activities were noted in a letter from Lt. Stroh to his mother and sister dated June 18th.

> The big event is old news now—just another
> mission to be flown. Guess it is still mighty hard
> for the boys on the ground over there though. Been
> keeping up with Dad's movements and so far his outfit
> is winning the war over there. If they don't make the
> headlines after a few days I will be mighty surprised.
> Felt pretty proud yesterday when we went over and
> gave the outfit direct support—really put my heart and
> soul in the work we had to do.
>
> Yesterday we went to a landing strip in France
> and operated out of it all day. We were next to an
> ex-German strong point—one that they apparently
> abandoned in great haste. We collected all kinds of
> souvenirs—so many that we couldn't carry them back.
> The place was apparently a cavalry unit because
> there were about 100 fine looking horses around. One

Frenchman is selling each horse and saddle for 20 francs or about 40 cents. Sure hope we move across soon so I can get one of those horses.

Guess you have been reading in the paper about the new "secret weapon" the Jerry is sending over. They are going right over our field day and night. They sure are funny things to watch. Everybody takes a few pot shots at them, but few hits are made. The first night they came over we stayed up all night watching the tracers go through the air. It was a wonderful show...

Had a nice letter from Dad the other day written the night before he went across. He seems very confident and that is half the battle. Personally I don't see how they can lose with all the stuff they have on the beach.

How do you like the news of the B-29's bombing Japan? That's pretty good I'm thinking. The way the boys are doing over there in that theater there won't be anything for us to do when we get there. I sure would like to get in on some of that—drop a few bombs right in all those paper houses.

Unaccustomed to accolades in the press though they were, the soldiers of the 9th Division were elated to finally see mention of their unit in the papers regarding their recent military successes; a real morale builder. Articles were published in the *New York Times, New York Post, Time* magazine, *Washington Star,* and the *Chicago Daily News,* and covered by the Associated Press, all praising the rapidly advancing 9th Division in their drive to the sea.[2]

Several counterattacks were launched against the 60th Infantry's zone by the German 77th Division on June 18th in their desperate attempt to escape being trapped on the peninsula. The first was stopped by a withering artillery barrage by regiment and division batteries against the motorized German column on the Bricquebec-Barneville road. Virtually all the vehicles in the column were destroyed or rendered inoperable. The survivors fled on foot in disarray, but later reorganized and attempted another breakthrough to the south. This attack was launched late that night and was halted by infantry units closely guarding and denying all road intersections. A third attack of regimental strength supported by armor was a thrust across a small bridgehead of the Seye River. It was eventually contained by elements of the 39th Infantry and 60th Infantry, supported by division artillery. Thus, by June 19th, the containment of the now greatly weakened German 77th Division was successful and the 9th Division turned north toward Cherbourg. The press kept pouring it on for the 9th Division.[3]

The division's drive to the north was arrayed in regiments abreast proceeding up the western side of the peninsula. The 60th Infantry was on the left, closest to the coast, the 47th in the center, and the 39th, with the 4th Cavalry attached, on the right in contact with the 79th Infantry Division. Rounding out the VII Corps further to the east was the 4th Infantry Division, which had been holding the eastern edge of the Quineville Ridge. Advance northward by the 9th and 79th Divisions was rapid, as the exhausted remnants of two German divisions were barely executing delaying actions while they withdrew to fortress Cherbourg. But by the end of the day, as the Americans drew within range of the outer line of the main Cherbourg defenses, resistance increased dramatically, anchored by a ring of hardened emplacements on high ground.

On June 20th, 9th Division plans to attack further northeast with the 47th Infantry and 39th Infantry were thwarted by heavy concentrations of German direct and indirect artillery fire. On the left flank, the 60th Infantry was to drive northward to the west of Cherbourg

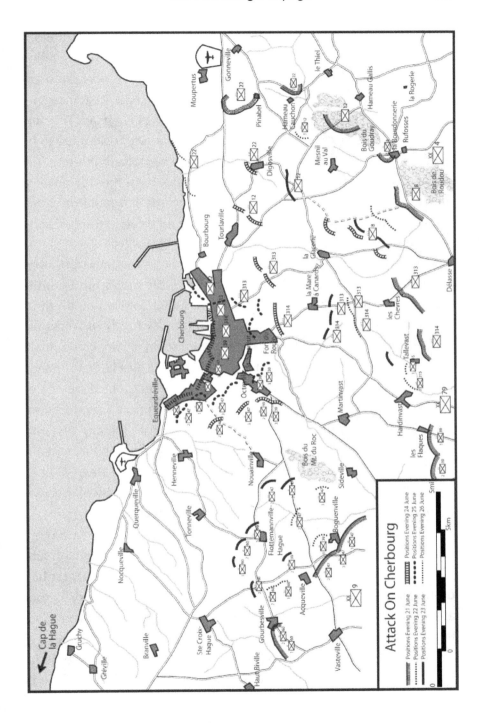

Attack On Cherbourg

Positions Evening 21 June
Positions Evening 22 June
Positions Evening 23 June
Positions Evening 24 June
Positions Evening 25 June
Positions Evening 26 June

and seal off the Cap de la Hague peninsula, but two of its battalions were diverted to assist the 47th Infantry. The remaining 3rd Battalion continued north. By the end of the day, the 9th Division's rapid advances of the past week had come to a screeching halt. Road marches were over for the time being, and intense fighting lay ahead. The next day was devoted to patrolling, consolidating, and repositioning to be ready to execute the Corps' coordinated plan to attack the city. The 39th Infantry assumed the division right flank from the 4th Cavalry, which in turn moved to the west to assume the left flank responsibilities from the 60th Infantry, thus allowing all three of the division's infantry regiments to be available for the final assaults.

On June 21st, while the 9th and 79th Divisions held positions for the most part, the 4th Division, on the east, caught up with the rest of the Corps' advance. By that night, Gen. Collins had all three of his infantry divisions drawn up tight and ready for the final assault on Cherbourg. The German garrison commander, Generalleutnant Karl-Wilhelm von Schlieben, had been ordered by Hitler to defend Cherbourg to the death. Von Schlieben had reorganized his forces into four regimental-size groups. They stood behind an array of concrete fortifications beginning four to six miles from the city on commanding ground with observation of all approaches. The Americans faced man-made and natural tank obstacles including steep-banked stream beds. Within the fortifications was a complex array of firepower including dual purpose artillery batteries as well as heavy guns.

The urgency of Cherbourg's capture had been given even more emphasis because of a major disruption to the movement of supplies across the beaches. A major storm from June 19th to 21st had destroyed the recently completed and functioning Mulberry harbor at Omaha Beach, making the facilities at Cherbourg an even more important strategic objective.

The June 22nd assault was to be preceded by a massive aerial bombardment, with British tactical bombers, eleven groups of the IX

Bomber Command, and twelve P-47 groups, one of which was the 362nd. The primary objective of the bombing was the demoralization of the defending troops, although each flight had specific target assignments. The infantry assault was immediately to follow the medium bombers, who were to lay down a rolling barrage, making their runs parallel to the front from west to east. The bombardment was preceded on June 21st with a multilingual propaganda broadcast where Gen. Collins explained the hopelessness of the enemy position and demanded the garrison's surrender. The demand received no response from Gen. Schlieben.

The bombing began at 12:40 P.M. Prisoners later reported the effectiveness of the barrages in weakening morale. Twenty-four of the tactical airplanes were knocked down by flak, including three from the 378th Fighter Squadron (one pilot was recovered). The rolling bombing in front of the attacking troops was followed by artillery barrages, the 9th Division Artillery being particularly effective. The infantry units jumped off immediately following the artillery. The action is described in Joseph B. Mittelman's *Eight Stars to Victory.*

> The 47th jumped off ...on Sideville. Stubborn opposition greeted the Raiders, for the enemy had possession of the high ground and strongpoints. It was necessary to reduce these prepared positions one-by-one; and the day's battles followed a pattern: meeting strongpoint, reducing by artillery and tank-destroyer fire, assault, and then on to the next strongpoint. Bougainville was captured in this manner. It was here that General Stroh showed his mettle; he was all over the area, directing fire and spreading encouragement.
>
> Over to the left the enemy had excellent observation on the 60th, and his artillery was having a field day... Despite two counterattacks and

the obstacles of terrain and shelling, the regiment
advanced as planned.[4]

By the end of the day, the 60th Infantry had captured the town of
Acqueville and advanced to just shy of Flottemanville. The 47th advanced to just west of Bois du Mont du Roc. During these advances,
the 39th Infantry fought "a battle within a battle," cleaning out pockets of resistance bypassed by the other regiments.

The fighting on June 23rd remained heavy, as all three regiments
continued to advance on the city, smashing through the outer ring
of enemy defenses. The 39th continued to clear fortified positions
bypassed by the 47th and moved into positions just southwest of
Octeville less than two miles from the seaport section of Cherbourg.
The 47th completed the reduction of enemy defenses on Hill 171 and
captured 400 prisoners. The 60th followed air and artillery bombardment in the Flottemanville area and occupied the town by evening.
The VII Corps' noose was tightening around Cherbourg and the inevi-
tability of its capture was apparent to both sides.

The 39th and 47th continued their attacks along the ridge line
leading into Cherbourg through Octeville on June 24th and overran
three defended Luftwaffe installations in their way. The 60th Infantry
meanwhile cleared and held the northern flank. After fighting their
way through Octeville, by evening the 2nd and 3rd Battalions of the
39th had established positions just north of the town and were halted
by Corps direction, while the 79th Division on their right fought to
catch up. The 47th turned to the north and advanced toward the old
fort of Equeurdreville, the coastal batteries to the north, and Redoubte
de Fouches. Attacks on those positions were postponed. Not unlike
the latter stages of the Bizerte campaign, the 9th Division had its
advance halted by Corps headquarters in order to allow its flanking divisions to catch up. Just prior to midnight, the 9th's next day's
field order, typically written by Gen. Stroh, was promulgated and

included this line, "This Division will attack on 25 June and capture CHERBOURG."[5]

The 47th Infantry claimed the honors of being the first to enter the city of Cherbourg proper. They started the day with the 2nd Battalion taking the fort at Equeurdreville, before which they had halted the night before. After that engagement, two companies pressed forward into Cherbourg and one platoon made it all the way to the beach before being recalled. Simultaneously the 3rd Battalion reduced the defenses at Redoubte de Tourches after a heavy artillery barrage.

On the right, the 39th Infantry jumped off at 1000 toward the city, although 3rd Battalion continued house-to-house fighting in Octeville against stubborn resistance where the desperate enemy employed anti-aircraft guns, light artillery, snipers, and small arms. The infantry-men cleared that up by early afternoon and continued forward, taking up positions just outside the city abreast of 2nd Battalion. Over the course of the day, the 9th Division took over 1,000 German prisoners.

The three divisions of VII Corps continued to constrict the noose on June 26th with the 9th Division advancing across the entire western hemisphere of the front. The 60th Infantry still commanded the left flank to oppose any attempt of the enemy to slip out of Cherbourg and onto the Cap de la Hague, where there was still a considerable German garrison. In the middle of the 9th's sector, the 47th Infantry advanced steadily through the streets, reducing a bevy of enemy holdouts who utilized an array of small arms and sniper fire. On the right, the 2nd and 3rd Battalions of the 39th Infantry captured the subterranean fortifications at St. Sauveur in the center of the rim of fortifications. There they forced the surrender of 842 German prisoners including Gen. von Schlieben and Admiral Hennecke, the naval commander of Normandy. The coup de grâce was firing tank destroyer rounds directly into one of the tunnel entrances to the fortress. Von Schlieben refused to sign a general surrender, claiming he did not have adequate communications to inform his remaining troops, so the 39th Infantry continued their advance. They fought their way northward all the way to the harbor, capturing another 400 prisoners who had been holed up in City Hall. With the forced surrender of von Schlieben's deputy to the 47th Infantry the following day, all organized resistance in Cherbourg ceased.

During the Cherbourg fighting, VII Corps commander, Gen. "Lightning Joe" Collins, was interviewed by Don Whitehead of *The Saturday Evening Post*. The ensuing article highlighted the general's nickname and thrust Collins into the limelight from which he never retreated. In the article, among many salient remarks, Collins expounded on the role of the infantry battalion commander.

> Battalion commanders have the toughest job of any officers in the Army. They must carry the ball. No matter how well planned an operation is, it still must be carried out in the field. The battalion commander is the key man in the infantry. These fellows win the D.S.C. two or three times a week.

The fighting around Cherbourg was not over. The 60th Infantry and 4th Cavalry Group had succeeded sealing off Cap de la Hague to the west, where intelligence reported that some 3,000 German troops were still entrenched. On June 28, the 4th Division took over the occupation and defense of Cherbourg, relieving the 9th Division to sweep the remaining German defenders from the cape. The division sent out patrols to reconnoiter the ground to the northwest on June 27th and 28th. They attacked in force on the 29th with the 47th Infantry on the right advancing up the coast, the 60th on either side of the main highway down the center, and the 4th Cavalry along the coast on the left. The 39th Infantry was in reserve. The division was opposed by German artillery batteries as they progressed up the cape, capturing strong points along the way and taking hundreds of prisoners. By the end of June 30th, the German commander had been captured, and organized resistance ceased. However, one more engagement remained: the capture of the German garrison at Auderville on the northwest tip of the cape. This task fell to Lt. Col. Stumpf's 3rd Battalion of the 39th Infantry.

July 1st marked the end of the Cotentin Peninsula campaign. The Falcon 3rd Battalion had moved up during the night previous to launch a daring early morning attack against Auderville. Supported by Company A of the 899th T.D.'s, Troop C of the 4th Cavalry, and fully motorized, the battalion passed through the 60th infantry and into unknown country. It was dark and dangerous to the front and the terrain was strange.

At midnight the group reached... just beyond Joburg, and the Falcons dismounted. It was a foot march now, with armored support from the vehicles of Troop C close by. The troopers reached the edge of Auderville before the foot soldiers, captured several prisoners, interrogated pro-Allied civilians and obtained the location of enemy positions.

Coming in from the north at 4 A.M., the 3rd Battalion surprised the town completely and had captured it one hour later... By 10 A.M. the 3rd had captured 1,000 prisoners (3,000 that day), two 10 inch railway guns, four 155mm howitzers, four 88mm self-propelled guns, two 47mm guns and ten Flak guns! In addition, the victorious 3rd reported the peninsula was cleared of the enemy "as far north as Auderville and west [from] there to the coast."[6]

Later on July 2nd, the 9th Division, having captured 6,000 prisoners, double the number that intelligence estimated as being on the cape, reported to Corps that the peninsula was secured and all operations ceased; mission accomplished. During the Cotentin campaign, the 9th Division captured 18,490 prisoners, out of the VII Corps total of 39,000, in addition to vast quantities of weapons, supplies, and vehicles. Losses to the division were 390 killed and 1,851 wounded. Thirty-ninth Infantry casualties for its first three weeks in action on the continent were seventy-nine killed and 329 wounded, about 14 percent. Seven soldiers were put in for the Distinguished Service Cross, seventy-five for the Silver Star, and seventy-one for the Bronze Star. Accolades in the press, and elsewhere, continued to proliferate, including articles in the *Boston Globe, San Francisco Examiner*, and *Newsweek,* as well syndicated reporter Ernie Pyle.[7]

Captain Harry R. Stroh, June 22, 1944:

> Congratulations are well in order I guess. I always knew that your outfit is the best in the whole Army. Some people I know thought you had shot your wad in Africa and Sicily, but the last few days have changed their tune. I go around all the time now with my chest way out. You have done a mighty fine job and I know everybody is mighty proud of you.

Imogene Stroh Stumpf, June 20, 1944:

> You can't complain about not hitting the headlines now. Mother will send you several clippings. Why, you're even referred to as the *crack* Ninth division. All they say about the preparation and training given the men months before, we know can be accredited to you. I just know it has been all your foresight and that just

makes us all the more proud of the great success of the division. I don't have to say keep it up because that will go on. You're making yourself and the division one of the most famous in the greatest war of all times.

Back at the 362nd Fighter Group, newly promoted Captain Stroh had been following the movement of his father's division with great pride and excitement. However, after his exciting missions of June 17th, he was essentially out of supporting the intensive ground campaign, due in large part to the same storm that had laid waste to the Mulberry harbor. On June 18th and 20th, he flew a total of four "beach patrol" missions, basically hunting German aircraft over the expanding Allied beachhead, but those flights were uneventful. On the 22nd, he flew a dive-bombing mission south of Cherbourg that was not recorded in his flight log, but after which he submitted an official report.

I was flying Yelo Leader, at 8,000 feet, top cover for Right-Field Blue section over Dreux. My second element had aborted and I had but two ships left. I was watching a contrail coming towards me from the west at about 15,000 feet. I turned into the contrail and then flying instinct warned me to look behind me. I skidded around and saw the ME 109. I immediately called Right-Field Blue Leader and broke down and to the left. Just as I broke I caught a burst from the 109. I called Blue Leader and told him I was going to the Beach Head with Yelo two. On the way to the Beach Head Blue three and four joined me and gave me cover. I landed at B-5. Damage—left aileron control cable cut, and left gun ammunition bay hit, rudder and elevator damaged. Engine ran rough probably due to the fact

that I landed with no oil pressure as it was all over me.
I came back on a British Ensign landing at Northolt.
Here Captain Cline picked me up [in the UC-78] and
bought me back to the base.

Stroh flew a dive-bombing mission on the 24th and a B-26 bomber escort on the 25th. He related some of his recent excitement to his father in a letter dated June 26th.

Been getting quite a few compliments the past few
days from all the boys and am feeling mighty proud.
The War Department General order on your Legion of
Merit came into the orderly room and everybody read
the citation. By the phrasing of the citation I don't see
why you didn't get the DSM at least.

Spent a few days in France last week due to a
forced landing on one of the strips. I tried to get a lift
up to the frontlines to pay you a little visit, but nobody
would give me a lift. I did get pretty close to the lines
and saw a little of the action. I really have to hand
it to the doughboys—they can take it and then still
dish it out. I realize now what a soft life I am leading
compared to them.

The plane I had the forced landing in didn't
seem to be very lucky for me. About the first of last
week I was jumped by a 109 and had my rudder
and propellor damaged. Then three days later I was
jumped again and the ship was so badly damaged I
couldn't fly it home. It is times like that when I'm
glad we had some landing strips over there. I did
get a shot at the two planes, but didn't knock either
one down. That sure made me mad. I got out of both

without a scratch, but those 109's don't look too
inviting from the front end.

On June 27th, Capt. Stroh was Blue leader on a squadron dive-
bombing mission near Verneuil, France, when his four-ship flight was
bounced by twenty-plus FW-190s from two o'clock at 5,000 feet. He
described the ensuing air combat in a letter to his mother and sister
dated July 2nd:

Had my big chance to become an ace the other
day. We were going out on dive-bombing and just
before reaching the target, my flight was jumped by
20 enemy planes. There was nothing to do but drop
our bombs and start fighting. I must have used all
my ammunition nearly but didn't knock any planes
down. I damaged several of them but didn't knock
them down. I had a good wingman that day because
he sure kept those Jerries off my tail during the
whole engagement—that was his first mission too—he
was soaking wet when we got back—don't blame him
though —pretty rough on a new man. There were so
many Jerries around you couldn't concentrate on any
one plane—sure would have liked to have gotten a few
of those boys.

So the Stroh family is famous, eh! Don't know
whether Dad's name has been mentioned in any of the
news reports but that outfit will go down in history
and his name will always be connected with it. I didn't
know my landing on the other side would raise so
much publicity as it did—can't imagine it being given
over the radio and everything. As a matter of fact I
didn't have to land—my wingman was the person short

of gas and I just went in with him so that he wouldn't
have to go home by himself. That boy was shot down
last week so he isn't here to share that little clipping
you sent. He was a good boy—hated to see him get it.

It is likely that the mission on June 27th is the one for which Capt.
Stroh was later awarded the Distinguished Flying Cross, although his
medal citation reads "for extraordinary achievement in aerial flight
against the enemy... on 21 June 1944." According to his flight log,
378th Fighter Squadron mission reports, and the Group history, Stroh
did not fly a combat mission on June 21st, nor did the descriptions of
the missions that were flown on that date resemble the circumstances
described in the citation, or in Stroh's letters to his family.

Capt. Stroh and the squadron mission report both state that his
"flight" was jumped by twenty enemy fighters: four P-47s versus
twenty FW-190s, with the 190s having positional and energy advantage at the onset. (The mission report actually states, "Blue flight was
bounced by 20 *plus* FW-190's.") At low altitude and forced to jettison
their bombs, the P-47 pilots fought for their lives. It was a melee, a
"fur ball." It was impossible for the vastly outnumbered Americans
to saddle in on any one bandit without they themselves becoming
predictable targets for the bad guys. They could make only slashing attacks using short gun bursts, then immediately turn away. In
the pandemonium, it is remarkable that Stroh was able to get hits
on "several" of them, but there were no opportunities to "follow the
kills" and document them with gun camera film. Nor were his wing-
men in any position to verify kills. The FW-190 was quite vulnerable
to fifty-caliber machine gun fire. The P-47s' converging gunfire was
concentrated at the point of impact for a target in range. So if a target
took any hits from a P-47's eight .50 cals, it took a lot of hits. Stroh's
guns were working fine, as he used up nearly all his ammunition.

All things considered, it is feasible, even likely, that Capt. Stroh had multiple kills that day. But the rules for kill claims were very specific and strictly enforced; the actual physical destruction of the aircraft or the bailout of the pilot had to be visually witnessed or documented by gun camera film. And Capt. Stroh, by his very nature and code of honor, would never have "pushed" a claim. Likewise, it was so in character of him to credit his rookie wingman in the day's work. In a letter to his father, he remarked wryly that "they are the ones that withdrew, even outnumbering us 5 to 1." His DFC citation further reads:

> With complete disregard of the dangers involved in attacking the superior numbers of hostile planes, he fearlessly engaged the enemy and repeatedly pressed home his attacks in the face of great odds. His outstanding airmanship was in large measure responsible for the dispersal of the enemy formation and the protection of his squadron.

The squadron's last mission of June was on the 30th, an armed recce in the vicinity of Orleans where railroad tracks and vehicles of opportunity were bombed and strafed. It had been a costly month for the 362nd Fighter Group; twenty-six pilots were reported MIA, of which seven eventually returned to the group. Some of the non-operational highlights of the month included the appearance over their airfield of German V-1 "buzz bombs" on the way to targets mostly in and around London. A welcome diversion was the abundance of fresh strawberries and cherries coming into season. The former could be had for two shillings a pound and the latter for one.

Capt. Stroh, along with most of his 378th Squadron mates, had quite an active month in terms of missions and flight hours. His totals are difficult to calculate exactly because his multi-mission day of June 17th was not entered into his log book. His total flight time is estimated to be sixty hours on thirty-one flights, and twenty-seven combat missions, all of which were in the P-47. As with the group, the June squadron price tag was high. The 378th lost ten pilots out of about thirty, although two of them eventually made it back.

After the hectic weeks of the Cherbourg campaign, the 9th Division stopped moving for a few days, and mail from home began to catch up. Gen. Stroh's letters from Imogene gave him an idea of what the campaign had looked like from the home front.

June 4, 1944

It seems strange not to have word from any of you but we'll be patient and someday, maybe, know the reason why. Bob's of the 11th of May was the most recent of all of you.

Last evening... over the radio came the message that Eisenhower had landed in France. The first thing I could think of was to be home with Mother, but about 45 mins. later the announcer said it was an error. Can you beat it. That's the kind of thing that gets the old endocrine gland upsetting the digestive tract. The commentators have an awful time now giving any news. It is too calm to be natural and I'm awfully suspicious about you all.

Had my accepted credits awaiting me when I arrived this morning. As far as I can see, G. W. has given me credit in full for everything I took at Lindenwood.

June 11, 1944

We read that the 9th Air Force is in France, and only the 1st, 4th, and 29th Div. were in. So little is told that we honestly don't know a thing. We're just hoping that you got in the first fling. Gen. Bradley's army went in first so we're hoping that means the 9th, also.

Although it's hard just to sit and hope we are so proud of you and glad the three of you are in it together. Also, now that the dreaded invasion has begun, we feel that there is an ending when you'll be coming home. It was awful not seeing any ending of the mess because there hadn't been a beginning.

June 17, 1944

We don't know one thing about the division and we wonder so about you both. I have the feeling you're not out of England yet, for some reason.

I know Bob enjoyed that bottle of Scotch if you were able to give it to him. It is always so nice for you to tell me about things Bob does. He doesn't write in detail or much about his accomplishments so what you tell I pass on to his family.

P.S. Oh Pappy, we just heard that you're in, at least Bob's is in because they mentioned the hat insignia or whatever. Mother just called it down the stairs after hearing it on the radio. Boy, oh boy, oh boy! It's so exciting. I'll turn on the short wave and see what London has to say. As of now you're helping the 82nd going West on the Cherbourg peninsula. Yeah, Army!

June 20, 1944

...yesterday your first mail started to dribble in. I received yours of June 3rd and Bob's of the 5th. From these we knew for the first time that you weren't in the first landing. Now we'll wonder when you did land. We can tell a little because things started happening over there on the 17th. Keep your head down, Pappy.

June 25, 1944

General Handy has come back telling what wonderful things he's heard about your work. Of course, he doesn't have to tell us because we already know, but thought you'd be interested.

We haven't heard from you or Bob since you left England, but Harry's latest of the 11th said he gets hourly reports of your position and he's taking good care of you.

You know this wondering about you all is sort of hard on the stomach activities at this address. Mother never says anything and I don't either because we just kid and are as happy as we can be, but if she feels like I feel and I know she does—I'll be glad when we can all sit around the same table again.

The "hat insignia or whatever" Imogene mentioned in her June 17th letter referred to the 39th Infantry motto, "Anything, Anywhere, Anytime, Bar Nothing." This motto was coined by Col. "Paddy" Flint, the beloved C.O. of the 39th. He abbreviated it "AAA-O" with the dash or "bar" depicted as an arrow through the entire insignia. He stenciled it on his helmet in bold white letters, and his soldiers followed suit—maybe not the most tactically sound idea, but it typified and reinforced the esprit and morale of the regiment after Paddy took over in Sicily.

Major General Donald A. Stroh

Colonel Robert H. Stumpf

Lieutenant Harry R. Stroh

Imogene "Genie" Stroh, Harry Stroh, Imogene "Jerry" Stroh Stumpf, 1943.

**Generals Eddy and Stroh, 9ᵗʰ Division command
car, Bizerte, Tunisia, May 9, 1943.**

Prime Minister Winston Churchill, Generals Eisenhower, Bradley, Collins, Eddy and Stroh. (Colonel "Paddy" Flint leaning in.) Winchester, England, March 24, 1944.

General Stroh and Lieutenant Stroh at Pitt Manor, Winchester, May 1944.

Lt. Col. Stumpf, England, spring 1944. Note 39th Infantry motto on the side of his helmet has been censored.

Lt. Stroh in his P-47 cockpit, spring 1944.

Captured German General Hermann Ramcke, Generals Canham and Stroh, at Crozon, France, September 19, 1944.

**39th Infantry soldiers breach the "dragon's teeth,"
September 1944.**

Gen. Stroh and Lt. Col. Stumpf, 8th Division Headquarters,
Wiltz, Luxembourg, November 3, 1944.

Lt. Col. Stumpf directing infantry combat operations, February 1945.

Gen. Stroh congratulates Lt. Col. Stumpf after the 424th Infantry presentation review, St. Quentin, France, March 25, 1945.

Prisoner of war temporary enclosure near Bad Ems,
Germany, May 1945.

15

———◆———

Breakout

Following their victory at Cherbourg, the 9th Division moved into bivouac about three miles southwest of the city in an area called Les Pieux. They cleaned up, rested, recuperated, restocked, cleaned, maintained and repaired equipment. There was a ceremony on July 4th with a cannon salute and the presentation of awards. Capt. Stroh sent a letter to his father dated July 3rd indicating how much he had been paying attention to the division's stunning progress. "Guess about now you must be resting and licking your wounds. The whole outfit did a swell job and deserves a world of credit. If you don't go down in history now or at least get the jump on the 1st [Division] something is radically wrong."

The 362nd Fighter Group spent the early part of July on a variety of missions, mostly in northwestern France; armed recce—especially against the German transportation system, escort of medium bombers, fighter sweeps, and dive-bombing gun emplacements. Many of the targets were in the areas south of where the First Army was massing for the offensive to break out of the heretofore slowly expanding beachhead. On most of the escort missions, some of the P-47s also carried bombs to be used against specific targets or targets of opportunity. The pilots were occasionally seeing large formations of German Me-109s and FW-190s, but favorable engagement opportunities were still relatively few. Often the "Jerries" attacked from above when the P-47s were low to the ground in their bombing profiles. Capt. Stroh sent a letter home on July 9th, one of his rare days off from flying.

Had a letter from Dad last week—the first since he went across. He didn't tell me much of what was going on but being over his area I could see plenty of activity. Bob must have done a mighty good job those first few days because that's all Dad talked about. Glad to see Bob make good.

Finally got myself a new airplane the other day—after losing mine [to battle damage] several weeks ago. It is the newest model out with a bubble canopy which looks just like a blister on top of the plane. It is a wonderful ship and I sure am going to take good care of it. That other plane I had was just unlucky or something. Things are picking up as far as running across Germans in the air too. They come up in mass formations now so maybe if I am lucky I might get the advantage on one of them and chalk one up to my credit.

Sure are getting a lot of new faces in again. We took a check of all the old boys who came across originally with the group and found that there are only 12 of us left in the Sqd. [out of 27] Kinda felt funny reading off the names and not finding them here. Have to expect things like that though.

On July 9th, the 9th Division moved out to an assembly area about three miles southeast of Carentan, a march of about sixteen miles. There they relieved elements of the 30th Division and the 113th Cavalry Group and anchored the left flank of the VII Corps front, oriented toward the south. They were in the middle of hedgerow country, facing a formidable enemy who was reinforcing for a powerful counterattack, the goal of which was to break through the Allied lines from south to north, splitting the expanding beachhead. Directly opposite the 9th Division was the Hitler's veteran Panzer Lehr Division. *Eight Stars to Victory* provides a good concise description of the *Bocage*.

> Hedgerows formed a multitude of defensive lines upon which the retreating Nazis could fall. This was Bocage country, the battlefield composed of small compartments (fields) separated by hedgerows... solid earthen mounds, rising to a three foot bank and then capped with four or five feet of hedge. These natural walls were two to three feet thick and contained brush, briars, vines, mud and sometimes wire. Unless the hedgerows were blasted, neither 57mm anti-tank guns nor tanks were able to move forward safely; and the former were of little use anyway except on the roads. The enemy was often just on the other side of the hedgerow—listening, planning, and heckling. After taking one row, the slow, torturous procedure had to be repeated... time after time. It was dangerous fighting... and often 300 yards constituted a good day's gain.[1]

A humorous anecdote about fighting in the bocage was told by a 39th Infantry soldier, Private Leo Banks, and related to an army buddy by his widow, who shared it with this author.

> Enclosed is an article that was in the "Octofoil." Leo laughed when he read it, and told me the story

of how he first met Robert Stumpf. The division was advancing when German troops came towards them. Leo said he jumped into the hedge-row, and was followed by an officer. When he saw this huge (6'4") man jumping in, he got out of his way fast. The officer laughed and said, "It's okay, soldier, you don't have to stand up because of me."

Another anecdote of the bocage was shared with this author by Staff Sergeant Leon Lowery, a squad leader in K Company. The battalion was advancing through the hedgerows when they began taking machine gun and rifle fire from the upstairs windows of a house in a small village. They were too close to request artillery fire. Sgt. Lowery described the action.

Col. Stumpf ordered the Company K commander to send some men on patrol and attempt to enter the rear of the house. The company commander chose me and four other soldiers to do this. We entered the back of the house, cleared the downstairs, crept up the stairs and confronted two machine gunners and five riflemen. The only chance the enemy soldiers had and their only option was to surrender because we had cover and they did not. All seven surrendered. We destroyed the guns and they became prisoners. I have often thought that this was probably the best thing that ever happened to those young soldiers. The battalion then advanced.

The reason I remember this so vividly is because of this action, Col. Stumpf recommended that I receive the Silver Star and the four other soldiers with me receive the Bronze Star. Later, Col. Stumpf presented

me the Silver Star and I mailed it home. I often saw
him mingling with soldiers and asking them their
hometowns, etc. After the Silver Star incident, he
always recognized me and said, "Keep up the good
work, Sergeant, and good luck." At times I saw him
with Paddy Flint.

The battle to push south by VII Corps began the morning of
July 10th with the 9th Division on the left of the three-division advance. To their left was the 30th Division of the XIX Corps. The 9th
Division was strongly reinforced by the 18th Field Artillery Group, the
113th Cavalry Group, and Combat Command A of the 3rd Armored
Division. The 9th's regimental alignment from west to east was the
60th Infantry, 47th, and 39th on the left.[2]

The division jumped off all across the front at 0800 and was met
by spirited enemy resistance. It was classic hedgerow fighting, a
slow slog through fields and marshes, battling mostly small arms and
heavy mortar fire throughout the day. During the fighting, division
headquarters was visited by Lieutenant General Courtney M. Hodges,
assistant commanding general, First Army, who conferred with Gen.
Stroh and Gen. Collins, who was also visiting. Gen. Hodges remarked
in the First Army diary entry for the day "that the attitude and military bearing of the 9th was a pleasure to see; that it was one division
which had remembered all it had been taught, and that discipline
and self-confidence were the natural result." By day's end the division
had advanced several thousand yards and were dug in along a front
roughly northwest to southeast from Haute Verne, occupied by the
60th Infantry, to Le Desert, occupied by the 39th.

During the night, forward elements of the 39th Infantry and the
30th Division heard noises of tracked vehicles moving behind the
lines to the southwest. Ninth Division artillery prepared for action
in the early morning hours. Shortly afterward, a combined armored/

infantry column of the Panzer Lehr Division crashed through 39th Infantry positions at Le Desert, splitting the 1st and 2nd Battalions, and maneuvered behind the 3rd Battalion in an effort to capture St. Jean-de-Daye. Simultaneously, a second column attacked up the road to La Charlemenerie, overrunning one battalion CP and forcing the 47th Infantry to withdraw some 600 yards. This created a gap and loss of communications between the 47th and 39th Infantry. Confusion reigned for some hours as division and sub-headquarters figured out what was happening and rushed reinforcements up to battle the enemy tanks, including the 899th T.D. Battalion on the right and the 3rd Battalion 39th Infantry on the left. The extent of the German penetration behind the American lines was approximately 2,000 yards.

Throughout the day, the entire 9th Division and its attached units fought back furiously, attacking the tanks from their flanks and taking them out piecemeal. Generals Eddy and Stroh were in nearly constant contact with the front. They were supported by American dive-bombers attacking close to the front in the 39th area.

During the melee, Lt. Col. Stumpf organized bazooka teams to supplement the tank destroyers. From Gen. Eddy's diary: "1350—To Paddy's CP, then to Stumpf's CP, arriving there at 1400. Saw 2 destroyed German tanks, 1 U.S. Tank Destroyer and 1 U.S. tank burned out. Evidence of bombing and strafing mission mentioned above were found prevalent."

By nightfall, the 9th had regained all of the ground lost to the Panzer Lehr columns earlier in the day. They dug in for the night in similar, but stronger, positions to the night before; 3rd Battalion moved into the center of the 39th Infantry front. It appeared that the division had destroyed the fighting capability of the pride of the German armored force. Gen. Eddy scribbled a note at the bottom of his official diary, which was otherwise typewritten by one of his aides.

A very hectic day—one of the most hectic. Hit by the Panzer Lehr Division with 40 tanks between the 39th and 47th [unreadable] Some got behind 39th right. 39th fell back some 800 yards. Attack then stopped cold. In all 10 German tanks knocked out by [unreadable] and many more by air. 39th retook all ground lost and 47th's advance in our counter attack which was very slow getting started. Because of attack changed my plans. Directed 47th to attack south of 60th to take out 47th objective to east.

The official tally of tanks destroyed in the 9th Division sector that day was thirty-six, a combined effort of infantry, tank destroyers, division artillery, and air support.

Gen. Eddy's diary entries for July 11th include personal or phone conferences with Gen. Stroh five separate times on battlefield issues from coordination of counterattacks to close air support. This was indicative of the close and effective working relationship between the two that had developed over the preceding two years, including three combat campaigns. As it turned out, those entries were the last mention of Gen. Stroh in the document. He had reached a seminal moment in his career and his life, and we have reached a turning point in our story. At the end of the Panzer Lehr battle, Stroh was ordered by First Army to proceed to and assume command of the mightily struggling 8th Infantry Division, some fifteen miles to the west in the vicinity of la Haye-du-Puits. From this point on, we will feature the activities of the 8th Division, while continuing to spotlight the 39th Infantry and the 362nd Fighter Group. References to the entire 9th Division will be limited only to those required for context.

The 8th Infantry Division came ashore at Utah Beach on July 4th, very well trained, but having no combat experience. They became part of Major General Troy Middleton's VIII Corps. By July 8th, they were organized and put on the line between the 79th and 90th Divisions, north of la Haye-du-Puits. For the next four days, they made insignificant progress toward their assigned objectives along the Ay River and suffered a series of casualties and reliefs of division leadership, including the assistant division commander, who was killed in action, the relief of two regimental commanders, and two wounded battalion commanders. By the end of July 11th, Gen. Middleton had seen enough and relieved the commander, Major General William C. McMahon. Gen. Stroh received a phone call late that night from Gen. Bradley's Assistant Chief of Staff, his friend Gen. Henry "Monk" Lewis, informing him of verbal orders to proceed to the 8th Division. He carried out those orders the following day. Interestingly, the 8th Division artillery commander, Brig. Gen. Pickering, was senior to Stroh by a few months.

Breakout and Pursuit provides a good summary of Gen. Stroh's first several days commanding the 8th Division. When he arrived it was both inept and demoralized, despite the courage and initiative of individual soldiers.

> Advocating side-slipping and flanking movements, he [Gen. Stroh] committed his reserve regiment immediately in hope of gaining his objective quickly. Without special hedgerow training, the division learned through its own errors how to solve the problems of attack and soon began to manifest that steady if unspectacular advance that was feasible in the hedgerows. The troops moved with increasing confidence, maintaining momentum by bypassing small isolated enemy groups. Despite continuing resistance, the division occupied the ridge overlooking the Ay River on 14 July and began to reconnoiter for crossing sites.[3]

By the 15th, the 8th Division occupied a three mile front from west to east between the Ay and Sèvres Rivers, the 79th Division on their right and 90th Division on their left. This constituted the VIII Corps sector of the massive First Army front that stretched from the Atlantic coast on the west to the city of St. Lo on the east. The American army was positioning for an epic push to the south, followed by a pivot to the east, and a breakout across France in the direction of Berlin.

For the next several days, the 8th Division dug in and readied itself for the big push south, while the rest of First Army got into position and waited for the weather to clear. Division artillery shelled enemy strongpoints across the river. At night they lifted their fire to allow patrols to reconnoiter south of the river and to clear gaps in the minefields. When weather permitted, Allied air harassed the enemy during daylight hours. For their part, the enemy shelled 8th Division positions regularly in return, at one point forcing Gen. Stroh to move his command post. True to form, just as his new outfit was digging in, Gen. Stroh took a moment to collect his thoughts and penned a letter to Imogene describing the current situation.

Hq. 8th Div. APO 8
July 15, 1944

    Things are changing so fast in this outfit that it's far beyond me to keep track of them. Having been here for three days I already feel like an old timer, as there have been two senior officers report since then, the last one only a few minutes ago. [Colonel Charles D. W. Canham] This last gent is to be my assistant, in place of another of the same rank who arrived the day before I did, and is now being relieved today. It's a real merry-go-round, and if I'm not a lieutenant colonel within two weeks I'll be much surprised.

    A new broom always sweeps clean, so of course I

have found many changes to make. The first major one was to saw eight inches off the bottom of the private latrine seat. My predecessor was a tall, lanky character, who perhaps fitted this establishment quite well, but my short legs merely dangled over the edge. So this should be an improvement. The next change was to organize a mess. My predecessor, in addition to being long and lanky, was also of a Spartan nature who liked to squat down in front of his tent in the rain and partake of some cold C rations out of the pristine can. This did not particularly appeal to me, so we are organizing along the lines that Matt used. We will never be able to match his wine cellar, presided over by the French speaking Maxwell, nor his flair for gracious entertainment, but at least we have a tent, a table "donated" by the French, a gasoline range, and some table wear. In a few days we should be doing right well. The high command here was used to sleeping in converted trailers, complete with spring bunks, radio, and electric lights, but much too susceptible to shell fire for my timid nature. So I have gone back to my nice hole in the ground, and I notice that all others really followed suit.

The wrench in leaving the 9th was not too severe, but I did hate to be separated from Bob. With him in the same division I felt that I was in a position to help him along from time to time, and to give you some news of his doings. Not that he needs helping particularly. Don't get me wrong. He is doing alright by himself. But it doesn't hurt to have a friend in court where it will do the most good. I felt badly that I had to leave without saying goodbye, but my summons was urgent, and I could not get out to his battalion which was out on the front line at the time. I talked to Paddy, who promised to pass it along to Bob.

Do you know a lad named [Eph] Graham, of Bob's class? He reported in today as the commander of an attached [artillery] outfit. One word led to another, and he said he not only knew Bob, but Jerry also. I assume he was referring to you. Anyway, he said that you and his wife were also acquainted. It's getting to be a small army, after all.

Bob's outfit, and others of the division, celebrated the glorious Fourth by holding ceremonies for the presentation of decorations to individuals who had earned them during the current campaign. I was unable to attend any of them at the last minute, being tied up at the time by preparations for the next move, so was not privileged to see Bob get his bronze star for heroism. He may already have received an oak leaf cluster or palm for a second star, awarded for achievement.

During our brief stay near Flamanville [the first week of July] we inherited part of a 1650 model French chateau, complete with dungeons, keeps, and moats. The present owner and his family still lived in part of the building, and one evening invited a few of us down to what he called a "reception." Quite an interesting evening, with cakes, fresh strawberries, and Normandy cider for refreshments. The old gentleman is a retired French major, who was an instructor in the United States during the last war. We had the crowd in to dinner the next night, and put on a private showing of mine the next night, so you can see that Franco-American relations are already firmly cemented.

There have been a thousand interruptions to this letter. Please excuse.

Gen. Stroh's inbound mail would probably have taken a while to catch up with his change in APO number, but he may have received a letter from Imogene written on July 2nd, and probably waited for her letter of the 9th. He also had one en route from his son, written July 12th, although mail service could be intermittent for those units engaged at the front.

3416 Ingomar Pl.
Washington, D.C.
July 2, 1944

I received your letter of June 17th the other day and it almost seemed unreal to hear about Bob's exploits. He wanted to tell me something in his June 20th letter of his personal experience but couldn't for 14 days, but he sounded so excited. Just imagine you watching him take a village. It is too wonderful to be true. Then Harry thrilled us when he said he was your cover one day and he had put his heart and soul into it. Isn't it grand that you're in the same theater?

The antiaircraft has folded up with a flurry. We had a nice luncheon for our shift given by our supervisor in her apartment, and the Army gave us a grand dance at the Shoreham with a very excellent Army Air Force Band.

July 9, 1944

It's wonderful Harry's been promoted. Mrs. Bell said you'd better watch out or your sons would catch up with you. Little does she know.

Since I last wrote you I've signed up to be in an organization called the Jangos. It consists of Army and Navy juniors who do volunteer work. I'm going to work one evening a week at Doctor's Hospital generally putting people to bed and making them comfortable by giving back rubs, giving bed pans, seeing if they have ice water, arranging flowers, and any nice easy things like those. It will be fun.

Just got a gorgeous certificate from the Antiaircraft Artillery Command with my name on it and no. of hours that I've "loyally and patriotically" with "unselfish contributions to the war effort" and on and on.

If the war isn't over soon, I'll have to transfer all your letters to the next larger drawer. They are all so very interesting. I don't see how you write so well to everyone at any time.

APO 141, England
July 12, 1944

Finally got a letter from you written since you were on the other side. Everybody takes as much interest in you as I do. I practically have had to read it aloud to them just to give the boys an idea what was going on over there. I was kinda expecting to see the return address with the title of Maj. Gen. on it. According to Mother your name is to appear on the next promotion list whenever that comes out.

The group has been hitting the jackpot lately— running into all kinds of Jerries in the air and on the ground. So now we are running up our score and almost doubling the past record. I still haven't shot any in the air but I did manage to knock off one or two on the ground. Knocking them off on the ground doesn't count though—just like shooting ducks then. We are going into pretty fat territory on our missions now so one of these days I'll get lucky and let one of those boys have a short burst.

Been giving the old doughs some pretty close support the past couple of days. At first I was rather worried about the skill of the pilots in dropping the bombs on the enemy instead of on our own troops but so far our group has done darn well in that respect.

The wheels want to send me off on a seven day leave now—they say I have 150 combat hours now and ought to take a little rest. I'm trying to stall them off until I get on the other side and then I might have a chance to visit you. It will probably take me seven days to find you, but I keep pretty well informed as to your whereabouts. Hope I can work the deal because I would like to see you again and hear the big story first hand and see how you made out.

3614 Ingomar Pl.
Washington, D.C.
July 16, 1944

I think your last letter was July 2nd or 1st; I sent it to the Stumpfs immediately since you had described working with Bob in it.

I know how thrilling it was for you to work directly with him, and I think he is doing a wonderful job... He just must be a born leader and soldier and it is a grand thing that he is able to show himself.

My last letter from him was the 29th and he
was able for the first time to mention Quineville and
Fontenay-sur-Mer. He praised his men and said he was
lucky, but it was all very modest and if it weren't for
your letters we wouldn't know more of the details.

Well, the other night we were watching intently for
familiar faces in the capture of Cherbourg news reels,
when who should be leading the two German Generals
in the Corps Commander's HQ., but old Pappy! We both
recognized you at the same time and we both squealed
and I know disturbed the audience around us. You
looked very tired and had that grim expression on
that you always have in times of public appearances.
It sure was swell. You must have been on the screen a
full five or six seconds.

July 24, 1944

It was a thrill to get the first letter from you in
your new command today written July 15. It gets me
how you can pick out such funny things to talk about
and make us laugh so. Guess that it is the way you can
keep your mind normal is to think of the funny parts
of life. It is pretty wonderful.

I also got a letter from Bob of July 5th in which he
mentioned that he didn't know why he got the Bronze
Star (modest) and that there were rumors about your
floating around but that he hadn't heard from you.
Between the two of you it must be terrific keeping up
with all the personnel changes. I don't see how the
Army keeps moving.

I certainly hope things break well for you right at
this important time. It must be very hard for you. We

haven't been told what divisions are in action since
Cherbourg. Today the 29th was mentioned being
around St. Lo. We don't know anything about your
division.

We are all quite upset that you have left Bob. It will
probably be easier personally and socially not to be in
the same division, but it did help him professionally.
He has a great deal of leadership and ability and you
have given him a chance to show it. I'm glad that you
got to know each other better.

Just had a letter from Frances. Frank *has* to
take 10 days leave to be eligible to go overseas. He
hasn't had any leave since January when they had
10 days. Isn't that just too, too bad! She sure did a lot
of explaining why he was taking it and all. The more
she says the worse it gets in my opinion. And you men
over there living in holes! She's always talking about
when Frank was overseas. He was over three months
safely in a hospital in Trinidad because he jumped off a
truck on a bum knee. What a sissy.

We left the 39th Infantry the night of July 11-12 after the "hectic"
struggle to turn back the Panzer Lehr Division south of Carentan. The
battle continued on July 12th as VII Corps attempted to push forward
toward their objectives along the Périers to St. Lo highway, roughly
four miles to the southwest. As the 39th fought methodically through
the hedgerows on either side of Le Désert road, they were harassed
by small groups of roving German infantry with mortars and self-
propelled guns. At one point a company was flanked and received a
brutal barrage inflicting heavy casualties including all the company
officers. As the American infantrymen began to fall back in confusion, 1st Lt. Jack Hubbard, a tank destroyer officer nearby, assumed

command and organized the survivors to hold their position until another company was brought up to disperse the enemy. Overall progress for the regiment on the 12th was insubstantial. Despite heavy weather on the 13th, the 39th jumped off once more with heavy artillery support and made substantial progress of up to 2,000 yards. After being pinched out, the regiment was held in division reserve on July 15th. On July 16th the 3rd Battalion led an early morning reconnaissance of the town of Esglandes. As the other battalions moved up, they received heavy machine gun and tank fire from the town and consolidated positions for the night. The next morning 2nd and 3rd Battalions continued the attack on the town, but were unable to take it and waited for air support to suppress its defenders. That night, 39th Infantry patrols penetrated across the Périers-St. Lo highway, cutting it for the first time. The 3rd Battalion attacked to the southwest the next morning and achieved its objective that afternoon.

For the next three days, the 39th Infantry continued patrolling to determine enemy positions and consolidate its own. Air support was minimal due to adverse weather. Shelling the enemy was limited due to low allotments of artillery ammunition, while the American lines continued to absorb regular shelling from the enemy.

First Army was getting set to launch its great offensive breakout, code-named Operation Cobra. The objective was to open a significant gap through the German lines with the three infantry divisions of VII Corps, the 9th, 4th, and 30th, along a five-mile front west of St. Lo, which was by this time in American hands. Once the opening was achieved, a second wave of two armored divisions and one infantry division was to stream through the gap and fan out to exploit the breakout. The starting line was the Périers-St. Lo highway behind which the lead divisions had been consolidating. The kickoff event would be a massive aerial bombardment along the five-mile front, south of the highway. The 9th Division was on the right flank of the VII Corps front. Its objective was to attack through the German defenses

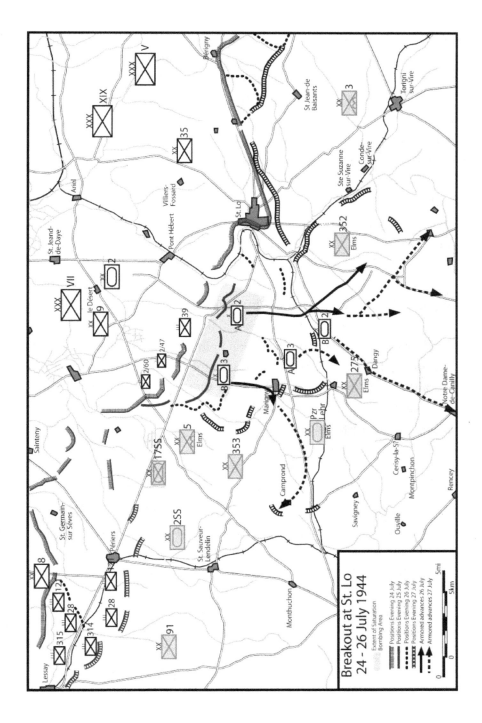

Breakout at St. Lo
24 - 26 July 1944

and pivot to the west, holding down the western edge of the breakout corridor as the second wave passed through, defending against
German attempts to close the opening from the west.

Ninth Division units, including the 39th Infantry, withdrew 1,200
yards on July 24th into the safety zone anticipating the aerial bombardment to occur that day. The bombers were scrubbed for poor
visibility, so the regiment had to retake its former positions and wait.
During this re-attack, Col. Flint was mortally wounded by sniper fire
and died the next day. Gen. Stroh wrote of this "picturesque regimental commander" in a letter to Imogene: "A fine soldier, a great leader,
and one whom it will be difficult to replace." Flint's executive officer,
Lt. Col. Van Bond, assumed command of the regiment.

With the weather clearing up, D-Day was set for the next morning, July 25th. The preliminary bombardment was to be delivered by
a total of over 2,000 Army Air Corps aircraft, beginning with fighter-
bombers, followed by medium, then heavy bombers. By this time, the
362nd Fighter group had moved across the Channel to an expeditionary airfield called A-12, not far from Omaha Beach, within enemy
artillery range, and within earshot of the battle at St. Lo. From the
362nd Group history:

> For many days our ground forces had been poised
> north of the St. Lo- Périers highway, ready to strike.
> For several days our own group had been briefed for
> its part. One fighter group after another was to go
> across a narrow strip just south of the highway, drop
> white phosphorous and HE and fragmentation bombs.
> The medium bombers were to hit a strip of enemy
> defenses just south of those taken by the fighters. And
> south of that was a wider territory to be bombed by
> the thousand or so heavies.
>
> On the 25th we took off as a group at 1038 hours.

Our thirty-four planes carried two 250-lb frag clusters each and one 100-lb white phosphorous. We did not head straight for the target which was only five minutes away, but went from one strip to another, picking up other fighter groups, and these groups, flying one behind the other, then went over the target in sequence. Just how effective our own bombing was will never be known. Such was the dust and smoke and haze that the pilots could see very little. The planes were not all back until 1215, but in the rest of this very busy day, the group ran seven [additional] squadron missions, three by the 378th and two by each of the others.[4]

This "carpet bombing" tactic was similar to the one used for the final assault on Cherbourg, with mixed results. The British had also used it for assaults on Caen. First Army and the Air Corps had gone to considerable efforts to make sure this epic barrage fell only upon enemy positions and not at all on their own troops. In the first place, the highway itself was a very distinct visual boundary that only the most inept bomber would have trouble dropping on the appropriate side of—if he could see it. Secondly, the more accurate fighter bombers were brought in first, dropping not only high explosive and fragmentation ordnance, but also white phosphorous—also known as "Willy Pete," used as a target marking device. Other color-coded targeting smoke was delivered by American artillery, marking both friendly and enemy positions. Thirdly, the entire ground assault force was withdrawn an additional several hundred yards north of the highway, adding a further margin of safety. Most importantly, the whole operation painstakingly waited until the weather at last cooperated. The success of Operation Cobra depended on the accuracy of the bombardment.

As mentioned in the 362nd account of the action from the pilots' perspective, even before the fighters had finished their runs, visibility had been severely reduced by "dust and smoke and haze." A total of 550 fighter bombers made the initial attacks. As the waves of a total of 380 mediums laid down their sticks, the visibility continued to deteriorate. Worse yet, a southerly breeze began to blow this combination of dense white Willy-Pete smoke, black high explosive detonations, dust, flak and other artillery smoke across the highway and safety zone and over the leading elements of the American lines. By the time the 1500-plus Fortresses and Liberators arrived, the highway was totally obscured, and some bombardiers simply released their loads into the smoke. Allied casualties were substantial, especially in the 9th and 30th Divisions. The 47th Infantry alone suffered fourteen killed and thirty-three wounded. The 3/47th, with thirty casualties, lost its entire command team, except the CO, and was so badly mauled, it was pulled from the line and replaced by the 1/39th, which itself had taken casualties. The 3/39th also sustained casualties but remained organized and stayed on the line. Among the dead was the U.S. Army Ground Forces commander, Lieutenant General Leslie J. McNair, who was visiting the front observing the action from a foxhole. One infantry company commander later recalled:

> The dive-bombers came in beautifully and dropped their bombs right where they belonged. Then the first group of heavies dropped them in the draw several hundred yards in front of us... The next wave came in closer, the next one still closer. The dust cloud was drifting back towards us. Then they came right up on top of us... We put on all the orange smoke we had but I don't think it did any good, they could not have seen it through the dust. The shock was awful.[5]

Ironically, the color-coded smoke used by American air, artillery, and infantry to define the targets, and friendlies, caused more problems than it solved. In all, bombs from thirty-five heavy and forty-two medium bombers dropped within American lines, out of 1500 and 380, respectively.

Despite these setbacks to friendly forces, the enemy took an order-of-magnitude worse pounding. The bombardment buried men and materiel, smashed tanks and artillery batteries, and completely disrupted communications by destroying radios and antennas, cutting lines, and killing or disabling messengers. Soldiers were dazed and confused; perhaps 1,000 or more perished. Roughly one-third of the front line and first reserve line, including remnants of the Panzer Lehr Division, were casualties. The vast majority of tanks and tank destroyers were destroyed or inoperable.

The 9th, 4th, and 30th Divisions, shaken by the friendly air bombardment, rallied and jumped off on time, crashing through the hobbled German defenses on both sides of the highway across a three-mile front. They established a complete rupture of the German lines, progressing by nightfall more than a mile south of the highway. On the morning of July 26th, the 1st Division and Combat Command B of the 3rd Armored Division crossed the road through the breech cleared by the 9th Division and began their breakout maneuver to the southwest. A mirror image maneuver was executed on the left flank of the breach with a breakout to the southeast. That same day, a minor incident occurred that illustrates some of what was going on behind the scenes during the chaos at the front. Capt. Charles Scheffel had just returned from a hospital in England to the 39th Infantry after being wounded aboard ship off Utah Beach:

I was still at 39th Regimental Hq. sort of listening
to news of the advance... Went over to find my medical
Dr. friend. Couldn't find him, but did find the dental tent

so went in to see if all my fillings were OK. While there, Lt. Col. Bob Stumpf came in, at the time the 3rd Bn. Commanding Officer, with a tooth ache that seemed to have him in great pain. The Dental Dr. told him that he had one that needed pulling right then, but it seemed that putting the Col. to sleep or lack of a deadening agent kept them from doing the pulling right at the moment. Col. Stumpf started to go out of the tent and back to his Bn. and continue the battle with his bad tooth. All of a sudden he turned around and in effect said to pull the damn thing right now without any pain killer. Believe they gave him a good drink of either Scotch or Calvados, he sat down in the portable dental chair. The Dental Officer, a 1st. Lt. did just that. The Col. wobbled out of the tent back to duty. I thought to myself that here is a man with a lot of guts. He had a good reputation, a West Point graduate, taller than myself at 6'2" and looked and acted the combat officer.[6]

For three days, the 39th Infantry continued to advance south and southwest against stubborn resistance. On the night of July 27th, the 2nd and 3rd Battalions of the 39th launched an attack on a road junction near La Buissonet, capturing it in the predawn hours, then pushing on through stubborn resistance to Potigny. By the morning of July 28th, they achieved their objectives as part of the 9th Division pivot to defend the right flank of the breakout. They were then pinched out by the 83rd Division as it advanced southward, and moved to assembly areas near Marigny as VII Corps reserve. From a First Army after-action report: "The 9th Division not only held its flank position, but made some advances to the west to widen the breach."[7]

For the month of July, the 39th Infantry sustained heavy casualties: 144 killed, 597 wounded, twenty-five missing, for a total of 746 out of a normal strength of about 3,000, about 25 percent. Medal nominations included four Distinguished Service Crosses, fifty-two Silver Stars, and 116 Bronze Stars.

The objective of the western arm of the breakout was to isolate the German forces facing VIII Corps, which moved forward—south— against the Germans in conjunction with the breakout forces on July 26th. Some twelve miles west of the 39th Infantry's jumping-off point on the July 25th, the Gen. Stroh's 8th Division was at the center of the VIII Corps' line of advance. *Breakout and Pursuit* describes the set-up and the action on July 26th:

> Two good highways lead south... and converge at Coutances. The terrain between those roads was in the 8th Division zone. Between the Ay and Séves Rivers it was thick with hedgerows, though the least unfavorable on the corps front for offensive action. General Middleton chose to make his main effort there with the 8th Division, which was to attack frontally to the south and effect a penetration.
>
> Early on the morning of 26 July the VIII Corps Artillery delivered twenty-five prearranged missions during a one hour period, laid down counter battery fires, and prepared to fire on call... As the 4th Armored Division helped by delivering supporting fires, the other divisions of the VIII Corps moved out.
>
> Attacking with two regiments abreast [28th and 121st Infantry] General Stroh's 8th Division met strong small arms and mortar fire at once. The zone of advance was thick with antitank and antipersonnel mine fields, and German tanks contested the attack. By sideslipping and out flanking, by employing tanks and tank destroyers to enfilade hedgerows defenses,

and by engaging enemy armor with bazookas and
antitank grenades, the 28th infantry, on the right
(west) advanced more than a mile and by evening
secured the high wooded ground just north of the
Lessay-Périers highway.

The other assault regiment, the 121st Infantry
on the left (east), attacked along the axis of the main
road to Périers... During the attack, two battalion
command posts received direct enemy artillery hits.
At the height of the crisis German tanks appeared. A
tank platoon, called forward to challenge the German
tanks, lost one Sherman to a mine and two others to
the mud of a marshy bog... Taking heavy casualties
from small arms and mortar fire, the infantry fell
back.[8]

During the night, patrols found evidence that the enemy lines
would remain in place. As both attacking regiments of the division
began their advance the morning of July 27th, they met stubborn
resistance that required some regrouping. In the afternoon the regiments came abreast and attacked across the Lessay-Périers highway,
and occupied the high ground one to two miles south by the end of
the day. The 79th and 90th Divisions followed through the gap created by the 8th Division, fanning out east and west to pursue the
retreating German forces.

On July 28th, the 8th Division continued south with little resis-
tance for another seven miles and set up in the vicinity of Coutances.
Clearly the Germans had withdrawn from the field south of the VIII
Corps advance in an attempt to escape envelopment between the
Corps front and St. Lo breakout forces.

At this point, First Army ended Operation Cobra with the successful breakout of several divisions of armor and infantry through the gap

created by VII Corps west of St. Lo. on July 25th. The breakout had gone more or less according to plan with all objectives achieved and the enemy in retreat. Only the glaring misstep of Air Corps bombs falling on friendly positions during the preliminary bombardment marred the otherwise splendid American performance. From a purely military perspective, however, the bombardment had achieved its goals, providing the springboard for large-scale breeching of the German lines. The next chapter will discuss the continuing attempt by both the western and eastern arms of the breakout to entrap their respective German opposition.

16

Pursuit

Since even before the Normandy invasion, the fighter-bomber boys of the 362nd Fighter Group had been laying the groundwork for the breakout at St. Lo and the ensuing entrapment of the German armies facing the Allied invaders. As they perfected their skills at bombing and strafing tactical targets, they set about methodically destroying the German transportation system in France. Railroad trains and marshaling yards were prime targets, as were road junctions, bridges, railroad tracks, vehicles of all kinds, and ammo dumps. As the big breakout push became imminent, enemy gun emplacements made the list. As was the case on June 17th, the squadrons began to operate temporarily out of expeditionary airfields in France. Capt. Stroh was quite busy flying missions in the beginning of July, then got a few days off. He wrote home on July 16th.

It doesn't seem possible that this is the middle of July. I'm beginning to feel like an old timer over here now. I can imagine what Dad feels like with over a year and a half overseas.

Flew a few extra missions over the rest of the flight leaders and got a little ahead of them on time this month so they won't let me fly until they catch up with me. So since I wasn't doing anything I thought I would take a few days off and go to London. I did a little more sightseeing and managed to see the formal guard mount at Buckingham Palace. I thought the U.S. Army had a pretty formal guard mount, but this one took the cake.

Didn't have a letter from Dad all last week, but I imagine he is all right. He is no doubt in the semi-rest camp taking things a little easy after what they have been through—they sure deserve it.

Saw in the paper that Gen. Roosevelt died. He was a pretty good friend of Dad's in North Africa, wasn't he?

I was talking to a paratrooper in London and I asked him how Chambliss and Eberly made out. According to the paratrooper Chambliss is dead and Eberly was wounded—they both got it during the initial phase of the invasion. I was sorry to hear about them—they were pretty good boys.

The 378th Fighter Squadron mission reports indicate that Capt. Stroh led the whole squadron in combat on July 18th, the first mention of him in this role.

Mission No. 133—Armed recce southeast of Paris. Led by Captain Stroh. Twelve A/C dispatched. T/U—1400, TOT—1515, T/D—1715. Red and Blue flights strafed and bombed two trains. One train had 30 flats with armored vehicles and one train had 30 cars, part passenger. Over half of armored cars destroyed, train burning, locomotive blown up X-6476. Yelo flight, one single locomotive blown up at S-6205, 20 car train destroyed. All cars hit heavily and burning. Tracks split at S-5506.

The next day, the 362nd P-47s were flown for the last time out of their base at Headcorn, Kent, landing at their new home in France, an expeditionary field designated A-12, not far from Omaha Beach. They were one of the first, if not the first, U.S. group to operate out of France. Life was very different for everyone, operating so close to the front; Allied artillery firing over their heads at German positions, and Germans returning the favor. Capt. Stroh could scarcely contain his enthusiasm.

378th F.S., 362nd F.G., France,
(Near Omaha Beach)
July 24, 1944
Dear Mother and Jerry:
    Well we are finally in the war—and I mean right in the middle of it. That old stuff about the Air Corps being 100 miles behind the line is a lot of talk—we are even closer to the lines than some of the artillery. This is a lot of fun though—more exciting and more to keep you occupied. The first thing I did was dig myself a nice big foxhole. It was a good thing I did, too, because the first night the Jerries threw a few shells over at us. They didn't hit any of the planes though, but did get a few men.
    The weather has been a little bad lately so I decided to take a little trip and visit Dad. About 5 of us went over to the 9th and much to my surprise

they informed me that Dad had gone to another outfit. Had a big time talking to all the people I knew in the 9th and learned all about the experiences of the past month. Saw an old friend from Leavenworth days—George Rice. He recognized me immediately but at first I couldn't quite place him. Yesterday I took another day off and finally found Dad. He seems in fine spirits but looks a little tired to me. Hope he can make a go of the new division and get his second star in a hurry. We'll all know in a few days and I am sure he will make good.

Dad had a lot of praise for Bob, Jerry. He must be doing pretty well. I tried to see him when I was visiting the 9th but he was in the front lines and Bob's C.O. [Col. Flint] didn't want me to go up. Maybe I'll get to see him again sometime.

Kinda like the life we are leading now—living in pup tents and really roughing it. At least we will be in condition for the other theater if we go over there. We don't do any long missions anymore—do nothing but close support about 1,000 yards behind the enemy lines and then head right home. We only log about an hour on each mission so we will be here a long time to get in our required hours before going home. I'd like to stay a while longer anyway—things are beginning to break.

The next day, July 25th, the 378th Fighter Squadron was part of the epic breakout bombardment in front of the VII Corps assault forces, including the 39th Infantry. The squadron flew three additional missions before the sun went down. For the next week or so, all the fighter-bomber groups were busy assisting the breakout armor and infantry units as they chased down the retreating Germans. As Gen. Stroh's 8th Infantry Division continued their southerly advance through Coutances toward Avranches on July 28-29, the 4th and 6th Armored Divisions passed through the VIII Corps sector trying to head off the German retreat to the south. The 13th RCT of the 8th Division was motorized and temporarily attached to the 4th Armored Division to support their thrust. All this pressure on the German retreat caused mayhem, and the P-47s pounced, adding to the chaos on the ground.

> German hopes for an eventual concerted breakout attempt were largely destroyed on 29 July by Allied tactical aircraft. The destruction that occurred went far beyond Allied anticipations. On the afternoon of 29 July pilots of the IX Tactical Air Command discovered a "fighter-bomber's paradise" in the Roncey area—a mass of German traffic, stationary, bumper to bumper, and "triple banked." Pilots estimated at least 500 vehicles jammed around Roncey, and for six hours that afternoon the planes attacked what became known as the Roncey pocket. As squadrons of fighter-bombers rotated over the target, American artillery, tanks and tank destroyers pumped shells into the mélange. More than 100 tanks and over 250 vehicles were later found in various stages of wreckage, other vehicles had been abandoned intact... the fact was that the Germans had fled on foot in the hope of escaping the devastating fire rained down upon them.[1]

The fighter bomber groups continued their unrelenting attacks on German positions and infrastructure for the rest of the month and into August. For the 362nd, as one would expect, July was especially active in terms of missions flown and flight hours amassed. But it is clear that flight record-keeping was not keeping up with actual numbers being flown. There are missing and incomplete entries in individual flight records and inconsistencies between group and squadron mission reports. For example, the mission that Capt. Stroh led on July 18th is not entered in his flight log. These types of omissions may have been due to the frenetic pace of flight operations and perhaps the confusion surrounding the move across the channel to A-12 and subsequent "combat" conditions. Nonetheless, Capt. Stroh's flight log indicates sixteen operational missions, all but one in his new bubble canopy P-47D-27, for 35.4 hours. It also reflects two non-operational P-47 flights and four in the UC-78, for a total of forty-one hours.

The last days of July, the 8th Division continued its southerly advance, following the 4th and 6th Armored Divisions. By August 1st, they had passed through Avranches to an assembly area southeast of the city. There, the 13th Infantry rejoined the division. On August 2nd and 3rd, the division continued the advance, clearing pockets of resistance, capturing German prisoners, and securing road networks. The 13th Infantry was again assigned to the 4th Armored Division.

By August 4th, the division was on the outskirts of Rennes, the provincial capital of Brittany. Gen. Stroh ordered outposts to defend all road and railroad approaches to the city. The division would maintain occupation of Rennes until August 13th. On August 12th, Gen. Stroh had an unexpected visitor about whom he wrote in a letter to Imogene.

> Capt. Harry Richard Stroh dropped in to spend the morning with me today. Can you beat it? Just as casually as if he were still in school and living at home. Not having heard from him for nearly three weeks, I sent Berry out in search for him, and in less than two hours the two returned in the Potomac III [Gen. Stroh's jeep]. By the most fortunate coincidence in

the world, Harry's outfit, two days ago, moved into
a new field not five miles from our present C.P.! The
squadron cooks being A.W.O.L. at breakfast time this
morning, Harry's morning meal had not gotten beyond
the coffee stage, with a backing of "K" rations during
the preceding forty-eight hours, so it didn't take much
urging for him to partake of a ten o'clock breakfast
here, consisting of a cup of fruit juice, two fried eggs,
a large piece of steak, toast, four cups of coffee and
a large slab of raisin pie. After a chocolate bar to
stave off starvation at eleven, he had no difficulty
in disposing of chicken salad, lettuce, soup, cocoa,
dessert, and some of Mother's cookies shortly after
noon. I sent him on his way rejoicing soon after with
a German machine pistol, and two cases of captured
German cognac for his buddies.

What Gen. Stroh did *not* reveal in this letter about his son's visit to
his C.P. was related to the author in a conversation with Capt. Stroh's
squadron-mate and good friend, Bob Kennedy, on March 31, 2006.
Kennedy, who accompanied Stroh that morning, also enjoyed the lavish spread at the general's mess, but added another wrinkle to the story. Apparently, the division, in their occupation duties in Rennes, had
appropriated a large quantity of local wine, so large in fact, that the
general had a 500-gallon tanker truck converted to store it. So, in addition to the other refreshments, everyone in attendance enjoyed par-
taking of French wine from tin cups. Kennedy added that the ground
troops they encountered were delighted to see pilots and expressed
their gratitude for the close air support. Gen. Stroh continued:

[Harry] seems to be enjoying his adventures
immensely. He is now squadron operations officer, but

gets in on about every other mission, and is line for a majority.

I know where the 9th is, but can only guess what it is doing.

Do you mean to say you are saving my letters? I have good reason to save yours, but why save mine?

Don't you worry about Bob and me being separated, as it will probably turn out better for him in the long run. He is fully able to take care of himself, is well established by now, and has made a fine reputation for himself. I was glad of the opportunity to give you some first-hand accounts of his exploits, but you'll just have to educate him along those lines.

While the 8th Division was busy in the west, the 9th Division had turned its sights to the east. After their right flank blocking maneuver for the breakout at St. Lo, the 39th Infantry, with the rest of the 9th Division, had gone into VII Corps reserve at the end of July, assembling near Marigny, about five miles west of St. Lo. After a few days of rest, reorganization, and maintenance, it was time to reenter the fray, as reflected in the regimental ops report of August 4th that stated, "at 1710, the Combat Team was attached to the 1st Inf. Div. with instructions to move at 1900 motorized to vicinity of MORTAIN... C.P. established at 2230, balance of Combat Team closed in by 0300, 5 August." Mortain was about thirty miles south southeast of Marigny. The move was essentially a looping right flanking maneuver to support the rest of the 9th Division, whose objectives were north of Mortain. It required the regiment to pass through the zones of other units, including the 1st Division and the 3rd Armored Division, before hooking up with the rest of the 9th Division from the south. In the big picture, these operations were part of First Army's eastward drive to the Seine.

Action for Lt. Col. Stumpf's 3rd Battalion was swift in coming, just a few hours after taking up their new positions about five miles northwest of Mortain on August 5th. From the 39th Infantry ops report of that day:

> Attacked at 0800 with 3rd Bn. on right and 2nd
> Bn. on left... passed through bridgehead of TF-2, 3rd
> Armored Division at LE ROUSSEL and advanced
> under mortar and artillery fire, and also received
> small arms and tank or SP [self-propelled gun] fire
> in the afternoon... Counterattack received at 1725 on
> the left flank of the 3rd Bn. by tanks and infantry, and
> then extending along entire front, air support called
> for but marking smoke drifted before planes were
> over target and bombing was inaccurate. Another
> counterattack received at 2125 on front, but was
> repulsed. All Battalions consolidated for the night.

The following day was relatively quiet for the 39th Infantry, as the battalions consolidated their lines just north of Le Roussel, facing east. The regimental CP, artillery battalion, cannon, and anti-tank companies were about a mile and a half to the southwest. Facing them were the 116th SS Panzer Division and the 2nd Panzer Division. At noon, the 39th reverted to 9th Division control whose other regiments were to the north. Units of the U.S. 30th Division were deployed to the south, in and around Mortain. Units of the 4th Division were situated to the west, just behind the 9th Division. Opposing the 30th Division were two more SS Panzer divisions. The enemy was preparing a counterattack of two armored columns, the objective of which was to break through the American lines with two armored columns, then advance to and retake Avranches, some twenty miles to the west. The northern of the two prongs was aimed at the small town of Mesnil Tove, which was between the 39th CP and the front lines. The first inkling of the enemy assault came early on August 7th per the 39th Infantry ops report.

At 0130 "B" Co. reported vehicular movement in vicinity and at 0230, 9th Rcn. Plat. reported that they had run into enemy armored column... moving west toward MESNIL TOVE on road south of 1st Battalion. Forward switchboard in MESNIL TOVE reported 0312 that MG fire was hitting around their location and that all troops had left town; 1st and 3rd Battalion field trains were overrun and set afire...

3rd Battalion at 0328 instructed to send their reserve Company "K" and tank destroyers down road from LE ROUSSEL toward MESNIL TOVE. One Platoon of the cannon company was located directly north of the enemy axis of advance, and after dismantling their guns and disabling their vehicles, the men moved north and the platoon leader remained as a listening post. At 0422 [he] reported twenty track vehicles, and at 0507 advised of an additional 35 vehicles, including some personnel carriers from which the enemy was unloading. The axis of the enemy advance cut directly across the Regimental axis of communication with the battalions north and Regt'l C.P., Cannon Co. (less one platoon), A. T. Co. (less two gun platoons), and 26th F.A. south of the enemy.

At 0600, "K" Co., a short distance south of LE ROUSSEL, reported heavy enemy resistance and fell back... As soon as observation was possible, fire was laid [on the enemy] by the artillery...

At 0900, Co. "K" was pinned down by artillery fire

in LE ROUSSEL, but continued attempts to move south toward MESNIL TOVE.

Fire continued until about 1100 on both Co. "K" and the road block south of the road, when pressure lightened in the sector as the enemy armor moved to the west, although enemy infantry still held sector at MESNIL TOVE and along axis road west from town.

By 1300, the situation had stabilized and plans were made to move all installations then south of the enemy around through 4th Division area to come in behind Battalions with line facing the East. Pressure continued on all battalions from the front for the balance of the day from infantry and tank or SP fire.

By 1500, a new regimental CP had been established behind the front lines of the battalions which remained essentially the same as the previous day. Lacking direct contact with the rest of the 9th Division, the 39th Combat Team was attached to the 4th Division. During the night, a company-size enemy force successfully infiltrated the gap between the 1st and 3rd Battalions, and after a firefight, "M" company withdrew to an alternative position. Throughout the day and into the next night, the battalions repulsed a series of attacks, both along the front and from pockets of infantry in the rear and along the enemy axis of advance. Support was rendered by 4th Division artillery and the Air Corps. By noon on August 9th, contact was established with the 9th Division, and the 39th Combat Team reverted to their control. Prisoner reports indicated that the two-prong armored attack had been initiated with seventy tanks and that thirty remained at the end of the battle. The 39th Infantry claimed fourteen of the tank kills. It had played a decisive role in the defeat of the major German counterattack at Mortain by absorbing the northern of two armored thrusts, both of which succeeded initially in breeching the American lines. Thwarting these attacks enabled the momentum of the Allied offensive east of the breakout at St. Lo to continue.

Capt. Stroh was granted several days' leave the first week of August in recognition of his overseas combat service, but unlike his bomber pilot contemporaries, he was still quite a way off from a trip back home. Back at A-12 with the 378th Fighter Squadron on August 6th, he wrote about his leave in letters home and to his father.

APO 141, France
August 6, 1944
Dear Mother and Jerry:

Guess you are kinda wondering what has happened to my letter of last week. As a matter of fact I did write you a letter and that's as far as I went. You see I had a short leave—five days to be exact—and I went back to England. I was staying at a town where I couldn't mail the letter—there being no censors in the town to OK the letter. Besides I was afraid to mail it with a Red Cross return address because you might think that something had happened to me and I was in a hospital or something.

Those five days were mighty fine and I really did enjoy myself. This is the first fair size leave I have had since coming across and I took full advantage of it. I spent four of the days at a summer resort that had been recommended by Dad the last time I saw him... I will tell you the name of it at a later date. It was mighty nice to sleep all morning, play tennis and swim all afternoon, and then sit on the terrace of the hotel drinking a nice cold beer or scotch and watching the sunset or maybe going inside and dancing a little. The war seemed millions of miles away, but now I am back to reality.

I haven't seen Dad for several weeks now and the first chance I get I'll try to get a jeep and drive down to see him. They are moving so fast I don't know if I can find them or not but I'll sure try. If the situation keeps up as it has in the past few weeks I think we'll all be home for Christmas.

Yes, Jerry, Dad told me that Bob is getting the Bronze Star, but he didn't say anything about the cluster. Bob must be doing a bang-up job. Gen. Quesada was down here today and he wanted more recommendations for DFC's and Silver Stars from this group. So I guess I'll have to get busy and start writing up some of the boys. It makes me mad the way the 8th Air Force [bombers] gets their DFC's automatically while we of the 9th have to earn ours the hard way. The 8th gets theirs for 25 mission and most of the boys who came over with this group have about 65 or 70 missions to their credit and no sign of a DFC, and I figure we are doing more work right now than the 8th ever thought of doing. There are only 10 of the original 28 [pilots] in this squadron that came over last year. Now we have 41 pilots in the sqd. so you can see how many strange faces there are.

Dear Dad:

The situation is kinda looking up in the past week. I have been keeping my eye on the 8th and it looks as though you will be getting that second star before long.

I kinda feel like a draft dodger or something. Here a great push has been going on and I have been basking in the sun in England. I finally decided to take a little rest—not having had any for 8 months... thought I would take you up on the recommendation of that

summer resort in Southeastern England. It was all
you said it was. However, there are loads of people
from London escaping the buzz bombs so the town was
a little crowded. That didn't matter much though—I
still played a lot of tennis and did a lot of swimming...
The view was wonderful... Guess by this time you
could stand a little rest yourself, but if things continue
as they are, I don't see how the Dutchman can stand
up much longer—then we can all take a long rest.

Well, take care of yourself and I'll be down to see
you one of these days. We have so many pilots in the
sqd. now that I am on duty 24 hours and off 24 so you
see I can come down anytime I am off—all I have to do
is find some transportation.

After returning from leave, Capt. Stroh got right back in the saddle,
leading mostly armed recce missions, where the squadron worked
with local tactical controllers when communications could be established, or going after targets of opportunity when not. On August 7th,
the squadron attacked the German airfield at Chartres, where they
destroyed seven aircraft on the ground and damaged three others in
addition to bombing airfield facilities. They began to fly "column support" missions, essentially airborne escort of armored columns. On
August 11th, the boys flew the airplanes to their newest home base,
the former German airfield at Rennes, the city then occupied by Gen.
Stroh's 8th Division. Once again, he was in charge of setting the place
up, as related in a letter to his mother and sister.

APO 141, France
August 13, 1944
What a week this has been—never seen anything
move so slow in my life. After I got back from leave I

found I had a new job—that of Operations Officer of the squadron... Once we get settled in it won't be bad, but two days after getting the job we made another move and I had to come to this new base and get it set up before the main body of the sqd. came down. I have never seen so many dumb people in my life as the kind I have run across lately—if I tell them to do something once, I must tell them a hundred times until they get it done. This is a good job though and if I make out OK I might even get a promotion in time.

Our group really hit the jackpot on fields this time. We have an old German permanent base—the biggest in this part of the continent, as a matter of fact. Hardly know how to land on a concrete runway again—and hardly any dust. The field is so big that one can hardly get around without some sort of transportation...

Also Dad is only about 7 miles away—just like being next door to him. Went over to him yesterday and spent the morning with him. They are doing a swell job and it looks as though Dad will be getting that other star pretty soon. Hope he stays around this area for a while 'cause then I could get over there quite a few times.

Thought I might have a chance to get home for 30 days. They are sending 12 men home tomorrow for 30 days and then come back. Those going back have 200 [combat] hours to their credit so I figured I might get on the next list after these come back. However, this is the only bunch going home—high command is going to think up some new system. So now I'll just have to sweat out the new system and see what happens. Jim Rippin is going home and rubs it in every time I see him.

Earlier that day, August 13th, the Group began to fly interdiction missions in the Brest area, about 120 miles west of Rennes. The 378th mission report on that date stated, "Flak intense, heavy, and accurate over Brest." This fortress city on the tip of the Brittany peninsula was the second largest port in France and a strategic objective for Gen. Patton's Third Army. The 378th would visit there regularly until its capture.

While the 8th Division kept Rennes occupied, VIII Corps, now part Third Army, detached the 121st Infantry to the 83rd Division on August 6th for the conquest of St. Malo and vicinity. The 121st's objective was the port town of Dinard, just west across the wide Rance River from St. Malo. The combat team left immediately by motor for the forty-mile march, sending a small force to Dinan while en route to accept the surrender of the small German garrison there. As the regiment approached Dinard on August 7th, it came under heavy machine gun fire from roadblocks, and was forced to fight its way ahead against pillboxes, mines, booby traps, and barbed-wire entanglements. The advance slowed as the combat team was pounded by heavy mortar and tank fire. On August 9th, the 3rd Battalion was cut off from the regiment. For three days it received almost constant shelling, but was able to repulse all assaults. Late in the day on August 12th, the regiment regained contact with 3rd Battalion. The consolidated regiment was then able to drive through the remaining defenses and occupy Dinard on August 14th. They mopped up the following day and reverted to 8th Division control.

In the meantime, on August 13th, the 8th Division wrapped up its occupation of Rennes and moved to Dinan, where it remained until August 17th. Gen. Stroh sent the reinforced 3rd Battalion of the 28th Infantry to the Cap Frehel peninsula to assume positions of the local French Forces of the Interior and reduce the enemy in the area. The objective was about twenty miles northwest of Dinan as the crow flies. The remainder of the 28th Infantry followed up the next day. The regiment took 300 prisoners. On August 17th, the 8th Division moved 120 miles to the west to an assembly area outside of Brest. For three days activities were limited to patrolling and preparations for the attack on Brest, before moving into the battle sector on August 21st.

Back in the eastern sector, in the days following the repulsion of the German counterattack at Mortain, the Allied strategy to cut off the German retreat was coming to fruition. First and Third U.S. Armies formed a southern pincer while British and Canadian armies formed the opposing northern pincer. The Germans were attempting to retreat eastward through a fifteen-mile gap between Falaise to the north and Argentan to the south, roughly 120 miles west of Paris. This became known as the Falaise Gap or Falaise Pocket. The ultimate Allied objective was to cut off the retreat, entrap and destroy the entire German force, while the Germans battled to delay the Allied advance, attempting to keep their lane of retreat open.

The 39th Infantry's role in this massive scheme was part of VII Corps' northerly attack on the southwest sector of the pocket. On the afternoon of August 14th, the combat team departed their assembly area near Mortain by motor transport to Couptrain. There they dismounted and the 2nd and 3rd Battalions attacked north with little opposition. They continued advancing the next day until encountering enemy armor to the north heading east at 1740. At 1800 they came under enemy artillery and tank fire and dug in. The German armor continued to move eastward that night. On the morning of the 16th, the 39th continued to advance north while facing increasing levels of small arms fire. That afternoon they faced more tanks and by the end of the day were under mortar and artillery fire. On August 17th, the combat team advanced slowly with all three battalions on the front against limited resistance. At the end of the day, they held a line about a mile south of Briouze. The next day they made contact with the British 11th Armored Division crossing their front from west to east, which essentially pinched them out of the battle. For the next several days, the 9th Division remained in place as it resumed area patrols in Corps reserve status.

While some German units managed to escape the pocket to be later reconstituted across the River Seine, they nevertheless took a pounding from Allied air and artillery. Casualties and losses of weapons and equipment were great. Gen. Eisenhower later summarized the action.

> Back inside the pocket, the confusion was still greater, and the destruction assumed immense proportions as our aircraft and artillery combined in pounding the trapped Germans. Allied guns ring the ever-shrinking "killing ground," and while the S.S. elements fought to annihilation, the ordinary German infantry gave themselves up in ever increasing numbers. By 20 August the gap was fully closed near Chambois, and by 22 August the pocket was eliminated... What was left of the Seventh and Fifth Panzer Armies was in headlong flight toward the Seine, and a further stand west of the river was impossible.[2]

From August 13th until this time, the 362 Fighter Group had been splitting their missions between Brest in Brittany and the area west of Paris including the Falaise Gap. Beginning on August 16th, they concentrated on the growing drama surrounding the pocket. Excerpts from group and squadron mission reports reflect a vivid description of the pandemonium of the German retreat.

> August 16, 8 missions were flown in support of the 7th Armored and 5th Infantry Divisions... 13 enemy vehicles were destroyed and one oil dump hit.

August 17, Nine missions were run to the same area west of Paris... seven tanks were claimed for the day, six of them by the 378th from just one mission.

August 18, the Group flew missions in the Brest area.

August 19th, The whole group went south of Paris to the area around Melun... to concentrate on barges... they claim to have damaged no less than 60 of these along the upper Seine. One locomotive and some cars were destroyed and another damaged, and a flak tower silenced.

August 20, Six 8-plane missions supported our columns around Dreux. [west of Paris] The 377th claimed six tanks destroyed by bombing and strafing. On their second mission the 378th met 12 109's and 20 190's destroying six and damaging one. The 377th bombed two tanks on the next time around and the 379th claimed 3 destroyed. That evening the whole group went out to the bend in the Seine SW of Rouen, where the squadrons dumped six-hour delay bombs on three ferry sites to somewhat dampen the German evacuation during those hours of darkness when our planes could not bomb and strafe fleeing troops.

August 21, Each squadron ran three 12-plane missions supporting our columns from Melun to Mantes-Gassicourt. The 377th bombed 18 camouflaged trucks for "Quick Dive," who said: "On the button." The same controller had 18 more tanks for the 378th. The 379th found about 25 enemy vehicles and destroyed 15, damaged 5. They also got a tank. That evening "Beagle" vectored the 377th to 25 vehicles, of which they destroyed about 17. The 378th

believed they put 7 heavy guns out of action along the
Seine.

August 22, the 378th flew three missions, the
first in support of the 5th and 7th Divisions, vectored
by Quick Dive on a single tank. Armed recce in
the Chartres area, vectored by Quick Dive on 18
tanks in the woods. Dropped three 500's and six
clusters of frags—NRO. [no results observed] Gun
emplacements... Five heavy batteries and many light
guns observed. Damaged 10 of them considerably.

August 23, The whole group took off for the area
around Mens and Troyes. The 378th and 379th
bombed RR targets and got a locomotive with steam
up. The 378th destroyed 20 freight cars. The 377th
bombed gun positions as controlled by "Gaysong."
They then proceeded to controller Beagle's position
which was being strafed, and destroyed two and had
one probable of the five Me-109's they found there.

August 24, Three squadron missions were run to
support the 7th Armored and 5th Infantry Divisions
around Fontainebleau. The 378th destroyed one
armored car, 12 trucks and two tanks.

Capt. Stroh took time out from aerial artillery duties to write letters to his mother and sister on August 20th, and to his father on the
21st, which was a group day off due to bad weather.

Haven't heard from Dad lately, but he is still in this
neck of the woods so I'll have to drop down to see him
sometime. As a matter of fact I bought him 6 pair of
new stars which his aide said he needed.

Did I tell you about my boost—I am now Ass't. Sqd.

C. O. The job calls for a Maj. but I don't think I will get it for some time since the C. O. is still a Capt. Our old C. O. was shot down which was a big loss [Maj. Sherwin Desens, on August 3rd, POW], so now the present C. O. and I are pretty green at the job, but are trying hard. Maybe if the war lasts long enough—I might get the boost in rank.

Dear Dad,

What a day this has been—nothing but rain and more rain. Kinda take pity on you doughboys on this kind of day—guess you are getting the same bad weather we are, only we rest and you have to continue working. Thought I might drive out and look you up yesterday but it was too wet to take any extended jeep ride. One of these days I'll take a day off and see you— have to do it soon or we will be too far away again.

About 12 of the boys from the group left for home last week for their 30 day leave. I didn't feel so bad until they actually left and then I realized how much I wanted to go back—even if it were just for a short time. I know how you feel now, only you have more reason to go back than I—you're going on two years now and that is a long time.

Went to a nearby town yesterday and had a real French dinner. I must admit these French know how to cook—and in great quantities—too much for me to eat, and pretty cheap too. I'll have to go out more often...

Our Sqd. got fat on enemy aircraft again yesterday—shot 6 more down—that makes us the hottest squadron in the group now. We lost a couple doing it, but that's to be expected. As usual I wasn't on the mission when the boys ran into the Jerries. I'm about the most unlucky person I know of.

Take care of yourself. I'll try to see you soon.

From August 25th through 27th, the group flew exclusively in support of VIII Corps, as the battle against the German garrison at Brest intensified. Capt. Stroh flew at least four of the five missions. He was well aware of his father's business there and upped his game; despite his previous routine of twenty-four hours on, twenty-four off, he flew on all three days.

After closing the Falaise Gap on August 22nd and the subsequent destruction of German forces within it, the Allies began chasing the speedily retreating surviving German armies across northeast France. On August 20th, the 9th Division took up positions covering a thirty-mile sector on the left flank of the First Army from Sees, southeast of Argentan, northeast to Vernuil. There they patrolled the hilly, wooded area with Mortagne as the headquarters. On the 24th, they joined the rapid advance of VII Corps, which now included the 1st Division, the 3rd Armored Division, and the 4th Cavalry Group. By the 25th, they had made their way to Arpajon, about twenty miles south of Paris, and began staging for a crossing of the Seine.

In an interesting aside, the highly regarded VII Corps team under Gen. Collins led all the American armies to Germany. Commanding the 3rd Armored Division, upon whose tanks the doughboys of the 39th Infantry often rode, was Major General Maurice Rose, for whom Lt. Col. Stumpf had served as executive officer in the Sicily campaign. The Corps further developed and refined the concept of tank-infantry coordinated team operations that Rose's Combat Command "A" had introduced in Sicily.

The 39th Infantry's Seine crossing site was at Melun, some thirty-five miles south of Paris, but before they could begin, on August 26th, Paris was liberated by French and American forces. The celebrations were monumental. The joy of the French people, now free from four years under the heel of the cruel Nazi regime, spilled out into the streets as they welcomed the American liberators with open arms.

The Germans had blown all the bridges across the Seine, so combat engineers built pontoon bridges for the American army to cross. The 39th Infantry crossing at Melun early on August 27th was uneventful. As VII Corps advanced, the 3rd Armored Division led the way, charging ahead and leaving pockets of resistance to be cleaned up by the infantry. The next day the 9th Division crossed the Marne and pushed northward. They were riding on trucks, tanks, and tank destroyers, at times covering scores of miles a day in contrast to daily advances in the bocage measured in hundreds of yards.

The 39th Infantry crossed the Aisne River on August 30th and continued on toward Belgium. By August 31st they were in Dizy-le-Gros, having advanced more than 400 miles since August 1st. Such a dizzying pace had stretched the supply chain thin and probably could not be sustained all the way to Germany. Conversely, the enemy supply lines were shrinking and they were planning a more robust defense to stop the Allies as they grew closer to the homeland. For the 39th Infantry, that line in the sand would be in Belgium, crossing the Meuse River, some 50 miles to the northeast.

For the month of August, the 39th Infantry lost eighty-five killed in action, 455 wounded, and forty-one missing, a casualty rate of nearly 20 percent. Recommendations for medals included four Distinguished Service Crosses, twenty-one Silver Stars, and twenty-three Bronze Stars.

Lt. Col. Stumpf's twenty-ninth birthday, September 1st, came as the 39th Infantry advanced north, part of the 9th Division's right flank position on VII Corps. Their objective was the town of Hirson along the heavily wooded frontier on the French-Belgian frontier. The regiment was held up early in the drive by a blown bridge forcing an alternate route. Early in the afternoon, they received a barrage of heavy artillery but, with the assistance of tanks from the 3rd Armored Division, achieved their objective by nightfall.

Elements of the 9th Division entered Belgium the next morning, the first of all Allied forces to begin the liberation of that country. At that time, the 39th was following a 3rd Armored column northward when the tanks were halted by mines and small arms fire. The 39th took care of the opposition while the mines were cleared, and the column moved out. Not long after, the tankers ran out of fuel, so the doughboys continued on their own. Third Battalion encountered the enemy in the early evening, engaged them, and drove them off, taking out two tanks in the process. The regiment reached the village of Eppe-Sauvage by the end of the day and dug in.

The following day, September 3rd, the division changed course to the east toward the Meuse River city of Dinant. It was in this area that the Germans were planning to make a determined stand and force a delay in the Allied advance, which would give them time to reinforce their fortified defenses along the Siegfried Line. Conversely, the American strategy was to speed quickly across Belgium and breach the vaunted West Wall—as the Germans called it—before the enemy could adequately man it. During the day's advance, the 39th Infantry encountered only scattered resistance. Third Battalion was halted after securing the town of Florennes, in order for the other battalions to catch up to return to line abreast positions.

The 39th's advance toward Dinant the following day was swift, facing only spasmodic resistance. The doughboys rode on tanks and all manner of other vehicles, although there were some slowdowns due to throngs of Belgians turning out to gratefully welcome their liberators. Many called out warnings to the Americans against attempting an assault crossing of the Meuse. The 3rd Battalion arrived at the west bank of the river in the afternoon near the village of Anhee, about four miles north of the fortress city of Dinant. Preliminary reconnaissance found all the bridges blown and no suitable daylight crossing sites.

The regiment was ordered to cross that night. Mittelman described the river from a military perspective:

> It is as wide as the Rhine in places, and on either side for many miles are steep rises—some sheer and others pitted with natural landings. Even in 1944, this river presented an overwhelming problem to any invading force headed eastward.
>
> The Germans knew full well the value of the river line, and it was here that they planned to halt the speedy American advance, thus gaining time to reach the Siegfried. Enemy defenders blew the bridges from Namur southward, then retired to the heights. Here, sitting behind machine guns, flame-throwers and mortars, they could wait confidently. The Americans would have to climb down one side of the gorge, attempt to ford a river under fire and then have to launch an assault uphill ... under direct observation![3]

The 9th Division plan called for a diversionary feint from the 47th Infantry against Dinant, with the 60th Infantry crossing the river to the south and the 39th crossing at three points to the north near Anhee. The 39th was then to hook to the south and assault Dinant from the rear. After dark, Lt. Col. Stumpf made a personal reconnaissance of the 3rd Battalion's crossing area, and discovered a temporary narrow catwalk crossing the river that, inexplicably, the enemy had failed to destroy. After crossing to the other side alone, he began to reconnoiter the area where the battalion would establish a beachhead, but was interrupted by an enemy patrol. He was able to remain undetected, evade the patrol, and complete his reconnaissance. He then withdrew back across the catwalk to the western side.

The division operation was to kick off at one minute after midnight on September 5th. The 47th Infantry began their barrage on Dinant right on schedule, while the other regiments moved toward the riverbanks with rubber assault boats and pontoon bridge equipment. It took the 39th Infantry three hours to get set up for the crossing at water's edge. The first wave of 1st Battalion's assault of fifteen boats received withering bursts of machine gun fire from the enemy on the heights across the river. Twelve boats were sunk. One company commander did make it ashore with twenty men. They fought valiantly until their ammunition ran out, and then the group was wiped out. Further attempts by 1st Battalion to get across were cancelled. Meanwhile, 2nd Battalion made an attempt to cross the damaged bridge at Dinant, but was repulsed by heavy fire.

At about 0500, Col. Stumpf led 3rd Battalion on its tricky single-file quick-step across the catwalk, the soldiers spaced about five yards apart. As platoons gradually made it to the east bank, Stumpf directed them to the positions he had selected earlier during his reconnaissance. While the ranks of the battalion on the east bank began to fill, they started to push out to the east under heavy machine gun, mortar, and artillery fire. Meanwhile, the regiment had rerouted 2nd Battalion, which looped around to the left and followed 3rd Battalion over the catwalk, assisted by smoke cover and artillery fire. This took all day, but the beachhead grew as more and more units made it across. Right away, it was clear that supply would be a huge problem, especially ammunition. The troops had only what they had carried into the battle. Any resupply would have to be hand carried across the catwalk until a more substantial bridge could be constructed. With the two battalions across, the engineers attempted construction of a pontoon bridge, but were thwarted by heavy enemy fire.

As dawn broke on 6 September, 2nd and 3rd Battalions had further secured their positions and continued to expand their foothold, with supporting fire from the 1st Battalion on the west bank heights. At 1000 Col. Bond sent "B" Company across the catwalk to take up positions on 3rd Battalion's right flank. This was accomplished by 1645. "A" Company made a similar move after dark. During the day, slow progress was made under heavy pressure at the front. Meanwhile, the 3rd Armored Division at Namur to the north sent Task Force King to clear the enemy all the way to Dinant. The task force arrived at 1430 and the resistance broke. The task force was then attached to 3rd Battalion for the attack on Dinant. Lt. Col. Stumpf formed two armored columns, one to proceed down the east bank river road to the city, the other to loop southeastward and attack from the east.

Third Battalion, with Task Force King attached, continued the attack on Dinant at dawn on September 7th. The city was cleared of the enemy and secured by 1030, including its imposing citadel which overlooked the main bridge. By that time a Bailey bridge had been completed south of Dinant over which tanks and tank destroyers moved into the city. The exhausted soldiers of 3rd Battalion hitched rides with them as the 39th Infantry was ordered to an assembly area near Purnode, about four miles north-northeast.

It was not until December 22, 1944, during the Battle of the Bulge, that Lt. Col. Stumpf was officially cited for his performance crossing the Meuse and taking Dinant. By that time, it must have seemed like ancient history; so many more battles behind him, so many more soldiers lost. The Silver Star citation reads:

ROBERT H. STUMPF, Lieutenant Colonel, 020707, 39th Infantry, who distinguished himself by gallantry in action against the enemy on 5 September 1944 in the vicinity of Anhee, Belgium. Moving forward alone on a reconnaissance of the Meuse River for a crossing site, Colonel Stumpf observed an enemy patrol approaching him. Skillfully evading the enemy group, he continued on his voluntary mission. He notified all Company Commanders of his plans and then personally led the Battalion to the site he had selected. Successfully making the assault crossing of the Meuse River, Colonel Stumpf repeatedly exposed himself to heavy enemy fire to effectively maneuver and deploy his companies. Colonel Stumpf's aggressive leadership, devotion to duty, and courageous actions contributed materially to the success of the operations and were a credit to himself and the Armed Forces of the United States.

If the men of the 39th Infantry thought they were going to get a little rest before moving out again, they were sadly mistaken. The chase was still on. The Germans who withdrew from Dinant were hustling toward the border and their fortifications at the West Wall. All along the front, the Allies pursued them in a race to get to the Wall before the Germans had time to man it properly. The 39th moved out on the morning of September 8th. Third Battalion, drained and battered from the Meuse/Dinant fighting, remained behind the other two battalions and in a quasi-reserve status for the next six days. Though they were on the move, this grace period gave Lt. Col. Stumpf the opportunity to reorganize the battalion, placing new faces in leadership positions to replace losses, and integrating replacements into their units.

The regiment met only sporadic resistance as they completed the final leg of the journey to Germany's doorstep on September 12th in the vicinity of Eupen, Belgium. The race across France and Belgium was over. Fighting through the bocage and lightning single-day advances were behind them. They were about to enter a new, very ugly phase of the war, with advances measured in casualties per yard, where weather and terrain only accentuated the enemy's furious defense.

17

———◆———

Brest and Crozon

During the latter weeks of August 1944, as the bulk of the American armies sprinted across northern France toward Germany, VIII Corps moved into positions around Brest. This port city's strategic importance was gaining emphasis even then, as difficulties in logistics supporting the growing Allied presence on the continent became more acute. Although some supplies were arriving through Cherbourg, most were still coming across the landing beaches. As the more unpredictable and severe autumn weather approached, attaining suitable ports became paramount. Furthermore, the German garrison at Brest contained a substantial and effective enemy force of 50,000, and was home to the largest of several naval bases that accommodated the German submarine fleet. Both needed to be eliminated.[1]

The battle for Brest bore similarities to Cherbourg: a heavily fortified port city with significant manpower and firepower. Its commander, Lieutenant General Hermann Bernhard Ramcke, a seasoned airborne commander, had been ordered by Hitler to fight to the last man. His defenses included three German divisions and a number of naval units and labor battalions. The city was ringed by layers of fortifications and plenty of artillery, including heavy coastal artillery turned inland. In addition to fortresses and strongpoints throughout the layered defense, there was a massive old city wall in the heart of downtown. Each day the Germans delayed the fall of Brest meant another day tying up three U.S. infantry divisions needed to the east where Allied forces were approaching the German border.

The American VIII Corps was commanded by Major General Troy Middleton, whose plan was a three division assault, advancing on three sides, with Gen. Stroh's 8th Division in the center, advancing north to south. On his left was the 2nd Division advancing from the northeast, and on the right, the 29th Division from the northwest. Stroh had been working with Middleton since he assumed command of the 8th Division in early July. On August 24th, forward elements of the 13th and 28th Infantry regiments were in contact with the outer ring of enemy positions just south of the town of Gouesnou, about three and a half miles north of the inner city fortifications. Those regiments would be first in the line for the 8th Division with the 121st in division reserve. Gen. Middleton ordered a coordinated Corps attack for the afternoon of August 25th following artillery and aerial bombardment to soften up the defenses. He also arranged for at least four fighter-bombers to be on call during the ground operations, controlled by local air liaison officers. The 13th and 28th Infantry jumped off on time against very stiff resistance and posted gains of about 1,200 yards by the end of the day.

The 362nd Fighter Group launched four full-sized squadron missions to Brest on the 25th. Some of the targets were in support of the ground attack, but most were on maritime targets in the harbor. The 378th, including a flight led by Capt. Stroh, scored two direct hits on an enemy cruiser, sinking it, and two more on a beached cruiser. They

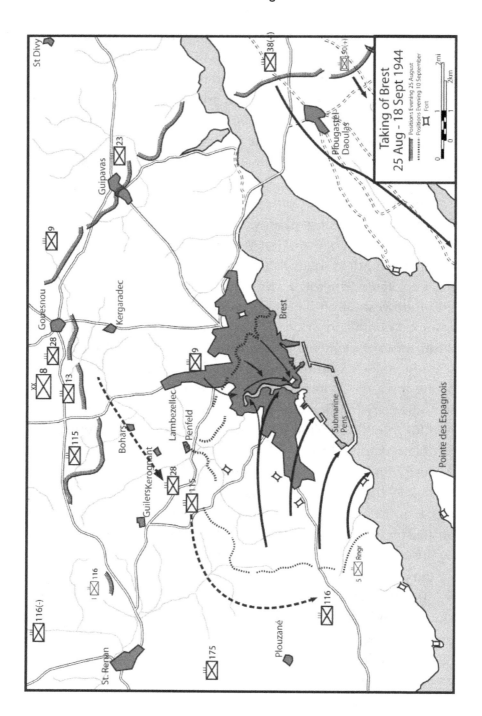

Taking of Brest
25 Aug - 18 Sept 1944

- - - - - Positions Evening 25 August
········· Positions Evening 10 September
⊠ Fort

reported, "Flak intense, accurate, heavy from ships." This mission re-sulted in a Presidential Unit Citation, which reads in part:

> Although the target was partially obscured by a
> heavy overcast and the harbor formidably defended
> by coastal batteries and heavy and light anti-aircraft
> installations and concentrated fire from naval and
> ancillary vessels, the flights of the 362nd Fighter
> Group fearlessly and repeatedly bombed and strafed
> the shipping and harbor installations at dangerously
> low altitude...
>
> Direct hits were scored on two cruisers, one of which
> was left beached and burning, and twelve addition naval
> and merchant vessels including heavily laden troop
> transports attempting to evacuate enemy personnel
> from the harbor were vigorously attacked and left
> damaged or in flames. In addition, objectives impeding
> the advance of Allied infantry and armor in the Brest
> area were successfully attacked and the progress of the
> units of the ground forces greatly facilitated.

That night, RAF heavy bombers attacked enemy positions in preparation for the next day's attack. American and RAF aircraft again blasted the enemy the next morning, but, despite the bombing efforts, the situation changed little and the enemy resistance remained firm. The following days' attacks might best be characterized as a long slog.

> The attack on 26 August displayed the kind of
> combat that was to predominate during the siege
> of Brest. Because ammunition stocks were low,
> the artillery reduced its activity to direct support

missions. As the Americans came to a full realization
of the strength of the German opposition, and the
pattern of the enemy defense system emerged,
commanders on all echelons saw the necessity of
changing tactics... The nature of the battle changed
from a simultaneous grand effort to a large-scale
nibbling—a series of actions dictated by the local
problems of each sector commander.

The divisions began to probe to locate and
systematically destroy pillboxes, emplacements,
fortifications, and weapons, moving ahead where weak
spots were found, overwhelming pillboxes with flame
throwers and demolitions after patient maneuver
and fire. Small sneak attacks, the repulse of surprise
counterattacks, mine field clearance and the use of
smoke characterized the slow squeeze of the American
pressure.[2]

On August 26th, Capt. Stroh led a flight of Thunderbolts on another
maritime search-and-destroy mission in Brest harbor, dropping bombs
on freighters and one armed ship. His flight was controlled by "Kleenex
Able," who submitted this report to 8th Division headquarters.

Date 26 Aug 44
To C-G 8th Div
Firebrick Blue leader after bombing ships asked
for strafing tgt. Was put on strong point 973027—said
it was well dug in & a lot of activity—would send next
flight of bombers for it—Requested I give his regards to
Gen. Stroh.
Time signed 1345
Landis Maj AC

That night, Gen. Stroh, after the second day of the bitterly fought battle for Brest, found time and strength to write his regular letter to Imogene.

> I have been trying to get to your letter all day, but what with almost constant air and artillery activity, kicking the boys along up front, conferences with the corps commander, etc, etc, it is now nearly eight in the evening and I'll have to hurry. I think everything is pretty well buttoned up for the night, and there should be no interruptions but you never can tell.
>
> The biggest thrill of the day came this afternoon, when an air liaison officer handed me the enclosed message. "Firebrick Blue leader" is undoubtedly Harry. Can you beat it? That kid was evidently pushing around one of the planes we saw today, and operating directly over our sector. We run across each other under the most unusual circumstances. He also gets around. Just the other day I was reading that his squadron was jumped by about 20 Heinies while jamming the German retreat across the Seine. Score 6 Heinies, 2 Americans.
>
> Pink envelopes or otherwise, I sure like to receive letters from you. Two came this week, —August 6 and 13. Thank you very much for remembering Mother's flowers for Harry's birthday. [his 24th, August 31] To be quite honest in the matter, I had completely forgotten the matter in the stress of things which have been happening quite strenuously in recent weeks, and it would have been a catastrophe if she had not received them. Let me know the cost and I'll write it on my cuff. I don't have any bank account, and I imagine

you wouldn't have much use for French invasion francs.

Yes, you're right, I do love to eat, and I see no reason why we shouldn't eat well while we can, so long as we don't deprive others. A recent dinner, when we had a couple of the regimental commanders as guests, was really a humdinger. Went something like this. Gin, cognac or rum highballs, with choice of fruit juice or Vichy water. Clear soup. Fresh crab cocktail with drawn butter. Stewed chicken with dumplings, peas and French fried onions. Lettuce onion and radish salad with mayonnaise. White wine. Chocolate meringue pie. Coffee or cocoa. Benedictine. Not bad for the field. And everything delicious.

The mess has accumulated a new pet, a small grey rabbit, which would fit in the palm of your hand when we got him, her, or it in Normandy, but has by now prospered and about trebled in size despite the frequent change in scenery. The bunny is very tame, enjoys being picked up, and delights in licking your hand. It is remarkable how soft hearted otherwise tough soldiers really are.

Wish I could give you some news of Bob, but we are now separated by a good two hundred miles or more [closer to 500], and I don't know when we'll see the old outfit again. This push is something isn't it? And to think it only started a month ago yesterday.

The next day, August 27th, the 8th Division made little progress against the entrenched German defenders. Division chief of staff Col. Cross's personal diary entries on that day and the next:

27 Aug. Division attacked at 0930 hrs. Limited
objective only. Heavy ground haze early morning
hours lifted about 1000 hrs. Air support expected
later in day. German resistance still strong. Only 22
prisoners taken.

28 Aug. Stubborn resistance encountered all day...
fire heavy and accurate indicating that all barrels had
been zeroed in and adjusted. Hand to hand fighting
with bayonets and grenades. Little ground gained
except 13th Inf. which reached its objective. 28th
Inf. did not gain any ground. Both second and third
battalions under constant shell fire. 1st Bn. 28th Inf.
put in to pressure Hill 80.

The 378th Fighter Squadron continued to provide support across the Corps front, launching in shifts of four or six planes so that the battlefield had continuous on-call presence. The close support of bombs and bullets on enemy positions was a morale boost for the doughboys below. But even without delivering ordnance, the P-47s' mere presence overhead had a noticeable negative effect on the enemy's willingness to open up with its artillery. On August 27th, 8th Division air liaison officer, Maj. Landis, made seven separate reports to division headquarters reflecting the staggered nature of the flights.

1150—Bombed German C.P. & signal center E
of church in Lambezellec... Hit 88 3-gun position at
943009—only one gun firing... said arty was knocking
hell out of church.

1210—Bombed gun positions N barracks 963026 in
wooded plot... all bombs hit in wooded sector —

1315—Bombed tgt #1 gun positions.. Klondike...

Yellow saw gun positions—yellow 2 saw gun flashes,
laid violet smoke, yellow three got flak direct hit on
88, yellow one overshot, yellow four put two guns out.

1430—Bombed tgt #1 with jellied gas or napalm
bombs... all bombs in tgt area—smoke seen for approx
5 minutes.

1515—Bombed gun positions 945016, observed the
guns firing, strafed on way down—direct hits oh the
ESE gun positions with 1000 pound bombs—results
very good.

1630—Fire bombed gun positions at Q944022...
two bombs failed to burst. Dropped first on low cement
bldgs.

It is likely that Capt. Stroh was on one of the first of the day's rotation, possibly the one mentioned in the 1150 report; Lambezellec
was smack-dab in the middle of the 8th Division sector. Catching his
breath between missions, he took a few minutes to write his regular
weekly letter to his mother and sister.

France, Aug 27
Dear Mother and Jerry:

Now that was a mighty choice cake you sent—it
wasn't crushed or anything when it got here and
it was still moist... the rest of the boys enjoyed it
also. It came just in the nick of time because all our
rations seem to be held up because of transportation
difficulties, so you can imagine how much we did
enjoy it.

Wish I could see Dad today and tell him a few things.
For the past two days I have been doing nothing but
give him support—at least his division. They give me

some target that the division wants knocked out and I try my darnedest to knock it out. I flew behind the front lines to try and locate the division headquarters but they must be too well camouflaged for me to spot. Yesterday I told the ground controller to give my best regards to Dad so maybe he knows that I'm up above him. As soon as he gets through with the present operations he might be moving back this way so I might be able to see him—right now he is up to his neck in work and I wouldn't want to bother him.

I sent you a magazine that had an article on our group. It is a British magazine but at least we are famous now and finally broke the print. I don't see why we aren't written up more because we are the best 47 outfit in the 9th Air Force and that ain't hay...

Now that Paris is free I'm kinda anxious to see what the place looks like from the ground—probably just as the movies predict it.

The mail is finally catching up with us—we must have gotten 2 mail bags full yesterday with 4 letters in it for me from home and a box of cookies from Grandma. Funny how your morale goes up when you get a letter from home.

Received a letter from Joe Dover yesterday. He is in New Guinea but is now in the hospital in Australia. His engine exploded over the jungle and he hurt himself in several places when he jumped. He had quite an experience, according to his letter, staying in the jungle until he was rescued.. Hope he gets well because he is a pretty good egg.

Take care of yourself.

Love, Harry

The 378th's last mission of the day was armed recce in the Brest area with sixteen aircraft dispatched. They bombed and strafed gun positions assigned by their respective controllers at four different locations, all of which were damaged or destroyed. Gen. Stroh watched the action with some satisfaction, hoping to take advantage of the damage to enemy gun batteries. As the flight of four in front of his division began to retire from the battlefield, he observed one P-47 leave the formation, fly very low over the German lines once, then do another orbit for a second run, during which it was hit by ground fire and crashed in a farmyard. The general turned to his aide, Lt. Berry, and said, "Thank God Harry is not flying today." He knew that Capt. Stroh had flown the day before, and believed this was his day off. The general received the air liaison officer's final report of the day shortly afterward.

> No. 7 Date 27 Aug 44
> To C-G
>   Bombed gun positions at 973027—some hits on positions—Firebrick Yellow Leader reported some activity & ambulances in Lambezellec in woods to N.E.—Firebrick Yellow Leaders ship exploded at 1000 ft.
>   Time signed 1800
>   Landis Maj AC

As the battle for Brest continued to rage, the weather deteriorated and the P-47s were unable to provide support for three days. Gen. Stroh had no contact with the 362nd Fighter Group or his son's squadron, and no knowledge of the following three reports for weeks.

378th Fighter Squadron

August 27

Mission No. 206—Armed recce in Brest area. Sixteen
A/C dispatched. T/U-1620, TOT-1700-1745, T/D-1830.
Captain Stroh NYR...

CONFIDENTIAL

HEADQUARTERS ARMY AIR FORCES

MISSING AIR CREW REPORT [form]

1. ORGANIZATION: Location St. Jacques, France
   [Rennes]; Command XIX Tactical Air Command;
   GROUP 362nd Fighter Group; Squadron 378th
   Fighter Squadron

2. SPECIFY: Point of Departure St. Jacques, France;
   Type of Mission Ground Support

3. WEATHER CONDITIONS: Clear 5 to 6 miles
   visibility

4. GIVE: (a) Date 27 August 1944; Time 1730 hours;
   Location Brest, France
   (b) Specify whether ( ) Last Sighted; ( ) Last
   contacted by radio; ( ) Forced down; (XX) Seen to
   Crash

   5. AIRPLANE WAS LOST AS A RESULT OF: Enemy
      anti-aircraft or our own shells.

   6. AIRPLANE: Type P-47 D...20; AAF Serial
      Number 42-76597

   9. THE PERSONS LISTED BELOW WERE
      REPORTED AS: Battle Casualty

   10. NUMBER OF PERSONS ABOARD AIRPLANE: 1
       1. Pilot Stroh, Harry Richard Captain

362nd Fighter Group
Captain Harry Stroh Missing in Action
Witness—Lt. Edwards

While flying Yelo Three position in Firebrick Squadron on Aug. 27, 1944, affording column support in vicinity of Brest, Captain Stroh, who was Firebrick Leader, called in to the ground controller to be assigned a target just before reaching the area. He made contact with the controller Albright and we were given a target to dive-bomb. After we had dropped our bombs the controller called Firebrick Leader and asked him to go down in the area two or three miles Northeast of the city of Brest to look for some enemy troops reported to be there. Firebrick Leader called Firebrick Yelo Three to take charge of the flight while he went down. I saw him go down to a couple of hundred feet and fly over the area and then climb back up to 3,000 feet. At that time I was right back of him with the flight and thought he was trying to get back into position, but instead, we completed another orbit and he went down again. Was watching and he flew pretty low right over the same area for about three-quarters of a mile, and then started to pull up again when something struck his ship and caused an explosion. Immediately the plane went out of control and crashed about three hundred yards from where it was first hit, and exploded.

Lt. Edwards' account makes it clear that Capt. Stroh was leading not just his flight, Firebrick Yellow, but the entire squadron; Edwards refers to him several times as "Firebrick Leader." What is not clear in the reports is what actually struck Stroh's P-47. Both sides' artillery batteries were active, but the German anti-aircraft barrels were purposely targeting enemy planes. It is likely that every German soldier with a gun who could see it was firing at the low-flying P-47. The chance that a stray American artillery shell struck Stroh's plane is a possibility, but a remote one.

As was always the case when pilots were lost, there was a mix of negative emotions for the surviving pilots. It was especially painful with the loss of one of the original cadre who had been together in this greatest adventure for well over a year. The loss of Capt. Harry Stroh was one such time. This is how it is remembered in *Mogin's Maulers*: "His loss was deeply felt by the organization and was more tragic because it occurred over his own father's, General Stroh's, 8th Division."[3] Many years later, 378th pilot John Baloga, who was on the mission, but in another flight, wrote, "The death of [Harry Stroh] was the only one that caused mass discussions and sorrow... We talked about it when we got back. The extra shock was when we found out that his father was the Gen. in charge of the infantry attack and the artillery support."[4] Capt. Stroh's good friend Lt. Bob Kennedy, who was one of the surviving original pilots of the 378th, and Stroh's wingman on their breakfast visit to Gen. Stroh's CP only two weeks before, remembered him with fondness.

> Harry joined the squadron shortly after me in Connecticut in 1943. He was one of the few West Pointers in the group, the complete opposite of typical Pointers; just the nicest, best liked, most congenial. I went to London on leave with Harry; toured the town, visited some bars. Played a lot of poker with him at the Group mess and officers club.[5]

The 362nd Fighter Group public relations officer, Paul Mitchell, became friends with Stroh when he was assigned as the group assistant ops officer in the spring of 1944. Mitchell wrote a memoir for *Mogin's Maulers* in 1980 where he recalls his most enduring memories of the war, one of which was "joyriding about England to RAF bases in a twin-engine Cessna flown by tent-mate in Kent, the late and great West Pointer, Capt. Harry R. Stroh."[6]

Last page of Capt. Stroh's flight log. Note second flight of 27 August 1944 is missing.

The furious battle for Brest continued for several more days with limited progress against the German defenses. After three days of miserable flying weather, on September 1st, the 362nd Fighter Group resumed near daily missions in support of VIII Corps forces as they slowly degraded the German outer ring of strong points. Gains by the 13th and 28th Infantry regiments were measured in hundreds of yards per day. On the morning of August 29th, the 28th Infantry had arranged a truce with the Germans to evacuate wounded during the battle for Hill 80 and Hill 88, so named for the 88mm artillery pieces defending it. Previously E and G Companies had advanced beyond their adjacent units and, during the truce, were cut off, captured, and marched into Brest.

The next day, August 30th, Gen. Stroh relieved the 28th Infantry with the 121st, which had been in division reserve. Gen. Middleton visited the division CP and, among other business, promoted Stroh to major general, a milestone that he had fretted over for more than a year. On that day and the next (Harry Stroh's birthday) the division consolidated small gains and reorganized the lines in preparation for a major corps attack. The attack on September 1st was successful and all objectives in the 8th and 2nd Division sectors were achieved. The following day, attacks by the 13th and 121st Infantry forced the enemy to abandon some positions in their outer defense ring. A shortage of artillery ammunition then necessitated a slowdown of large-scale offensive operations for several days. Operations were limited to patrolling and strengthening occupied positions.

On September 8th, with adequate artillery support, the 121st Infantry attacked and seized the heavily defended eastern edge of the Lambezellec Ridge, the northern gateway to Brest. They continued on to the town of Lambezellec, about two miles north of central Brest, and entered into street fighting with the defenders. The 13th Infantry, on the 28th's right flank, attacked simultaneously to the south as the two regiments advanced abreast through the town and continued south the next day. Gen. Stroh took a break to write to Imogene the evening of September 9th, still unaware of his son's demise.

According to the crazy numerical prediction that I sent to Mother two or three weeks ago, the war was supposed to end at two o'clock this afternoon. [below] If it has, the news has not reached this sector yet at any rate, although it is after six. I guess predictions are not as valuable as guns. Will have to wait for better news later.

You must indeed feel relieved after hearing from Bob. As I have said before, you cannot expect regular and comprehensive correspondence by junior officers when things are moving as fast as they have for the past six weeks. Their time is less and less their own as you go down the scale.

If we could not get a few crumbs of humor sometimes out of our experiences I think everyone would blow up. Some of this is furnished by the prisoners we pick up. The other night two German privates, the orderly and driver of a German officer, stole the latter's clothes, complete with medals, and walked into our lines, thus gloriously arrayed. On another occasion a German lieutenant, bringing up his company's ration of cigarettes, took the wrong turn and blundered into our lines to be captured. Recently an adjacent division captured a German truck convoy with 2500 rations en route to one of their outlying garrisons. I suppose those poor krauts are still wondering what happened to their chow. It's a great war.

	CHURCHILL	HITLER	ROOSEVELT	IL DUCE	STALIN	TOJO
BORN	1874	1889	1882	1883	1879	1884
AGE	70	55	62	61	65	60
TOOK OFFICE	1940	1933	1933	1922	1924	1941
YRS IN OFFICE	4	11	11	22	20	3
	3888	3888	3888	3888	3888	3888

END OF WAR—1/2 of 3888 is 1944

DATE AND TIME—1/2 of 1944 is 972: 9th Month, 7th Day, 2 o'clock

TO FIND SUPREME RULER, TAKE FIRST LETTER IN EACH LEADER'S NAME

C H R I S T

Meanwhile, the two attacking regiments of the 8th Division reached the strongpoint of Fort Bouguen on September 10th. The fort, only about a mile from the German naval base, was part of the old French inner city wall defense. It was a formidable structure featuring a moat, high walls, tunnels, and a sheer cliff leading down to the Penfeld River. After an artillery barrage, an infantry attack was repulsed. Also on the 10th, control of VIII Corps shifted from Gen. Patton's Third Army to Lieutenant General William H. Simpson's Ninth Army.

Gen. Stroh prepared a more elaborate attack for the following day. A heavy pounding by direct large caliber artillery fire, in an attempt to create a major breach in the walls, was not especially effective. As a result, the Corps commander decided to suspend further operations against that portion of the inner defenses and contain the garrison troops in place. As the American noose around Brest tightened considerably over the last several days, the maneuvering room had become insufficient for three divisions. Gen. Middleton directed the 2nd Division to relieve the 8th Division units before Fort Bouguen, pinching out the 8th. After withdrawing from contact with the enemy at Brest on September 12th, the division began moving to the Crozon Peninsula, as close as three miles across the harbor, but fifty miles around the bay by land. This large and strongly held promontory was a direct artillery threat to Brest, as well as the destination of German troops attempting to retreat from the Brest garrison.

The Crozon campaign was an example of an operation by an independent division. Conventional wisdom before the war held that such operations would be extremely rare, that divisions would habitually operate as parts of much larger masses. But this war in Europe provided many occasions when units of this size found themselves entirely on their own for tactical dispositions. Written shortly after the war, Gen. Stroh published a detailed study of the battle, excerpts of which provide the following narrative of the operation.[7]

This was one of the few campaigns in my experience for which ample time was afforded for plans, orders, and reconnaissance; when the various troop units moved into position methodically and without interference; which was amply supported with the necessary means; and which worked out almost exactly as originally planned.

The Crozon Peninsula was estimated to contain from 1,500 to 3,500 German defenders who had the advantage of formidable permanent fortifications and large amounts of artillery. [The number of defenders was grossly underestimated.] This force had been contained for some weeks by an improvised American unit known as Task Force "A," Brigadier General Herbert L. Earnest, consisting largely of mechanized cavalry, combat engineers, tank destroyers, light tanks, and armored light artillery.

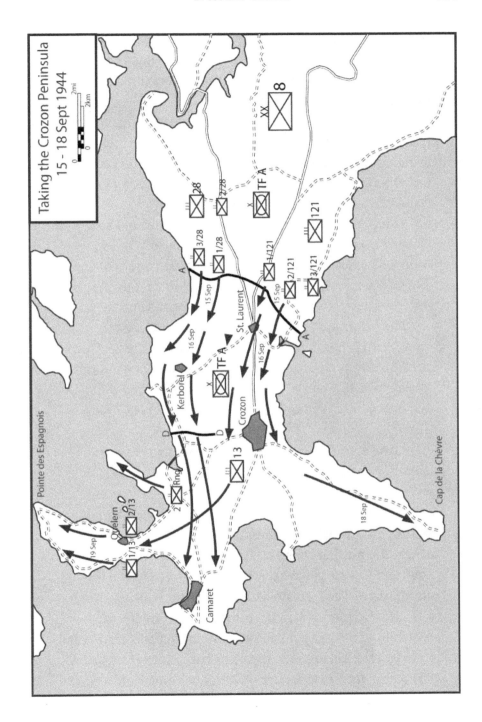

Taking the Crozon Peninsula
15 - 18 Sept 1944

Incidentally, included in the Force was the 17th
Cavalry Reconnaissance Squadron, the successor to
the cavalry regiment of the same number with which I
had served during World War I.

Task Force "A" with commendable aggressiveness
had driven west along the peninsula until it held the
line about 15 miles from the tip. Beyond this point it
had been unable to advance because of strong enemy
resistance.

The Crozon Peninsula completely dominates the
water approaches to the port of Brest. It bristled with
seacoast defenses. Until these could be reduced, the
use of the port would be completely denied to the
Americans even after they were in possession.

The peninsula itself is shaped like a forearm,
wrist, and a hand of three fingers and a thumb. The
principle town, Crozon, lies at the wrist. The thumb
is represented by Ile Longue; the fingers by Pointe
des Espagnols, the Camaret Peninsula, and Cap de la
Chèvre.

After a complete study of the topography and
German defenses it was decided to attack initially
with two regiments in assault, each to operate from
east to west along one of the forearm ridges, thus
taking advantage of the high ground to take the bulk
of the German defense in flank. The flat, wide valley
between the ridges would be mopped up by the light
elements of Task Force "A," advancing abreast of the
assault regiments and maintaining direct contact
between them. The initial attack was to continue until
the westernmost extremities of the parallel ridges
had been captured in the vicinity of the wrist. The

left assault regiment would then halt and consolidate its positions while Task Force "A" would push to the southwest and clean up the German defenders in the Cap de la Chèvre. Simultaneously, the right assault regiment would resume its advance for the capture of the Cabaret Peninsula.

Strongest resistance was expected in the Pointe des Espagnols where the most formidable defenses were located and where the German garrison was expected to retire for its final stand. The reduction of this finger was to be the job of the remaining regiment, kept in reserve for that purpose.

As the division was relieved by echelon from in front of Brest it was moved to assembly areas east of the line held by Task Force "A," itself passed to control of the division forty-eight hours before the attack started. Other reinforcements were strong and ample, bringing the strength of the division to approximately 25,000 men. Reinforcements included a medium tank battalion, a tank destroyer battalion, two companies of a chemical battalion, the 2nd Ranger Battalion, an anti-aircraft artillery battalion, and seven field artillery battalions.

The division was also authorized to call direct on Thunderbolts operated by the aggressive pilots of the 378th Fighter Squadron, 362nd Fighter Bomber Group, based at Rennes.

All elements of the reinforced division were in position by 14 September except the 13th Infantry (division reserve) which arrived on the 15th.

On the evening before the battle was to begin, as Major General Stroh stood before the most daunting challenge and potentially greatest triumph of his life, he received the news that he had been dreading; Harry had been killed in action on August 27th. He would later write, "This was the most tragic moment of my life." Twenty-five thousand men and his country were counting on him; there was nothing he could do but fight on. Stroh's narrative of the Crozon campaign continues:

The 28th Infantry, Colonel Merritt E. Olmstead, attacking in the north zone, started its assault at 0800, 15 September. It attacked with the 1st and 3d Battalions, right to left in assault, and the 2d Battalion in reserve.

The 121st Infantry, Colonel John R. Jeter, attacking in the south zone, also employed two battalions, the 1st and 2d, in assault. Its 3d Battalion occupied excellent firing positions on the high ground in the vicinity of Kersaniou, from which it supported by fire the attack of the remainder of the regiment.

The first day's fight was a typical hammer-and-tongs affair through hedgerow country with which the division had become thoroughly acquainted during its operations in Normandy and the attack on Brest. By dark both regiments had advanced an average of 800 yards against stiffening resistance and believed themselves in contact with the German main line of resistance.

The 28th Infantry renewed the attack at 0700 on 16 September and progressed slowly but steadily throughout the day, registering a gain of about 1,100 yards by dark. The 121st Infantry, renewing the attack at 0800 on the 16th, succeeded during the day in capturing an enemy strongpoint at St. Laurent, and in making an appreciable breach in the main line of resistance in the southern portion of the regimental zone. The Germans reacted vigorously against the 1st Battalion on the right during the afternoon, launching three successive counterattacks, all of which were repulsed. Both regiments were now abreast and in a position to exploit the success the following day.

Progress on 17 September in both regimental zones was rapid. On the right, the 28th Infantry, still attacking with the 1st and 3d Battalions abreast, and aided by an early morning ground fog, quickly overran the airfield near Kerborel, continued to sweep along the northern ridge, and by dark had seized a position nearly 5,000 yards west of its jump-off in the early hours of the morning. Its 3d Battalion moved forward by bounds in rear of the assault battalions cleaning up bypassed pockets of resistance. The 121st Infantry, likewise without change of formation, made even more rapid progress on this date and by dark had seized its regimental objective in and around Crozon, an advance of about 7,000 yards during the day.

Task Force "A" was having difficulty keeping contact with the rapidly advancing assault regiments, due primarily to the lack of suitable east and west roads through the valley. As darkness (1900) approached it was evident that it would be unable to advance beyond the road running north from Crozon.

At dark the division was buttoned up with the 121st Infantry disposed with one battalion in the vicinity of the fort northwest of Crozon, one battalion on the high ground about 1,000 yards southwest of the town, and one battalion on Hill 96. The 28th Infantry had the 1st and 3d Battalions abreast along line DD, with its 2d Battalion on Hill 73. Task Force "A" was in contact with the interior flanks of both regiments. The 13th Infantry, still in division reserve, had been moved forward by bounds during the day and was at dark disposed with its leading battalion on Hill 60.

The operations of 17 September had witnessed the complete collapse of the German defenses as far west as the wrist of the Peninsula. The withdrawal had assumed the proportions of a rout. Nearly 1,500 prisoners were captured, including thirty officers. One of these unfortunates had in his possession the German field order for the occupation of the new positions during the night 17-18 September, complete with the location of command posts, assembly areas, and lines of resistance.

The stage was now set for the beginning of Phase 2 of the operation. Prior to daylight on 18 September one battalion of the 13th Infantry was to advance and seize Hill 70 and protect the advance of the 28th Infantry to the west against interference from the southwest. The 28th Infantry was to continue its advance to the west, seize Hill 61 and continue its attack into the Camaret Peninsula. The 2nd Ranger Battalion, attached to the division on 17 September, was to move in rear of the 28th Infantry, swing to the north as soon as uncovered, and reduce the defenses at Ile Longue. The 121st Infantry was to hold its positions in the vicinity of Crozon and to cover the debouchment of Task Force "A" into Cap de la Chèvre.

Operations on 18 September progressed most satisfactorily. Hill 70 was occupied by one battalion 13th Infantry prior to daylight. Under its protection the 28th Infantry swept forward, captured Hill 61, and occupied the entire Camaret Peninsula before dark.

As soon as the 28th Infantry had passed Hill 61 on its way to the west, the 13th Infantry occupied this hill and advanced with the patrols of one battalion as far as the wall across the neck of the Pointe des Espagnols.

The 2nd Ranger Battalion had no difficulty in occupying Ile Longue, where it released several hundred American prisoners of war previously captured during the Brest campaign [including E and G Companies, 28th Infantry].

It had been planned previously that Task Force "A" would use routes southeast of Crozon in moving into the Cap de la Chèvre. This was found unnecessary due to the feeble hostile reaction and the stout defense maintained by the 121st Infantry on the high ground in the vicinity of the town. All day the numerous mechanized and motorized vehicles of Task Force "A" streamed through Crozon on their way to the southwest. Given elbow room, this highly mobile force rapidly spread out over the entire cape. This proved to be a cavalryman's holiday. By dark, advanced elements of the force had reached the tip of the cape, and gathered in several hundred bewildered German prisoners, including Lieutenant General von Rauch, commander of the 353d German Division.

This officer had had a busy three months previously. His division had been cut to pieces by the advance of the 9th Division [during the Cherbourg campaign], whence he led the remnants to Brest and thence to the Crozon Peninsula, only to be finally hunted down and captured at last.

With the forearm, wrist, thumb, and two of the three fingers of the Peninsula in American hands by dark on 18 September, it remained only to raise the curtain on the last act of the drama on the 19th. It was estimated that the reduction of Pointe des Espagnols would not be child's play. The old but formidable French fort and the wall across the neck were strong. During the night of 18-19 September the bulk of the artillery with the division was moved to the west to be within easy support range of the attack on the following day. Brest had already fallen to the 2nd and 29th Infantry Divisions. Arrangements were made with the American artillery based on the peninsula north of Crozon to add its weight to the other fires. The 378th Fighter Squadron was to participate, with planes in the air at all times. The 13th Infantry, Colonel Robert A. Griffin, fresh and eager, was in position ready for jump-off in the vicinity of Hill 61.

All night, and until 1100 on 19 September, artillery of all calibers battered at the wall and at the fort, but were unable to effect a breach. Accordingly, at that time the 3d and 2d Battalions, 13th Infantry, attacked abreast. These troops, with magnificent elan, scaled the wall, overran the fort, and continued their advance to the north. The men advanced with parade-ground precision following closely behind successive concentrations put down by the overwhelming American artillery and closely supported by the dive-bombers of the Air Force, which strafed and dropped their bombs repeatedly only a few hundred yards ahead of the advancing infantry. Strongpoint after strongpoint fell, and by dark the victorious troops had reached the northern point. The intrepid young pilots of the 378th were still longing for a fight and were disappointed when, at about 1800, they were told that there were no more targets and that the final objective had been reached.

Near the tip of the point, in a dugout seventy-five feet deep, the men of Company I, 13th Infantry, captured Lieutenant General Ramcke, surrounded by the last remnants of his 2d Paratroop Division. Ramcke had led the German invasion of Crete in 1941, and was commander of the fortress of Brest before he escaped therefrom by water in the last days of the siege of that city to make a last ditch stand on Crozon.

Crozon Peninsula, consisting of approximately fifty square miles of as heavily organized an area as any that existed in France, had been cleared in five days of a whirlwind campaign. A total of 225 officers, including two lieutenant generals, 895 non-commissioned officers, and 6,316 privates were captured. This number represented more than twice the estimated maximum of German defenders. In addition, some hundreds were killed.

Careful planning; time for orders, reconnaissance, and movement; the necessary means to accomplish the job; maximum coordination between artillery and infantry, and between ground and air forces; and finally, the irresistible aggressiveness of the American soldier paid dividends.

A footnote to this remarkable campaign is a more detailed description of Gen. Ramcke's capture, a story that lives on in American military lore. A platoon leader of Company I, 1st Lt. James M. Dunham, while leading his men in clearing out the last German holdouts in a coastal area, spotted white flags. A German officer announced in English that Gen. Ramcke was in a dugout below and wished to discuss terms with the American commander. Brigadier General Charles D.W. Canham, Assistant 8th Division Commander, Col. Griffin, 13th Infantry, Lt. Col. Earl L. Lerette, 3rd Battalion, and Lt. Dunham arrived and were escorted into the dugout where Gen. Ramcke was waiting. The haughty German commander spoke to Gen. Canham through his interpreter. "I am to surrender to you. Let me see your credentials." Pointing to his rifle-toting doughboys waiting at the dugout entrance, Canham replied, "These are my credentials."[8] The surrender instrument was signed by Gens. Stroh and Ramcke early that evening.

It is worth noting that Brest was never used as a major supply port for the Allies during the war. Between the Germans' thorough sabotage along with massive Allied aerial and artillery bombardment, the facilities were completely destroyed. In addition, the strategic situation had changed because of the Allies' whirlwind advance across France and Belgium to the German border which had vastly increased the length of supply lines. High command determined that it was not worth the effort and expense to rebuild. But they deemed the campaign a success; destruction of the naval base and many vessels, and the annihilation of the entire German garrison.

At the height of the battle on September 17th, back in Washington, Imogene wrote to her father about the terrible news that she and her mother had received three days earlier. A telegram from the Secretary of War had officially informed them that Capt. Stroh "has been missing in action since 27 August over France." This, of course, was different than the news given to Gen. Stroh, who was informed, probably unofficially, that his son had been killed in action. As the letter clearly indicates, she took the MIA news quite literally.

> It is so hard to write you when I know it will be two weeks or more before you get this letter, and by that time if I should say anything halfway consoling it will sound awfully silly if you and Harry happen to be enjoying steak and champagne.
>
> It is bad enough for us to worry, but it is worse that you must know because you've been so close to him this last year and been running into him so much. Then, too, you have that tremendous responsibility to think about. Mother's been wanting you to come home so much these last few months, but now she wants you to stay so that you may all come back together.
>
> Wherever Harry is he must be madder than anything that he can't get word to any of us because he knows how concerned we'd be. He can pout, but I'll bet he is pouting now like he's never pouted before...
>
> It's going to be fun hearing you three tell some of your experiences and won't Harry puff up when he's got something over you two. He's just so proud of the fact that the Air Corps roughs it as much as the "gravel agitators."

September 24, 1944

> I think if Mother knew that you knew about Harry she'd feel so relieved because she'd know you would be doing everything in your power to find him, especially now that we know you are around Brest and that that was Harry's last mission.
>
> Even when we got that poop-sheet of Harry's that

arrived from his C.O. last week we couldn't believe that
you were near Brest. Mother says she sure didn't G-2
your position very well... And say, as soon as you get
Harry stuffed with steak, you'd better hike yourself
over there with that division and help those Armies
over in Germany. Those Germans are beginning to
fight back awful hard and your keen military mind has
to get in there to outsmart them.

It is difficult to imagine the emotional extremes endured by Gen.
Stroh in the days that followed. While his division regrouped, cleaned
up, repaired equipment, and rested for a few days before preparing
to move east, Gen. Stroh secured endorsements from his Corps commander, Gen. Middleton, and Army commander, Gen. Simpson for
a two-week leave to the United States. He visited Harry's crash site
outside the little town of Kergaradec, just north of Brest, a small farm
of the Quéféléan family into whose farmhouse parts of the stricken
plane had come to rest. One of the family members present at the time
of Gen. Stroh's visit was eighteen- year-old Marie, who described the
scenario in a letter to Imogene, nearly fifty years later. The letter was
transcribed into English by Marie's niece, Jacqueline.

Monday, February 7th, 1994
Madame QUÉFÉLÉAN Marie
KERGARADEC   To Major Harry R. STROH's sister
29850 GOUESNOU
(Finistère)

Dear Madam,
    I have just been told that you have been looking for
reminiscence of your brother who was killed in August
1944 during the siege of Brest. His plane crashed on

our house and pieces of it were scattered all over the property. I had the painful surprise of discovering remains, part of his foot and leg that had remained in the cabin. [cockpit] We buried it and warned the local authorities so that they did what was necessary. A few days later I saw your father who had come to collect his thoughts on the place where we had laid down his remains.

I can well remember seeing your father who, then, was a 'field' officer. Since then, I have known that he became a general.

I was eighteen then. I was born in 1926. The whole tragedy had affected us very much: a young man of our own age who died so far from his homeland while he was defending our country. The field where he was killed has remained the same since then. Nothing has been changed.

I still live in the same place in Kergaradec (in Gouesnou). I know that you will be informed of all this by the authorities but I really wanted to tell you about it myself, for this tragedy has been deeply rooted in my mind since then.

If you come to France and to Kergaradec, I will be very pleased to welcome you at home.

Yours respectfully

Kind Regards.

J. Quéféléan

(Mrs. Quéféléan's niece)

Imogene, clearly moved by this letter, responded almost immediately after being away on travel. At the time, she was planning a reunion trip to Brittany with a group of veterans and their families to commemorate the 50th anniversary of the battles there. This is taken from a rough draft of her letter:

> 5840 Lowell Avenue
> Alexandria, Virginia, USA
> 1 March 1994
> Dear Madam Quéfélean,
>
> Such a lovely letter from you has been sent to me by Colonel Dwan. I am sorry to be so late to answer, but I have just been in Florida taking care of my grandchildren.
>
> Your letter has deeply affected me. I have wanted to see the place where my brother, Harry Stroh, crashed for some years. I visited Crozon in 1985, for ceremonies in September, but did not get to visit your area.
>
> It was as if he just died to receive your letter to know you were there afterwards and knew about it has really shaken me. I am planning to be there in September and look forward to meeting you. I wish I had studied French!
>
> Before he left home, Harry told me he was just cannon fodder. This I did not want to hear and being young I thought nothing could happen to him. He was pleased to see my father sometimes in England, and through that winter and he, my father, and my husband were together for Christmas 1943. He and my father must have communicated often the summer of 1944 and they must not have been very far apart.
>
> Brest was so heavily defended that the Allies had to virtually destroy it and the surrounding area. How did you survive? I wonder how you lived.
>
> I will look forward to seeing you.

Thus began a correspondence and friendship that lasted for many years. Marie provided more insight into the military and civilian situation outside of Brest during and after the battle in her next letter to Imogene, dated March 10, 1994.

When I learned that some Americans were investigating about the very place where your brother died, I was overwhelmed for we had had been talking about it for ages in the neighborhood. It was a complete mystery!

Yet, we had been providing a lot of details to such an extent that in the family your brother was known as "our American pilot." It was the only plane that had crashed in August 1944 in Kergaradec.

My elder brother... was of the same age as your brother. He was also there when your father came to our place as well as one of my sisters. We were standing near your father who was with two civilians who spoke French. They were the ones who told us that the American officer was the pilot's father.

It has been nearly fifty years now since I kept a piece of the plane of your brother as a token... If you wish, I will give it to you when you come.

To answer your question 'how did I survive?' here are a few details: in our village of Kergaradec, there were three farms, three families that were very close to one another. In August 1944 many German soldiers were occupying our neighborhood. Among them, one very humane officer said to our father: "If my wife and my children lived in this area, I would take them away from here for the fighting will be dreadful." (for that was already the situation) I remember mum saying:

"I spent one night in the shelter but I won't spend one more night, I'd rather die in my bed."

The German officer then said: "You have to leave today." That was on 14th August 1944. "I will write a pass for you" he added. Then we moved about seven kilometers from our place.

My father and the other two heads of the families stayed there until August 20th when the first house was shot down. They came and joined us thanks to a pass written by the same German officer. Before leaving they had penned in all the cattle in the same field where there was a watering place. I think that the wooded patch your father alludes to in his account was next to that field. (of course, all the cattle was killed)

It was where we had taken refuge that we saw the first Americans. That was also where we had been told that a plane had crashed on our house towards the end of August.

We came back to Kergaradec on 8th September. It was soon after we were back home that I discovered what I told in my first letter. It was after we warned the local authorities in Gouesnou that we saw your father arrive with the two civilians. We sympathized with him.

Then we built sheds and lived there for about four years. Our house was rebuilt in 1948.

A series of events marked the administrative trail regarding Capt. Stroh's death during the days and weeks following the shoot-down, which led to the notifications to Gen. Stroh, and separately, to Mrs. Stroh on September 14th. The crash occurred the evening of August

27th. The missing aircrew report was required to be filed to Army Air Corps Headquarters within forty-eight hours of the incident. A report from the 8th Division Graves Registration Officer to Gen. Stroh dated November 9th established a timeline for the following events. On September 3rd, the remains of an "unidentified" pilot were evacuated through medical channels to the 8th Division graves registration collecting point. A further identification was attempted at the collecting point, but none was found. The remains were then evacuated to the VIII Corps collecting point for processing to the St. James American Cemetery about 200 miles to the east. At the Corps collecting point, an ID bracelet was discovered bearing the name Harry Stroh and his Army serial number. The body was buried as Harry Stroh, rank unknown, and a Report of Burial was sent to Ninth U.S. Army on September 9th.

Meanwhile, by 9th Air Force Special Order number 251, Harry R. Stroh was promoted from captain to major as of September 7th; his status at that time was Missing in Action. As we know, Gen. Stroh was informed of Maj. Stroh's death on September 14th, the eve of the Crozon campaign. Gen. Stroh's chief of staff, Colonel Thomas Cross, dispatched the division G-1 to bring back the officer who witnessed the crash, presumably Lt. Edwards. Also on the 14th, Mrs. Stroh, at home with her daughter Imogene in Washington, received a telegram from the Secretary of War informing her that her son was missing in action as of August 27th.

A week or so later a VIII Corps search team led by the Corps GRO returned to the crash site and discovered, among other things, Major Stroh's West Point class ring. Around this same time, Gen. Stroh visited his son's grave at St. James and the crash site at Kergaradec. He mentioned these events in his first letter to Imogene since learning of her brother's death.

Sept 23, 1944

It has been all that I could do to write to Harry's
mother and grandmother during the past two weeks.
I find it equally difficult to write to his sister now. I
have never seen you in the face of real tragedy, and
have no way of predicting what your reactions will
be. Knowing your tender heart I can but fear the
worst, but knowing also your courageous spirit I am
comforted by the certain realization that you have
been a real help to Mother during these dark days. I
don't know how she could have stood the blow if you
had not been near to comfort her.

I took a trip of nearly four hundred miles early
in the week to visit Harry's grave. It is located on a
green hill-top, overlooking a beautiful valley, near the
little village of St. James. The surroundings are still
crude, as you can judge from the enclosed pictures,
but the cemetery will receive the tender care always
shown where American dead are buried, and it will
undoubtedly be a beautiful spot by another spring and
summer. I am sending you these pictures, and will
leave it to your judgement whether you show them to
Mother, as I am not sure of her reaction. Personally,
I was much comforted to see with my own eyes that
Harry was tenderly interred, and his grave marked
and decorated. It might have been quite otherwise had
he been buried by the Germans on the battlefield. The
officiating clergyman is our division Chaplain, and
the four respectful onlookers are soldiers who work
in the cemetery... I am also enclosing some sprigs of
flowers and greens. The peony and the greens were
taken from the wreath you see in the photos. The

poppies, similar to those which made Flanders Fields so notorious, were picked within a few feet of where Harry's crashed plane landed.

Harry sleeps in an heroic company, a company of American boys, united in death, and without regard to creed, color, birth, or rank. The graves on either side of Harry's are those of enlisted men.

"On Fame's eternal camping ground
Their silent tents to spread,
And Glory guards, with solemn round
The bivouac of the dead."

So ends, on this hill-top, all the love and ambition which I lavished on your brother, a love and ambition which he repaid a hundred fold. I have only realized since his death in the long night hours when I cannot sleep, how much he loved me, admired me, and tried to please me. He died, as a matter of fact, trying to show me that he could take it. As if I didn't know! He had more courage in his little finger than I have in my body. Do you remember when I used to look forward to the day when he would give me his first salute as an Army officer? When I said good-bye to him at St. James the other day, I told him that he was a better man than I am, and saluted him before I left. I hope that this leaving will be au revoir and not adieu. I do not know how Mother will feel about it, but I should like, after the war, to bring him back to sleep in the Long Grey Line at West Point which he loved so well. I keep his photograph and yours prominently displayed in my tent, so I can say hello in the morning and sleep tight at night. His ring is also a great comfort to me.

I thought, on this Saturday afternoon, that I would

be halfway across the Atlantic, and would be with you in time for church tomorrow. I started out all right yesterday morning, all packed and clothed for the journey, but didn't get very far. With the enthusiastic approval of my corps and army commanders I was certain that my leave would be approved at the highest headquarters, but there I met a stone wall, and returned here this morning. It was a bitter, bitter disappointment, and I know it will be for you at home. I did my very best, taking the matter to Eisenhower in person, but got nowhere. He, and other senior officers there, had heard of Harry's death, and expressed their sympathy. While this was appreciated, I would have been more receptive to a more concrete expression of their feelings.

Your homey, cheerful letter of the 3rd reached me since I last wrote you. It is always a great pleasure to receive them, and a special comfort now.

The verse Gen. Stroh quoted in his letter of the 23rd is from a poem written in 1847 by Theodore O'Hara called "Bivouac of the Dead." It commemorates Kentucky troops killed in the Mexican War and is on display at various national cemeteries. Today, the St. James American Cemetery is a beautiful, pristine, quiet place, meticulously attended. From the bell tower, one can see the ocean about six miles to the northwest, the spires of Mont Saint-Michel rising just offshore.

Apparently Gen. Stroh made the long trip from the Crozon Peninsula to St. James on the day after the Crozon campaign ended, Wednesday, September 20th. It is not certain on which day he visited the crash site at Kergaradec, but it was probably the next day, the 21st. Col. Cross's diary entry of September 22nd: "Gen. Stroh departed on leave of absence for the United States." The next day's entry includes: "Got a call from Gen. Stroh that he would return, apparently leave not approved by headquarters." He returned to the division CP at 1200 and this message was waiting for him:

> FROM SHAEF FORWARD SHCOS
> TO 8TH INF DIV
> FOLLOWING MESSAGE WAS RECEIVED FROM YOUR
> WIFE JUST AFTER YOU LEFT. (TO COMMANDING
> GENERAL NINTH ARMY. PERSONAL FOR GENERAL
> STROH EIGHTH DIVISION FROM SMITH SIGNED
> EISENHOWER CITE SHCOS) MESSAGE FOLLOWS:
> "HARRY HAS BEEN MISSING IN ACTION OVER
> FRANCE SINCE AUGUST TWENTY SEVEN. HOPE
> YOU CAN GET DETAILS ON HIS WHEREABOUTS. WE
> ARE PRAYING FOR HIS SAFETY. ALL ARE WELL AT
> HOME. LOVE. GENIE." I WILL GLADLY RELAY ANY
> MESSAGE YOU WISH TO SEND HER.

Gen. Stroh, now fully aware that his wife did not know of their son's death, responded with this cable, apparently relayed through Gen. Eisenhower's Chief of Staff, that Mrs. Stroh received on September 26th: "Harry died heroically. Full details in my letters of September 15th and 19th. Cannot get home. Courage." Imogene responded on the 28th.

> I never thought that I would have to write this letter to you. Mrs. Handy brought your cable over about noon yesterday.
>
> It seems that Mother had been expecting that news all along but it is hard to believe even when it does come. You worded the cable so well, but Mother is terribly disappointed you can't get home.
>
> We're awfully anxious for your letters and feel such

a satisfaction that you were there to get the details. It has been so wonderful that you both have seen each other so much this past year and even worked together. Harry always wanted to be a credit to you, Daddy, and he certainly has proved himself that you may always be proud of him.

This has always been an exceptionally happy family, and as Mother says, you can remember Harry as strong and healthy and that big grin on his face.

I'm so sorry you have to be there alone and I wish Bob could be with you, but I guess that's impossible.

18

---◆---

The Siegfried Line

Reichsfuhrer S.S.   10 September 1944

Certain unreliable elements seem to believe that the war will be over for them as soon as they surrender to the enemy.

Against this belief it must be pointed out that every deserter will be prosecuted and find his just punishment. Furthermore, his ignominious behavior will entail the most severe consequences for his family. Upon examination of the circumstances they will be summarily shot.

(signed) HIMMLER

On September 13th, the men of the 39th Infantry were poised to attack into the vaunted Siegfried Line, a colossal series of fortifications just inside the German border stretching from the Dutch frontier to the Swiss border.

Known as the West Wall to its German constructors, the Siegfried Line consisted of a series of mutually supporting small fortresses known as pillboxes. Hitler began construction of the barrier in 1936 and by the end of 1938, there were more than 500,000 men working on it, using a third of Germany's total cement production. More than 3,000 concrete pillboxes, bunkers, and observation points were built. The pillboxes typically were twenty to thirty feet wide, forty to fifty feet deep, and twenty to twenty-five feet high. At least half of the structure was subterranean. The walls and roofs were three to eight feet thick, made of steel reinforced concrete. Inside were living quarters, weapons, ammunition, and communications equipment. Pillbox density averaged about ten per mile, 200 to 400 yards behind anti-tank barriers. In 1944, after four years of neglect, these structures were overgrown with foliage, giving them natural camouflage that made them difficult for aerial reconnaissance and attack.[1]

The wall complex was protected by a multitude of natural and man-made barriers like rivers and lakes, thick forests, ravines, and railroad cuts. In clearer areas, the Germans constructed fields of anti-tank barriers that became known as "dragon's teeth." They consisted of reinforced concrete pyramids, five feet high, in five alternating rows. Roads leading through the dragon's teeth were protected by steel and concrete obstacles and gates which were usually within fields of fire of one or more pillboxes.[2]

As VII Corps approached the German border from the west and southwest, the 1st Division and 3rd Armored Division were in the north near Aachen, the 9th Division was in the middle, south of Eupen, and the 4th Cavalry Group covered the right flank. On September 13th, the 39th Infantry was in a column of battalions advancing to the east toward the German city of Roetgen, with 3rd Battalion in reserve. A detailed study of the activities of this battalion, one of the first Allied units to breech the Siegfried Line, was prepared by 2nd Lt. Fred L. Hadsel of the 1st Army's Information and History Service. This account, which covers the period from September 14th until October 26th, represents in microcosm VII Corps' initial breach of the

Siegfried Line and the first two phases of what would become known as the Battle of the Huertgen Forest. The study is based substantially on interviews with Lt. Col. Stumpf and Capt. A. V. Danna, commanding I Company, and their logs. The remainder of this chapter consists of verbatim and paraphrased excerpts from Lt. Hadsel's report.[3]

13 Sept. (cont.)

The 3rd Battalion stopped in the vicinity of Muetzenich at nightfall. They spent the night on the road because the ground was too muddy to permit pulling off to the side.

14 Sept.

At daylight the battalion renewed its advance, with the immediate plan of joining the two leading battalions as soon as possible. The battalion moved with two companies on tanks and TDs and shuttled the third, while the heavy weapons and headquarters units were on trucks. Three trucks had been stuck the night before, and the column was short on gasoline.

As they advanced through the woods of the Konzener Wald, a few snipers and one machine gun were encountered, but these were dusted off when the tanks fired into the trees along the road. At RJ 942234, the 1st and 2nd battalions had turned sharply northwest in the direction of Roetgen, but the 3rd continued east 800 yards before hitting another road leading north which would connect them with the rest of the regiment. This section of road had not been cleared of the enemy.

As the battalion approached the highway it encountered the first enemy roadblock, consisting of a locked iron gate and a number of mines. A platoon of the 15th Engineers, attached to the battalion, came up and cleared the mines, and the tanks crashed through the gate. Col. Stumpf had put out a security squad on the flank of the column in the direction of Konzon, and it engaged the enemy at a range of 500 yards in a fire fight. The skirmish did not develop into anything too serious, and the column continued north at 1000, having been held up about an hour.

Before the tail of the column passed the point of the first road-block, the leading elements hit another obstacle, felled trees across the road, but it was neither mined nor covered by fire. The tanks looped cables around the trees and pulled them off. 500 yards further they hit a third roadblock, felled trees and mines, as well as a large crater in the middle of the road. The crater was made passable by a tank-dozer. Stumpf radioed for engineers to make the road suitable for heavy traffic, while the engineers pulled the mines and the tanks dragged off the logs.

Early in the afternoon the column rendezvoused with the rest of the regiment, and Stumpf was given a further mission. The bulk of his battalion would follow 1st Battalion north out of Lammersdorf, with K Company instructed to run patrols east out of Lammersdorf towards Rollesbroich. K Company pushed through the rear of 1st Battalion supported by one section of tanks, and proceeded east on the main road through the town. As it reached the edge of town about 1600, it came under enemy mortar and 75mm AT fire. The tanks fired at the AT gun and probably knocked it out, but the area also took artillery hits and the sergeant making the hit was killed.

As K Company came under fire, Stumpf decided to commit I Company into the fight on the left side of the road, while at the same time he secured permission to abandon the plan of following C Company, to concentrate on the opposition facing K Company.

K Company moved forward along the scattered houses as the enemy continued to use mortar and AT fire on their positions. It advanced about 200 yards, with one platoon on each side of the road, and almost reached the Dragon's Teeth. Since it was getting dark, it did not try to breach the obstacles and held this position for the night.

Meanwhile I Company attacked in two columns up parallel to

the trails leading northeast from the main road. The plan was for I to conduct a flank movement from the north on the enemy position and thus secure the area from the rear. I Company was under fire from the pillboxes and emplacements to its front as soon as it left the highway in Lammersdorf. The enemy used only small arms at this time. The company was able to advance more than 200 yards before it became too dark to see. It then held its position for the night.

Throughout the development of this attack, the entire right flank of the battalion was open to the southeast. Therefore, Col. Stumpf brought up L Company to act both as a reserve for the battalion and protection on the right flank. L Company set up a thin line from the railroad track to the west to a small trail near the Dragon's Teeth on the east, and began to receive some fire from the southeast.

By nightfall the entire battalion was thus employed and under fire. One section of heavy machine guns were, as usual, employed with each company, and mortars were set up in the rear. The section of tanks with A Company fired at enemy positions, while the other section remained in the town with the TD platoon to guard the road crossings. The AT guns were set up to bolster the defense on the right flank. L Company began to receive long range artillery fire, but the other companies nothing heavier than 50 mm mortars.

15 Sept.

The regimental commander, Col. Bond, ordered that the entire line of 3rd Battalion probe for weak points in the enemy defenses. If one company made a break, the other two would quickly withdraw and follow in its path.

K Company in the center of the battalion front met the strongest resistance. Under heavy fire, which dominated the open ground at the gap through the Dragon's Teeth, the company went through the gap and captured the entrenchment just east of the concrete obstacles. It fought from house to house to get to the Dragon's Teeth, but resistance in the gap itself was not especially heavy.

While K Company moved slowly throughout the morning across the Dragon's Teeth, I Company attacked on the left flank. It came under heavy mortar and small arms fire, and likewise could not move fast, advancing no more than 200 yards and not crossing the Dragon's Teeth. I Company did succeed in surrounding some pillboxes on the near side of the obstacles, but even though employing TDs against them, the pillboxes would not fall.

L Company also jumped off early. It sent a flank patrol down the trail southward towards the village of Paustenbach, while the bulk of the company attacked down the road just east of the railroad towards the same objective. The town itself was reached with surprisingly little opposition, and the main body of the company moved down the main street and cleaned the houses of scattered opposition. Meanwhile the patrol on the east flank turned sharply east and worked up a defiladed trail towards the Dragon's Teeth until they came in the open within 200 yards of the obstacles. Here, they came under heavy fire and were unable to advance further, and held this position as the left flank of the company front.

Having cleared out most of the town and the orchards behind the houses, L Company continued the attack to the next objective, Hill 554. This ground dominated the entire area, including the town of Lammersdorf. It was considered vital to a successful penetration of the Siegfried Line that the hill, with its excellent observation, be in American hands. Col. Stumpf directed L Company to attack east to Hill 554. Leaving one platoon to guard Paustenbach, it began its attack with two platoons. With fire from pillboxes and emplacements on the hill, the enemy responded with such intensity, that L Company could not advance much beyond the line of houses along the eastern edge of the village.

As the battalion tied in for the night, it had secured a good observation post in the area taken by K Company. Thereafter, artillery called in by the battalion helped considerably in the attacks. Three 75mm AT guns and two 20mm gun emplacements were targeted with some success.

16 Sept.

L Company renewed its attack on Hill 554. The two platoons on the left of the road on the northwestern slope forced their way up to the Dragon's Teeth, engaging in hand-to-hand fighting. One platoon got into the entrenchments and managed to cross the concrete obstacles and the enemy pulled out. However, a pre-zeroed in mortar barrage then came down on their position, while enfiladed fire hit the platoon from the left flank. This advanced position could not be maintained because the platoon was cut off from the rest of the company by enemy fire. It therefore withdrew to the entrenchments just west of the Dragon's Teeth.

I company was attacked at dawn, but lost no ground and continued to move up the two trails to the Dragon's Teeth. It took one pillbox, and in the afternoon secured a foothold beyond the Dragon's Teeth. The tanks and TDs were brought up to fire at the pillboxes to make them button up, while the infantry enveloped them. Total advance of the company for the day was not over 300 yards, and the enemy small arms and mortar fire continued to be heavy.

K Company likewise continued the attack. It pushed approximately 300 yards from its position at the Dragon's Teeth and reached a pillbox to the right of the road, which it reduced and took up positions there.

17 Sept.

Early in the morning I Company, whose position beyond the Dragon's Teeth exposed it to enemy fire on three sides, received a very strong counterattack. Enemy infantry, but without mortar support, hit the company from the northwest, north and northeast, took prisoners and pushed in the outpost. Friendly mortar fire and company rifles stopped the attacks. Col. Stumpf sent tanks up to support a counterattack by I Company. About two hours later, around 0900, the company and tanks attacked and the enemy broke. The entire area to the northeast fell to the company. A large number of prisoners were taken, and the position consolidated by noon. I company held this ground for the afternoon while E Company of the 2nd Battalion worked its way down from the northwest, making contact late in the afternoon.

K Company in the center of the battalion zone of action continued to experience difficult going along the road where it received small arms and well observed AT and artillery fire. It found that in addition to pillboxes on the right of the road, it received fire from two on the left which it attacked and cleaned out during the day. It did not advance its position very much before nightfall. In attacking these pillboxes, it had a smoke screen laid down and was materially aided by mist. However, AT fire from the east and southeast was still so effective that tanks could not be brought up into the fight.

L Company held its position throughout the day. Stumpf sent a 155mm gun east up the main road from Lammersdorf into a position where it could fire on some of the pillboxes in L Company's sector.

18 Sept.

With the arrival of 2nd Battalion, Col. Stumpf could make different plans of attack. K Company would continue its drive to the east along the main road from Lammersdorf until it reached the first road junction where it would turn south for about 400 yards. At this road juncture it would turn southwest and encircle Hill 554 from the east. I Company was to be pulled out of its present position on the left flank of the Battalion and brought around to assist L Company with its attack on Hill 554 from the west and northwest. The objective for I Company was the northern part of the hill with the first pillbox with a steel dome. L Company would take the southern part of the hill with a second steel domed pillbox.

L Company's attack did not go off as planned because the lead tank escorting them through the gap in the Dragon's Teeth was disabled by mines and AT fire in the gap. Most of the afternoon was spent trying to clear the gap so the attack could proceed. When a TD hooked up to the tank to pull it out, more mines were detonated and the front end of the tank was blown off. L Company's position did not significantly change during the day.

K Company, in the meantime, had launched its attack on Hill 554. As it turned southwest at the second RJ, it came under fire from a pillbox. On the map, the arrow of the pillbox had it pointed the other way, indicating an entirely different field of fire. The company commander radioed, however, "To hell with the arrow, it's shooting on me." The company was held in open ground by this fire temporarily.

After being relieved by E Company of the 2nd Battalion, I Company was required to reduce one more pillbox before it could follow its route to Hill 554. By noon, it was in position to join L Company on the attack on the hill, but as L Company was delayed by the tank in the gap, Col. Stumpf directed I Company to proceed up the trail in the direction of the pillbox that was holding up K Company. In approaching the position from the west, I Company elements found themselves on top of the pillbox without realizing it.

Some soldiers called in to the pillbox and told the Germans to surrender, but the reply was a rifle grenade fired out of the door. It was impossible to blow the door because the enemy could fire through it when it was open, and the machine guns were deep in concrete tunnels, not reachable by grenades. K Company, which had edged closer, had a prisoner who went up to argue with his comrades inside. He told them to think of their families rather than the war, but still they would not surrender. Col. Stumpf directed that a tank-dozer be sent up from the western part of the position. It approached the pillbox from the rear and pushed dirt from the top over to fill the entrance half-way. Another call was made to the men inside to surrender. They were given five minutes to decide. When that time was up, the pillbox was sealed up. It was now dark, and the 3rd Battalion held its positions. The next day, K Company soldiers found the Germans in the buried pillbox still alive and ready to surrender for the privilege of being unearthed.

19 Sept.

Weather severely reduced visibility throughout the day which restricted the use of supporting weapons. I and L Companies attempted another coordinated attack on Hill 554 with tanks again escorting L Company through the Dragon's Teeth. Three tanks moved though the gap as planned. As they came up the slope with I Company, the lead tank was fired on by a bazooka, which took it out. Thereupon, the other tanks withdrew. Throughout the fight the enemy was in trenches around the pillboxes, and from the pillboxes themselves, they called in mortar and artillery fire on the hill.

K Company maintained their positions throughout the day. Col. Stumpf formulated plans for the renewal of the attack the next day.

20 Sept.

The situation for the battalion was becoming more critical since the enemy, by his observation from Hill 554, was able to throw fire into the entire area. Jump-off for a new attack was planned for 1000. A P-38 bombing mission proved ineffective; one bomb hit on the hill, one in the valley, and two on M Company, about 100 yards northwest of the hill.

The attack was preceded by smoke. There were now three tanks in support, including a 105 SP gun, and the infantry reached the top of the hill. One tank was hit by AT fire, while the other two tanks shot up the trenches. The enemy fled from the emplacements back into the pillboxes. It then called in a terrific shelling on its own position. L Company was in the trenches immediately west of the pillboxes on the hill, while I Company was about 1,000 yards to the north. Both companies caught the artillery fire and by 1200 the attack had to stop.

Col. Stumpf informed regiment that a continued assault on Hill 554 would result in excessive casualties. He was directed to hold positions of L and I Companies, while an attack by K Company in another direction took place to the east.

21 Sept.

The strength of the enemy resistance in the vicinity of Hill 554 would be undermined if the high ground to the northeast could be secured. As part of 3rd Battalion's mission to the South of Lammersdorf and in conjunction with 2nd Battalion's mission in the direction of Rollesbroich, K Company was given the task of attacking to the east and seizing that ground.

K Company's attack began at 0900 and was preceded by a barrage of mortar, artillery and smoke on the wooded areas all along the slope in front of the objective. The company worked its way up the wooded slope without serious opposition. It came up to the pillbox dominating the hill to the west, and the enemy in the fortification came out and surrendered. From this point the company began to work around to the north of the hill. As it approached the pillbox that dominated the road towards Rollesbroich, it encountered resistance. Simultaneously it observed more than a company of Germans retreating south and east around the northern nose of the hill. These forces were giving way in front of an attack by E Company 2nd Battalion. The A Company forward observer called in artillery and mortar fire upon the slope over which the enemy had to traverse, and it came down with devastating effect. In addition, a machine gun was set up near the pillbox which also fired with good effect. The result was to disorganize the enemy completely, who broke under the fire of 3rd

Battalion, only to rush back into the fire of 2nd Battalion. A few escaped to the east, while others surrendered to E and K Companies, but a large number were killed. A small group managed to dig in along the road to Rollesbroich which prevented the complete union of the flanks of E and K Companies.

K Company could not advance because of one remaining manned pillbox to its right. It worked up close to the emplacement and attempted to breach it using pole charges. Two failed to detonate and the third exploded but had little effect. The effort was then postponed due to darkness.

22 Sept.

In the morning K Company was to continue its advance to the east but had to reduce the pillbox before it could get very far. Initially, they exploded 75 pounds of TNT inside the first door with little effect. White phosphorous grenades were dropped down the ventilators with equal lack of success. Five gallons of gasoline were poured down the ventilator and set on fire, as were oily rags. Neither brought any response. A series of teller mines were blown up on top of the bunker without success. Finally, after dark, a tank-dozer was brought up, the 15th Engineers put 300 pounds of TNT and two captured "beehive" mines into the hole made by previous detonations. The tank-dozer packed dirt all around and over the explosive. The ensuing explosion was tremendous and the enemy inside at last surrendered. An officer had prevented the soldiers from surrendering earlier. The entire day had been spent reducing this one pillbox.

23 Sept.

A planned attack to the east towards Rollesbroich by 2nd Battalion was repulsed by a series of counterattacks before it could get started. Consequently, 3rd Battalion held its positions.

24- 28 Sept.

Throughout these days, the entire battalion held defensive positions. The weather was very wet and movement of vehicles was limited to hard roadways. Active patrolling continued. Positions of units changed very little.

29 Sept.

During the lull, plans had been perfected for an attack on Hill 554. L Company, which was on the right of the battalion zone of action, was to attack east from Paustenbach, with the pillbox on the crest of the hill as its objective. I Company was to swing around the open ground on the eastern slope and attack from the southeast. K Company was to attack from the North, forming the left flank. A platoon of tanks was to go with the leading elements.

The attack was to begin at 0930 following aerial and artillery preparatory bombardments. After waiting thirty minutes for a smoke screen, the tanks led the assault through the Dragon's Teeth on the northwest part of the hill. The tanks moved much faster than the infantry and they shot up the pillboxes and entrenchment with considerable success. Heavy enemy artillery fire hit them when they reached the southeast slope. One tank was taken out, but the others stayed there to fire on the enemy.

The progress of K Company south along a trail was rapid. It met only moderate small arms fire opposition until reaching the pillbox on the southeast slope, where it came under heavy fire from the direction of Witzerath and Simmerath, towns about a mile to the southeast. The company then built up a position where they could face to the southeast.

I Company was held up for a time on the south slope by the same artillery barrage that was targeting the tanks. At 1500 the company reorganized and attacked again, this time taking the pillboxes on the southern slope. By the end of the day, it had taken four pillboxes and its patrols had made contact with K Company on the left.

When L Company moved back into position following the bombing and artillery preparations, they could observe no opposition in the
vicinity of their objective. Col. Stumpf had them attack immediately
and they seized the objective before the enemy could recover suffi-
ciently to offer a determined resistance. L Company held the ground
for the rest of the day and in the evening sent a patrol to reduce one
final pillbox. By nightfall, 3rd Battalion held all of the objective area
except for the road just south of the hill.

30 Sept.

During the day, the battalion made little changes to its position. It
ran patrols and improved its defensive positions. At 2000, the enemy
launched a strong counterattack from the south. In the darkness it
penetrated considerably into L Company's positions and retook one
of the pillboxes. The attack was stopped by 0100, although small enemy groups of infiltrators were still being cleared out. The moon came
out and by its light L Company attacked the pillbox, recapturing it by
0400. The enemy soldiers who had been behind the lines were killed,
captured or escaped to the east.

1 Oct.

K Company, which had withdrawn under the enemy attack the
night before, reoccupied its former positions and took 15 or more
prisoners in the action. There were too many pillboxes in the area
for the battalion to hold satisfactorily, so Col. Stumpf shortened its
lines. L and K Companies withdrew from the pillboxes to the bottom
of the hill on the south, while I Company pulled into a position near
the crest of the hill on the southeast. This repositioning was done in
conjunction with the engineers, who began to blow up the pillboxes
being vacated. They used six 50 pound boxes of TNT on each. In the
darkness, however, one case of C rations got mixed in with one set

of six boxes, so the pillbox was blown with five boxes of explosives and one box of C rations. I Company found the next morning that for breakfast it was issued a box of TNT.

2-5 Oct.

The battalion remained on the defensive until it was alerted to move north to take part in the drive in the vicinity of Germeter and Vossenack.

So ended the first phase of the Siegfried Line campaign for the 39th Infantry. After four days of rest and reorganization, they would venture deeper into the Huertgen Forest for phase two. For the month of September alone, which included the Meuse crossing and Siegfried Line operations, the regiment lost 85 men killed, 380 wounded and 38 missing, for a total casualty count of 503, something north of twenty percent considering they were not at full strength when they started. Recommendations for decorations included 18 Silver Stars for 17 enlisted men and one officer, presumably Lt. Col. Stumpf; and 77 Bronze Stars.

The regiment had been engaged almost constantly since June 12th; the Cherbourg campaign, the breakout at St. Lo, closing the Falaise pocket, the race across France and Belgium—including cross-ing the Meuse, and two weeks hammering away at the Siegfried Line. The men had slept exclusively in holes in the ground, had very few opportunities to bathe, had subsisted mostly on C and K rations, and, of course, had watched their friends die or be horribly wounded. They were exhausted, physically and emotionally. Their ranks were depleted. Replacements were not keeping up with attrition, and re-placement soldiers, lacking combat experience, were rarely as effec-tive as those they replaced. Likewise, their equipment was, even if not in disrepair, certainly not in the best of condition, including vehicles, armor, artillery, even small arms. The question was, how much longer could they keep going? Perhaps the answer was in realizing that the Germans had it even worse.

19

The Huertgen Forest

Commander-in-Chief West

Headquarters,
1 October 1944

SOLDIERS OF THE WESTERN FRONT!

You have brought the enemy to a halt at the gates of the Reich. But he will shortly go over to new super attacks. I expect you to defend Germany's sacred soil with all your strength and to the very last. The homeland will thank you through untiring efforts and will be proud of you.

New soldiers will arrive at the Western Front. Instill into them your will to victory and your battle experience. All officers and N.C.O.s are responsible for all troops being at all times conscious of their great responsibility as defenders of the Western approaches. Soldiers of the Western Front!

Every attempt of the enemy to break into our Fatherland will fail because of your unshakable bearing.

Heil the Fuhrer!
VON RUNDSTEDT,
Field-Marshal.[1]

The 9th Division was the first of a steady stream
of American units which in subsequent weeks were
to find gloom, misery, and tragedy synonymous with
the Huertgen Forest. Few could distinguish one dank
stretch of evergreens from another, one abrupt ridge
from another. Even atop the ridges, the floor of the
forest was a trap for the heavy autumn rains. By the
time the American and German artillery had done
with the forest, the setting would look like a battlefield
designed by the Archfiend himself.[2]

On the night of October 4th, the 39th Infantry was poised to
launch its next offensive to crack the dogged German defenses in
the Huertgen Forest. Their immediate objectives were Germeter and
Vossenack with a final objective of seizing the high ground in the
vicinity of Schmidt. They also were charged with protecting the north
flank of the division front from possible counterattack from the town of
Huertgen, just a couple of miles to the northeast. The planned jump-
off at noon on the 5th was postponed because the weather was too
poor for the preparatory air bombardment. The next day brought fair
weather and the air strikes began at 0930, two groups of P-47s bombing and strafing targets marked by red smoke from the artillery. This
was followed by two separate artillery barrages, after which six battalions of infantry attacked abreast through the woods, the 39th Infantry
on the left, the 60th to their right. Third Battalion 39th Infantry was
in the center of the regimental zone heading straight for Germeter.[3]

The rate of advance was painfully slow and costly. Enemy artillery
rounds were fused for air-bursts which produced wicked showers of

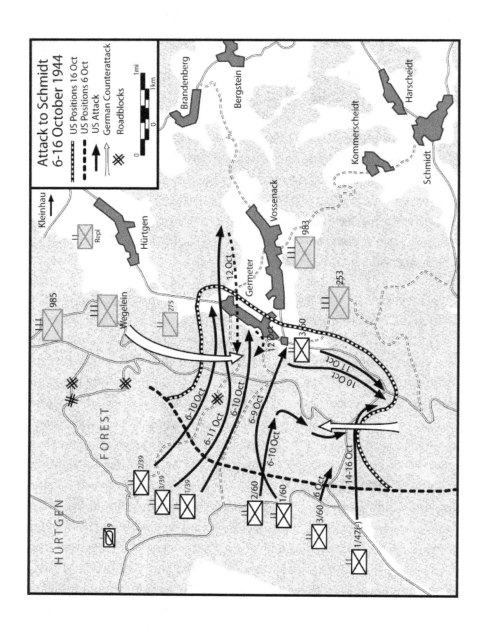

Attack to Schmidt
6-16 October 1944

US Positions 16 Oct
US Positions 6 Oct
US Attack
German Counterattack
Roadblocks

sharp wooden shrapnel from the dense fir trees as they exploded. The regimental sector contained only one trail leading to Germeter, which was subject to booby-trapped roadblocks and mines, as were the firebreaks. As a result, the infantry generally did not have the support of tanks and TDs. Furthermore, it was difficult to adjust supporting artillery fires because of the density of the trees and because the engagements tended to be close in. At the end of the first day of fighting, really only half a day, the 39th Infantry lost ten killed and thirty-nine wounded. The regiment had started its initial drive through the Huertgen Forest in September at approximately 85 percent strength, about 2,425 men.

Progress on October 7th continued at a similar pace, as the battalions advanced towards the edge of the forest around Germeter. Third Battalion jumped off early in the morning moving through thick brush and trees. They came upon a pillbox to the southeast, fire from which slowed their process substantially. Enemy shelling from the north continued all through the day and night. Col. Stumpf directed L and K Companies to plan for an attack on the pillbox in the morning. That second day, the regiment lost another six killed and ninety-one wounded. Replacement troops were dribbling in, but these green soldiers had to learn the art of forest warfare, and survival, on the fly. They learned, for instance, that a foxhole was of no use against tree shrapnel from above unless it included a roof of logs and sod.

The next morning, L Company maneuvered around the pillbox to its rear and resistance folded. K Company then took the position from the front. All battalions continued to make slow but steady progress throughout the day. By the end of October 8th, some heavier weapons had made their way forward and plans were prepared for an attack through the clearing and into Germeter as soon as all battalions had made their way to the edge of the forest. The 39th Infantry casualties for the day: fourteen killed, seventy-seven wounded, and five missing.

On October 9th, the 39th Infantry continued to consolidate its positions at the edge of the woods. In the morning, the 3rd Battalion continued moving east and advanced to the edge of the woods northwest of Germeter. Late in the afternoon, L Company cut the Germeter-Huertgen road and I Company swung to the north to cut the road at Wittscheide. There, with coming darkness, they dug in and endured continuous mortar and artillery fire from the enemy. I Company got one platoon across the road, with the balance staying on the northwest side. Regimental casualties for the day: eleven killed, sixty-nine wounded, three missing.

At dawn on the 10th, the Germans launched a heavy counterattack on I Company positions from the north and east, overrunning two platoons, which were mostly destroyed. Forty-eight men were lost. Col. Stumpf regrouped the remaining companies and, with the help of tanks brought up from the west, spent the rest of the day retaking I Company's lost ground. On this day, 3rd Battalion alone suffered 104 casualties. Meantime, 1st Battalion occupied Germeter after the Germans had withdrawn. The 39th Infantry losses for the day: twenty killed, eighty-five wounded, and forty missing—mostly from I Company.

The next morning, the plan was for both attacking battalions, 1st and 3rd, to advance across the open ground between Germeter and Vossenack and occupy the latter in preparation for an assault on Schmidt, the ultimate objective. Second Battalion was to protect the northern flank. At this point, no battalion in either the 39th or 60th Infantry regiments could field more than 300 men.

First Battalion's attacks across the open ground were repulsed by the enemy; they made no progress. Meanwhile, Col. Stumpf directed his companies to proceed eastward through the forested ridge line just north of Vossenack to attain positions for an attack on the town from the north. Just prior to jump-off, a shell hit K Company's command group and the entire company had to be reorganized before the attack could begin. Once underway, the battalion advanced in a column of companies led by L Company, then K, then what was left of I. By late afternoon, it had advanced nearly a mile and was in position to emerge from the ridge line to the northeast and take Vossenack from the rear. Stumpf sent out a patrol which slipped undetected into the town itself. The patrol observed large numbers of Germans there but made no contact.

Regimental casualties for October 11th: seven killed, sixty-nine wounded.

Third Battalion's extended formation along the ridge line put it in an ideal position to execute the attack on Vossenack in coordination with 1st Battalion, which was supposed to attack more from the west. But Col. Bond was concerned about its northern flank, which was exposed to a possible counterattack out of the Huertgen area. Therefore, Stumpf was given the order to tie in his position and make contact with E Company, which was protecting the road north out of Germeter. Even as these preparations were being made, Col. Bond's premonition about a counterattack from the north was becoming a reality. During the night of 11-12 October, 2,000 men of the Kampfgruppe Wegelein had moved into position for an attack from an area just west of Huertgen. This enemy regiment, named for its commander, was fresh and well equipped with heavy machine guns and mortars. Half of the veteran soldiers were of such quality that they were training to be officers. The ensuing battle is grippingly described in Charles Whiting's *The Battle of the Hurtgen Forest: The Untold Story of a Disastrous Campaign,* beginning at dawn on October 12th just north of the 39th Infantry 2nd Battalion positions.

The day grew lighter. Here and there a noncom or officer came through the trees and issued orders for the coming day in a whisper. They always whispered now, as if there was a Kraut hiding behind the very next tree, and they didn't want to attract attention to themselves, for attention could mean sudden death. Most of the men had become passive and apathetic, but a few men started cleaning their weapons, while others primed grenades for the day's new battle.

Smoke started to rise slowly behind them where the cooks were attempting to prepare a hot meal, and there was the creak of handcarts sloshing through the ankle-deep mud of the trail. It seemed like any other morning in the Green Hell of the Hurtgen: cold, damp, and boring, with the prospect of more violent action to come.

A whine. A groan. A sound like a diamond being scratched along a piece of glass. Then the frighteningly familiar, baleful shriek of the German multiple mortar was heard. Fingers of black smoke poked their way up into the leaden sky, and suddenly, all was chaos and confusion. The rockets ripped great steaming holes in the earth like the work of gigantic moles. They snapped the trees, flinging their crowns high into the air, and sent huge shards of jagged metal hissing lethally to all sides.

The survivors said later that the barrage seemed to last for hours. In truth it took only a matter of minutes. But it sufficed to sever communications, knock out several gun pits, and force the men of the 39th to cower in their holes, the gravel and dirt pattering off their helmets like heavy rain on a tin roof. To their front the whistles shrilled. Hoarse voices cried commands in German, and then they came streaming out of the trees in their camouflaged jackets, firing from the hip as they came.

Kampfgruppe Wegelein was attacking!

Attacking along a wooded plateau, the officer-cadets swiftly enveloped the first over-extended battalion of the 39th it encountered. The jubilant enemy poured down the Regiment's main supply trail, headed toward Germeter. Colonel Bond, the 39th's commander, realized immediately what the Germans intended. Their move was "aimed at the left rear exposed flank and designed to cut off the 3rd Battalion that had crossed the Germeter-Huertgen road and had a patrol in the far edge of Vossenack."

Bond reacted correctly. Although his 2nd Battalion was yelling for help, he concentrated on getting 3rd Battalion to carry out one of the most difficult tactics in the book—to turn around completely and attack to its rear. If the 3rd Battalion made a mess of it, the resultant confusion might well be followed by panic and flight.[4]

As the battle raged around Germeter, the 3rd Battalion was poised to launch its coordinated attack on Vossenack. Col. Stumpf, at a forward position on the ridge line, waited for the signal for the battalion to jump-off, smoke on the enemy positions to his south, unaware of the situation to his rear. The smoke never came. Inexplicably it seemed, in the late afternoon he received an order by runner—radios were not being used for security reasons—to attack back toward Germeter! He was at first dumbfounded, but endeavored to carry out the order and began moving the companies. By dark, he had established positions about 300 yards west of the Germeter road, an area they had occupied two days before. For the 39th Infantry, October 12th claimed another eleven killed, and sixty-nine wounded.

Unbeknownst to Col. Bond, the German counterattack had been

costly for the enemy as well. There had been communications problems and as many as 500 casualties throughout the initial attack. Then German higher headquarters issued an immediate order to withdraw all officer candidates from the field. Col. Wegelein was suddenly down to less than half of his original force while the 39th Infantry maneuvered to set up for a counter-counterattack of their own.

As the morning of Friday the 13th dawned, 3rd Battalion jumped off to the west with the depleted K and L Companies. The latter ran into a devastating ambush and had two of its understrength platoons wiped out. Col. Stumpf then turned K Company around to attack back east against the ambush position. About 1100, the remnants of L Company were pinned down and K was beginning its attack to attempt to regain contact with L. Meanwhile I Company, across the Germeter road to the northeast with E Company, was under attack. K Company fought back and regained contact with L. At this time, heavy mortar fire rained down on the enemy salient that protruded into the regimental position. The enemy was now facing units of all three battalions on three sides. L Company was on the east, now down to forty riflemen. The butcher's tally for the regiment was the highest of any single day in the campaign: forty killed, sixty-nine wounded, forty-nine missing.

After these harrowing fights and countless others throughout the war, only a few veterans of the original 39th Infantry roster made it this far. One who did was Sergeant Herbert Taff, the radio and communications sergeant in L Company.

> I had many opportunities to speak to the 3rd Battalion Commander, Col.Stumpf. I was the liaison between the Bn Commander and my Company Commander most of the time during combat. Everyone respected Col. Stumpf and he was a great leader who took us through many hazardous situations.

I served in Company "L" till war's end in Europe
except for two months that I was in 1st General
Hospital, Paris from March 1945 till May 1945, for
wounds received in Germany.[5]

The next day, K and L Companies were pinched out of the fight by other units and went into regimental reserve. During the morning skirmishes, a soldier in G Company shot and killed a solitary German soldier walking in front of his position. It was Col. Wegelein. The 39th Infantry regained all ground lost to the German counterattack. It spent the next several days regrouping, consolidating its positions, and patrolling the front. Relief of the regiment by units of the 28th Infantry Division began on October 26th. The 9th Division passed to V Corps control and began movement to a rearward position in the vicinity of Camp Elsenborn, Belgium, about twenty-five miles to the southwest. The 39th Infantry monthly casualty count in the Huertgen was 154 killed (including thirty-two who died of wounds), 698 wounded, and 102 missing. The regiment's cumulative total since landing at Normandy on June 10th: 547 killed, 2,459 wounded, and 206 missing, for a total of 3,212, about 110 percent of authorized strength.

The surviving soldiers of the 39th Infantry, and their brothers in the other 9th Division regiments, were spent and depleted. While fighting valiantly, they had failed to achieve their primary objective, the high ground around Schmidt. They had advanced a total of 3,000 yards at the cost of over 4,000 casualties, and inflicted a somewhat lesser number on the enemy. Neither side could claim victory. The 9th was the first, but would not be the last American division to get chewed up in the Huertgen.

Lt. Col. Stumpf's executive officer beginning early in the Normandy campaign was Major Richard Kent, a 9th Division veteran since Fort Bragg days. He reminisced about his relationship with Stumpf in a letter written in 1991 to fellow 39th Infantry veteran Col. Don Lavender.

The language in his letter reflected the brutal nature of what they endured during those months, perhaps never so grim as what they experienced in the Huertgen Forest.

> For years I was stationed with and got well acquainted with Robert Stumpf and we shared stories. Stumpf was a huge Neanderthal man. I didn't like him much at first, but I admired and understood him. Stumpf suffered from the loss of every man and often was in tears. I slept next to him in combat and, as his executive officer, was the telephone orderly. As part of my job, I was required to give him the bad news. He often took out his frustration on me rather than take it out on his fighting men that he admired so much. He was never abusive, but often plain damned ornery.
>
> After the war, Stumpf was on the faculty at the Command and General Staff College when I went through. He treated me like a king. The tactics taught there were straight out of the 9th Division handbook.
>
> There were years when I was stationed with and became a close friend, hunting and fishing partner of Bob Stumpf, when the booze and stories flowed, usually to our wives' distress.[6]

Total casualties accumulated by Col. Stumpf's 3rd Battalion during the nearly five months of continuous combat since June 12th amounted to approximately 1,070 men, including 180 killed, or close to 120 percent of the battalion's authorized strength. That's a lot of suffering.

20

---•---

Luxembourg

After the Crozon campaign, Maj. Gen. Stroh received orders to move the 8th Infantry Division to the front along the Germany-Luxembourg border, still part of VIII Corps (Gen. Middleton), and Ninth Army (Gen. Simpson). The journey would take them some 600 miles across France, passing close to the recently liberated Paris. The Duchy of Luxembourg is about forty miles long north to south, nestled in rolling, wooded country, south and east of Belgium. The Our River defined its border with Germany, to the east of which stood the completely intact and manned Siegfried Line. The 8th Division's three regiments were to be thinly spread out over twenty-three miles along what was considered to be a "quiet" sector of the German front, in positions on the right flank of VIII Corps.

Preparations for the move took about a week and included the usual post-campaign clean-up and maintenance activities, and a little rest for the troops, who had been engaged with the enemy almost continuously since early July. This lull afforded Gen. Stroh the opportunity to visit his son's grave and last battle site, to investigate the circumstances of his death, and to attend to his final affairs. It is surprising that, given this rather quiet time and the equally quiet sector of the front to which the division was bound, Gen. Eisenhower did not grant the two-week leave that Gen. Stroh requested, and which was favorably endorsed by his corps and army commanders. It would certainly have been most beneficial to Stroh's mental and emotional state, and that would only have been beneficial to the division as a whole. Furthermore, Stroh would have been back on the job at about the time the division took operational control of its positions at the front. This occurred on October 3rd, two weeks to the day from when Stroh had wrapped up the Crozon Campaign. It is worth mentioning that he had a highly capable staff to run things in his absence, including two brigadiers and an excellent chief of staff. During this period, Imogene sent an "extra" letter, dated October 1st, describing her brother's memorial service in Washington.

General Handy said our letters of last Wednesday were to be delivered to you this week in person. You'll never know how much we've missed you this last two weeks and there was an empty space at church this morning at Harry's service.

As Mother would, she carried off this service just like she always does big things. She had white mums at the altar in the two vases and that was absolutely all. Dr. Lowry followed the Holy Communion service as you know it and added very lovely prayers at various appropriate places. At one place he mentioned Harry's name.

I don't know exactly who was at church, but I'll name as many as I can think of. There was General and Mrs. Handy, General and Mrs. De Witt, Gen. Cocheu, Gen. Sweet, Mrs. Endicott, Mrs. Collins and Nancy, the Gilbert girls, Frances Stone, the three

Brannons, Mrs. King, Mr. and Mrs. Taylor, Mrs. Quails and Frances (Guy lost a leg in France and is now in England waiting to come home). Mrs. Levy, Mrs. Bell and Peggy, Col. and Mrs. Skinner.

Flowers have been coming and most of them are glads. The Bells's called yesterday afternoon and brought some lovely peach glads and some gold dahlias. The dahlias make a beautiful frame for Harry's picture and we've kept some of the glads for the dining-room table. The Taylors sent some gorgeous coral glads with cream centers and Mother has some in that battery glass jar on the radio. Frances and Mrs. Lewis sent a box of white glads to the church and Mrs. Collins will take them to the men at Walter Reed tomorrow. The Gilberts sent white glads. We took Mrs. DeRowan over with us to the hospital yesterday and filled four vases with all those we haven't used and put them in four different wards. The men got such a kick out of them.

Yours and Mother's friends have been just grand and you don't know how much they think of you until trouble comes.

Yesterday Mother got a promotion list from Harry's C.O. stating that Harry was promoted to a Major August 17th.

Mother has been just fine and not sick a bit. She talks to everyone on the phone and receives everyone when they come to call on her. She's acted exactly as Harry would want her to. You'd be awfully proud of her.

We're so terribly anxious to hear from you since your last letter was Sept. 5th, and Bob's was Aug.

25th. Gen. Handy can't understand why the mail should be held up. I know the Stumpfs are nearly frantic. As for me, I just hope for the best and go about my daily business. That is all any of us can do. All the more now I want to do the best of my ability to be a good wife and daughter.

Daddy, I keep thinking of you and can't imagine what your thoughts must be. Yesterday in the hospital looking at those maimed men I am so thankful Harry wasn't one of them. He'd be so unhappy and that would make you feel worse than you do now.

You have a job now you never dreamed you'd ever have a few years ago and we are all so proud of you. Harry was so honored to have helped you. Col. Skinner the other evening said that folks say that the unsung heroes of this war are Don Stroh and Matt Eddy. Of course we know who made the latter. You were Harry's ideal so try not to let this hurt you.

We hope you'll be able to come home soon.

The 8th Division began its move on September 26th by rail and motor convoys. Once in Luxembourg, Gen. Stroh deployed his three regimental combat teams along the Our River and held division artillery alongside his division CP in Wiltz, some ten miles west of the center of his sector. At the north end he placed 13th Infantry, whose CP was in Ouren, Belgium, where that country's territory bulges into Luxembourg and Germany, straddling the river. G-2 considered this sector the most likely site of German offensive action. The 28th Infantry was headquartered in Consthum, due east of Wiltz. The 121st Infantry was headquartered at Medernach, toward the southern end of the sector. All three combat teams were reinforced with additional armor and artillery units.[1]

Not having an actual division reserve, Gen. Stroh organized a provisional rifle battalion made up of division special troops. This 1,500-man force was organized into eight companies, five of which were rifle companies. The battalion began daily training on October 8th. They provided defense of the division headquarters in Wiltz and were available as a mobile ready force to respond to any German incursion along the thinly manned front. Similarly, Division Artillery was available to provide rapid support from Wiltz to any developing hot spot along the front. Gen. Stroh described his setup in a letter to Imogene dated October 8, 1944.

> Somewhere in Luxembourg
>
> Luxembourg is a very beautiful little country, with mountains and woods which remind me of Western Pennsylvania or North Carolina. The towns are neat and clean as a pin, particularly the city of Luxembourg, the capital, which I have visited briefly. The people are friendly and enthusiastic.
>
> We had a long and interesting trip getting here, during which I had a couple of hours in Paris. Guided by a motorcycle M.P. we made a flying trip through some of the famous boulevards, which are as beautiful as they are pictured, and paused briefly at the Arc de Triomphe, where the French unknown soldier is buried, and the Eiffel Tower. Also saw many other famous buildings as we hurried by... On one night we bivouacked among the still evident trenches in the heart of World War I battlefields, and saw several large French cemeteries of that struggle.
>
> Three of your lovely letters have reached me since I last wrote, including that of September 28, which made the trip in about eight days through the

kindness of my old boss at Benning in '39-'40. [Gen.
Handy] I am very much comforted that you and
Mother are bearing up so well under the shadow of our
tragedy. I had no criterion from which to judge just
how it would affect you. I personally find it difficult to
recover from the shock, but am doing my best to give
all I have to the job, always trying to remember that
the lives of thousands of other people's sons depend
largely on my judgement. How it will all turn out I
cannot tell as yet.

The enclosed photos will give you an idea of the
luxury in which we are now living. When you get a
mahogany desk with a glass top in the field it is really
something. All were inherited from the Germans, so
our consciences do not trouble us a bit. Our living
quarters are equally fine. We occupy a completely
modern house, which would take at least $25,000 to
duplicate at home, with several modern baths, electric
stove, steam heat, electric lights and a fireplace, all of
this after nearly three [four] months of tent life in the
woods and apple orchards is certainly too good to last.

I think you are perfectly right about your decision
to take some cultural subjects, such as history
or government, in lieu of home ec. as you say, a
knowledge of which will be useful and valuable as you
travel around the world with Bob during the years to
come, and in all probability the Regular Army will be
largely employed in duties in foreign countries for as
many years to come as is possible to contemplate. We
used to think that tours in Hawaii, Panama and the
Philippines just about exhausted any foreign stations.
We will look back on those days and smile at such

silly thoughts. If Mother can join me, I could relish some additional foreign service in times of peace, and I think you will enjoy it also. The Handys must think a great deal of you two. I wrote him a letter of thanks the other day for his sympathy and cooperation. I see that he accompanied Marshall on the first non-stop flight from the United States to France since the days of Lindbergh.

You can see Harry's ring quite clearly in the picture.

The primary combat activity for the 8th Division troops on the front line was patrolling in order to keep tabs on the German frontline positions. The enemy was doing the same thing. This resulted in occasional skirmishes as opposing patrols would inevitably run into each other. It was stressful work, and because the long front was so thinly manned, most of the men were continuously involved. After a few weeks, they were growing increasingly weary. About that time, the division received reinforcements of several units of the 9th Armored Division, which had arrived in the VIII Corps sector primarily as Corps reserve. These fresh units supplemented a rotation protocol whereby units were relieved for three days' R and R in the rear. The 8th Division established a rest camp in the picturesque town of Clerveaux for this purpose. The men were provided hotel rooms, recreational opportunities, and free time, warm and out of the increasingly biting weather.

Army Chief of Staff, General Marshall, Ninth Army commander Lt. Gen. Simpson, and VIII Corps commander Maj. Gen. Middleton made command visits to the division during this period. During formal ceremonies, Marshall awarded the Silver Star medal to Major Donald R. Ward of the 28th Infantry, the unit Marshall had served with in World War I. He later mingled with the troops. A few days later Gen. Eisenhower and 12th Army Group commander Lt. Gen. Omar

Bradley paid a visit to the division and formally presented another seven Silver Stars to gallant soldiers of the 8th. On both occasions, Gen. Stroh briefed his bosses on division strategy for managing the front and possible future Allied offensives involving the 8th Division.

The hilly and forested Luxembourg countryside, together with the spread-out nature of the American line, allowed the Germans plenty of opportunities for infiltration. In one such instance on October 7th, American Lt. Colonels Bailey and Usher of the 28th Infantry were traveling in a vehicle well in the rear of the front when they were flagged down by what appeared to be an American captain and sergeant standing beside a jeep. As they pulled alongside the jeep, they heard the "captain" speaking in German. The Americans opened fire and killed the two men. At the same time, a machine gun and rocket launcher opened fire from the edge of the forest. The officers dismounted and began shooting it out with the Germans. Col. Usher was killed in the ambush. Col. Bailey continued to fire on the enemy until they withdrew. The American driver had disappeared, presumably captured. Gen. Stroh quickly changed the policy so that no vehicle would go forward of the division CP without at least two armed passengers in addition to the driver. At night, an additional escort vehicle was required.

Another feature of this period was the growing presence of German V-1 "buzz bombs" flying over the front lines. Some of them landed in the rear regimental positions and as far as the division CP at Wiltz, but did little damage.

While physically comfortable and busy with matters at hand, Gen. Stroh was clearly still raw emotionally over his son's death and the worry associated with his own absence from home for nearly two years, especially in light of the family tragedy. Daughter Imogene further addressed the situation directly in her letter of October 8th, after receiving her father's letters explaining the circumstances of Harry's death. As in her previous letter, she ends with a plea that her father come home soon.

I received your letters of Sept. 9th and Sept. 23rd
this week. Also Mother received yours of the 15th and
Meade Dugas brought the one of the 19th. We were
very worried how this shock would affect you, but
after reading your beautiful letters we have no fear
that you have pulled through. Mostly, I think you're
able to carry on because Harry would want you to and
you never wanted to let him down, even now.

It seems dreadful that you had to be all alone all
through it even to visiting the cemetery, but it is a
help to you as well as us to know everything. I didn't
even hesitate to show Mother the pictures of his grave
and the flowers. By the way, they still had their color.
Mother wants to know every detail and is so thankful
we know where he is.

I'm so glad you found Harry's ring and he'd be
so proud that you want to wear it. Daddy, he never
wanted to be a better man than you, but just as good.

We are even more disappointed than you, that you
can't get home right now. Mother needs you so much
and I can't even begin to take your place.

I'm glad we had to move now. That other house
would always remind Mother of his visits and that
Christmas and graduation leave. It must have been
hard for you having seen him so much this last year
and in such danger. I'm glad you became so close and
did have the opportunity to be in the very same place.

We keep thinking of you receiving our letters
while we still thought Harry was missing. You mustn't
worry about us. There are so many grieving families
all over the world and we must all remember those
boys. I'll never be able to forget Harry.

Take care of yourself and come home as soon as
you can.

Understandably, Imogene underestimated the impact of Harry's
death on her father's mental and emotional state about which he
elaborated in a letter to her dated October 22nd. The division was
entering its third week of what was becoming routine operations with
only minor contact with the enemy, and the headquarters staff was
enjoying comfortable accommodations. A far cry from everything he
was accustomed to since arriving on the continent, these conditions
may have set him up for unusual opportunities for introspection, perhaps contributing to his somber disposition.

Although I have heard from you and Mother as late
as October 12, I still feel that we are so far apart, and
hear from each other infrequently, as to make it most
unsatisfactory and distressing. When Mother wrote
last she had not even received my letter of September
19 by regular channels, not to say any of those written
after that date, and all of which I am unusually
anxious that you both should see for what degree of
comfort they can give you. There are also numerous
enclosures which I feel you will find of interest.
Perhaps this shock has made me unduly impatient, but
it now seems that mail from here is taking longer to
reach home than the reverse. It is a screwy business.
Three of your grand letters arrived since I last
wrote, and that's a consolation. You were still keeping
a stiff upper lip when you wrote on September 24,
hoping that I'd someday be able to "stuff Harry
with steak," but it won't work out that way, will it? I
never sit down at my place at our mess table without

remembering with tears in my eyes how he sat at the very place, only fifteen days before he died, and ate like a glutton of steak and eggs, for a mid-morning breakfast. How he relished it, and commented on the unusual luxury after days and weeks of 'K' and 'C' rations! At least you will know after Mother receives my letter of a couple of weeks ago, that Bob was all right late in September. Haven't heard from him since, but hope to make a trip, if things continue quiet, to see how he's doing. Maybe this week.

I can see you and Mother and Miggles [the cat] in front of the fire wrapping Christmas packages. A very vivid description. Christmas will be a very sad affair this year unless we are all together...

Thank you for the account of Harry's memorial service, and especially the list of people who were there and the prayer. It is nice to know that so many of our friends were there, and that so many of them sent flowers to you and Mother. Expect to see Monk L. [Lewis] tomorrow. I have had several kind letters, and Mother writes that she has received many more that she will send me.

Honey, you flatter me, you really do. Unsung hero indeed! Russ Skinner has been kidding you. But I know what you're driving at. You're trying to cheer me up, and to try to cushion the awful blow with your own courage, fortitude and optimism. And it works, too. Every time I think about my citation for the DSM I say to myself that Harry helped me get it. Yesterday I even received a letter of congratulations on the Brest campaign from Patton. And Harry helped me get that, too. How proud and happy he would be if he only knew it! Knew it? He does know it. I have only to rub his ring, as Aladdin did the magic lamp, to know he is beside me, to see his grin, and to feel the grip of his hand. His life and death are an inspiration to me, even though I think of him through a mist of tears. But I like to hear what you have to say. My only concern is that I did not succeed in making him understand that I approved of all he ever did. I am almost afraid, that in his overwhelming desire to please me, and to make me approve of him, that he was almost afraid of me. How bitter a thought that would be. It was I who should have put out an effort to keep abreast of his loyalty, his generosity, and his nobleness.

I shudder to think how Mother will get through her birthday this week, when we remember what happened a year ago. [Harry's surprise visit before he shipped out.] There is absolutely no chance of my getting home now, so there is no use in waiting for me. I will make the supreme effort at Christmas time, but even that is very doubtful.

Was thrilled this morning at the opportunity to pin second lieutenant bars on three brand new officers, just commissioned from sergeants for heroic action in battle. That is what you call coming up the hard way. All had won their spurs in the greatest of all competitions. One had been wounded three times. Just ordinary American boys who were putting out above and beyond the call of duty.

The congratulatory letter from Patton was in addition to a sympathy note that was included in Gen. Stroh's papers, and which arrived shortly after.

Third United States Army
Office of the Commanding General
25 October 1944

My dear Stroh:

I only learned today that your gallant boy was killed during the Brest Operations. Please accept my sincere and heartfelt sympathy.

Most Sincerely,
[signed]
G. S. Patton, Jr.
Lieut. General, U.S. Army
Commanding

On October 30th, Gen. Stroh made the roughly fifty-mile trip north from Wiltz to Camp Elsenborn, Belgium where the 39th Infantry was bivouacked and trying to recover from their ordeals in the Huertgen Forest. There he met Lt. Col. Stumpf for dinner at the regimental mess. It is very likely that he heard plenty about the Huertgen and got an earful more when he met with the 9th Division commander, Maj. Gen. Craig, who had taken over from Gen. Eddy when the latter was promoted to XII Corps commander. Back at his 8th Division CP, the staff was making big plans to celebrate his 52nd birthday on November 3rd. Gen. Stroh described the occasion in his letter to Imogene of November 5th.

As you might guess from the enclosure [note from Col. Stumpf], there is nobody else sitting beside me but your overgrown husband, believe it or not. He says that he cannot decide whether you will be displeased at receiving such a short note as this, or overjoyed that he has written more than once this week. In any event, I think that this is the first time that we have ever collaborated in writing a letter to you.

I have seen a lot of this big hunk of man this week, and hope to have him around for two more days before he will have to go back to the job. We do not have much to amuse him with here, and I do not propose to give him a busman's holiday by taking him up to see our front line dispositions, but we do have all the facilities for giving him a complete rest, change, and relaxation, which he is taking advantage of. I had to give him special instructions in how to turn on a hot water faucet, and how to flush the toilet, neither of which he has had to do since Hector was a pup, but he finds a return to civilization a pleasant operation which is not too difficult. I think he should be benefitted by the break, which he richly deserves.

I can tell you truly that he loves you. Nothing gives him more pleasure than to talk of you, and of how he desires to get back to you. His favorite picture of you is the snap you had taken with the capitol as a background, which he carries over his heart. I have never seen him more sentimental than when he showed me this picture the evening of his arrival, as we were getting ready for bed.

I must tell you also, however, of a fact against which you must be on your guard. I think it incumbent upon me as your father to warn you against this thing which may even result in wrecking your romance and ruining your life. Are you ready? Bob is wearing green underwear! The G.I. variety of wool which is issued in lieu of white so that it will not be too conspicuous when the boys wash it and hang it out to dry. I cannot imagine anything so harmful to a loving relationship than a husband attired in green underwear, except it

be the young officer bridegroom who couldn't get his
new boots off on his honeymoon all the way from New
York to San Francisco. So guard yourself.

I first saw Bob when I visited his outfit last
Monday, and we had dinner together at his regimental
headquarters. He had on about eight layers of clothing,
which is getting to be necessary while engaged in the
pleasant pastime of jeep riding in this rugged weather.
But by the time he had peeled off a few I discovered
that he was looking as fine and robust as ever, despite
the fact that he has been in action almost continuously
since I left the division, during which time he has made
a perfectly fine record. When he went to bed here on
Friday night he said it was the first time he had had
his clothes off to sleep since early in July. So you can
imagine how hard he has been going. If ever a man
deserves a furlough and a return to the arms of his wife,
it is your own Bob.

Arranged with his division and regimental
commanders to let him visit me for a few days as soon
as he could be spared, but did not anticipate that this
would be as early as four days hence. But on Friday
afternoon, without previous notice, he arrived. Berry
bumped into him by mere chance on the road, hid him
from me until dinner time, and then produced him as
the best surprise of a surprising day as a member of my
birthday party that evening. Torres had succeeded in
pressing his blouse during the afternoon, Bob soaked
off three [four] months accumulation of dirt in our
luxurious bath tub, Berry mellowed him with Scotch,
and by the time the party was due to start your hubby
was all set to add glamor to the occasion... The crowd

included my usual mess, an artillery commander, and
our six Red Cross doughnut girls, who don't look so bad
when they get their best uniforms on. All this was a
surprise party for me, and as we had a merry evening,
despite the absence of a certain sweet and wonderful
boy, who was lying alone so many miles away. I guess
he would want me to do these things. I know he would.
But my heart was heavy as I proposed the toast, "To our
absent loved ones, living, and dead."

Bob received a forty-eight hour extension to his
leave this afternoon, so we hope to have him with us
until Tuesday. We may make a sightseeing trip to the
Verdun area tomorrow.

The surprise party was quite a lavish affair with everyone in dress
uniforms, and an extensive menu that reflected substantial preparation by the staff. They started off with highballs, canapés, and hors
d'oeuvres, including Russian caviar and pate de foie gras. The buf-
fet consisted of an assortment of meats—venison, turkey, chicken,
beef, and pork; salads—asparagus tips, "perfection" potato, tuna
fish, chicken, and fruit gelatin; other treats—hardboiled eggs, deviled
eggs, deviled ham, American cream cheese, and "fromage Ramcke."
Beverages included chocolate malted milk, vin rouge Chateau Pavie
'24, van blanc Moselle, champagne Dare-Noel '37, and coffee. In
addition to rum cakes, dessert included a large decorated sheet cake
whose twelve candles Gen. Stroh dutifully blew out, then cut with a
saber. The cake bore the inscription, "Happy Birthday General Stroh"
and the 8th Division emblem. Gen. Stroh's aide-de-camp, Lt. Berry,
was the master of ceremonies, while his orderly, Cpl. Torres, busily
kept glasses filled and dishes served. Besides the Red Cross ladies,
others in attendance were assistant division commander, Brig. Gen.
Canham, artillery commander, Brig. Gen. Pickering, chief of staff,

Col. Cross, and Lt. Col. Stumpf. After supper, with drinks and cigars, the twelve gathered around the table for a game of hearts.

Gen. Stroh's apparent admiration of and devotion to his son-in-law appeared to have grown since Harry's death. It was as though Bob in some way became a substitute for Harry; the recipient of a father's love for his son that had no other outlet.

Juxtaposed to the quiet routine of the 8th Division in early November, the 28th Division was frantically engaged in the same area of the Huertgen Forest where the 9th and 4th Divisions had already withstood its terrors. After the 28th had retaken Vossenack and Schmidt, the Germans launched a furious counterattack, pushing the Americans out of Schmidt and partially out of Vossenack before the attack was repulsed. Crippled by overwhelming casualties, the 28th was forced to withdraw. Now it was the 8th Division's turn. They began departing their positions on November 16th for the 100-mile motorized march to the now infamous battlefield as part of V Corps, effecting a complete exchange of positions with the 28th Division.

While preparations for the coming action were being formulated, Gen. Stroh's demeanor had not improved. If anything, the pain of Harry's death continued unabated, as did his worry over the state of his wife's well-being, in addition to the stress induced by the impending battle. By mid-November, he apparently was approaching what he considered his breaking point. He composed another formal request for leave in the United States to the army group commander, Gen. Bradley, this time elaborating on his mental state.

Headquarters, 8th Infantry Division

15 November 1944

SUBJECT: Leave of Absence

TO: Commanding General, Twelfth Army Group. (thru Commanding General V Corps.)

    1. I request leave of absence for twenty (20) days

in the United States, effective on or about 10 December 1944.

2. On that date I will have completed two years' continuous overseas service in the North African and European Theaters; on that date also I will have completed six months' continuous service in France, Luxembourg and Germany. All of this service has been in combat divisions. With one or two exceptions I believe myself to be the only general officer involved in the initial African landings, or their first follow-up, who has been engaged continuously in the field since those dates, without the opportunity to visit the United States.

3. Two months ago today I learned that my only son had been killed in action before Brest, under particularly tragic and distressing circumstances. I have tried my best to recover from the effects of this blow. In this I have been unsuccessful. It has materially intensified the harmful results of the mental and physical strain of the past two years. I cannot escape the convictions that my efficiency has been lowered perceptibly. I have even begun to lose confidence in my ability to discharge my present responsibilities.

4. I feel that a brief period of complete rest, relaxation, and change of scene is essential and may be beneficial. If leave of absence cannot be granted, then a brief period of official duty in the United States may be possible.

D. A. Stroh
Major General, U.S. Army
Commanding

This letter was sent out just as the 8th Division was being transferred from VIII Corps to V Corps, commanded by Major General Leonard T. Gerow, hence his inclusion as an addressee. Regardless of possible career implications that it may have generated, it surely would not have been well received by Gen. Gerow on the eve of such a critical battle for the division and the corps. It is worth noting that Stroh was not asking to be absent for the coming battle, that it would in all likelihood be over before December 10th. No division had been able to withstand battle in the Huertgen for more than a few weeks. He also used the modifying phrase "on or about" to give his boss some wiggle room. It is interesting that he addressed the request to Gen. Bradley and not Gen. Eisenhower, knowing that it would probably end up on Eisenhower's desk as it had in September. In any event, by identifying his own mental and emotional issues, he knew he was risking command of the 8th Division and the future of his career. Ironically, the following letter went out the very next day.

HEADQUARTERS VIII CORPS
OFFICE OF THE COMMANDING GENERAL
16 November 1944

Major General Donald A. Stroh,
Commanding General, 8th Infantry Division,
APO 8, U.S. Army.
My dear General Stroh,

On the eve of the departure of the 8th Infantry Division from the VIII Corps, I desire to take this opportunity to express to you, your officers, and to your enlisted personnel my sincere appreciation for the splendid work accomplished while a member of the Corps which I am privileged to command.

The entire service of the 8th Division since landing in France has been with the VIII Corps. The work of the division near La Haye du Puits, its subsequent break out of the Cherbourg Peninsula, its operations near Avranches, Rennes, St. Malo, Brest and on the Crozon Peninsula is sufficient to establish the division as one of the best in the U.S. Army. In all of the enumerated operations, the division acquitted itself in a manner in keeping with the best traditions. It never failed to gain its objective. It has killed, wounded, and captured large numbers of the enemy. It has been able to take its losses and the hard knocks of combat without complaint. Its esprit and morale has always been the best.

In taking leave of the VIII Corps, the division will be missed. We shall miss the fine spirit of cooperation which has always been so evident. We shall watch your continued progress. If the wheel of fortune should ever return the division to the VIII Corps, it will be our gain—and you will be welcome.

I desire to express to you personally my appreciation for your good work and the superior manner in which you have commanded the division. I regret that I cannot convey personally my thanks to all ranks of your command. My best wishes go with the 8th Division in its future battles.

Cordially yours,

Troy H. Middleton,
Major General, U.S. Army,
Commanding

In the left margin, Gen. Stroh scrawled, "One of the nicest letters I've ever received. Harry assisted me materially in getting it."

Throughout his time in Luxembourg, other nice letters continued to arrive from Imogene, mail that he clearly valued deeply and may have helped keep him from going completely off the deep end. Excerpts:

3614 Ingomar Pl.
Washington, D.C.
October 15, 1944
    Yesterday, Mrs. Irwin took Mother over to call on Mrs. Handy. When she got home again, she said Gen. Handy [Lt. Gen. Thomas Handy, Vice Chief of Staff of the Army] was expected home that day. About nine o'clock who should call but "the old boy himself." He apologized all over the place that he didn't see Bob—Bob would have fallen all over himself if he had—and that Bob's Corps commander [Gen. Collins] and division commander [Gen. Craig] had many words of praise for him. Then he started off to Mother how good you are and you were fine and all that sort of thing. It certainly bucked us 100% to have such a nice man go to all that trouble his first night home to call us up.
    Since I last wrote I've received three letters from Bob the last written Sept. 30 in Germany. He had just heard Harry was missing in a letter from me... I never have told him the details because you will want to tell him when you get together. We haven't the slightest notion where you are. Your Army hasn't been mentioned since Brest. I'm wondering if Bob is around Aachen. He wrote that they went through Belgium so fast he didn't even have a chance to write from there.
    The flowers are still coming and the house is full of lovely mums. Shirley Ridgeway, daughter of the general [Mathew Ridgeway, 82nd Airborne Division],

who dragged Harry in Boston and at the Point several times, sent some. She was very fond of Harry, but in time Harry got awfully indifferent toward her. She was too good he said.

October 22, 1944

We called on the Handys last night and were treated to a bottle of "captured beverage" drinking out of glasses there were part of Gen. B. Smith's property with G.R. IV on them for George Rex IV. The bottle was opened for our benefit. Gen. Handy got an officer on the problem of Harry's estate and Mother got a phone call just a while ago. She asked me to write you that nothing could be done until the official notice from the War Department arrives and then the AG takes care of everything. Mother will be told just what to do and all. This officer called again just now saying that the Chief of Staff of the War Department is on it so official news will probably come soon.

October 29, 1944

We planted a whole slew of bulbs yesterday in our funny little rock garden and wondered if we'd be here to enjoy them in the spring. I have a feeling we'll still both be here, still waiting. Maybe you will have been here for a visit, however. That would be nice.

We went to the movies the other night for the first time for a long time to see a real cute show "Janie." We both enjoyed it. The newsreels are sort of hard to look at now. It must be hard for you to keep on going. It's the only thing to do, but it is wonderful of you to be able to.

Hope Bob and you have seen each other by now.

November 3, 1944

Mother and I haven't heard from you since Oct. 11th and I haven't heard from Bob since Sept. 30th. It is hard to be realistic about it when the postman goes by. I know you're both alright, but those letters mean so much. I hope Bob has been able to be with you by now.

General and Mrs. Handy came by last night while I was at the hospital, to give Mother the pictures you sent with General Handy. There you are with the big boss [Gen. Marshall] giving out all your stuff. It seems so strange that General Handy should be with us so often and just having seen you and yet you've been away so long. They have been just grand to Mother.

There is the best article about "Joe Lightnin" [Gen. Collins] in the Saturday Evening Post this week. It is nice to see articles about good soldiers that deserve recognition. They haven't written anything about you in a popular magazine yet, but I just wish you could hear just some of the things people say about your abilities.

November 12, 1944

The mail really must be tied up. It has been a month yesterday since we heard from you all, and Sept. 30th is still Bob's last letter. It is awful not hearing from you all. Army life is glorious and glamorous with bands and flags and uniforms of peace, but war is becoming more terrible than we ever dreamed.

Mr. Thomas Henry [*Washington Star* reporter] came by yesterday to interview Mother about putting a photo and history of Harry in the Star. He told us little things about you, and it was quite nice to know he'd known Bob well, too. He seems to be very modest and will write a nice conservative piece for Harry.

Mother just received the official notice from the War Department on Thursday. It took a long time, and every day we're so thankful you were there, though it must have been simply awful for you. There is nothing anyone can say or do.

The official notice was in the form of a letter to Mrs. Stroh from the War Department, Adjutant General's office, dated 11 November 1944. She also received a personal letter from Gen. Marshall dated 10 November.

About the time Gen. Stroh was setting up his Huertgen Forest command post in Rott, Germany, and preparing the battle plan, he sat down at his desk to share his latest thoughts with Imogene in a letter dated November 18th.

Believe it or not, your envelope postmarked October 9, and containing two of Harry's 1939 letters to you, did not arrive here until yesterday. I appreciate you sending them to me, as they vividly brought back the carefree days of that long ago, when the only thing I had to worry about was whether Harry was going to get through West Point, and you through Lindenwood. Can you imagine anybody's being worried about trivialities like that?

Nice of you to think about my birthday. I mailed Mother a nice collection of excellent pictures taken here on that day, with the suggestion that you have one or more in which Bob figures prominently.

"Joe Lightning" takes his honors very modestly and

seemed very embarrassed that he should appear in two articles almost simultaneously. He said something about assuring Gladys that he would never be quoted in print, and that he shuddered in anticipation of receiving her next letter, after she has seen the *Post* article. And it will be even worse when *Yank* reaches her. Between you and me and the gate post, however, I don't think that the young man is too averse to a little publicity. He has it coming, in any event.

It is mighty fine that you have been given some film of Harry's activities...

I'm in a pretty good position to know where Bob is. Unless he gets knocked down by a jeep you don't have to worry about him for a while at least. By the time you get this letter, of course, everything may be different.

I think Bob enjoyed his forty-eight hour extension two weeks ago, and I have no doubt that his outfit was still on the up and up when he got back to it, despite the absence of his guiding hand for the first time in over a year. Did he tell you that he is the only battalion commander in the outfit who had that job that long? We had a nice trip to the Verdun area in my sedan on Monday, despite the efforts on Bob of a class reunion with young [Eph] Graham the night before. I tried to get him to sleep late on Tuesday, as it would be his last opportunity for some time, but he insisted on getting up to eat breakfast with me. He looked around the house all morning except for a brief visit to the officers' sales store here... After lunch I sent him on his way in the Lincoln Zephyr, followed by his jeep, in which he had arrived. I imagine it created a mild sensation when he rolled up in the mud in front of his C.P.

21

———◆———

Huertgen Redux

14 October 1944

ORDER OF THE DAY.

Soldiers of the Army Group!

The battle in the West has reached its peak. On widely separated fronts we must defend the soil of our German homeland. Now we must shield the sacred soil of the Fatherland with tenacity and doggedness... The Commandment of the hour is: None of us gives up a square foot of German soil while still alive.

Every bunker, every block of houses in a German town, every German village must become a fortress which shatters the enemy. That's what the Fuhrer, the people and our dead comrades expect from us. The enemy shall know that there is no road into the heart of the Reich except over our dead bodies...

Egotism, neglect of duty, defeatism and especially cowardice must not be allowed room in our hearts. Whoever retreats without giving battle is a traitor to his people...

Soldiers! Our homeland, the lives of our wives and children are at stake!

Our Fuhrer and our loved ones have confidence in their soldiers. We will show ourselves worthy of their confidence.

Long live our Germany and our beloved Fuhrer!

MODEL,

Field Marshal.[1]

The months-long battle of the Huertgen Forest is perhaps the most controversial campaign of World War Two. Some military scholars are convinced that capturing this impossibly difficult piece of terrain was entirely unnecessary, that it could have been bypassed, its defenders held at bay. But the senior military leadership at the time were convinced that the Germans could have used it as a launching point into the flanks and rear of American forces if they had passed it by. Further, at the onset of the campaign, no one understood just how difficult and deadly it was. The thinking was that a single infantry division would be sufficient to seize and secure all the key objectives in short order. Instead it required four infantry divisions, the 9th, 4th, 28th and finally the 8th, over a period of almost three months, to finally get the job done. All these divisions sustained heavy casualties.[2]

The 8th Division objectives for the attack were the towns of Huertgen and Kleinhau, and the high ground between them. The little cow town of Huertgen sits about fourteen miles east southeast from the center of Aachen, and about a mile south of the even smaller village of Kleinhau. Both are within three miles north of Vossenack, where the 39th Infantry had fought its last furious battle in the forest in mid-October. Because of defensive positions inherited by two of the 8th Division's combat teams in the vicinity of Vossenack, the burden for the attack fell to a single combat team, the 121st Infantry, commanded by Col. John Jeter. Combat Command R of the 5th Armored Division was attached to the 121st for the battle, and another battalion from the 13th Infantry would join them as the battle progressed. The entire division artillery was available for their support as well. Unfortunately, when Gen. Stroh received the attack order late on November 19th, which specified an H-hour at 0900 on the 21st, the 121st Infantry was still in Medernach, Luxembourg, some 107 road miles to the south. Stroh ordered the regiment to move out immediately, but the earliest they could reach their line of departure would be late on the 20th, leaving little time and no daylight for terrain evaluation, reconnaissance, battle planning and proper briefings. A stickler for proper battle preparation, Gen. Stroh found himself with these substantial handicaps before the fighting even started. All appeals to his new corps commander, Gen. Gerow, for more time were denied. Gerow himself was being pressured by First Army commander, Lt. Gen. Hodges, to jump off on the set date and time.

Battling rain, fog, mud, and darkness, the last infantrymen of the column dismounted their vehicles at the staging area just before dark on the 20th. They then faced a seven-mile foot march to the assembly areas behind the 12th Infantry positions through which they would pass during the jump-off in the morning. They were fatigued by the journey, the march, then shelling, and further challenged by having to stage into tactical positions in the dark, in a dense forest. The last units arrived at their assigned positions exhausted, only a few hours before daylight. Still, higher leadership had high hopes for quick success in the coming action. From Sylvan's *War Diary* entry of Monday, 20 November 1944:

General Hodges motored to see General Stroh in the afternoon and came back exceedingly well pleased with the tactical planning which had evolved. General Hodges especially noted the fact that General Stroh thought he was being supported by a remarkable amount of artillery—18 Bns—and was confident of success. Their attack will jump off at nine o'clock although General Hodges said he could wait until eleven o'clock if it looked as if there would be more favorable weather.[3]

He was pinning much hope on the success of the 8th Division attack tomorrow. If the attack should fail, the advance of the VII Corps to the north could be seriously hampered. He has the greatest confidence in General Stroh's tactical ability and believes that with a half-way break in the weather—one that would allow at least the Cubs to function—we should push the Boche back a good piece.[4]

Gen. Stroh convinced Gen. Gerow to delay committing the armored combat command, leaving it indefinite pending developments on the ground. The objective area was defended by four German battalions that had fought the 112th Infantry for ten days, and were somewhat depleted. But intelligence officers failed to discover that the entire German 344th Infantry Division had arrived only hours before jump-off. At 0800 on the 21st, artillery from V Corps, VII Corps, CCR, and 8th Division all began a barrage against all known and suspected enemy positions. The effectiveness of these fires was difficult to evaluate because of a dense overcast. *The Siegfried Line Campaign* richly describes the initial stages of the battle for Huertgen.

With all three battalions on line, the 121st Infantry attacked at the scheduled hour... One battalion headed up the Weisser Weh valley, another moved astride the bloody plateau, and the third attacked along the Germeter-Huertgen highway.

Hardly had the artillery finished its bombardment before the pattern the ground fighting would take for the next four days emerged. On the first day, no unit made any appreciable advance except one company east to the Germeter-Huertgen highway, which gained a meager 500 yards. The woods were as thick as ever with anti-personnel mines, with log bunkers bristling with automatic weapons, with barbed wire, and even more than ever with broken tree trunks and branches that obscured the soggy ground and turned any movement, even when not under enemy fire, into a test of endurance. Any hope that the enemy might not have much fight left was quickly dispelled. For all the good the American infantry could detect, the attempt by American artillery to silence the enemy's big guns and mortars might have been made with peashooters. Not until last light of the first day did Colonel Jeter's regiment complete even a passage of the 12th Infantry's lines.

For three more days the 121st Infantry plodded on, absorbing sometimes alarming casualties, enduring conditions that made men weep, and registering daily gains that varied from nothing to 600 yards. On the second day, a cold driving rain mixed at intervals with snow, added to the other miseries. Visibility was so poor that no planes could operate. On 23 and 24 November Colonel Jeter committed attached light tanks along the firebreaks, but they bogged helplessly in the mud. Other tanks trying to move up the Germeter-Huertgen highway fell quiet, prey to German guns in Huertgen.[5]

Meanwhile, Gen. Stroh was under increasing pressure from his bosses to create a breakthrough, especially Gen. Gerow, who, of course, was under pressure from both his boss, Gen. Hodges, and his counterpart, Gen. Collins, VII Corps. The progress of Collins' own advance hinged on the 8th Division securing his southern flank. Initially, General Hodges was all right with the slow progress as per Sylvan's diary entry of November 21st: "The General had instructed General Stroh to go slowly, buttoned up, and to avoid mine casualties. Consequently, he was not disappointed in the limited advances..."[6] However, by the 23rd, Thanksgiving Day, his patience was running thin. That morning he held a powwow at the 8th Division CP.

[Generals Hodges and Kean] started early this morning for the 8th Division where they met General Collins and General Gerow in addition to General Stroh. To the latter the General said in emphatic terms that he was not satisfied with the progress being made; that the minefield had not proven to be as much of an obstacle as people feared and that the progress, or rather the lack of it, made by the division showed lack of confidence and drive. He made it quite clear that he expected better results on the morrow. As if to prove his point that the division was not going ahead as it should, one battalion went out later that afternoon and captured 90 prisoners.[7]

The next day, the 121st Infantry's left flank battalion made some headway up the Weisser Weh valley by sending a company on a flanking maneuver that racked up some significant gains. The company, however, soon came under intense artillery fire whose deadly tree bursts were followed closely by a spirited counterattack. The company broke and fell back, giving up all the ground they had gained.

Col. Jeter relieved both the company and battalion commanders. He had to appoint another company commander the next day when one was lost to artillery fire. And he relieved still another battalion commander; two out of three in two days.

Justified or not, the reliefs took place under extenuating circumstances imposed by the misery and incredible difficulty of the forest fighting. It was attrition unrelieved. Overcoats soaked with moisture and caked with freezing mud became too heavy for the men to wear. Seeping rain turned radios into useless impedimenta. So choked with debris was the floor of the forest that men broke under the sheer physical strain of moving supplies forward and evacuating the wounded. The fighting was at such close quarters that grenades often were the decisive weapon. The minefields seemed endless. A platoon could spend hours probing, searching, determining the pattern, only to discover after breaching one minefield that another lay twenty-five yards ahead. Unwary men who sought cover from shellfire in ditches or abandoned foxholes might trip lethal booby traps and turn the promised sanctuary into an open grave.

Added to all the other miseries was a constant reminder of the toll this bloody little plateau already had extracted. Because concern for the living had from the first taken precedence over respect for the dead, the swollen bodies of the fallen of three other regiments still lay about in grotesque positions. At the end of the fourth day of fighting on 24 November, the 121st Infantry had deposited fifty known dead of its own on the ground and incurred a total of about 600

battle casualties. Almost as many more had fallen prey
to the elements or to combat exhaustion.[8]

The regiment had lost nearly 40 percent of its effective soldiers
and had not gained the objective of the edge of the forest overlooking
Huertgen. During the day on the 24th, another conference was held
at 8th Division CP, described in longhand notes in division chief of
staff Col. Tom Cross's diary.

24 Nov 1944
    Meeting held at Div CP (Rott) General Collins,
CG VII Corps, General Gerow CG V Corps and other
general officers of Corps, Div, Arty, etc. Decision
finally reached, both corps to attack at 0730. Main
push to be made by CCR 5th Arm. Div. followed by
121 Inf. to seize Hurtgen and Kleinhau and hold
them against enemy attack from the north, east, and
southeast. Before this can be accomplished, the road
leading to Hurtgen from the south must be cleared of
Boche mines etc. by engineers and 121 Inf (1st and
3rd Bn) assisted in clearing the road. Much trouble
was experienced during the night. Destroyed tanks,
craters and mines caused delays all night and early
AM. Bridges (treadway) were brought up to bridge
craters. Many inaccurate reports received during
early morning hours causing confusion as to the
situation, hearing mortar and art fire continuously
rain on our positions. Meeting referred to above was
again dominated by General Collins as usual. Col.
Anderson CCR did not indicate much enthusiasm for
the job ahead in the morning.

The die was cast for an armor attack up the Germeter-Huertgen highway, which was badly damaged and still exposed to German artillery. But failure to secure the Weisser Weh valley and its road left no other alternative. Col. Anderson's skepticism was well founded. Be that as it may, Gen. Stroh ordered CCR to proceed up the road before daylight on the 25th, with the assurance that the combat engineers, with the infantry's help, would have the road passable by then. In addition to mines, there was a large bomb crater in the road at the southern end of the woods that would have to be repaired or bridged. Sometime after midnight, the 8th Division engineer personally assured Col. Anderson that the crater would be bridged, or a path cleared around it by first light.

As dawn was breaking on the 25th, the lead tanks arrived at the crater. It was not repaired, bridged, nor had a pathway been cleared around it. Its dimensions were so great that it halted all vehicular traffic. The lead tank commander attempted to "jump" the crater, a foolhardy gesture that resulted in the tank lying disabled on its side. The Germans reacted to the activity by plastering the Americans with mortar and small arms fire in the increasing daylight. In less than an hour, CCR's armored infantry took over sixty casualties. As the commanders pushed to get the armor moving, supporting artillery poured over 15,000 rounds into the enemy positions. A break in the weather provided the opportunity for three squadrons from the 366th Fighter Group to attack suspected artillery and tank positions. Although the crater was bridged by mid-morning, further armored advances were also repulsed by the Germans. The armored infantry attempted to advance, but were turned back. CCR withdrew.

Although the infantry battalions made some progress that afternoon, Gen. Stroh decided to make a change and relieved Col. Jeter. He appointed his trusty chief of staff, Col. Tom Cross, to assume command of the 121st Infantry. In light of the Germans continued success in stopping the American tanks, Stroh directed that the infantry alone would continue the advance. Despite the bloody fighting and slow progress of the first five days, he felt that the German defenders were also tiring and knew that they had been rousted out of many of their best defensive positions. Further, they were being flanked by elements of the 4th Division attacking on the regiment's left. Stroh juggled some of his battalions in defensive positions, and freed up the 1st Battalion, 13th Infantry to reinforce the 121st. Col. Cross directed this fresh battalion to make its way around the 121st's left flank through 4th Division positions and be prepared to attack Huertgen from the woods line northwest of the town on November 27th.

While the battalion was shifting its position on the 26th, the 121st attacked again and made surprisingly rapid progress against much lighter opposition. By 1100, the regiment was at the woods line overlooking Huertgen from the west and southwest. Intelligence reports indicated that the Germans had withdrawn from Huertgen. Col. Cross ordered an immediate attack, but it was repulsed by heavy opposition coming from the town itself.

On the 27th, tank destroyers took positions along the woods line and spat supporting fire into the town. Medium tanks joined the lead battalion in the attack. Artillery began scoring hits on German guns and tanks, yet still the enemy clung to their tenuous positions in mere shells of buildings. By nightfall, the Germans still held on to most of what was left of Huertgen, although 1st Battalion, 13th Infantry had severed the highway north of the town and had established solid positions in the northeast part of the town. A few units of the 121st occupied some buildings along the western edge. The fanatical German defenders would fight on for one last day.

For Gen. Stroh, it was the end of his role in the campaign. Assured that the battle for Huertgen was won, Gen. Gerow had forwarded Stroh's request for leave to Gen. Hodges the day before, after apparently having held the request in abeyance for the previous ten days or so. Hodges endorsed the request and forwarded it to General Bradley. This is reflected in Sylvan's diary entry of November 27.

> General Stroh, worn out from two years of steady combat duty, and saddened by the death of his son... requested 20 days leave in the United States. A request, approved by General Gerow who believed that under the existing circumstances General Stroh could not do justice to a divisional command, was put in yesterday and General Hodges recommended to General Bradley at least two months in the States. This was approved...[9]

Gen. Hodges, having known Gen. Stroh for many years, and with great mutual respect between them, likely recognized the stress Stroh was under and thus made the duration of the leave two months rather than twenty days. He did so knowing that should Stroh return to theater at the completion of leave, he may not be reassigned to command the 8th Division. It appears Gen. Eisenhower was the final approval authority. In a cable to Gen. Marshall Eisenhower wrote, "I am sending him home to see whether he can recover his spirits and again feel equal to the task of leading a division." Further explaining his rationale for granting the leave, Eisenhower later wrote to Gen. Marshall:

> I enlisted Handy's help in the question of checking up on our division commanders that I send home for a rest. It is always possible that one or two of them will not completely recover. Both Stroh and O'Daniel have lost only sons in the war, and this shock and distress, coupled with abnormal strains always borne by an active Division commander, are nearly more

than any one man should be called upon to bear. But
with anything like a recovery to their usual spirits
and vigor, I hope to get all these men back... because
each is an outstanding leader. Corps and Army
commanders stand up well... spared the more direct
battle strains of a Division commander.[10]

As expected, Huertgen fell the next day, November 28th, but not
until after a brutal finale of street fighting, often hand-to-hand. Over
200 German prisoners were taken with many more killed. Scores lay
buried beneath the rubble of the little agricultural town. After more
than two months of ghastly fighting for this little piece of real estate,
four divisions had been largely depleted and thousands had died, one
of the most costly battles in the history of the United States Army.

In the voluminous literature that since has analyzed the campaign, some authors speculate that Gen. Stroh was sacked for not
having achieved a more rapid victory. But this is a simplistic conclusion to a complex situation. The bottom line is that Gen. Stroh's 8th
Division finally defeated the enemy at Huertgen, despite the serious
limitations imposed on him by his superiors before the start. He had
asked for the short leave out of a sense of duty, recognizing that his
mental and emotional states were in danger of affecting his combat
efficiency. Clearly Gens. Hodges and Eisenhower realized this and
agreed with Stroh's own assessment. Perhaps Charles B. MacDonald
stated it most succinctly.

About the time Huertgen fell, the 8th Division
commander, General Stroh, was departing the division
on a leave of absence. A veteran of the fighting since
the North African campaign, General Stroh had seen
his son shot down and killed while flying a fighter-
bomber in support of the 8th Division at Brest. Higher

commanders had deemed it time General Stroh had a rest, with the proviso that he return later to command another division.[11]

The remark about commanding "another division" may have been a little off the mark. Writing later about a meeting with Gen. Eisenhower at SHAEF headquarters on his way back to the States, Gen. Stroh reported, "...it was stated when I left for home that I'd get the 8th back."

There is ample evidence of the high esteem in which Gen. Stroh was held by his soldiers, and his superiors. After the war he received a gift from the man who, more than any other, manifestly assisted him in the successes of the 8th Division, Col. Tom Cross. It was a book, *The Gray Bonnet, A Combat History of the 121st Infantry Regiment.* An inscription inside the front cover reads:

> To Major General D. A. Stroh, whose able command and leadership guided the fortunes of the Blue Bonnet Regiment on the battlefields of Europe, always attaining their objectives, never losing ground. T. J. Cross, Colonel 121st Infantry, 5 July 1946

22

---◆---

Winter Warfare

In December 1944, while Gen. Stroh was recharging his batteries back home in the States, Lt. Col. Stumpf and the 39th Infantry were back on the front lines, still slogging it out in the same general area where the fighting had begun when they first crossed into Germany in September. The differences, however, were pronounced. The weather had turned bitterly cold; the coldest winter in memory for northern Europe. At times, surviving the cold was as difficult as surviving the enemy. A second major difference for the 9th Division was that they were once again fighting a war of maneuver, albeit limited, in contrast to the near stalemate of the Huertgen Forest. They were well rested, at full strength, and well trained; in much better shape than when they were pulled out of the Forest in mid-October. The enemy they faced was a combination of very good veteran combat divisions, and Volks Grenadier divisions, essentially light infantry made up of a skeleton crew of veteran officers and NCOs and fleshed out by remnants of other branches, the very young, and the very old. The Germans remained fanatical in their resistance, though, as evidenced by their last stand at Huertgen. And they still had a lot of punch and motivation because they were defending their homeland. They also brought new weapons into the fight, including the monster 70-ton King Tiger tank.[1]

The 9th Division was back with "the first team of the First Army," Gen. Collins's VII Corps, whose objectives included the city of Düren, which had been a Corps objective since September. Düren lies about eighteen miles east of Aachen, on the east bank of the Roer River. Another thirty miles to the east flows the Rhine River, the Third Reich's last major natural barrier against defeat from the West. The orientation of the Corps attack would be west to east following major roads and railroads just north of the Huertgen Forest.

On December 5th, the 39th Infantry began moving from Camp Elsenborn, their home for the last six weeks, to assembly areas south of Langerwehe, about five miles west of the Roer River. They relieved the 26th Infantry, and were temporarily attached to the 1st Division while awaiting the arrival of the bulk of the 9th Division. The attack was scheduled to jump off on the morning of December 10th, so ample time was available for planning, reconnaissance, and coordination with adjacent units. A combat command of the 3rd Armored Division was attached to the division, and Gen. Collins insisted that the infantry and armor work closely together, something that both units had done extensively in the successful drive across France and Belgium. The 1st Division had taken a beating in this sector only weeks prior, so all 9th Division commanders were being extremely thorough in their preparations. The mission for the attack was stated clearly in the division Report of Operations.

> Attack to the east in conjunction with the 3rd
> Armored Division, to seize and hold initially the towns
> of KONZENDORF, ECHTZ, SCHLICH, AND MERODE.
> It was estimated that the enemy's resistance to our
> advance would be strong. His defense consisted of
> centers of resistance formed by built-up communities

in the sector and dug-in positions between these communities. The enemy line, which at some points was only 75 yards from our own, was held by the Fifth Parachute Regiment in the southern sector, with two battalions on line and one in reserve, and the Eighth Parachute Regiment in the northern sector... The Ninth Parachute Regiment was in reserve... Enemy artillery was expected to be heavy and for the most part observed.

This push to the Roer River began on the morning of December 10th with the 39th Infantry delaying in their positions south of the railroad line until the 60th Infantry was ready to go. At 1515, the 2nd Battalion, 39th Infantry attacked southeastward in column of companies under cover fire and demonstrations from the other two battalions. The villages of D'Horn and Geich were captured in short order, setting the stage for the attack on Merode. The castle town, which had proven so deadly for the 1st Division, was captured that evening by the 2nd Battalion and Company "K" of the 3rd. On December 11th, the attack resumed at 0800, toward the Derichsweiler, while spending the day mopping up and consolidating prisoners in Merode and Schlich.

The next morning, December 12th, Lt. Col. Stumpf and the 3rd Battalion attacked along a line of departure from D'Horn to Schlich under the cover of smoke. They advanced eastward toward the objective Derichsweiler against long-range artillery, mortar, and machine gun fire. The doughboys were fighting in the streets by 1430 and succeeded in clearing half of the town by nightfall, then consolidated their positions after taking 146 prisoners of the German 942nd Infantry. The next day, the 3rd Battalion continued to clean out the remainder of the town, moving slowly, while taking heavy artillery and mortar fire from the town of Gurzenich, about a mile to the southeast. The battalion had Derichsweiler under complete control by 1535. The regiment captured an additional eighty German prisoners from the 501st Anti-tank Battalion, 8th Paratroop Regiment, and 942nd Infantry.

On the 14th, the 39th Infantry held their positions while clearing out isolated pockets of resistance that might interfere with the impending operations. They continued to take intermittent shelling, most of which fell on the nearby 3rd Battalion. The wet weather had turned colder, adding to the miserable conditions that prevented the regiment from fully benefiting during its temporary breather. That night, the 39th received orders to attack the next day and seize all ground west of the Roer River in their sector. The regiment began planning for yet another river assault crossing. The Report of Operations for 15 December, however, read, "Attack scheduled for 1300, but held up awaiting coordination with unit on the right; finally called off for the day." A likewise entry was made the following day, December 16, 1944. To the south, the Panzers were on the move. Hitler's last gasp, the Ardennes counteroffensive that would become known as the Battle of the Bulge, was underway.

Half a world away in Washington, D.C., Gen. Stroh was enjoying being at home with his wife and daughter for the first time in two years. After a stop at SHAEF Headquarters in London on November 29th, he and his trusty aide, 1st Lt. Causa Berry, traveled across the Atlantic on official SHAEF orders to proceed and report to the Adjutant General at the War Department for sixty days "for the purpose of carrying out instructions of the Theater Commander." They were authorized a baggage allowance of sixty-five pounds each, and Gen. Stroh was allowed an additional 150 pounds. Clearly, the temporary duty orders were strictly for rest and rehabilitation and would require little or no official duties, but they provided a per diem stipend of $7.20.

Shortly after the Strohs' emotional reunion, they attended the Army-Navy football game in Baltimore on December 2nd with Gen.

Collins' wife, Gladys. The Collins' son, a West Point cadet, was able to score four tickets. On a bitterly cold Saturday afternoon, the game featured the nation's top two college teams. The heads of the military branches, General Marshall, Admiral King, and General Arnold, were in attendance. Much to the delight of the Stroh/Collins party, number one Army prevailed, 23-7.

The following week, Gen. Stroh consented to an interview with *Washington Post* reporter Charles Holstein, who ran a story in the December 8th edition. In it, the general described the circumstances surrounding the loss of his son during the battle for Brest, and his great admiration for the soldiers who were enduring great hardships in the global fight against tyranny.

Among Gen. Stroh's generous baggage allowance were Christmas presents for the family, including Imogene's in-laws in Barberton, Ohio. The Strohs enjoyed Christmas at home, albeit tempered by the absence of Harry and Bob. All were deeply concerned about the latter as the 39th Infantry was likely at the front stemming the onslaught of the Germans' massive counteroffensive. Imogene's last letter from him was from December 4th, although she received an undated cable that read, "LOVE AND BEST WISHES FOR CHRISTMAS AND THE NEW YEAR TO ALL AT HOME. ALL WELL. B STUMPF." On December 27th, Imogene flew to Barberton to be with Bob's parents. She mentioned in a short letter home that Bob's dad was especially "tickled" with his gift that Gen. Stroh had spirited back, a German military pistol. The presence of that particular souvenir probably violated some regulation or other along the way.[2] Imogene returned to Washington on January 2nd.

Mrs. Stroh received letters of condolence from Secretary of War Henry L. Stimson and General H. H. "Hap" Arnold, Commanding General, U.S. Army Air Forces, both dated January 6th. The Strohs attended a ceremony on January 12th sponsored by the Central High School Alumni Association to honor six graduates with Certificates of

Distinction. Ironically, the only military men of the six were a private and a general, the former having been wounded in battle. There were nice write-ups with photos in the *Post* and *Star*. Mid-month, Gen. and Mrs. Stroh and Imogene enjoyed a getaway at the Greenbrier Resort in White Sulfur Springs, West Virginia. The famous landmark was purchased by the Army in 1942 and served as a detention facility for German and Japanese diplomats and their families after the onset of hostilities, then converted into a hospital. The property maintained visitors quarters for senior officers. They celebrated Imogene's 25th birthday on January 29th, after which Imogene left with her friend Mary Louise for a visit to the Big Apple while her father packed up and left to return to the war. She picked up on her correspondence protocol with her father as soon as she got back.

3614 Ingomar Pl.
Washington, D.C.
February 2, 1945

I've gone and returned from my trip to New York, and the house didn't seem the same without you here. It seemed as if I'd been away for a long time and that there had been a lot of changes made.

Mother still has the remains of your cigars complete with ashes in the big brass irons here in the den.

I hope you didn't mind me not going down to see you off. I didn't think you would. I wanted Mother to have all the show because I hung around all the time and besides it was probably easier to take for her.

The War Department called today to say you'd arrived safely and gave your cable. Mother has been relieved and so happy you had those sixty days. It's grand you got your old job. I'll bet everyone was glad to see you, too. I'm wondering if you saw Bob but imagine you have not had the time. Haven't heard anything more from him since that letter written the 13th. I still can't get over how his birthday greeting reached here right at the proper time.

Today was my first day in the next semester. Now I'm a full-fledged senior on the last lap. You should see my gorgeous grades! You'd never believe your daughter was a B student at G. W... I can hardly believe it either. If Bob didn't come back before September, which he *will*, I'd get a B.S.

I can't begin to tell you how wonderful it was to have you home. Surely Harry must have been with us because we were all so happy. Thank you for all the big things like Christmas, my birthday, the trip to White Sulphur; and for the little things like helping me hope for a letter each day, and carrying those two little logs up that last day, and struggling with the cork on the champagne bottle. We were all very happy, and we're still happy remembering.

On December 17, 1944, the 39th Infantry was preparing to move south toward the northern flank of the huge German counteroffensive. However, 3rd Battalion began taking small arms and artillery fire from pockets of resistance just north of Guerzenich. Lt. Col. Stumpf directed K Company to attack under the cover of smoke, jumping off at 0750. They had cleared out all resistance by late in the afternoon. The next day, they were still taking isolated sniper fire from the surrounding area, which they dispatched and were then relieved by the 329th Infantry. The regiment began movement at 0830 the following morning to the vicinity of Elsenborn-Kalterherberg. Their route of about twenty-five circuitous miles around the Huertgen Forest took them through

Gressenich, Stolberg, Brand, Aachen, and Eupen. Upon arrival they took over positions occupied by the 9th Reconnaissance Troop and began improving defensive positions while tying in with the units on their flanks. Their job was to hold the line against an expected German attack to expand the northern shoulder of their massive encroachment.

Under the overall command of Field Marshal Karl Rudolf Gerd von Rundstedt, the Germans' lofty objective was to capture Antwerp, the Allies' only northern supply port. They aimed to cut a salient through the American lines in the Ardennes and advance rapidly to Liege on the Meuse River, capturing American supplies to sustain the offensive, then continuing northwest to the sea. They had been planning and hoarding troops, equipment, and supplies for months, including elite SS and Panzer Divisions, for this last massive gamble. If it succeeded, the Germans would isolate the American First and Ninth Armies and their British and Canadian allies to the north with the possibility of defeating them in detail. On the other hand, if the Americans could halt the advance, then counterattack into the Germans' flanks and rear, they could turn the tables, isolating the German armies.

The onslaught began on the morning of December 16th with the German armor and Infantry making rapid advances, blitzkrieg style, before the Americans could mount a meaningful response. After several days of bitter fighting, the advance had been slowed, and halted in some areas. The defensive sector to which the 9th Division was proceeding on December 19th was from Konzen south through Monschau and Hoefen to Kalterherberg. The southern flank of this line was only about five miles north of Elsenborn, where they had spent the month of November. The 9th Division Field Order #49 of December 19th was, for most, the first solid indication of the extent of the German attack: "The enemy has pushed back our lines along a sixty mile front... attacks have been characterized by armored thrusts followed by infantry to consolidate gains."[3]

On the afternoon of December 21st, the 39th Infantry was attacked by two regiments of the 3rd Panzer Grenadier Division. Apparently, the enemy was not aware of the extensive defensive preparations by the Americans over the previous thirty-six hours. The attack was stopped cold by the infantry's small arms and mortars, and massed fires from the 9th, 2nd, and 99th Division artilleries which caught at least one entire battalion completely in the open. The carnage was hideous. Second Lt. John Adams of I Company, a replacement platoon leader, recalled, "They came down the center of the valley making a lot of racket as though they had no warning." He added that German prisoners captured that day "could not believe that we were there." His company commander, Capt. Anthony Dana, reported that the German medics were so numerous, he worried that they had fired on a large hospital group.

Undeterred, the Germans attacked again the next day; a relatively small attack at 1300, and a heavier one at 1730 that overran forward elements of the 99 Recon Troop. E Company was able to reinforce the troopers and assist their withdrawal. In response, Lt. Col. Stumpf moved 3rd Battalion up in preparation for a counterattack in the morning to regain the lost ground. They jumped off at 0750 in column of companies and engaged the enemy in a running small arms fight. The battalion recovered all the ground lost the previous evening and repulsed another attack at 1700 from the same direction. Sixteen prisoners were taken that day representing the 990th and 991st Infantry and the 29th Panzer Regiments.

These and other engagements in the 9th Division sector during this three-day period are significant because they represent in microcosm the last attempts of the German counteroffensive to break through the Monschau area front. Had the Germans been successful they would have had a clear road to Liege, whose capture may have provided a much-needed boost to the campaign's flagging momentum. Besides the heroic efforts by the infantry and artillery, the Air Corps provided valuable support to the ground troops on good weather days. From the First U.S. Army Report of Operations for that period:

> Von Rundstedt had sacrificed the best part of four divisions... in his repeated attempts to assault the Elsenborn Ridge and the Monschau area... His hopes of reaching Liege through Verviers were smashed by the stalwart resistance of the troops defending along the norther shoulder of the Gap and at St. Vith.[4]

For the next several days, the 39th Infantry continued to improve their defensive positions by adding minefields and wire barriers. They also patrolled regularly to maintain contact with the enemy and occasionally engaged German patrols in firefights. Christmas was like any other day—cold, snowy, the men on the front lines existing in miserable holes chopped out of frozen ground. Lt. Col. Stumpf was one of the dwindling number of Falcon men spending their third Christmas overseas. He managed to write letters home on December 26th. This one to his parents is reflective of his dour sensibilities, perhaps an indication of five and a half months of near continuous combat, and nearly twenty-seven months since he last saw his bride.

> Spent a fairly quiet day yesterday sleeping and visiting the companies which were consolidating after a local counterattack we put on. We have restored the lines in our present sector and are at present holding— but don't imagine it will be long before we're pushing again. Came here after taking part in a drive up north.
>
> Hope you like the stationery. A couple of 155's [howitzers] removed the store from around this package in one of the towns the battalion was "liberating." No Germans were available to make use of it, so I did. The only Boche remaining weren't interested in correspondence—as a matter of fact they weren't interested in anything.

Christmas packages are coming in from all you folks so fast that I'm worried about enough time to consume them all before we're on the move again. We even sent a package to the Nazis at 12:01 Christmas morning—5 rounds from each mortar in the battalion and the artillery kicked in ten. Peace on Earth... Will call for a repeat on New Years if we're still here.

Still in one piece and healthy.

Action at the front remained mostly static during the final week of 1944 with routine patrolling and occasional exchanges of artillery and mortar fire. The 39th Infantry Report of Operations for 28 December noted a "heavy artillery barrage at 0530 and small arms fire was received on Co. 'L' but subsided, although artillery continued heavier than normal for balance of the morning." Later that day an enemy patrol stumbled into L Company positions but were driven off. On December 30th, K Company sent out a combat patrol that generated a firefight. On that day, units of the 60th Infantry began relieving 3rd Battalion companies in the frontline defensive positions. The turnover was complete by the next day. During the month of December 1944, the 39th Infantry lost forty-five men killed in action, 245 wounded in action, and fourteen missing in action for a total of 306 battle casualties. A like number was lost to other causes, such as frostbite and disease.

January 1945 brought more and more snow, which complicated all aspects of units operating in the field, including supply, maintenance, and simply staying warm. The G.I.s improvised when needed. They burned charcoal in makeshift stoves to warm their foxholes, which they lined with raw wool from a liberated local felt factory. They lined the soles of their shoes with the felt—frostbite and trench foot were continuous problems. They fabricated snowplows, toboggans, and white coveralls for winter camouflage. Anti-freeze fluid made its way to the front lines to keep the armor and other vehicles moving.

The mission for the 9th Division and its 39th Infantry, until the very end of the month, was to maintain a solid defensive posture while demonstrating along the front, harassing the enemy with combat patrols and occasional company-sized attacks. They kept the Germans busy while other First Army divisions were continuing to attack against the German "bulge" as it was being called. During the first half of the month, the German momentum waned, stalled, and then finally stopped after about sixty-five miles of incursion. The 39th kept two battalions on line and one in reserve, rotating them so that the men could warm up, eat hot chow, and get dry at least a third of the time. One of the activities of these reserve elements throughout the month was to train in night attack, a tactic they would employ on the coming offensive.

On January 1st, the 39th Infantry received reports of enemy build-up opposite their sector of the front closest to 3rd Battalion. Lt. Col. Stumpf tapped L Company, supported by three medium tanks, to perform an armed reconnaissance to clear the area. They succeeded in destroying three machine gun and four mortar emplacements. During the skirmishes, one of the tanks became separated from the other two and was taken out by enemy anti-tank rocket fire. The infantrymen were unable to safely approach the tank to retrieve it, so it was abandoned and the company withdrew to the previous front line at nightfall. Next day, a patrol was sent out to destroy the tank to keep it from being retrieved by the Germans in working order. The patrol put four bazooka rounds into the tank and left it smoldering.

Daily patrolling along with active demonstrations in conjunction with American assaults to the south continued for the next three weeks. This period of cold defensive tedium was punctuated by a tremendous blizzard January 19-20 that dumped more deep and drifting snow throughout the area. About this time, von Rundstedt and his generals were coming to the conclusion that their massive offensive had been stopped for good. They began a hasty withdrawal lest the entire army group be completely cut off and destroyed. Also around this time, one of Lt. Col. Stumpf's company commanders received a dream-come-true assignment. Captain Orville K. Fletcher, M Company, scored orders to attend a school in the United States, and Imogene received an unusual letter.

February 1, 1945

Dear Mrs. Stumpf:

Recently I returned to the United States to attend a special school here in Leavenworth. I had the honor of serving under your husband, having command of Company "M." I was with him from Sicily until a few weeks ago when I left him in Germany.

The Colonel asked me to drop you a line to tell you he is fine. Personally, I want you to know he looks good, high in spirits and I'm sure you'd find him unchanged. Your husband is highly respected and well liked by officers and men of his Bn. He has stood by us and brought us through many a tight spot.

I hope you have been hearing regularly from the Col. I'm sure there is no cause to worry as they are well fed and clothed, but also <u>very</u> busy at this time.

If there are any questions please feel free to write me as I'll be here for another month.

From the looks of the news I'd say your husband will be home to you before so very long. I do hope it will be soon.

Sincerely,
Capt. Fletcher

602 Seneca Ave.
Leavenworth, Kans.

On January 28th the 9th Division received orders to prepare for a major V Corps offensive. The objective was finally to capture and control the five major dams of the Roer River system. Wresting them from enemy control was essential to the resumption of the Allied advance deep into Germany, lest the floodgates were opened and the low ground of the offensive inundated.

Planning for the attack and reconnaissance patrols began immediately to ascertain aspects of the terrain and latest enemy dispositions. On January 29th, L Company was struck by a massive food poisoning attack which swept through much of the unit, rendering it temporarily unfit for combat. As 3rd Battalion was to be one of the assault battalions, Lt. Col. Stumpf requested reinforcement. 1st Battalion was the designated division reserve for the attack, and B Company, under the command of Capt. Jack Dunlap, was attached to 3rd Battalion until L Company was well enough to return to battle.

Lt. Col. Stumpf moved his battalion out on schedule early on the morning of January 30th from the vicinity of Kalterherberg. The battalion arose at 0200 and had their last hot meal for the next several days. They moved out under bright moonlight and in waist-deep snow. From the 39th Infantry ops report of that day:

> 3rd Battalion moved from Line of Departure at 0415, and moved slowly in deep snow and over very difficult terrain, came under small arms fire from high ground at 0840 at close range due to limited visibility. Enemy log bunkers were located...and the reserve, Co. "K", was brought up to handle it releasing Co. "I" to maneuver to the southeast against resistance holding up Co. "B" on the right. Progress was slow to the front while Co. "K" cleared up the left flank and took PWs.

From the get-go, the battalion operated in darkness, practicing night tactics perfected in training during the preceding weeks. It is interesting to note that Company K, one of the 3rd Battalion's regular companies, was in reserve, while Company B, on loan from the 1st Battalion, was one of the assault companies. Despite the snow and rugged terrain, 9th Division gains for the first day were about 3,000 yards. Sixty years later, B Company commander Capt. Dunlap remembered how disgusted he was with the 3rd Battalion commander.

> It was a two company assault. I never thought I would be assigned as an assault company. I was supposed to be in reserve. I had a replacement platoon leader who had just shown me a photo of his new baby who he had never seen. He was killed leading his platoon up a hill into enemy fire. I have never forgiven Col. Stumpf.[5]

The next morning, 3rd Battalion was attached to the 47th Infantry for that day's assault, probably because of its relative position in the division front. It spent most of the next two days reducing enemy pillboxes in the Siegfried Line, made more difficult by the deep and drifting snow. During these operations, the warmer daytime weather began melting the snow, soaking the doughboys' clothing and shoes. At night, freezing temperatures iced the uniforms up and caused them to crack when they moved. Most of the troops were having problems with their feet, which were usually wet and very cold. On the morning of February 2nd, 3rd Battalion returned to 39th Infantry control and assembled near Hoefen. The next day, the regiment remained in assembly areas until receiving orders to proceed to the vicinity of Dreiborn six miles to the east, which had been taken by the 60th Infantry. They moved out at 1530 by foot and motor march, passing through Dreiborn at 2205 and attacking eastward toward Herhahn, a distance of about two miles. The road to Herhahn was found to be mined, so engineers were called up to clear the road to allow armor to support clearing the town. Approaching the town, they met intense fire from the houses and began mopping up operations.

Just after midnight on February 4th, enemy armor was reported to be approaching from the southeast. From the regimental ops report:

> ...difficulties in clearing artillery fires permitted two tanks to take up positions in town where they fired direct fire on the leading companies, holding up their progress. Interdicting artillery fire was placed on the road, and friendly armor began maneuvering to firing positions after observing enemy tanks by [muzzle] flash; two TDs hit mines passing around the tanks in front, and two belts of wooden box mines were located by the engineers and a gap made to allow passage... of the tanks and TDs by 0300 and after joining up with the leading companies, mopping up operations continued, although artillery and direct fire still continued at various intervals.

After the enemy armor threat had subsided about daylight, Lt. Col. Stumpf moved the 3rd Battalion north of Herhahn to Morsbach aboard trucks and tank destroyers. There, they rounded up civilians, whom they sent to the rear, and captured several prisoners, three artillery pieces with ammunition, three 120-mm mortars, and several anti-tank guns. For the rest of the day, the battalions consolidated on the high ground east of Herhahn and Morsbach, with special emphasis on anti-tank defense. They were now within a mile of the Urft River and about four miles of the Urfttalsperre Dam, second largest in the Roer system.

The 39th Infantry launched their February 5th attack at 0730 from high ground to clear the area to the river. In the course of the day, 3rd Battalion chased the retreating enemy all the way to the river, which the Germans attempted to cross. L Company took positions on the high ground and was able to inflict serious damage with concentrated small arms fire while the enemy was exposed during the crossing. The battalion consolidated their positions on the reverse slope, sent patrols to make contact with1st Battalion on their right, cleared the wooded area to their left, and established outposts on the forward slope. For the next two days, the assault battalions continued to consolidate their positions while sending out combat patrols to clean out any pockets of resistance and to recon bridges, crossing sites, terrain, and enemy dispositions.

On February 8th, the 39th Infantry was temporarily attached to the 2nd Division, remaining in defensive positions in the Urft River area until February 12th. On that day, Lt. Col. Stumpf said goodbye to the 39th Infantry and the 3rd Battalion that he had commanded for seventeen months. He turned the battalion over to his capable executive officer since the Normandy campaign, Major Richard Kent. Stumpf had been reassigned.

23

---•---

Golden Lions

After leaving Washington on January 30th, Major General Stroh arrived back in the ETO the first week of February. His first stop was SHAEF in London, where he met with Gen. Eisenhower on the 1st, then made his way to the continent. His travel orders from SHAEF, dated February 2nd, were to proceed to Gen. Bradley's 12th Army Group in Verdun, France, where he would receive orders to his parent Army headquarters and learn of his permanent assignment. His first letter to Imogene since the previous October was dated February 4, 1945.

> After nearly a week's wandering about the world I still haven't come to rest, and don't expect to until Tuesday [Feb. 6]. Two successive nights on the floor of a plane, and different every night for the rest of the period isn't my idea of a vacation, but I guess I should be thankful that they've been beds and nothing worse.
>
> You will note a definite change in my APO number, and my command [106th Division]. Both came as a

distinct surprise when I saw Monk [Lewis] Friday
evening [at Bradley's headquarters]. None of the
people at SHAEF nor ETO had said anything about
it, including Eisenhower when I saw him Thursday.
Although it was stated when I left for home that I'd get
the 8th back, there have been unexpected changes,
such as the promotion of my supposed temporary
successor, and the tough handling the 106th took,
including the illness and relief of its commander. So
I'm unable to decide whether this change is a knock
or a boost. I saw Hodges yesterday, who seemed
surprised by the development. If I have been a failure
as a division commander, I see no reason why they
trust me with another, particularly in combat. On the
other hand, I see no reason why my first pinch hitter
in the 8th couldn't take over the 106th. Certainly
he is less well dug in there than I. I feel that I turned
over to him a first class outfit, which he himself freely
admitted when I had lunch with him today. So it may
be that having succeeded in building up one outfit
from the dregs they want to have me try my hand
at another. I have gotten beyond the stage of caring
much, one way or another, but I am curious to know
what is behind it all. Whatever the reason, I have a
real job cut out for me. There isn't much left.

Despite his attempts at rationalization, this development had to
have been not only a shock, but a stinging disappointment. Gen. Stroh
had led the 8th Division out of the morass in Normandy and through
success after success on the battlefield, thereby securing its reputation
as a top-notch division of which he was very proud. Of course he knew
and respected the staff there and surely had been looking forward to

getting his old job back, especially in light of Gen. Eisenhower's comment before he went on leave. Taken in the best light, his superiors considered him just the right leader to rebuild the 106th Division, which had lost most of two complete infantry regiments in the opening onslaught of the German Ardennes offensive six weeks prior. Stroh was to replace Major General Alan W. Jones, who suffered a heart attack during the height of the Ardennes fighting. The division was still on the line, battling with one arm behind its back, with the American armies completing the recovery of all their lost ground.

After leaving Gen. Bradley's headquarters, Gen. Stroh reported to Fifteenth Army headquarters near Reims, France, commanded by Lt. Gen. Leonard Gerow, who had been Stroh's corps commander at Huertgen. Gen. Stroh continued in the same letter to Imogene:

> Had the pleasure of seeing Bob yesterday, but only for a few minutes, as his outfit was even then in the process of moving up. It was nearly dark, and had I been but a few minutes later I would have missed him. The division is operating in some of the wildest country I have ever seen, not far from the place where I last saw him! I think you will remember it on the map. Bob looked well, but somewhat thin, as well he might, after what he has gone through for the past three months especially. Delivered the bedding rolls to him, your letter, his father's letter, and the funnies, together with a bottle of Scotch I picked up on the way, for all of which he was grateful.
>
> I asked Bob how he would like to be a regimental commander in my new outfit. He'd like the job all right, particularly where he could grow up with the regiment, so to speak, but is not sure that his relationship with me would stand the gaff. In this I

could sympathize with him. He and I could work it out all right, but you know how others would talk. After all, a regimental commander at 29 is a rare bird, if not unheard of, not because it wouldn't work, but because nobody has ever thought of trying it. Anyway, I'd be glad to have Bob if the opportunity offers. The decision will have to be entirely his, and I told him to think it over and let me know. There is no rush, as things can't happen for a month or so.

It is apparent that Gen. Stroh was writing about one of the new replacement regiments that were to accrue to the 106th Division when they eventually were pulled off the line. In an ironic situation, the lone remaining regiment, the 424th Infantry, was commanded by one Col. John Jeter, who had replaced the previous commander after he was seriously wounded in the Ardennes. Jeter was the former commander of the 121st Infantry whom Gen. Stroh had relieved at Huertgen. Gen. Stroh dined with his friend and mentor, First Army commander Gen. Hodges, on February 6th, and they discussed the 106th Division situation.

General Stroh and Aide who have returned from two months in the states were the General's guests for dinner tonight. General Stroh tomorrow assumes command of the 106th Div. They are going to receive in the near future two more regiments, one the 3rd separate infantry regiment, the other one as yet unknown and thus come back to complete fighting strength.[1]

On February 3rd, the 106th Division was alerted for its next combat assignment: to anchor the right flank of the U.S. First Army in its drive eastward to the Rhine River as part of V Corps. Upon assuming command of the division on February 7th, Gen. Stroh found its combat units maneuvering into positions just on the German side of the Belgian border in a 7,000-yard-wide arc between the villages of Neuhof in the north to Losheim in the south. These positions were only a few miles from where the division had been decimated early in the Battle of the Bulge. On its right was Gen. Patton's Third Army, specifically the 6th Cavalry Group attached to the 87th Division; on its left, the 99th Division. The mission of the 106th was "aggressive defense," which meant continuous pressure, but not taking the offensive. Division headquarters and division artillery were located at Hunningen, Belgium, about five miles to the rear.[2]

> The zone ahead was a jumbled mass of hills and watercourses. Bisecting it progressively eastward were three streams... draining from north to south in winding valleys deepening to three hundred feet when they fed into the Kyll [River].
>
> It was no terrain to be taken frontally, organized as it was and backing against prepared Siegfried Line positions on the ridge east of the Grudsell [stream]. Each ridge could be turned from the north flank, but one lone regimental combat team of three infantry battalions could not be expected to do the job against determined resistance.
>
> The 2nd Battalion, 424th Infantry, with I Company attached, held the northern sector, including two hill masses 656 and 655, the latter a definite bulge into enemy territory. The southern sector slanting toward Losheim was held by the 1st Battalion. In reserve, at the deserted hamlet of Losheimergraben... the 3rd Battalion dug in. And on 12 February Lt. Col. Robert H. Stumpf was put in command of the 424th.[3]

Something had changed in Gen. Stroh's calculus as to which regiment he wanted Lt. Col. Stumpf to command. One thing is certain, Col. Jeter could not have remained in command of the 424th given Gen. Stroh's loss of confidence in him at Huertgen. Perhaps Jeter was originally assigned only as a temporary replacement during the Bulge and was moving on anyway. In any event, only five days after taking over, Stroh brought Stumpf on, not to command a future replacement regiment, but to command the 106th Division's only remaining regimental combat team. He later wrote, "I selected Lt Col Stumpf, from among a list of officers of that grade submitted by the First United States Army, to command the 424th Infantry." He also wrote Maj. Gen. Craig, commander of the 9th Division, to explain why he was pilfering his most experienced battalion commander. Craig replied, "I appreciate your letter… and of course understand your reasons for desiring the transfer of Lt. Col. Stumpf. He has the reputation of being a competent, energetic, and well qualified tactical leader." Besides the 424th Infantry, other active elements of the division at that time included two battalions of field artillery, a tank destroyer company, the division signal and ordnance companies, reconnaissance troop, engineer combat battalion, and medical battalion. There were no tank units attached, but they would not have been much help in this terrain.

The forward zone was a mess. In the first place the Kraut had scattered mines and booby traps in enormous quantities, with his usual ingenuity. Secondly, while the dense woods were crisscrossed by trails, these had become masses of mud from rain and thaw. Even jeeps could not negotiate them; the only vehicles which could be used off the main roads were a number of Weasels [jeep-sized tracked vehicles] which had been drawn for Division use. The engineers slaved endlessly, corduroying and laying wire matting on the principal routes.

Active patrolling at once disclosed the enemy to be well dug in in successive delaying positions.[4]

The month dragged on through a continuous series of small attacks and armed reconnaissance patrols by both sides. All the German assaults were repulsed, but there were some successes by the Americans. They made slow but steady progress in pushing the German lines eastward. The regiment and division continued to work on plans for a substantial attack and sent them up to Corps, but they were never approved. On February 24th, the 3rd Battalion moved up and relieved the 2nd, which left E Company in place, and moved back to defensive positions at Losheimergraben. The forward battalions continued to improve their positions and clear their fronts of mines, wire, and booby traps. They were successful in attacking and reducing those pillboxes they encountered. On both flanks of the division sector, other units were planning large-scale attacks and advances. But no such orders made their way to the 106th. Thus ended a frustrating month for the Golden Lions. In action most of the month with little to show for it, they lost eighteen killed, eighty-seven wounded, and twenty-one missing. At some point during the month, Gen. Stroh probably received Imogene's letters dated February 15th and 16th where she commented on his new assignment, and her follow-up a week later.

You could have knocked us over with a couple of feathers when Mother received your letter of Feb. 6th telling about your new job. We'd spoken of that division so much when you were home and were so concerned about it. It just goes to show that we never know what may happen next.

I'd say it was quite a feather in your cap to be given a problem such as that to get into working order, and don't try to tell us you don't think so too, and that you just love to get things running smoothly in your good methodical way. It's probably proving to be a most difficult task, but if anyone in the United States Army can fix it up, that person is you. We're so proud of you and so proud to tell people what they gave you, especially those we know who doubted why you came home.

February 16

I wrote yesterday before I received your cable... I *knew* Bob would accept the offer and it is a wonderful compliment and opportunity for him. I've no doubt that you will be as proud of him now as you always have.

I won't expect him home now until I see him. Just to know he is safe for a while and behind the lines a little is a grand relief as you well realize.

I received a letter from him, Jan. 25th, today and If I hadn't heard from you through cables I'd certainly be worried plenty. I'm so glad he is away for a while.

Thank you, Daddy, for giving him this splendid chance. Got Harry's eagles [colonel's rank insignia] in the mail today.

February 22

I haven't heard from Bob since the big proposition and decision and I'm certainly curious about all reactions.

I certainly am disappointed that I can't expect him home any time soon now, and then when he does come it will only be 30 days. Guess I should be so glad that he has escaped even a scratch and that he has a wonderful opportunity. Those two things really compensate the disappointment—almost.

You must be going through a difficult adjustment. The more I think of it, the more I'm convinced that giving you that division is a compliment. You know that no one has your background, experience and temperament to get a division in the 106th fix back into shape. You're just what they needed.

Say hello to Gen. Perrin [Gen. Stroh's assistant] for me. He is very nice and I'm glad you have another friend there.

As March dawned, the 106th Division finally got their chance to go on offense. The division was part of a much larger attack across the First and Third Army fronts to commence on March 5th. On the eve of battle, Gen. Stroh sat down to compose his regular Sunday letter to Imogene.

Your big hubby was here for a conference early this afternoon, which delayed me writing until this hour, and I'll have to hurry to get through before dinner time. He's just as big and sassy as ever, and has taken hold in good shape... Had a long talk with Bob last Monday morning, principally about regimental affairs, but in the course of it, I gave him the copy of the Silver Star citation, which you sent, and which he had never seen before. It seemed to buck him up no end. It is a fine citation...

I am particularly relieved to know of your reaction to Bob's transfer, as expressed in your letter of

February 16... Now that you feel everything is all right, it must be all right and everyone is happy. The change, as I have explained, will probably deprive him of a chance to get home for an indefinite time in the future, but his chances in the old outfit were not much better, if any, and the new job has many advantages.

Glad you think my new job is a compliment, because I can't honestly make up my mind even yet that it is. As a matter of fact there has been no opportunity yet to begin the main job which is confronting us. We have been engaged in more strenuous activities ever since I joined, and the end is not yet. I'm looking forward to a change in scene, climate, and activity.

You should see the palace we are living in at present. About half the roof has been blown off, but otherwise it is quite a nice house. Judging from the size of the manure pile in the front yard, which is always an indication of wealth in Europe, the place must have belonged to one of the most prosperous farmers of the community. The kitchen door opens into the stable, now occupied by several very dirty cows. I have a nice coal stove in my room, and a dresser with a vanity mirror. Can you tie that? Judging from the way we are knocking things apart up front, this may be the last relatively whole house we will get to live in for some time.

On the morning of 5 March 1st and 3rd Battalions, 424th Infantry, jumped off and advanced eastward, obtaining the first ridge line by nightfall. They were opposed by remnants of the 26th Volksgrenadier Division, which had suffered heavy losses in the fighting around

Bastogne during the Ardennes offensive. The next day, strong patrols advanced along the ridges all the way to the Simmer River. In
rapid succession, the 424th captured the towns of Frauenkron, Berk,
Kronenburg, and Baasem, its furthest advance in force. Although
mines and terrible road conditions were their most challenging obstacles, division artillery moved up behind the fast-moving infantry
as best they could. On 7 March, the 69th Division on the left of the
106th Division sector attacked in a broad arc to the southeast. As the
424th infantry moved forward, Lt. Col. Stumpf established his CP in a
knocked-out schoolhouse in the village of Berk.

The 1st and 2nd Battalions, 424th Infantry pushed forward almost
five miles, to near Baasem, and made contact with the 69th Division,
which in turn made contact with Third Army on the right near the
town of Stadtkyll, effectively pinching out the 106th Division. Thus,
the Lions' combat role in the war ended in victory, only seven miles
northeast of the position of the doomed 422nd Infantry in the Battle
of the Bulge eighty-one days prior. On this 7th day of March, elements of the U.S. First Army reached the Rhine.

The work of the 106th Division was not yet finished. Their next
mission was the reconstitution of the division to full combat strength
and readiness, a complex task of which Gen. Stroh and Col. Stumpf
were well aware. Once this was accomplished, they expected to be
back in action in Germany. Longer term, after the Germans finally
surrendered, they faced the possibility of moving to the Pacific theater
for the final assault on Japan. Because of mail delays, Imogene and
her mother were somewhat in the dark on the rapid developments
of their husbands' actions and whereabouts. Imogene's letters dated
March 15th and 23rd:

> I'm getting so used to your name in the paper,
> these important people! It is perfectly wonderful about
> that DSM especially because you have wanted it so

much and then the honor of receiving the [French] Legion of Honor which must have been a real surprise. In your last letter of March 8th you made no mention of the honors...

Bob's letter of the 8th was headed "Germany." You all seem surrounded with old friends' divisions and even Bob came out with a little information. He sounded so much like his old self which he hasn't been since last summer. He's probably "busier than a one-armed paper hanger" as he would say, getting on to the job and the responsibility but he is so bucked up. He says if the war ends he's going to ask the "old man" for leave home.

Your visit home has made Mother so different. She could tackle the world and lick it every time the way she goes about things now. She's so full of pep and ambition. You ought to see her handling this Red Cross drive... Now she's talking about doing volunteer work with the Motor Corps. I don't know what her limit is.

The division moved out of the battle zone on March 14th for St. Quentin, France, by forty-and-eight railcars and motor transport, a trip of about 140 miles as the crow flies. St. Quentin is about eighty miles north-northeast of Paris. Their mission was reorganization, re-habilitation, and training. They were to reconstitute new units with the same designations as those lost in the Ardennes. In Gen. Stroh's letter to Imogene of March 18th, he described the contrast between living on the battlefield and his new digs in St. Quentin.

The change from the mud and filth of last Sunday to the luxury of our present surroundings is really something. A day or two before I left I visited Bob's

CP and found him quite comfortably situated in a half-ruined schoolhouse. He was calmly shaving... The schoolhouse was in what must at one time have been a pretty little village in a peaceful little valley with a meandering stream through pleasant meadows, completely surrounded by concrete pillboxes and "dragons' teeth." The value of German real estate must take a decided drop when they begin construction of the first dragons' teeth in the vicinity because sooner or later a flock of high explosive shells is bound to drop in the area, and the surrounding houses are not improved thereby.

Bob may not write you that he is now sleeping between sheets in a hotel room with running hot water. This may be a partial compensation for his not getting home to you and missing a chance to be a hero. The 9th is now in a very interesting place. [It had crossed the Rhine and was advancing eastward.]

The Army Engineer was here on some official business yesterday, principally with Bob's outfit, and spent the night with us. He at once recognized Bob as one of his more brilliant students in physics at the Academy. I asked him if Bob had behaved himself there and he said "Oh, very well indeed." Coming from an engineer, this is something. This same gentleman was adjutant of Belvoir while we were at Hunt, and remembers us.

While at St. Quentin, the division was paid a visit by the Fifteenth Army commander, Lt. Gen. Gerow, who in a formal ceremony presented the Distinguished Service Medal to Gen. Stroh, an honor that he had been coveting for many months about which he noted in a scrapbook, "Career Climax." The recommendation and proposed citation had been submitted by Gen. Middleton, VIII Corps commander, in October 1944 and had taken all that time to work its way up to the top of the pyramid. The award certificate reads:

THE UNITED STATES OF AMERICA
TO ALL THOSE WHO SHALL SEE THESE PRESENT,
GREETING:
THIS IS TO CERTIFY THAT
THE PRESIDENT OF THE UNITED STATES OF AMERICA
AUTHORIZED BY ACT OF CONGRESS, JULY 9, 1918, HAS
AWARDED
THE DISTINGUISHED SERVICE MEDAL
TO
Major General Donald A. Stroh, United States Army
FOR EXCEPTIONALLY MERITORIOUS AND
DISTINGUISHED SERVICES IN THE PERFORMANCE
OF DUTIES OF GREAT RESPONSIBILITY
as Commanding General, 8th Infantry Division
GIVEN UNDER MY HAND IN THE CITY OF
WASHINGTON
THIS 20th DAY OF February 1945
[signed]
Henry L. Stimson
Secretary of War

On March 26th, the 424th Infantry held a formal awards presentation and review ceremony to recognize members of the regiment for heroism in combat. Gen. Stroh described the scene, among other things, in his April 1st letter to Imogene, written from the Savoy Hotel London on its stationery. He and his assistant, Gen. Herb Perrin, were in London conferring with the bigwigs about their plan to reconstitute the 106th Division.

What class! What luxury! I'll have a rude
awakening when I put on those silver leaves again, but
I'm certainly enjoying being a general while it lasts.
Packard limousine from the airport, a suite of two
bedrooms and sitting room for Herb and me, an official
car for the remainder of my stay, and the personal
plane of the army commander in which to make the
trip. This may be April Fool Day, but it is certainly
starting as if there was no foolishness at all.

Last night was one of the last that I'll spend in our
luxurious villa, so we decided to throw a little party.
We had Bob, the artillery brigadier, the two Red Cross
girls who are more or less permanently stationed in
the town, the French woman who occupies the house,
and the French lieutenant and his wife who have a
room there, in addition to our usual small mess, so we
had a group of twelve. It was the first time that Bob
had been in our place, and he seemed duly impressed,
as is the reaction of everyone who sees it for the first
time. Even the army commander, who lives in one of
the finest hotels in Europe, and who had lunch with
us the other day, said he "gave it up," meaning that
even he could not compete... Oh, we really put on the
dog. Bob liked the steak and French fries so well that
he had a second round, and later he proved himself a
fit subject to be hypnotized when he was tested by a
soldier who entertained us with magic and hypnotism.
He looked fine in his blouse with his campaign ribbons,
medal ribbons, and four service stripes. He will soon
be eligible for his fifth, you know, the only officer
in the division entitled to that number. He excused
himself quite early, stating that he had to get up early

this morning to go to church. I'll bet that surprises you.

We started on our series of presentation ceremonies last Monday with Bob's regiment. The afternoon was perfect, the parade ground nearly ideal, and the thing clicked like clockwork. It was a magnificent sight, and one of the most inspiring ceremonies I have ever seen. Bob had forty-eight men to be decorated with the Silver Star or Bronze Star, about three-fourths of the company guidons to be decorated with the white and blue streamer of the combat infantryman, and the same streamer to be affixed to the regimental color... It was Bob's first ceremony as a regimental commander, and you would have been proud of him... He confessed afterwards to being a bit nervous, but certainly gave no evidence of it while it was going on. He got a thrill when the band played the "West Point March."

After the regiment had fallen in and been mustered by the various commanders, they reported to the regimental commander. He in turn reported across the parade ground to the 106th Division commanding general, "Sir, the colors, guidons, and persons to be decorated are present." Whereupon the band struck up a march, and Gen. Stroh and Col. Stumpf "trooped the line," inspecting the ranks. They then returned to the forefront where, smiling broadly, the general presented the streamers and medals to his brave soldiers. The ceremony concluded with a "pass in review" of the entire 3,000-man regiment before Gen. Stroh and his senior staff, Col. Stumpf marching at the head of the column.

Simultaneous to their other duties at St. Quentin, the 106th Division began to prepare for assignment as tactical reserve for the

66th Infantry Division guarding the German holdout garrisons at Lorient and St. Nazaire on the French Atlantic coast. This required the division to move closer to those locations. Thus, on April 6th, the troops moved again, this time to Rennes, the capital of Brittany, some 240 miles to the west and about sixty road miles north of the German garrisons. Rennes was familiar ground for Gen. Stroh, whose 8th Division, which he then commanded, captured that city in August 1944 prior to the Brest campaign. There, too, he had visited with his son for the last time, and it was from the St. Jacques Airfield at Rennes that Capt. Harry Stroh flew his last mission.

It was a busy time for everyone as the division rolls began to swell. They welcomed two independent infantry regiments, the 3rd and the 159th, the latter veterans of the Aleutians campaign, and two field artillery battalions, all newly arrived from the States. In addition, individual replacement soldiers poured in; more than 6,600 officers and men, 2,200 from infantry replacement centers in the States, and the rest drafted from other service branches in the ETO, having undergone a crash six-week infantry training course in theater. During this massive influx of personnel, reorganization, and training, Col. Stumpf and his 424th Infantry, along with the 591st Field Artillery Battalion, were on five-hour alert to reinforce the 66th Division.

On April 14th, the entire reinforced division of more than 22,000 men formed up on St. Jacques Airfield for the solemn reconstitution of the five units lost in the Ardennes. The next day, Gen. Stroh described the ceremony in a letter to Imogene dated April 15th.

> We had one of the most impressive and thrilling ceremonies yesterday afternoon that I have ever seen, participated in by the largest group of dismounted soldiers in my experience. Its principal purpose was to transfer the colors, standards and guidons from the survivors of last December to the newly formed outfits

of the same numbers who will carry on the fight. The division was formed on three sides of a hollow square, with the reviewing post on the fourth side. On my right were the veterans, formed by units (one represented by one man), with the colors, standard and guidons in their possession. On my left, directly opposite, were the new outfits. On the third side, opposite me were the remaining division units, and those now attached. Bob, being the junior regimental commander in this group, had his regiment on the left of the other two. Herb commanded the works. I delivered a five minute oration over the PA. To the tune of "Kings of the Highway," the veterans advanced from one side, bearing the flags, and the color bearers and guides from the other, all halting when they met in the center of the square (which was about 200 yards on a side with battalions in line of masses). All presented arms, followed by the American and French national anthems. While still at present [arms], the flags were handed from the old to the new. Then to the "Official West Point March" (in Harry's honor) the color guard returned to their posts, and the old men joined the new. Afterwards, to the division march, the entire command passed in review, requiring 35 minutes, even with the battalions sixteen men abreast. Old Bob's regiment brought up the rear of the infantry, but they marched like the veterans they are. The affair was held on the very airstrip from which Harry took off on his last flight. How proud he would have been to attend.

Gen. Stroh's address:

Today we are taking the first step to rebuild the 106th Infantry Division. It will be a task which will require the best efforts of every officer and man here. I am counting on you to do your usual good job.

Our division emerged from the shock of the Ardennes last January to snap back vigorously, take the offensive, and assist in breaking the Siegfried Line in March.

Like a boxer knocked groggy but not out in the first round, you came back in the second, took the fight to your opponent in the third, and are now awaiting the gong for the knockout. Further victories lie ahead. We will be in at the kill.

Our division will be formed from various sources. On my right are the survivors of the 106th Reconnaissance Troop, 422d and 423d Infantry, and 589th and 590th Field Artillery Battalions, the units which fought to the death near St. Vith last December and held the line until additional American forces could be formed behind them.

On my left are the officers and men of the new units of the same numbers who will carry on the heroic traditions of Belgium and Germany established by their predecessors. Some of these men have come from other units of the division, some from our attached units. Already the blood of the old division flows in the veins of the new.

In front of me are the remaining units of the division and certain attached units, which we are happy to welcome into our official division family.

They are the 3d and 159th Infantry and the 401st and 627th Field Artillery Battalions. The 3d Infantry is one of the oldest regiments in the Army and has a combat record starting with the War of 1812... We will be proud to have all of them wear our shoulder patch.

Today we will transfer the colors, standards, and guidons from the survivors of St. Vith to the new units which will carry on the fight. It is fitting that we do this, because these bits of silk and wool are symbols of the pride and esprit of the regiments, battalions, and troops which they represent.

Old soldiers know well the sentiment which attaches to the colors and standards especially. In former wars they were carried in battle by the strongest and bravest men available. Many men gave their lives that the colors should not fall or be captured. Today we no longer carry the colors into battle, but they still deserve our utmost respect and admiration. They represent the heroic achievements of the past, and the hopes for a victorious future.

So when, in a few moments, the veterans of the Schnee Eifel, who have figuratively carried these colors through the hell of combat, transfer them to the newest units, I charge you with receiving them with the pride and reverence which they deserve. Your color guards are armed with weapons captured from the Germans. This too is symbolic of the fact that these colors will accompany us into Germany. They will be present when the last enemy soldier is killed or surrenders.

Additional comments from Gen. Stroh's April 15th letter to Imogene:

...another move is imminent. Each time we move we get one rung lower in the scale. At this rate, pretty soon we'll end up guarding prisoners. I can't leave this area too soon. It has entirely too many tragic memories for me.

When Torres left for home I inherited [Gen.] Jones' old striker, born in China, and who has fought the Japs there as a guerrilla. How he ever happened to wind up in the American Army is a mystery to me. He speaks and understands practically no English, so our conversation is usually restricted to a succession of OK's. He says OK and I say OK, and miraculously the thing gets done. I find that he has disturbed my life-long habits no end, such as wearing socks two days, underwear three days, OD shirt one month, etc. Every time I leave any garment lying around he grabs it, and launders it beautifully. My clothes will pretty soon be all worn out by being washed so much. He is a knockout with the shoe polish. I've never had such glistening foot gear in my life. I'm afraid I'll be spoiled by the time Torres gets back.

I am going to visit Harry tomorrow, as this may be the last chance available.

24

---·◆·---

Prisoners

Within a day or two of Gen. Stroh's wry comment to Imogene about having to guard prisoners, he was given the 106th Division's new assignment: movement to the Rhine to process German POWs, the huge number of which was growing precipitously every day. Very little planning or preparation had been accomplished to address the enormity of the problem or the suddenness of its onslaught. With the war still raging, apparently the 106th Division was the most available force to do the job. The irony was certainly not lost on Gen. Stroh that the division which had suffered the most POW losses in the war was now the American Army's principal unit responsible for handling German POWs. The division was to guard and process prisoners in enclosures in four zones along the Rhine River, from the Netherlands' border to Stuttgart, a span of nearly 250 miles.

The division began moving out almost immediately. The reconstituted units were left behind and attached to the 66th Division to continue training and provide support to the 66th. (They actually saw some action in the St. Nazaire area just before the Germans there surrendered.) Most of the rest of the division had closed on their positions along the Rhine by April 25th. Gen. Stroh set up his headquarters at Bad Ems, midway between the southern and northern extremes of the sector. Each of the four areas, Red, White, Blue, and Green, was commanded by a 106th Division regimental commander, or in the case of the Green Area, the division artillery commander. Col. Stumpf's 424th Infantry administered the Blue Area, headquartered at Ober Ingelheim, about thirty-five miles west of Frankfurt.

The actual guarding of prisoners was perhaps the most straightforward of the division's tasks. The POWs were demoralized, exhausted, hungry, and relatively docile. They were in no mood to organize mass escapes, or even solitary ones. The more challenging tasks for the division were logistical in nature. When the division arrived, the prisoners were crowded into massive "cages," mostly in the open with very rudimentary sanitation—think slit trenches—and no water or cooking facilities. The immediate requirements were to provide them sustenance, water, shelter, clothing, and urgent medical services. Then came the administrative chores: screening, cataloging, interrogation, segregation, and ultimately transferring and discharging. The numbers were staggering. By April 30th, less than a week after the division had arrived, it was administering more than 165,000 POWs in five enclosures. And that was only the beginning. As the German Army crumbled, prisoners arrived by the tens of thousands daily. By May 3rd the Red Area housed 129,000 prisoners, the White Area 250,000, and the 424th Infantry's Blue Area 160,000. The Green Area contained significantly fewer.

Gen. Stroh recognized early that he simply did not have enough soldiers to do the job properly. His infantry division had absolutely no training or experience for this mission. He asked for reinforcements. They came in the form of three hastily assembled Provisional Guard Battalions of 1,000 men each. In addition, another 10,000 individual replacement soldiers were assigned to the division, a hundred men to each company, troop, and battery. This influx of personnel was an astounding leadership challenge in its own right. With these man-power reinforcements, the guard-to-prisoner ratio was about one to 150.

The medical situation was perhaps the most alarming and included the grave threat of epidemic due to the presence of communicable diseases combined with the crowded, unsanitary conditions. The division arrived with its organic 331st Medical Battalion, which consisted mostly of combat medics trained for the battlefield. But this was a different kind of problem. Gen. Stroh again called for reinforcements. In response, the division was provided with seven field hospitals, several ambulance companies, and, finally, a complete ambulance battalion. The division medical statistics for the month of May bore out the severity of the problem.[1]

Cases treated on sick call	1,143,177
Cases evacuated to hospital units	26,366
Deaths in the enclosures	1,404
Deaths in hospital units	733
Communicable disease admissions	5,615

On April 28th, while he was preparing for a long, unspecified trip the next day, probably back to Rennes, drafting his words carefully lest he offend the censors, Gen. Stroh penned a letter to Imogene in which he alluded to what was going on with the division. He also mentioned 3rd Armored Division commander Gen. Rose, who had recently been killed in action near the front of one of his columns.

Yes, Bob was Rose's executive officer in Combat Command "A" of the 2nd Armored in Africa and Sicily. In fact Bob received his promotion to lieutenant colonel under Rose, I think.

Speaking of promotions, I am recommending Bob

tomorrow for advancement to full colonel. The policy requires him to have served in his present job for three months before becoming eligible. This period will be up May 12, so we are getting a head start on the date. We have found that it requires a month or longer for the promotion to go through in the case of field officers, so it may be well into June before I can pin on the eagles, which I have ready.

I heard it from a very good source today that "soldiers" who had fought both in North Africa and Europe would not be sent to the Far East. Whether that refers to officers, and especially to Regulars, I doubt very much. But you can take what little grain of comfort the rumor might bring you.

If I never admired that big husband of yours before, I certainly admire him for what he has done for the past ten days. He brought his outfit up here, over a good many miles of roads, all by himself, and so far as I know arrived in perfect shape. Immediately after arrival, he took over a very distasteful job with his regiment, which was without precedent and which required the utmost display of initiative and improvisation under the most difficult conditions imaginable. He is still carrying that load, and will continue to do so for an indefinite time in the future, without asking "What do I do now? Where am I going to get this? I can't find this in the books." Or anything else that a less able man would scream about. He has just gone ahead and done it. You'll be more proud of him than ever when I have a chance to tell you about it. He never will, I'm sure of that. And I won't forget him. At least he's reasonably comfortable, and about as safe as he would be at home, so you can take comfort in that.

Wonder where they [*Washington Star*] got that "doughboys' general" stuff. I'm afraid the rest of the division thinks I'm too much of a doughboy. It's a hard thing to teach an old dog new tricks. But I try to give the artillery, the medics, the engineers and rest a fair break.

News from Imogene during this time reflected her excitement over her husband's and father's growing responsibilities, and awareness that the end of the war was in sight. The possibility of a reunion with her husband at long last was a dream that she tried hard to control, but found it was difficult. Excerpts from her letters of April 1945, beginning with the 5th:

Mother received your letter with Bob's first DB [daily bulletin] in it with "by order of Lt. Col. Stumpf" on it. It is pretty wonderful for him. How I'd love to have seen that regimental presentation ceremony on March 26th. In Bob's letter of the day before he mentioned he'd hoped he wouldn't pull any boners.

Imagine such a high percentage of Inf. men's badges for the regiment. When I see one of those on a soldier I stare so that he probably thinks I'm making a pass. I can't help it though, because they mean so much.

It's just awful that you still don't mention your knowledge of the DSM. Won't you be thrilled when you learn of it? You're certainly getting a chest full.

We were all shocked by the news of Gen. Rose's death. It seems rather fishy how he was shot and the aide and all the rest escaped.

From little hints you've dropped we have fairly well gathered what your immediate task is and it is indeed unique if we're thinking right, but we can't guess what the future might be. Right now we're so thankful you are both safe and you can stay that way for ever more.

Referring to Imogene's mention of him, Maj. Gen. Maurice Rose, commanding general of the 3rd Armored Division, was killed in action on March 30th. He was leading a small convoy in a jeep, trying desperately to evade German armored vehicles during a running tank battle. He was shot by a Tiger tank commander with four bursts from a submachine gun. Rose was dismounted and attempting to surrender, along with his aide and driver, who both escaped in the confusion. The general died instantly. There is still some controversy about the circumstances of his death.

The Blue Area of the POW zone was manned by the reinforced 424th Infantry. Col. Stumpf's command included five POW camps, more than any of the other areas.[2]

Camp A-12,	Heidesheim;	2nd Battalion, 424th Infantry
Camp A-7,	Biebelsheim;	1st Battalion and AT Company, 424th Infantry
Camp A-6,	Winzenheim;	3rd Battalion, 424th Infantry
Camp A-3,	Bad Kreuznach;	6952nd Provisional Guard Battalion
Camp A-8	Dietersheim;	2nd Battalion, 3rd Infantry

With the addition of two battalions and another 2,000 or so individual replacements, the 424th ranks had grown to over 7,700 men, the largest regiment in the Army. The Blue Area on the map was about 125 by 45 miles, but the camps were mostly clustered on either side of the Rhine in the northeast quadrant relatively near to the regimental headquarters at Ober Ingelheim. The 106th Division headquarters at Bad Ems was roughly forty miles to the north. The five camps under the 424th Infantry, which included eight enclosures, would ultimately process over 400,000 prisoners.

On the larger scale, totals for the fourteen camps under 106th Division jurisdiction peaked at 917,217 prisoners under guard on May 17th, and more than 1,250,000 prisoners processed for the duration of the eleven-week detail. Included in these numbers were sixty-eight Axis general officers and 2,600 women. The ages of the prisoners ran from seven to eighty years old, and represented eighteen nationalities. The enclosures were segregated to some extent; one for women, another for Czechs, another for Russians, and so on.

After the initial mayhem, the camps gradually assumed a more efficient, more healthy structure. The prisoners were given some autonomy to self-govern within their separate enclosures. German medical personnel were used in the enclosure dispensaries, German clerks attended to administrative functions, and German financial people handled payments to those being discharged. Food was provided by the American Army, obtained through various methods and sources, including from captured German supply dumps and local bakeries. Improvised cooking facilities were set up within the enclosures so German mess crews could provide for their own. The Division's 81st Engineers were exceptionally busy with construction projects: perimeter fencing, guard towers, latrines, food storage facilities. German work crews were organized for supervised construction within the enclosures.

Several days after VE Day, Gen. Stroh returned to Rennes by air to check in on his reconstituted units, a trip he made routinely. It was 600 miles one way and added another layer of complexity to his responsibilities. Returning two days later in an L-5 aircraft, he composed his regular biweekly missive to Imogene with his briefcase on his knees serving as a desk. His normally elegant handwriting was a little more difficult to decipher than usual.

Well, we licked 'em again, and how we licked 'em. I hope this time that they'll stay licked. Since the final terms were signed in Eisenhower's office in the early morning of May 7, the surrender came exactly two years to a day after we first entered Bizerte. That has been a long while ago, but when you consider the distance we've come since then, it's been a very short time. As I told Mother, our boys took the end very calmly since they had no time to do anything else. But there appears to be evidence that at least some men were genuinely sorry that the division did not have another opportunity to show what it could do in battle. At least two officers have already applied for transfer to an outfit which is headed for the Pacific, and I am sure that many others would welcome the chance if they could know that it would be approved. There is by no means any guarantee that we will not head in that direction ourselves. I do not know where we will end up.

The Air Corps, having lost the usual outlet for their enthusiasm, have had a series of field days all week, flying up and down the Rhine Valley in dozens of four-motored bombers, at times just skimming the water and flying at 25 feet over some of our enclosures, playfully throwing out telephone books, empty bottles, and other items, thus scaring our charges to death. I am told that these flights represent a series of sightseeing tours for big shots from Merrie England, and our own pilots who are anxious to see the results of their labor of the past couple of years without the excitement of anybody shooting them. Four of these big brutes swooped down on one of our little cub planes in the air, and playfully chased it hither and yon. It was like four large lions playing with a mouse. Boys will be boys.

I spent the afternoon with Bob on Friday. Just before I left him to return to my CP we drove together to the top of the hills overlooking Bingen from the other side of the Rhine to visit a tremendous monument there of a female figure called the "Watch on the Rhine," symbolizing no doubt the German belief that no foreign army would ever be able to force its way across the river. It is sort of a travesty now, and to add insult to injury, it has been bombed by our people. No direct hits were scored, but it is somewhat damaged by bomb fragments, and the surrounding park is completely wrecked by bomb craters. Bob looks better than I have ever seen him I think. He is working like a dog, as we all are, but it is not the strain of combat, and his living conditions are better than they have been since we left England.

I have run into an unexpected snag in his promotion. Visited army headquarters the other day and learned to my astonishment that my recommendation had been returned with the curt remark "not considered favorably at this time." Upon inquiry I learned that they have a promotion board there, who believed that he was too young for the job, and that two "Very Satisfactory" ratings in his record were against him. Both of these contentions, of course, are wholly absurd. Accordingly I sent the recommendation back with a strong endorsement, copy of which is enclosed, and which Bob has seen. I visited Army again on Friday, looking to talk to the boss in person, but he was not available, so I discussed the matter with his chief of staff. He seemed impressed by the evidence, agreed that there were good grounds for reconsideration, and agreed to present it to the commander for a formal recommendation. Have not heard further from it.

The "strong endorsement" that Gen. Stroh mentioned in his letter was a two-and-a-half-page, single-spaced memorandum to his boss, Gen. Gerow, in which he explicitly laid out the case for Lt. Col. Stumpf's promotion. He first argued that Stumpf's young age should not be considered against him, but rather be in his favor because he earned and performed well in regimental command at that age, and being young, had the stamina and vigor to withstand the strains of combat. He then bluntly addressed the two not-so-good "very satisfactory" ratings, arguing that one was a clash of personalities with his commander for a short period in North Africa, and the other while serving in a staff position for which he was not particularly suited. Gen. Stroh went on, in great detail, to outline his service while in command of an infantry battalion, and later an infantry regiment, over a period of twenty months, nine of which were in combat. Perhaps his strongest arguments were made in the final two paragraphs.

11. Lt Col Stumpf has rendered superior service in commanding his regiment during the past two months. I have observed him closely during three long motor movements, during several weeks of intensive training activities when improvisation and ingenuity were required to secure results, and for the past two weeks in carrying out his present mission.

I have been impressed with his force and leadership during all of this time, but especially during that period spent in his present area. He now commands a force numbering more than 7,700 and is in complete charge of five large prisoner of war enclosures, with prospects of taking charge of two more. With no precedent on which to work, in the absence of detailed orders, in the face of severe shortages of nearly every item of essential supply, he has handled the situation with great enthusiasm and success. He has exhibited commendable ingenuity, resourcefulness and initiative, by which he has largely overcome the manifold difficulties involved in a discouraging and unpleasant situation.

12. I consider that this officer has completely demonstrated his ability to command a regiment of infantry under all conditions and is fully qualified for immediate promotion.

This very strong resubmission of a promotion recommendation after his boss had dismissed the first one out of hand may have rankled Gen. Gerow. Especially given the history between the two. Stroh was not one to be intimidated and felt it was his duty to speak the truth as he saw it. It was likely that they had strong words for one another at Huertgen. Stroh was clearly unhappy with the situation going into that battle and made his dissatisfaction very clear to Gerow. Then Stroh's request for leave, to begin "on or about December 10, 1944," had suddenly been forwarded by Gerow and approved on November 27th, before the current offensive was complete. This was construed by some as tantamount to Stroh being fired. In the current situation on the Rhine, Stroh was most probably giving his boss regular earfuls with regard to what he considered shoddy support from Fifteenth

Army for the very complex and critical POW operation.

Probably unbeknownst to Gen. Stroh at the time, Gen. Gerow had, on May 20th, submitted his officer efficiency ratings for the general officers of his Fifteenth Army. He gave Stroh an "excellent" rating, the first rating other than "superior" since at least 1936. His comments included, "thinks clearly but slowly; lacks imagination and has difficulty in adjusting himself to new situations; methodical, analytical, and thorough in approach to problems; works best when given precise and detailed instructions; by nature stolid rather than enthusiastic; better staff than commander; not recommended for promotion; do not particularly desire him in my command." These words could not have been more scathing in such a report. But despite his apparently low opinion of Stroh, Gerow recommended approval of Stumpf's promotion and forwarded it up the chain.

Back home, Imogene could not seem to muster much excitement over VE day. In her letter to her father dated May 10th, she wrote:

> We can't get very enthusiastic about V-E Day and V-E+2 day for that matter. We're delighted there is no immediate prospect of you fighting, but there is so much to be settled. Peace is so hard to obtain and from the looks of things we don't really have it.
>
> It makes me angry for people to so easily say that Bob will be home as if it will be tomorrow or next week.

> May 17, 1945
> Since V-E Day we've expected so much I guess, and we know nothing so the anxiety and tension is very great. I've honestly expected Bob to be getting home now, but even that hope is dimming since he is a regular officer with the particular job that he has. I

just won't expect him till he gets here.

Mrs. Collins hasn't heard from her husband since April 23rd, so that makes me feel better. This mail business is just as bad on this side and upsets us as much as it does you all.

May 24, 1945

I wonder if Bob will get his promotion now. Maybe, with you recommending it so early it might help. I'm so glad Bob is doing such a good job. He's very capable, but also doesn't want to disappoint you in your choice.

Following the prisoner population peak in mid-May, the transfer/discharge phase began to ramp up. The first groups to leave were those drafted for labor forces in France. Other transfers followed and then the major task of discharging began. Using German clerical personnel to speed the process, the outflow reached a daily average of 9,000 discharges. Transportation of this magnitude stretched the division's capability to fulfill the requirements. Prisoners whose residences were within a hundred miles, known as the Retail Zone, were shipped out by truck. Further than that, normally in the sectors of different armies, the Wholesale Zone, dischargees usually travelled by rail to army reception centers, then locally dispersed.

The 424th Infantry planned a special ceremony for May 30th to recognize a most unusual, if not unique, event. Gen. Stroh provided the background story in a letter to Imogene dated May 27th.

Bob's regiment had a very peculiar thing happen to it last week. You may know that the 106th relieved the 2nd Division near St. Vith just two or three days before the breakthrough last December. In the excitement which followed Bob's outfit lost their

national and regimental colors, captured by the
Germans. A few weeks ago, the 2nd Division entered
Czechoslovakia, and there, near Pilsen, recovered both
colors from a captured German soldier. Robby [Maj.
Gen. Walter M. Robertson] returned them to me, still
in perfect condition. It is a rare coincidence that his
outfit should have recovered these flags which were
captured in the very area that the 2nd had vacated
just in the nick of time for them.

Bob's recommendation for promotion has hurdled
the Army barrier successfully, and should be well on
its way to eventual approval at higher headquarters. I
have informed all and sundry at my place that I must
be the first to know when it finally comes back, so that
I can personally pin Harry's eagles on Bob.

June 10, 1945

Bob's regimental ceremony of the week before
last was a very appropriate one which he arranged
himself. He could only muster a composite battalion,
everyone else being busy. A designated color company
moved forward from the battalion mass to receive the
recaptured colors. Bob made a neat little speech over
the loudspeaker and handed the colors to one of his
battalion commanders, who in turn handed them to a
color guard. The battalion then passed in review.

The division is getting lousy with ex-76ers. You
already know of Herb, of course. Last week Jake
Z. [Col. Jake T. Zellars], who used to command the
417th in your day, arrived to take over the 423d,
the commander of which wasn't doing so well. I sent
for him for the purpose, knowing that he had the

necessary experience and personality to build a good outfit. So Jake and Bob, old enough to be father and son, and separated by 20 years in service, are now commanding regiments in the same division, while the other regimental commander [Col. William B. Tuttle] is one file senior to me on the permanent list. War certainly makes strange bedfellows.

Bob was completely surprised last Sunday when I made a special trip to his C.P. at Nieder-Ingelheim to pin on his eagles. I had arranged with my C of S and AG to tell me when his promotion came through, and not to tell him about it. The order arrived on the late evening of the 2d, coming through remarkably fast after it got started. The chief called me right away and I went down the next morning... I bet Bob is the first of his class to make the grade, always excepting the Air Corps.

As soon as our current job is over I am going to recommend him for the Legion of Merit, if he continues to keep out of trouble. Don't tell him yet, as it may not go through.

I guess you have now completed the first week of your last semester... Bob may return in time to interrupt it, but again he may not. We truthfully cannot say from one day to the next what is going to happen to us. I expect the division will be put in one of four "categories" before long, perhaps the first of July, which will give us more of an inkling than we have now.

There's hardly a day passes without some demand from higher headquarters for the transfer of one or more officers for some other job, many of them in the

States. The first one that comes along for which Bob is eligible, and which he wants, I'll recommend him.

This non-fraternization policy is certainly getting hard to control. These pretty young girls, bare legged, riding bicycles, and with their skirts blowing up around their hips, is more than our healthy young men (and some elder ones) can endure forever. The roads are full of temptation, and something is going to bust wide open before long.

Gen. Stroh included a clipping from the *Stars and Stripes* with this letter, across the top of which he wrote, "Who won the war?" The gist of the article was a matrix of the number of major units from each of the five Allied Armies that were on the ground in Europe at the end of hostilities.

	U.S.	Britain	Canada	France	Poland
Armies	5	1	1	1	0
Corps	16	4	2	1	0
Infantry Divisions	42	8	3	8	0
Armored Divisions	15	4	2	3	1
Airborne Divisions	3	2	0	0	0

While the division and its attached units were busy processing POWs, their reconstituted units moved from Brittany in late May to Nachtsheim, about twenty miles west of Koblenz. There, under the leadership of Brig. Gen. Perrin, they established a training camp which was christened Camp Alan W. Jones, in honor of the division's first commanding general.

On June 23rd Gen. Stroh submitted a recommendation for the Legion of Merit on behalf of Col. Stumpf. The recommendation went through Gen. Gerow to Gen. Eisenhower, and covered the period from when Stumpf took command of the 3rd Battalion, 39th Infantry in September 1943 until June 12, 1945. The narrative of the write-up explicitly describes Stumpf's activities in great detail during the periods when he and Gen. Stroh served in the same divisions, and to a lesser extent from July 1944 until February 1945 when they did not. The verbiage is very similar to his recommendation for promotion, in some cases exactly the same, only a month prior. Stroh probably figured since the promotion went through, why change it up?

Imogene shared an interesting "small-army" story with her father in a letter dated June 14th, and with it other gems from her letters of the summer of '45.

> I was having lunch with a group of girls when I spied across the room a 9th Div. patch with a string of service stripes beneath it on a lieutenant. Without consulting with myself one second, I went over to him to ask what regiment he'd been in. When he said 39th, I asked him if he knew Colonel Stumpf, and I nearly fell over after he got through falling over when I learned that he had a company under Bob and he never could get over me being Bob's wife. I asked him out for dinner and all evening we talked nothing but 9th Division. He is [1st] Lt. George Barfoot and he had been given I Co. just four days before his capture before St. Lo. He's been in prison ever since with Col. Goode and Col. Waters in Poland. Talk about bitter, that boy really is. He looks fine though and has gained 35 pounds back. He's on his way home to Denver.
>
> I learned a lot I'd never known and a lot I'll bet Bob doesn't know. He knew you were Bob's father-in-law. It seems everyone does, yet he couldn't get over you being my father. Anyway, I think he had a nice evening

and a pleasant introduction back to the States. He can't get over being home.

June 28

I'm afraid my schooling [at GW] isn't being taken very seriously... last night at the Watergate Lightnin' Joe accused me that I was getting my degree on my good looks. I accepted that rib and told him I had all male professors this summer and was sitting as far forward in classes as possible.

July 26

Colonel Raymond of the 8th Division came by for a few minutes this morning to call on Mother and he had quite a tale to tell how much the division misses you and needs you. He even wants to get out of it he is so unhappy about its future. He just raved and raved about you. You might see what you can do about getting it [back].

As summer came on, the massive nature of the prisoner problem for the 106th Division began slowly to subside. On June 12th, the British took over the enclosures and prisoners in the Red Area. The next day the 3rd Infantry moved to Wiesbaden and took over four enclosures housing non-dischargeable prisoners. On June 23rd Seventh Army took control of that regiment and its camps. Finally, on July 10th, the division, in a formal ceremony, handed over its remaining 128,141 prisoners to the French 10th Infantry Division. The remaining attached units were relieved. On July 14th, the Fifteenth Army commander, Gen. Gerow, sent a commendation to Gen. Stroh, apparently having mollified his previous assessment of Stroh's abilities as a commander.

My sincere appreciation for the outstanding
manner in which your duties were performed during
your assignment to Fifteenth Army. The thorough
and competent manner in which your responsibilities
in connection with prisoners of war were performed
is indicative of able command and staff supervision.
Your headquarters has manifested a high state of
training, commendable zeal and excellent cooperation.
The tact, efficiency, and spirit of cooperation displayed
by all units of your command in working with the
French military is worthy of highest praise.

Gen. Stroh sent a similar commendation to the Commanding Officer, 424th Infantry on July 10th which, when describing the POW operations, stated that it was "unparalleled in the history of the American Army. It has been difficult, arduous, and without precedent." He went on to describe the enormity of the job and the host of reinforcements assigned to the regiment, 3,400 individuals and a plethora of separate units including medical, military police, ambulance, truck, even infantry battalions. He then recorded the numbers of POWs processed by the 424th: peak total—304,253; total processed—445,000; most discharged in a single day —12,000; June daily average processed—3,700.

After the wrap-up of prisoner operations, the division began moving again on July 12th, this time to the Bruchsal-Karlsruhe administrative district on the Rhine just northwest of Stuttgart. There they came under control of Seventh Army for occupation duty. This occupation zone had never been "combed" thoroughly, so the 106th Division was tasked with that detail, code named Operation Tallyho. Its purpose was to check credentials of everyone in the district, civilian and military, to discover prohibited articles such as firearms and radio transmitters, and uncover any black market operations. The sweep was completed during a forty-eight-hour period beginning July 21st. The division utilized forty-six roadblocks and complete house-to-house searches. Apparently results were scant, but the job was done.

Letters between Imogene and her father during this period were primarily a series of schemes to get Col. Stumpf home, either for a leave period or through reassignment. The overarching consideration for everyone concerned was the expectation that the colonel would be going to the Pacific theater at some point, either with the 106th Division or by assignment to a stateside division slated to deploy. In any case, the minimum furlough in the States was thirty days. Another option they thought might be feasible was for the ladies to join them in Germany during occupation duty, as had been done after the last war. Of course no one knew anything about the Manhattan Project. Lacking the prospect of such a game-changer against Japan, they expected the final campaign against the homeland would be a long, brutal slog, much as it was against Germany. But with the detonations of the atomic bombs over Hiroshima and Nagasaki, on August 6th and 9th, everything changed.

After events in the Pacific sealed Japan's fate and ended the war, the 106th Division's days were numbered. Things began to happen quickly. On August 9th, Gen. Stroh received orders to proceed to Army Ground Forces, Washington, D.C., via surface transportation on August 17th. His last day in command was August 16th. The orders were modified at the last minute to detach and proceed by air transportation on August 18th. His new command was Army Ground Forces Replacement Depot Number 1, Fort Meade, Maryland. Apparently, he was home and checked in with AGF by August 21st, because his start date at Meade was September 21st, accounting for a thirty-day leave.

On August 9th, Col. Stumpf relinquished command of the 424th Infantry. He departed the next day as leader of a "packet" of high-time soldiers heading back to the States by sea, an evolution which became mired in mountainous red tape and complications. At one point he was stuck waiting in Le Havre for over a week. From there he sent Imogene a cable, "Air priority cancelled sailing twentieth Le Havre." His final communication was another cable dated August 27th: "Stuck in staging area. Air passage cancelled. May be home end of September. Not definite am taking troops." At the same time he penned a V-mail letter explaining his frustration and disgust in detail. However, somehow he was able to get relieved of his packet duties and secured a seat on a flight to the States. He arrived home on his 30th birthday, September 1st; two years, ten months, and one week after setting sail for the invasion of North Africa. He and Imogene enjoyed reading his last V-mail, together, in Washington.

—————•—————

Epilogue

G en. Stroh arrived home August 20, 1945. He went on to serve as commanding general of the 1st Replacement Depot at Camp Pickett, Virginia, until it closed down in February 1946. Thereafter he served as the president of the Army Records Board, which processed more than 130,000 officers' service records to determine their equitable permanent rank and rating status. He never reverted back in rank and was eventually transferred to the permanent general officer's list. In 1948, he and Genie had Harry's remains reinterred at the Military Academy Cemetery at West Point.

Gen. Stroh retired in 1949 as a major general on a medical disability. In 1951, he was conferred an Honorary Doctor of Letters by his alma mater, Michigan State University. Gen. Stroh died in 1953 and was buried at Arlington National Cemetery. After his death, Mrs. Stroh, Nana, devoted much of her life to her three grandsons. She died in 1985 at age ninety-two and was buried with her late husband at Arlington. Retired General Lightnin' Joe Collins, former Chief of Staff of the Army, attended the funeral.

After Col. Stumpf's arrival home, he and Mrs. Stumpf repaired to the Florida beaches for some richly deserved R and R. The colonel's first post-war duty was commander of the 7th Infantry Training Regiment at Camp Croft, South Carolina. Imogene received a bachelor of science in home economics from George Washington University at the fall convocation on October 17, 1945. Col. Stumpf's Legion of Merit recommendation, submitted by Gen. Stroh in June, was approved. In January 1946, he was ordered to Greece as the district commander of an Allied group to oversee that country's first democratic elections, a detail for which he was awarded an oak leaf cluster to his Legion of Merit. In June 1946, he reverted in rank to lieutenant colonel and reported to Pasadena, California, to study rocket science at Cal Tech and USC, graduating in 1948 with a Master of Science in mechanical engineering.

The Stumpfs had three sons: Harry, Robert, and Donald. (Harry followed in his father's and uncle's footsteps; he graduated from West Point in 1972, and served as a career infantry officer.) Imogene and the boys followed the colonel throughout the rest of his career, from White Sands Proving Ground, New Mexico, to Fort Leavenworth, to Ottawa, Canada. Then to Carlisle, Pennsylvania, the suburbs of Washington, Fort Lee and Fort Belvoir, Virginia. While at Fort Lee, Col. Stumpf commanded the Virginia Sector of the XXI U.S. Army Corps under Major General Van Bond, his former regimental commander in the 39th Infantry, 1944–45. Col. Stumpf retired from active duty in 1967. He died in 1971 and was buried at West Point.

Growing up, my brothers and I heard very little about the war from our father. The few conversations about his experiences generally involved something light-hearted or humorous, such as playing cards in a foxhole, bathing out of a helmet, or gorging on cherry tomatoes in a field during a mortar barrage. If we asked him something more graphic he would sidestep the question. The only exception that I clearly remember was when I, at about nine years of age, asked how many Germans he had killed. He grew quiet and thoughtful, then gently explained that a better question might have been, "What was your most difficult experience in the war?" So I posed his question back to him, fully expecting him to regale me with a story about a bayonet charge or grenade exchange. But his surprising answer has remained with me always. "Sending my men into battle knowing that some of them would die."

I had no appreciation at the time that he was a battalion commander during the war, or even what a battalion was; no idea what it must have been like to be responsible, as a young man of twenty-eight, for the lives of 900 men. Even today, how any of these young commanders dealt with the psychological trauma of watching their men get killed or wounded day after day, for weeks and months at a time, is a question for the ages. The scars must have run deep.

Imogene lived a full and active life, her final twenty years amongst many friends in a seaside retirement community in Florida. She doted on her five grandchildren, accompanying each on a trip of their choice "anywhere in the world," while in their early teens. Those journeys took her and the grandchildren to Europe (three times), Australia, and the Amazon. Imogene died in 2014, a month shy of her 96th birthday, and was buried with her late husband at West Point, a stone's throw from the grave of her brother, Harry.

Notes

Prologue

1. *The Army Almanac: A Book of Facts Concerning the United States Army.* (Harrisburg, Pa.: The Stackpole Company, 1959), p. 111.
2. Rick Atkinson. *An Army at Dawn: The War in North Africa*, 1942–1943. (New York: Henry Holt and Company, 2002), p. 8.
3. Ibid.

Chapter 4 The Kasserine Pass and El Guettar

1. Henry Gerard Phillips. *The Making of a Professional: Manton S. Eddy, USA.* (Westport, Connecticut: Greenwood Press, 2000) pp. 91-92.
2. Ibid. p. 96.

Chapter 5 Sedjenane to Bizerte

1. Phillips, *Sedjenane: The Pay-off Battle.* (Self-published, 1993) p. 2-3.
2. Ibid. p. 25.
3. Ibid. p. 43.
4. Ibid. p. 41.
5. Ibid. p. 87.

6. Ibid. p. 146.

7. *To Bizerte with the II Corps.* (U.S. War Department, Washington, DC, 1943) pp. 50-51.

8. Ibid. p. 52.

9. Phillips. p. 140.

Chapter 6 African Interlude

1. Barry Basden and Charles Scheffel. *Crack! and Thump: With a Combat Officer in World War II.* (Camroc Press LLC, 2007) p. 95.

2. Steven L. Ossad and Don R. Marsh. *Major General Maurice Rose: World War II's Greatest Forgotten Commander.* (New York: Taylor Trade Publishing, 2003) pp. 129-130.

Chapter 7 Sicily: Operation Husky

1. Ibid. pp. 130-137.

2. Joseph B. Mittelman. *Eight Stars to Victory: The History of the Ninth Infantry Division.* (Washington: Ninth Infantry Division Association, 1948) p. 130.

3. Ibid. p. 140.

Chapter 8 Sicilian Interlude

1. Ibid. p. 143.

2. Ibid. p. 145.

Chapter 10 Fighter Pilot

1. *Mogin's Maulers, The 362nd Fighter Group History of WW II (second edition).* (Chicago: Dan Gianneschi with permission of the 362nd Fighter Group Association, 1986) pp. 58-59.

2. Ibid. pp. 59-60.

Chapter 11 England

1. Joseph B. Mittelman. *Eight Stars to Victory: The History of the Ninth Infantry Division.* (Washington: Ninth Infantry Division Association, 1948) p. 149.
2. Ibid. p. 155.
3. Ibid. p.154.
4. Henry Gerard Philips. *The Making of a Professional: Manton S. Eddy, USA.* (Westport, Connecticut: Greenwood Press, 1995) p. 132.
5. Ibid. p. 131.
6. Ibid. p. 134.

Chapter 12 England: Phase Two

1. Ibid. p. 134-135.
2. *Mogin's Maulers, The 362nd Fighter Group History of WW II (second edition).* (Chicago: Dan Gianneschi with permission of the 362nd Fighter Group Association, 1986) p. 71.
3. Mittelman. p. 157.

Chapter 13 Normandy: Operation Overlord

1. Philips. p. 137.
2. Mittelman. p. 160.
3. The activities of the 362nd Fighter Group and 378th Fighter Squadron in this and subsequent chapters are taken from Group and Squadron Mission Reports, unless otherwise noted.
4. Mittelman. p. 165.
5. Philips. p. 140.
6. This paragraph and the following account of the battle for Quineville is based on an in-depth, typed, undated description of the action found in Gen. Stroh's papers, and supported by several other less detailed sources.
7. *Utah Beach to Cherbourg (6 June to 27 June 1944).* Washington: Department of the Army, 1947. pp. 114-115.

Chapter 14 The Cherbourg Campaign

1. This account of the 9th Division's activities in the Cherbourg campaign is primarily informed, unless otherwise noted, by Mittelman's *Eight Stars to Victory,* Harrison's *Cross Channel Attack, General Eddy's Diary,* and the 39th Infantry daily Report of Operations.
2. The press accounts are chronicled in Mittelman's *Eight Stars to Victory,* pp. 169-172.
3. Mittelman. p. 174.
4. Ibid. p. 177.
5. Ibid. p. 179.
6. Ibid. p. 186.
7. Ibid. pp. 186-187.

Chapter 15 Breakout

1. Mittelman. p. 189.
2. This and the following chapter's account of the 8th and 9th Divisions' activities in the July and August 1944 Allied offensive is primarily informed by Blumenson's *Breakout and Pursuit,* Mittelman's *Eight Stars to Victory,* and the 39th Infantry daily Report of Operations, unless otherwise noted.
3. Martin Blumenson. *Breakout and Pursuit.* (Washington: Center of Military History, Washington, 1961) pp. 125-126.
4. *Mogin's Maulers.* p. 89.
5. Blumenson. p. 237.
6. Charles Scheffel. From a letter to Imogene Stumpf dated February 1, 1992.
7. Mittelman. p. 202.
8. Blumenson. pp. 267-268.

Chapter 16 Pursuit

1. Blumenson. pp. 278-279.

2. Mittelman. p. 216.
3. Ibid. p. 227.

Chapter 17 Brest and Crozon

1. The 8th Division's role in the siege of Brest and the capture of the Crozon Peninsula is documented in Blumenson's *Breakout and Pursuit,* Chapter XXX.
2. Blumenson. p. 643.
3. *Mogin's Maulers.* p. 101.
4. John Baloga. E-mail to the author of March 26, 2004.
5. Robert Kennedy. Telephone conversation with the author on March 31, 2006.
6. *Mogin's Maulers.* p. 169.
7. Donald Stroh. "The Operation on Crozon Peninsula." *Military Review,* January 1946.
8. Marc Griesbach. *Combat History of the Eight Infantry Division in World War II,* 1945. (Nashville: reprinted by Battery Press, 1988) p. 27.

Chapter 18 The Siegfried Line

1. Charles MacDonald. *The Siegfried Line Campaign.* (Washington: Center of Military History, 1963) p. 31.
2. Ibid. p. 34.
3. Fred Hadsel. "Siegfried Line: 9th Infantry Division, 39th Infantry, 3rd Battalion, 13 September to 26 October 1944." 2nd Information and History Service, 1st U.S. Army, 22 November 1944. The Himmler quotation at the beginning of this chapter is included in Hadsel's report.

Chapter 19 The Huertgen Forest

1. Hadsel. p. 2.
2. MacDonald. pp. 94-95.

3. This chapter's account of the 39th Infantry in the Huertgen Forest is informed primarily by Mittelman's *Eight Stars to Victory,* MacDonald's *The Siegfried Line Campaign,* and 39th Infantry daily Reports of Operations, unless otherwise noted.

4. Charles Whiting. *The Battle of the Hurtgen Forest: The Untold Story of a Disastrous Campaign.* (New York: Orion Books, 1989) pp. 47-48.

5. Herbert Taff. Letter to the author of May 22, 2004.

6. Richard Kent. Letter to Donald Lavender. July 1991.

Chapter 20 Luxembourg

1. Marc Griesbach. *Combat History of the Eight Infantry Division in World War II,* 1945. (Nashville: reprinted by Battery Press, 1988) The activities of the 8th Division in this chapter are informed from pages 28-33, except as noted.

Chapter 21 Huertgen Redux

1. Hadsel. p. 2.

2. The primary source for this chapter is MacDonald's *The Siegfried Line Campaign,* except as noted.

3. William Sylvan and Francis G. Smith, Jr. *Normandy to Victory: The War Diary of Courtney H. Hodges & the First U.S. Army.* (Lexington: The University Press of Kentucky, 2008) p. 180.

4. Ibid. p. 181.

5. MacDonald. pp. 442-443.

6. Sylvan. p. 181.

7. Ibid. p. 184.

8. MacDonald. pp. 444-445.

9. Sylvan. pp. 187-188.

10. Dwight Eisenhower. Letter to George Marshall of December 5, 1944.

11. MacDonald. p. 448.

Chapter 22 Winter Warfare

1. The primary sources for the activities of the 39th Infantry in this chapter are Mittelman's *Eight Stars to Victory,* MacDonald's *Siegfried Line Campaign,* and the 39th Infantry daily Reports of Operations.
2. The pistol was a 9-mm Walther P.38.
3. Mittelman. p. 285.
4. Ibid. p. 291.
5. Jack Dunlap. Telephone conversation with the author on January 3, 2004.

Chapter 23 Golden Lions

1. Sylvan. p. 292.
2. Ernest R. Dupuy. *St. Vith: LION IN THE WAY: The 106th Infantry Division in World War II.* (Washington: Infantry Journal Press, 1949) p. 219. This will be the primary reference for the activities of the 106th Division, except as noted.
3. Ibid. p. 221.
4. Ibid. p. 221.

Chapter 24 Prisoners

1. Dupuy. p. 227.
2. Ibid. p. 229.

---•◆•---

Army Units

For readers unfamiliar with Army terminology, this is a brief discussion about U.S. Army organization and structure in World War II. The units in which our principal characters served may have familiar names such as battalion, regiment, and division, or Air Corps names such as squadron and group. We will explore the characteristics of these and other units and the relationships between them. When we discuss the number of troops and armament in these units, it is fitting to keep in mind that these are *full-strength* complements. Except at the beginnings of campaigns or the first combat of replacement units, the troop strengths were decreased commensurate with battlefield casualties and the rate at which replacements arrived. Often units were commanded by an officer whose rank was one below that called for, simply because of the lack of availability of someone of the standard rank. If the commander performed well and lasted long enough, his rank would typically catch up with him.

The WWII U.S. Army infantry **division** consisted of around 15,000 men, designated by a number, such as 9th Infantry Division (ID), and commanded by a major general (two stars). Infantry is the traditional term for foot soldiers, which is how these men fought, and often how they got from place to place. An infantry division was made up of three infantry regiments, division artillery (big guns), special troops (military police, supply, maintenance, communications), as well as attached battalions of combat engineers, reconnaissance, medical, armor (tanks), and anti-aircraft artillery. The division was further supported by headquarters staff personnel. Two or more divisions formed a **corps,** designated by a Roman numeral. Two or more corps formed an **army**. Two or more armies comprised an **army group** (four stars). During the war, corps were commanded by major generals and armies by lieutenant generals.

The infantry **regiment** consisted of around 3,200 men commanded by a colonel and designated by a number; 39th Infantry Regiment or simply 39th Infantry. (This can be confusing because a regiment and a division can have the same number. If an account does not specify "division" or ID, it is referring to the regiment.) The infantry regiments were made up of three infantry battalions and specialized companies: headquarters, service, cannon, antitank, and medical. The term **regimental combat team** or **RCT** is sometimes used to describe the regiment with its attached artillery battalion and other attached units.

An infantry **battalion** consisted of around 900 men, commanded by a lieutenant colonel and designated as 1st, 2nd, and 3rd, sometimes abbreviated as 3/39th which is the 3rd battalion of the 39th Infantry. Each battalion had three rifle companies, one heavy weapons company, and headquarters and support contingents. The battalion was considered the largest unit where the commanding officer was routinely within small arms fire of the front lines.

The infantry rifle **company** was manned at full strength by five officers and 187 enlisted men (weapons company, 166), commanded by a captain, and designated by a letter. A, B, C, and D companies made up the 1st battalion; E, F, G, H, the 2nd; and I, K, L, M, the 3rd. So if an account is referencing L Company, that would be part of the

3rd Battalion. A rifle company was made up of three rifle platoons and a weapons platoon. A heavy weapons company was made up of two machine gun platoons and a mortar platoon. The weapons companies were designated D, H, and M.

A rifle **platoon** was around forty-five men, led by a lieutenant and designated by a number, 1st, 2nd, or 3rd. Each platoon had three **squads** of about twelve men led by a sergeant.

So we see that there is some symmetry in this "triangular" organization: three regiments in a division, three battalions in a regiment, three rifle companies in a battalion, three platoons in a company. There was flexibility in manning and execution based on many factors, not the least of which was casualties. Often higher commanders would temporarily attach units of one division, regiment, or battalion to another depending on the tactical situation.

Besides the infantry divisions, there were armored divisions which were designed around tank warfare units, and airborne divisions whose soldiers were trained to arrive at the battlefield by parachute or in expendable gliders.

Depending on how one counts them, there were eighty-nine U.S. Army divisions in action at the end of World War II in Europe and the Pacific. Of those, sixty-seven were infantry, sixteen armored, five airborne, and one cavalry. The infantry bore the brunt of the fighting and suffered by far the most casualties. For the infantryman, there were only a few legitimate ways to go home: win the war, be killed, or endure a "million-dollar wound." A recoverable wound might get him a few weeks in a field hospital or a few more in England, but afterward, he would be back on the line.

Here is a brief look at the units of the Army Air Corps fighter force. The WWII fighter was a single-seat, single-engine (except the P-38, which had two engines) aircraft whose missions included bomber escort, air-to-air combat, close support of ground troops, and interdiction against ground targets. They were fast for their day, highly maneuverable, and extremely accurate in weapons delivery.

The basic unit of the Air Corps was the **squadron.** The 378th Fighter Squadron was built around sixteen operational P-47 aircraft in four **flights** of four. (There could be as many as thirty aircraft in the squadron at full strength.) The squadron was commanded by a major and manned by about twenty-seven pilots—all officers, eleven ground officers, and around 250 enlisted personnel. Three squadrons made up a fighter **group,** in this case the 362nd Fighter Group, commanded by a lieutenant colonel. The 362nd was part of the U.S. Ninth Air Force.

Glossary

Note: These definitions pertain primarily to World War II infantry and fighter aircraft operations. They have evolved since, and today may have slightly different meanings and connotations.

AAA: Anti-aircraft artillery.

Air Corps: AC. Aviation branch of the U.S. Army.

Air force: A unit of the Air Corps consisting of several fighter and/or bomber groups.

AG: Adjutant General.

AGF: Army Ground Forces.

APO: Army Post Office.

Armor: Tanks and other armored vehicles. The combat arms branch of the Army specializing in armored warfare.

Artillery: Arty. Large caliber guns, howitzers, and mortars.

AT: Anti-tank.

AWOL: Absent without leave.

Bazooka: 2.36-inch handheld anti-tank rocket launcher.

Brigadier General: Rank with one star.

Bomber: Aircraft used for delivering air-to-ground ordnance. Usually refers to larger, multi-engine planes such as the B-17 Flying Fortress.

Branch: Army designation of military specialty, e.g., Infantry, Artillery, Armor, Engineers.

Cal: Caliber. Small arms bore diameter.

Captain: Capt. Rank above first lieutenant and below major.

CG: Commanding General.

CIB: Combat Infantryman Badge.

CO: Commanding Officer.

COBRA: Code name for the American offensive beginning July 25, 1944 to break through the German front in Normandy.

Colonel: Col. Army rank above lieutenant colonel and below brigadier general.

CP: Command post: Temporary headquarters for a unit commander in the field.

Corporal: Cpl. Army enlisted man above private first class and below sergeant.

Corps: Unit of the army usually consisting of three or more divisions.

DFC: Distinguished Flying Cross.

DSC: Distinguished Service Cross.

DSM: Distinguished Service Medal.

Doughboy: Familiar term for infantryman.

EM: Enlisted man.

ETO: European theater of operations. Theater headquarters for American forces.

Field Artillery: FA. Combat arms branch of mobile large-caliber guns that directly support troops on the battlefield.

Fighter: Fast and maneuverable single-piloted, normally single-engine aircraft designed for air-to-air combat. Also employed in the air-to-ground role for tactical interdiction or in direct support of ground forces. Examples: P-47 Thunderbolt, P-51 Mustang.

Flak: Ground-based anti-aircraft fire. From the German *Fliegerabwehrkanone*.

Fw 190: Focke-Wulf 190, German fighter plane.

General: Four-star rank, above lieutenant general.

GRO: Graves registration officer.

HQ: Headquarters.

Howitzer: Artillery piece that normally utilizes arching trajectories and indirect targeting to fire over obstacles.

HUSKY: Code name for the Allied invasion of Sicily, July 1943.

ID: Infantry Division.

Infantry: Inf. Foot soldiers. A combat arms branch of the Army.

KIA: Killed in action.

Lieutenant: Lt. Most junior Army officer rank with two levels, first (senior) and second.

Lieutenant Colonel: Army rank above major and below colonel.

Lieutenant General: Three-star rank below general and above major general.

Major: Maj. Army rank below lieutenant colonel and above captain.

Major General: Two-star rank above brigadier general and below lieutenant general.

Me 109: Messerschmitt German fighter airplane. Also designated Bf 109.

MG: Machine gun.

MIA: Missing in action.

MP: Military Police.

NCO: Non-commissioned officer.

NEPTUNE: Code name for the amphibious operation from Britain to Normandy, June 1944.

OD: Officer of the Day. Also, the color olive drab.

OVERLORD: Code name for the Allied invasion of Normandy, June 1944.

Panzer: German word for "tank."

P/E: Port of embarkation.

PFC: Private first class.

Private: Pvt. Most junior army enlisted rank.

PW or POW: Prisoner of war.

QM: Quartermaster. Supply type.

RCT: Regimental combat team. An infantry regiment and its attached units.

Sergeant: Sgt. Noncommissioned officer.

SHAEF: Supreme Headquarters Allied Expeditionary Forces.

SP: Self-propelled, as in SP gun.

Sq: Squadron.

Strategy: The science of military command as applied to the overall planning and conduct of large-scale operations. In World War II there was a global strategy as well as a European theater strategy. Strategy is determined at a very high level of command.

Tactics: The techniques of securing the objectives designated by strategy, especially the art of employing troops and weapons against the enemy. Tactics are formulated at the lowest level of command commensurate with the mission.

TD: Tank destroyer.

TORCH: Code name for the Allied invasion of North Africa, November 1942.

Waffen-SS: Militarized wing of the Nazi party.

WIA: Wounded in action.

Bibliography

Books

Addis, Gregory A. *Fighting in the Great Crusade: An 8th Infantry Artillery Officer in World War II*. Baton Rouge: Louisiana State University Press, 2002.

The Army Almanac: A Book of Facts Concerning the United States Army. Harrisburg, PA: The Stackpole Company, 1959.

Astor, Gerald. *The Bloody Forest: Battle for the Huertgen: September 1944–January 1945*. Navato, CA: Presidio Press, 2000.

Atkinson, Rick. *An Army at Dawn: The War in North Africa 1942–1943*. New York: Henry Holt and Company, 2002.

Basden, Barry and Charles Scheffel. *Crack! and Thump: With a Combat Officer in World War II,* Camroc Press LLC, 2007.

Blumenson, Martin. *Breakout and Pursuit,* Washington: Center of Military History, 1961.

Dupuy, R. Ernest. *St. Vith: LION IN THE WAY: The 106th Infantry Division in World War II*. Washington: Infantry Journal Press, 1949.

Eisenhower, Dwight D., Joseph P. Hobbs (compiler), George C. Marshall. *Dear General: Eisenhower's Wartime Letters to Marshall.* Baltimore: Johns Hopkins University Press, 1999.

Gawne, Jonathan. *Finding Your Father's War: A Practical Guide to Researching and Understanding Service in the World War II US Army.* Philadelphia: Casemate, 2006.

Griesbach, Marc F. *Combat History of the Eight Infantry Division in World War II*, 1945. Nashville: reprinted by Battery Press, 1988.

Harrison, Gordon A. *Cross Channel Attack,* Washington: BBD Special Editions, 1951.

Howe, George F. *Northwest Africa: Seizing the Initiative in the West.* Washington: Center of Military History, 1993.

Lavender, Donald E. *Nudge Blue: A Rifleman's Chronicle of World War II.* Bennington, Vermont: Merriam Press, 2003.

MacDonald, Charles B. *The Siegfried Line Campaign.* Washington: Center of Military History, 1963.

Mansoor, Peter R. *The GI Offensive in Europe: The Triumph of American Infantry Divisions, 1941–1945.* Lawrence, Kansas: University Press, 1999.

Miller, Edward G. *A Dark and Bloody Ground: The Huertgen Forest and the Roer River Dams, 1944–1945.* College Station, Texas: Texas A&M University Press, 1994.

Mittelman, Joseph B. *Eight Stars to Victory: The History of the Ninth Infantry Division.* Washington: Ninth Infantry Division Association, 1948.

Mogin's Maulers, The 362nd Fighter Group History of WW II (second edition). Chicago: Dan Gianneschi with permission of the 362nd Fighter Group Association, 1986.

Ossad, Steven L. and Don R. Marsh. *Major General Maurice Rose: World War II's Greatest Forgotten Commander.* New York: Taylor Trade Publishing, 2003.

Phillips, Henry Gerard. *El Guettar, Crucible of Leadership*. Self-published, 1991.

Phillips, Henry Gerard. *The Making of a Professional: Manton S. Eddy, USA*. Westport, Connecticut: Greenwood Press, 1995.

Phillips, Henry Gerard. *Sedjenane, the Pay-off Battle*. Self-published, 1993.

Rarey, Damon Frantz, ed. *Laughter and Tears, A Combat Pilot's Sketchbooks of World War II Squadron Life, The Art of Captain George Rarey*. Santa Rosa, California: Vision Books International, 1996.

Sylvan, William C. and Francis G. Smith, Jr. *Normandy to Victory: The War Diary of Courtney H. Hodges & the First U.S. Army*. Lexington: The University Press of Kentucky, 2008.

To Bizerte with the II Corps—23 April to 13 May 1943. Washington: Military Intelligence Division, War Department, 1943.

Utah Beach to Cherbourg—6 June to 27 June 1944. Washington: Department of the Army, 1947.

Reports

Consolidated Efficiency Reports of Donald A. Stroh, 0-5845, Commencing Sept. 1, 1917.

Individual Flight Record of Harry R. Stroh, October 1942–August 1944, War Department A.A.F. Form No. 5.

Mission Reports, 378th Fighter Squadron, February 1944–May 1945.

Officer Qualification Record/Record of Assignments of Robert H. Stumpf, 0-20707.

Reports of Operations, 39th Infantry, June 1944–February 1945.

Statement of Service/Summary of Commissioned Service since 1 January 1937 through 1946 of Donald A. Stroh, 0-5845.

Stroh, Donald A. "The Operation on Crozon Peninsula." *Military Review*, Vol. XXV No.10, January 1946, pp. 3-8.

Stroh, Donald A. "World War II Lessons Learned." July 14, 1947.

Unpublished Memoirs and Letters

Baloga, John M. 378th Fighter Squadron, World War II memoir, undated.

Baloga, John M. E-mails to the author of March 26 and March 28, 2004.

Croonquist, Arvid P. Colonel, U.S. Army (ret.), letter to the author of March 6, 2004.

Cross, Thomas. Major General, U.S. Army (ret.), War Diary, 1944–1945.

Eddy, Manton S. Major General, U.S. Army (ret.), "Activities of General Eddy, 1944–1945."

Gunn, Frank. Brigadier General, U.S. Army (ret.), letter to the author of December 26, 2003.

Kent, Richard. Colonel, U.S. Army (ret.), letter to Col. Don Lavender, July 1991.

Lavender, Donald E. Colonel U.S. Army (ret.), E-mail to the author of January 2, 2004.

Lowery, Leon. K Company, 39th Infantry, letters to the author of September 15 and December 9, 2004.

Stroh, Donald A. Letters to his daughter, Imogene, 1942–1945.

Stroh, Donald A. The Story of Crozon. 1951.

Stroh, Donald A. War Diary. 1917–1918.

Stroh, Harry R. The letters of Harry R. Stroh to his parents and sister, 1930–1944.

Stumpf, Imogene Stroh. The letters of Imogene Stroh Stumpf to her parents. Jan. 1943–Aug. 1945.

Stumpf, Robert H. Letters to his wife and parents. 1942–1945.

Taff, Herbert. L Company, 39th Infantry. Letter to the author of May 22, 2004.

Interviews with the Author

Adams, John. I Company, 39th Infantry, January 21, 2004.

Baloga, John. 378th Fighter Squadron, March 28, 2004.

Cobb, Robert B. Colonel, U.S. Army (ret.) 39th Infantry, March 9-10, 2004.

Dunlap, Captain Jack. B Company, 39th Infantry, January 13, 2004.

Eubank, Perry. Colonel, U.S. Army (ret.) USMA '37, January 30, 2004.

Kennedy, Robert. 378th Fighter Squadron, March 31, 2006.

Scheffel, Charles. 39th Infantry, May 31, 2004.

Stumpf, Imogene S. November 23-24, 2003.

Van Valkenburgh, Robert. Colonel, US Army (ret.) USMA '37, January 31, 2004.

Acknowledgements

Letters to Imogene has been a work in progress since 2003 when I first interviewed my mother, the title character, with the intent of compiling the family's treasury of World War II memorabilia into a single volume. After completing much of the basic research, life events intervened, and the project was shelved until late 2019. The ensuing global coronavirus pandemic and the subsequent isolation provided an opportunity to concentrate on finishing the book.

In the intervening years, my mother had catalogued a library of family correspondence including all of her father's original handwritten letters to her. In addition, we had bound volumes of her letters to her father, and of all her brother's letters to his parents and sister, which Gen. Stroh personally typed up after the war. We also found some of my father's letters and V-mail to my mother and his parents. Because Harry Stroh's Air Corps pilot training took place during his father's and brother-in-law's participation in the war, we have included his accounts of that period, and hope they will be of interest to our military aviation brothers and sisters.

As I began actually writing the chapters from the beginning of my father's and grandfather's participation in the war, it became clear that these letters were providing a rich personal backdrop that made the historical accounts come alive. So rather than trying to recreate the back story, the characters tell it in their own words.

My grandfather, being an especially gifted and prolific writer, became the principal narrator, expounding on a general's life in World War II with accuracy, detail, and, in many cases, a lively sense of humor. Since all of his letters in our collection were to his daughter, Imogene, who had saved every one, we stumbled onto the theme of the book, and its title. Credit for the title is not mine, however, but goes to the Revd. Dr. Michael Hoffman, with whom I was chatting about the project when he asked the title. I explained that I didn't know yet and responded, "What's your mother's name?" When I told him, he didn't hesitate, "How about *Letters to Imogene*?"

My mother inherited her father's proclivity for saving and cataloging memorabilia about the war, a rich source of information. Thanks to the two of them, the availability of all this material will ensure that generations hence will have access to the original accounts. In addition, many of the published accounts that addressed the battles in which our characters fought were already in the family library. My wife, Susie, was my principal wordsmith, copy editor, and cheerleader, who discovered, with great regularity, errors that I had overlooked. She also kept me on track when I strayed into uncharted territory and steadfastly supported and encouraged me. Our daughter, Natalie, provided organizational skills and interview transcriptions during the early stages of the project. Later, her husband, Ari Solotoff offered helpful legal and other advice.

My brother Harry, proofread the entire manuscript at least twice. In addition to identifying typos, he provided invaluable insight on military perspectives based on his Army career. Former F/A-18 squadron-mate Brad Meeder, offered helpful comments throughout the manuscript, as did former infantry officer David Anderson.

Kudos to the book's mapmaker, U. S. Navy and Marine Corps

veteran Tom Houlihan, who created unique battle maps that emphasize the units represented by the principal characters, while depicting other units in the various campaigns for context.

Special thanks to 8th Division sons and historians Gregory Canellis and Jonathan Gawne; Brest, France historians Gildas Saouzanet and Ronan Urvoaz; Huertgen historian and mayor of Merode, Germany, Albert Trostorf; and 106th Division historian and webmaster Carl Wouters of Belgium.

The many veterans of the war who took the time to share their stories after so many years honored me beyond words. They all had some personal connection to my father, grandfather or uncle and their recollections leant great illumination and authenticity. Finally, I am grateful to all those who served in World War II, especially those who made the ultimate sacrifice, and those who supported them on the home front. They, quite literally, saved our planet.

CPSIA information can be obtained
at www.ICGtesting.com
Printed in the USA
BVHW031657070521
606757BV00001B/11

9 781977 236265